GenBench 2024: The Second Workshop on Generalisation (Bencharking) in NLP

Miami, Florida, USA
16 November 2024

ISBN: 979-8-3313-0847-6

Printed from e-media with permission by:

Curran Associates, Inc.
57 Morehouse Lane
Red Hook, NY 12571

Association for Computational Linguistics
209 N. Eighth Street
Stroudsburg, Pennsylvania 18360

Phone: 1-570-476-8006
Fax: 1-570-476-0860

acl@aclweb.org

Additional copies of this publication are available from:

Curran Associates, Inc.
57 Morehouse Lane
Red Hook, NY 12571 USA
Phone: 845-758-0400
Fax: 845-758-2633
Email: curran@proceedings.com
Web: www.proceedings.com

GenBench 2024

GenBench: The second workshop on generalisation (benchmarking) in NLP

Proceedings of the Workshop

November 16, 2024

The GenBench organizers gratefully acknowledge the support from the following sponsors.

Supported by

amazon

Order copies of this and other ACL proceedings from:

Association for Computational Linguistics (ACL)
317 Sidney Baker St. S
Suite 400 - 134
Kerrville, TX 78028
USA
Tel: +1-855-225-1962
acl@aclweb.org

Message from the Organisers

The ability to generalise well is often mentioned as one of the primary desiderata for models of natural language processing (NLP). Yet, there are still many open questions related to what it means for an NLP model to generalise well, and how generalisation should be evaluated. LLMs, trained on gigantic training corpora that are, at best, hard to analyse or might not be publicly available at all, bring a new set of challenges to the topic. The second GenBench workshop on generalisation (benchmarking) in NLP aims to serve as a cornerstone to catalyse research on generalisation in the NLP community. The workshop has two concrete goals: to bring together different expert communities to discuss challenging questions relating to generalisation in NLP and to establish a shared platform for state-of-the-art generalisation testing in NLP through our Collaborative Benchmarking Task (CBT). We started the CBT last year; this year's CBT is solely LLM-focused.

The second edition of the workshop was held at EMNLP 2024 in Miami, Florida. For this edition, we accepted 11 archival papers in our main track, 2 archival papers for our CBT, and 9 extended abstracts. The workshop also provided a platform for the authors of EMNLP Findings papers related to the workshop's topic to present their work as a poster at the workshop.

The workshop would not have been possible without the dedication of the programme committee, whom we would like to thank for their contributions. We would also like to thank Amazon for their sponsorship of 10,000 dollars, which we used to grant travel awards to allow participants who could otherwise not have attended to participate in the workshop, and to grant two best paper awards. Lastly, we are grateful to our invited speakers, Pascale Fung, Najoung Kim, and Sameer Singh, for contributing to our programme.

Organizing Committee

Workshop Organizers

Dieuwke Hupkes, Meta
Verna Dankers, University of Edinburgh
Khuyagbaatar Batsuren, Openstream AI
Amirhossein Kazemnejad, McGill University and Mila
Christos Christodoulopoulos, Amazon Research
Mario Giulianelli, ETH Zürich
Ryan Cotterell, ETH Zürich

Program Committee

Reviewers

Jonathan Brophy, University of Oregon
Lisa Bylinina, University of Groningen
Robert Frank, Yale University
Yangfeng Ji, University of Virginia
Jenny Kunz, Linköping University
Matthias Lindemann, University of Edinburgh
R. Thomas McCoy, Princeton University
Anmol Nayak, Bosch
Sanchit Sinha, University of Virginia, Charlottesville
Shane Steinert-Threlkeld, University of Washington, Seattle
Swetasudha Panda, Oracle
Koji Mineshima, Keio University
Tatiana Shavrina, Artificial Intelligence Research Institute
Jithendra Vepa, Idiap Research Institute
Rudolf Rosa, Charles University, Prague
Erenay Dayanik, Amazon
Antske Fokkens, VU University Amsterdam
Richard Futrell, University of California, Irvine
Djamé Seddah, Inria Paris
Lis Pereira, National Institute of Information and Communications Technology (NICT), National Institute of Advanced Industrial Science and Technology
Cassandra Jacobs, State University of New York, Buffalo
Marco Basaldella, Amazon
Houman Mehrafarin, Heriot-Watt University
Jean-Philippe Fauconnier, Apple
Deepanshu Gupta, Apple
Fabio Massimo Zanzotto, University of Rome Tor Vergata
Mira Moukheiber, Massachusetts Institute of Technology
Bryan Eikema, University of Amsterdam
Kate McCurdy, Universität des Saarlandes
Michal Štefánik, Masaryk University
Coleman Haley, University of Edinburgh
Michael Eric Goodale, Ecole Normale Supérieure de Paris
Rimvydas Rubavicius, Edinburgh University
Gautier Dagan, University of Edinburgh
Parsa Bagherzadeh, McGill University
Subham De, Meta AI
Churan Zhi, University of California, San Diego
Bogdan Kulynych, CHUV - University Hospital Lausanne
Jirui Qi, University of Groningen
Aditya Kaushik Surikuchi, University of Amsterdam

Keynote Talk
Invited Talk 1

Pascale Fung
Hong Kong University of Science and Technology

2024-11-16 – Time: **09:15 – 10:00** –

Bio: Pascale Fung is a Chair Professor at the Department of Electronic & Computer Engineering at The Hong Kong University of Science & Technology (HKUST), and a visiting professor at the Central Academy of Fine Arts in Beijing. She is an elected Fellow of the Association for the Advancement of Artificial Intelligence (AAAI) for her significant contributions to the field of conversational AI and to the development of ethical AI principles and algorithms", an elected Fellow of the Association for Computational Linguistics (ACL) for her "significant contributions towards statistical NLP, comparable corpora, and building intelligent systems that can understand and empathize with humans". She is an Fellow of the Institute of Electrical and Electronic Engineers (IEEE) for her "contributions to human-machine interactions" and an elected Fellow of the International Speech Communication Association for "fundamental contributions to the interdisciplinary area of spoken language human-machine interactions". She is the Director of HKUST Centre for AI Research (CAiRE), an interdisciplinary research centre promoting human-centric AI. She co-founded the Human Language Technology Center (HLTC). She is an affiliated faculty with the Robotics Institute and the Big Data Institute at HKUST. She is the founding chair of the Women Faculty Association at HKUST. She is an expert on the Global Future Council, a think tank for the World Economic Forum. She represents HKUST on Partnership on AI to Benefit People and Society. She is on the Board of Governors of the IEEE Signal Processing Society. She is a member of the IEEE Working Group to develop an IEEE standard - Recommended Practice for Organizational Governance of Artificial Intelligence. She was a Distinguished Consultant on Responsible AI at Meta in 2022, and a Visiting Faculty Researcher at Google in 2023. Her research team has won several best and outstanding paper awards at ACL, ACL and NeurIPS workshops.

Keynote Talk
Invited Talk 2

Najoung Kim
Boston University

2024-11-16 – Time: **11:00 – 11:45** –

Bio: Najoung Kim is an Assistant Professor at the Department of Linguistics and an affiliate faculty in the Department of Computer Science at Boston University. She is also currently a visiting faculty researcher at Google DeepMind. Before joining BU, she was a Faculty Fellow at the Center for Data Science at New York University and received her PhD in Cognitive Science at Johns Hopkins University. She is interested in studying meaning in both human and machine learners, especially ways in which they generalize to novel inputs and ways in which they treat implicit meaning. Her research has been supported by NSF and Google, and has received awards at venues such as ACL and *SEM.

Keynote Talk

Invited Talk 3

Sameer Singh
University of California, Irvine

2024-11-16 – Time: **15:00 – 15:45** –

Bio: Dr. Sameer Singh is a Professor of Computer Science at UC Irvine. He is working primarily on the robustness and interpretability of machine learning algorithms and models that reason with text and structure for natural language processing. Sameer was a postdoctoral researcher at the University of Washington and received his Ph.D. from the University of Massachusetts, Amherst. He has been named the Kavli Fellow by the National Academy of Sciences, received the NSF CAREER award, UCI Distinguished Early Career Faculty award, the Hellman Faculty Fellowship, and was selected as a DARPA Riser. His group has received funding from Allen Institute for AI, Amazon, NSF, DARPA, Adobe Research, Hasso Plattner Institute, NEC, Base 11, and FICO. Sameer has published extensively at machine learning and natural language processing venues and received conference paper awards at KDD 2016, ACL 2018, EMNLP 2019, AKBC 2020, ACL 2020, and NAACL 2022.

Table of Contents

Program

Saturday, November 16, 2024

09:00 - 09:15 *Opening Remarks*

09:15 - 10:00 *Keynote 1 by Pascale Fung*

10:00 - 10:30 *Oral presentations*

Is artificial intelligence still intelligence? LLMs generalize to novel adjective-noun pairs, but don't mimic the full human distribution
Hayley Ross, Kathryn Davidson and Najoung Kim

Investigating the Generalizability of Pretrained Language Models across Multiple Dimensions: A Case Study of NLI and MRC
Ritam Dutt, Sagnik Ray Choudhury, Varun Venkat Rao, Carolyn Rose and V.G.Vinod Vydiswaran

10:30 - 11:00 *Morning Coffee Break*

11:00 - 11:45 *Keynote 2 by Najoung Kim*

11:45 - 12:30 *Spotlight talks*

The SlayQA benchmark of social reasoning: testing gender-inclusive generalization with neopronouns
Bastian Bunzeck and Sina Zarrieß

MMLU-SR: A Benchmark for Stress-Testing Reasoning Capability of Large Language Models
Wentian Wang, Sarthak Jain, Paul Kantor, Jacob Feldman, Lazaros Gallos and Hao Wang

MLissard: Multilingual Long and Simple Sequential Reasoning Benchmarks
Mirelle Candida Bueno, Roberto Lotufo and Rodrigo Frassetto Nogueira

MultiPragEval: Multilingual Pragmatic Evaluation of Large Language Models
Dojun Park, Jiwoo Lee, Seohyun Park, Hyeyun Jeong, Youngeun Koo, Soonha Hwang, Seonwoo Park and Sungeun Lee

OmniDialog: A Multimodal Benchmark for Generalization Across Text, Visual, and Audio Modalities
Anton Razzhigaev, Maxim Kurkin, Elizaveta Goncharova, Irina Abdullaeva, Anastasia Lysenko, Alexander Panchenko, Andrey Kuznetsov and Denis Dimitrov

Saturday, November 16, 2024 (continued)

12:30 - 13:45 *Lunch break*

13:45 - 15:00 *Poster session*

Evaluating the fairness of task-adaptive pretraining on unlabeled test data before few-shot text classification
Kush Dubey

From Language to Pixels: Task Recognition and Task Learning in LLMs
Janek Falkenstein, Carolin M. Schuster, Alexander H. Berger and Georg Groh

Automated test generation to evaluate tool-augmented LLMs as conversational AI agents
Samuel Arcadinho, David Oliveira Aparicio and Mariana S. C. Almeida

Beyond the Numbers: Transparency in Relation Extraction Benchmark Creation and Leaderboards
Varvara Arzt and Allan Hanbury

CHIE: Generative MRC Evaluation for in-context QA with Correctness, Helpfulness, Irrelevancy, and Extraneousness Aspects
Wannaphong Phatthiyaphaibun, Surapon Nonesung, Peerat Limkonchotiwat, Can Udomcharoenchaikit, Jitkapat Sawatphol, Ekapol Chuangsuwanich and Sarana Nutanong

Towards a new Benchmark for Emotion Detection in NLP: A Unifying Framework of Recent Corpora
Anna Koufakou, Elijah Nieves and John Peller

MLissard: Multilingual Long and Simple Sequential Reasoning Benchmarks
Mirelle Candida Bueno, Roberto Lotufo and Rodrigo Frassetto Nogueira

MultiPragEval: Multilingual Pragmatic Evaluation of Large Language Models
Dojun Park, Jiwoo Lee, Seohyun Park, Hyeyun Jeong, Youngeun Koo, Soonha Hwang, Seonwoo Park and Sungeun Lee

OmniDialog: A Multimodal Benchmark for Generalization Across Text, Visual, and Audio Modalities
Anton Razzhigaev, Maxim Kurkin, Elizaveta Goncharova, Irina Abdullaeva, Anastasia Lysenko, Alexander Panchenko, Andrey Kuznetsov and Denis Dimitrov

The SlayQA benchmark of social reasoning: testing gender-inclusive generalization with neopronouns
Bastian Bunzeck and Sina Zarrieß

Saturday, November 16, 2024 (continued)

	MMLU-SR: A Benchmark for Stress-Testing Reasoning Capability of Large Language Models Wentian Wang, Sarthak Jain, Paul Kantor, Jacob Feldman, Lazaros Gallos and Hao Wang
15:00 - 15:45	*Keynote 3 by Sameer Singh*
15:45 - 16:00	*Afternoon Coffee Break*
16:00 - 16:30	*Panel*
16:30 - 16:45	*Closing Remarks and Best Paper Award*

Evaluating the fairness of task-adaptive pretraining on unlabeled test data before few-shot text classification

Kush Dubey
Independent
kushdubey63@gmail.com

Abstract

Few-shot learning benchmarks are critical for evaluating modern NLP techniques. It is possible, however, that benchmarks favor methods which easily make use of unlabeled text, because researchers can use unlabeled text from the test set to pretrain their models. Given the dearth of research on this potential problem, we run experiments to quantify the bias caused by pretraining on unlabeled test set text instead of on unlabeled, independently drawn text. Controlled few-shot and zero-shot experiments on 25 classification tasks and 3 language models—BERT, GPT-2, and Mistral 7B—do not find evidence of overoptimism. Furthermore, we demonstrate the importance of repeated subsampling when studying few-shot text classification, and recommend that few-shot learning benchmarks include multiple training folds. Code and data are available here: `https://github.com/kddubey/pretrain-on-test/`.

1 Introduction

It is common for NLP benchmarks to release text from the test set, as researchers can submit a file of predictions instead of submitting code. A potential concern is that researchers can use this text during training. Consider the Real-world Annotated Few-shot Tasks (RAFT) benchmark (Alex et al., 2021), which contains "few-shot" text classification tasks—tasks where the training set contains a relatively small number of labeled examples. Below is an excerpt from the RAFT paper (emphasis added):

> For each task, we release a public training set with 50 examples and a larger unlabeled test set. *We encourage unsupervised pre-training on the unlabelled examples* and open-domain information retrieval.

In the RAFT competition, a model is evaluated by scoring its predictions on the same set of unlabeled text which the model may have been trained on (using an unsupervised training procedure).

It is wrong to train a model on test set features with their labels and then evaluate on the test set when one needs to estimate performance on out-of-sample data. Test set performance would be overoptimistic (Hastie et al., 2009). This fact is widely known. But what if, as encouraged by Alex et al. (2021), a model is trained on test set features *without* test set labels? This paper studies this question for the domain of few-shot text classification.

2 Motivation

NLP benchmarks for few-shot learning are prevalent, as having only a handful of labeled examples is more realistic. One consideration when designing these benchmarks is that some few-shot approaches can—at least theoretically—use unlabeled text from the test set. With Pattern-Exploiting Training (Schick and Schütze, 2021), for example, one can train the final classifier on test set text with soft labels predicted by an ensemble of supervised models. With Pre-trained Prompt Tuning (Gu et al., 2022), one can pretrain the language model (LM) on unlabeled test set text before prompt-tuning on the labeled training set. A more classical approach would be to train a word2vec model (Mikolov et al., 2013) on unlabeled test set text, run this model on training text to get embeddings, and finally train a classifier on these embeddings with labels from the training set.

For other few-shot approaches, such as SetFit (Tunstall et al., 2022) and in-context learning with LLMs (as popularized by Brown et al., 2020), it is more common to only use labeled text.

While the ability to exploit unlabeled text is useful, applying this ability to test set text could be substantively different than applying it to text which is statistically independent of the test set. This difference in methodology may be more concerning in

Proceedings of the 2nd GenBench Workshop on Generalisation (Benchmarking) in NLP, pages 1–26
November 16, 2024 ©2024 Association for Computational Linguistics

the few-shot setting than in the many-shot setting. It is conceivable that differences between few-shot methods are due just as much to how unlabeled text is used as they are to how the few, labeled examples are used. This raises the question: does pretraining a model on a benchmark's unlabeled test set text inflate the model's performance on that benchmark?

3 Related work

As indicated by the quote in §1, the RAFT benchmark implicitly assumes that the answer is no. The validity of using test set features is not a fringe opinion. The popular textbook by Hastie et al. (2009) contains the following passage without a reference or evidence (emphasis added):

> There is one qualification: *initial unsupervised screening steps can be done before samples are left out.* For example, we could select the 1000 predictors with highest variance across all 50 samples, before starting cross-validation. *Since this filtering does not involve the class labels, it does not give the predictors an unfair advantage.*

The opposite opinion—that exploiting unlabeled test set features is unfair—may align more closely with best practices. For example, Gururangan et al. (2020) contains the following criticism of another study when comparing performances on a text classification task:

> Thongtan and Phienthrakul (2019) report a higher number (97.42) on IMDB, but they train their word vectors on the test set.

Jacovi et al. (2023) argue that benchmarks which release unlabeled test set text can be compromised, but do not discuss potential problems with using unlabeled test set text by itself.

Moscovich and Rosset (2022) contains experiments and theory for unsupervised methods which are common to tasks involving tabular data. They find that estimators of out-of-sample performance which were subject to these methods may be biased positively or negatively, depending on the parameters of the problem. They recommend further research on this bias in more domains, particularly when dealing with small sample sizes and high-dimensional data.

4 Experimental design

We study whether pretraining on unlabeled test set text biases test set performance for 25 diverse text classification tasks and two types of LMs: BERT (Devlin et al., 2019) and GPT-2 (Radford et al., 2019). Appendix A describes each task.

The goal of the experiment is to first establish that pretraining is beneficial, in line with Gururangan et al. (2020). Second, given that pretraining has a detectable effect, the experiment measures the accuracy difference between using test set text for the pretraining stage—an arguably unfair methodology—and using text which is independent of the test set—an inarguably fair methodology.

In more detail, the experiment starts by subsampling three separate sets of data from the full sample of data for a given text classification task:

- `extra`: n (either $50, 100, 200$ or 500) unlabeled texts which are optionally used for pretraining
- `train`: m (either 50 or 100) labeled texts for classification training
- `test`: n labeled texts to report accuracy.

Next, three accuracy estimators are computed. Procedures used to obtain them are described below.

4.1 $\mathrm{acc}_{\mathrm{extra}}$

1. Train a freshly loaded, pretrained LM on the n unlabeled texts in `extra` using the LM's pretraining objective—masked language modeling loss for BERT, or causal language modeling loss for GPT-2. Texts are passed independently, and padded to form batches.
2. Add a linear layer to this model and finetune all of the LM's weights to minimize classification cross entropy loss on `train`.
3. Compute the classification accuracy of this model on `test`.

Step 1 is task-adaptive pretraining—a procedure broadly recommended by Gururangan et al. (2020). Step 2 is a canonical way to train a transformer-based LM for a classification task, according to Section 2 of Zhang et al. (2021).

$\mathrm{acc}_{\mathrm{extra}}$ is clearly an unbiased estimator of out-of-sample accuracy because it never trains on `test`. In other words, the expected value of $\mathrm{acc}_{\mathrm{extra}}$ is the accuracy one would observe on independent, identically distributed data.

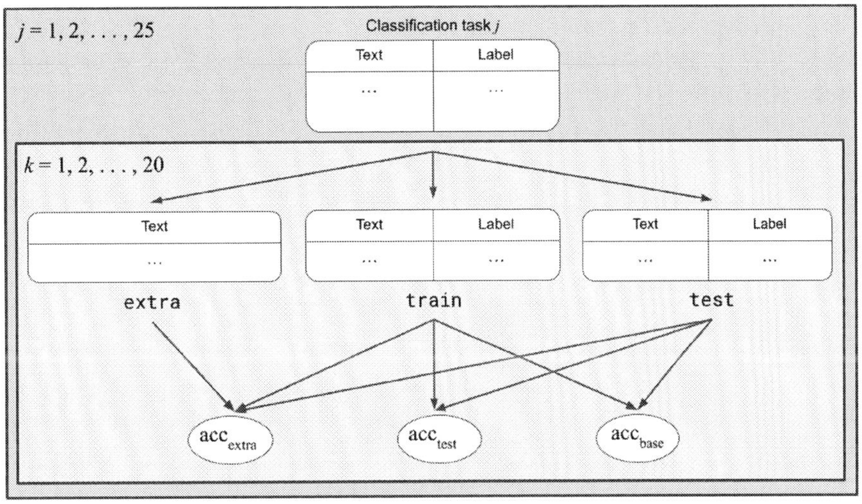

Figure 1: The experimental design (§4) for $n = 500$ as an example.

```
acc_extra = (
    language_model  # freshly loaded
    .pretrain(extra["texts"])
    .train(train["texts"], train["labels"])
    .evaluate(test["texts"], test["labels"])
)
```

```
acc_test = (
    language_model  # freshly loaded
    .pretrain(test["texts"])
    .train(train["texts"], train["labels"])
    .evaluate(test["texts"], test["labels"])
)
```

```
acc_base = (
    language_model  # freshly loaded
    # no further pretraining
    .train(train["texts"], train["labels"])
    .evaluate(test["texts"], test["labels"])
)
```

Figure 2: Pseudocode for the accuracy estimators defined in §4.

4.2 $\mathrm{acc}_{\mathrm{test}}$

$\mathrm{acc}_{\mathrm{test}}$ is identical to $\mathrm{acc}_{\mathrm{extra}}$, except that task-adaptive pretraining is done on unlabeled text from `test` instead of `extra` in step 1.

$\mathrm{acc}_{\mathrm{test}}$ represents what one might see in a competition like RAFT, where pretraining on unlabeled text from `test` is encouraged. It is unclear whether this accuracy estimator is unbiased, because it involved pretraining and evaluating on the same set of test set text. A reasonable hypothesis is that it is overoptimistic, i.e., $\mathrm{E}[\mathrm{acc}_{\mathrm{test}}] > \mathrm{E}[\mathrm{acc}_{\mathrm{extra}}]$.

4.3 $\mathrm{acc}_{\mathrm{base}}$

$\mathrm{acc}_{\mathrm{base}}$ does not do task-adaptive pretraining; it does not make any use of unlabeled text. It trains a pretrained LM on `train` to do classification, and then computes this model's accuracy on `test`.

This score provides a sanity check. If there is no boost from $\mathrm{acc}_{\mathrm{base}}$ to $\mathrm{acc}_{\mathrm{extra}}$, then it may not be surprising to observe no difference between $\mathrm{acc}_{\mathrm{extra}}$ and $\mathrm{acc}_{\mathrm{test}}$. A boost from $\mathrm{acc}_{\mathrm{base}}$ to $\mathrm{acc}_{\mathrm{extra}}$ would rule out undertraining as the cause of a null difference between $\mathrm{acc}_{\mathrm{extra}}$ and $\mathrm{acc}_{\mathrm{test}}$ due to insufficient pretraining epochs or too low a learning rate.

4.4 Repeated subsampling

The accuracy estimators are paired, because their classification training and test data are identical. The only difference is the source of unlabeled text for pretraining. For $\mathrm{acc}_{\mathrm{extra}}$, the source is independent of test data. For $\mathrm{acc}_{\mathrm{test}}$, the test set text is used. For $\mathrm{acc}_{\mathrm{base}}$, no unlabeled text is used.

A potentially important source of variation in this experiment is the particular subsamples, i.e., the particular realizations of `extra`, `train`, and `test` for a given classification task. To expose this variation, the experiment procedure is repeated tens of times for each task.[1] For example, for $n = 500$, and for each of the 25 tasks, 20 ($\mathrm{acc}_{\mathrm{extra}}$, $\mathrm{acc}_{\mathrm{test}}$, $\mathrm{acc}_{\mathrm{base}}$) triples are computed.

Appendix B explains more experiment choices.

5 Results

Appendix D.2 visualizes the distributions of $\mathrm{acc}_{\mathrm{extra}} - \mathrm{acc}_{\mathrm{base}}$ and $\mathrm{acc}_{\mathrm{test}} - \mathrm{acc}_{\mathrm{extra}}$. $\mathrm{acc}_{\mathrm{extra}} - \mathrm{acc}_{\mathrm{base}}$ is a control: it is the accuracy boost from pretraining

[1] For $n = 50$ and $n = 100$, the experiment is repeated 100 times. For $n = 200$, the experiment is repeated 50 times. For $n = 500$, the experiment is repeated 20 times. In total, $81,000$ finetuned BERT and GPT-2 models were evaluated.

on unlabeled independent text versus not pretraining at all. $\text{acc}_{\text{test}} - \text{acc}_{\text{extra}}$ is the main quantity of interest: it is the evaluation bias from pretraining on unlabeled test set text instead of on unlabeled independent text.

Table 1 contains means of these differences for each configuration of the experiment. It roughly suggests that while pretraining is consistently beneficial, pretraining on unlabeled test set text does not bias test set performance one way or the other.

	BERT	GPT-2
$n = 50$	4.1% / 0.19%	3.8% / 0.18%
$n = 100$	3.9% / 0.18%	4.1% / 0.11%
$n = 200$	3.9% / -0.39%	4.4% / -0.05%
$n = 500$	3.5% / 0.48%	4.6% / -0.08%

(a) $m = 50$

	BERT	GPT-2
$n = 50$	6.2% / -0.08%	2.2% / -0.05%
$n = 100$	6.1% / -0.37%	2.5% / 0.03%
$n = 200$	4.1% / 0.33%	6.3% / -0.01%
$n = 500$	6.1% / -0.16%	3.9% / -0.21%

(b) $m = 100$

Table 1: Means of accuracy differences taken across all subsamples of all 25 classification tasks. For each cell, the upper-left of the diagonal corresponds to the sample mean of $\text{acc}_{\text{extra}} - \text{acc}_{\text{base}}$, and the lower-right corresponds to the sample mean of $\text{acc}_{\text{test}} - \text{acc}_{\text{extra}}$.

6 Analysis

Reporting means is not enough, especially when studying few-shot learning. Appendix D.2 demonstrates that there is considerable variance, despite pairing the accuracy estimators.[2] While these visualizations tell us about how raw accuracy differences vary, they do not tell us how the mean accuracy difference varies. We seek a neat answer to the core questions: on this benchmark of 25 classification tasks, how much does the overall accuracy differ between two modeling techniques, and how much does this difference vary?

[2]One source of variance is intentionally introduced: the subsample splits, as explained in §4.4. The other source of variance is inherent: the added linear layer to perform classification is initialized with random weights.

One way to communicate the variance is to estimate the standard error of the mean difference across classification tasks. But the standard error statistic can be difficult to interpret (Morey et al., 2016). Furthermore, its computation is not completely trivial due to the data's hierarchical dependency structure: each triple, ($\text{acc}_{\text{extra}}$, acc_{test}, acc_{base}), is drawn from (`train`, `test`), which is itself drawn from the given classification dataset.

6.1 Model

This analysis does not aim to estimate standard errors. Instead, a hierarchical model is fit. Specifically, for each LM type (indexed by $i = 1, 2$ for BERT and GPT-2), each classification task (indexed by $j = 1, 2, \ldots, 25$), each of their subsamples (indexed by $k = 1, 2, \ldots, 20$ for $n = 500$, for example), and a control and treatment (indexed by $l = 0, 1$), the number of correct predictions is modeled ($*$ is short for $ijkl$):

$$Y_* \sim \text{Binomial}(n, \lambda_*) \quad (1)$$

$$\text{logit}(\lambda_*) = \mu + \alpha z_i + U_j + V_{jk} + W_{jl} + \beta x_l \quad (2)$$

$$\mu \sim \text{Normal}(0, 1) \quad (3)$$

$$\alpha \sim \text{Normal}(0, 5) \quad (4)$$

$$U_j \sim \text{Normal}(0, \sigma_U) \quad (5)$$

$$V_{jk} \sim \text{Normal}(0, \sigma_V) \quad (6)$$

$$W_{jl} \sim \text{Normal}(0, \sigma_W) \quad (7)$$

$$\beta \sim \text{Normal}(0, 1) \quad (8)$$

$$\sigma_U, \sigma_V \sim \text{HalfNormal}(0, 1) \quad (9)$$

$$\sigma_W \sim \text{HalfNormal}(0, 3.5355) \quad (10)$$

(1) number of correct predictions

(2) logit link for accuracy rate, additive effects

(3) prior for the global intercept

(4) prior for the effect of the type of LM (BERT or GPT-2)—a control variable

(5) prior for the effect of the classification task (partial-pooled to reduce overfitting)

(6) prior for the nested effect of the task's subsampled dataset

(7) prior for the interaction effect of the task and the intervention (to reduce underfitting)

(8) prior for the effect of the intervention

(9) prior for standard deviations

(10) prior for standard deviation.

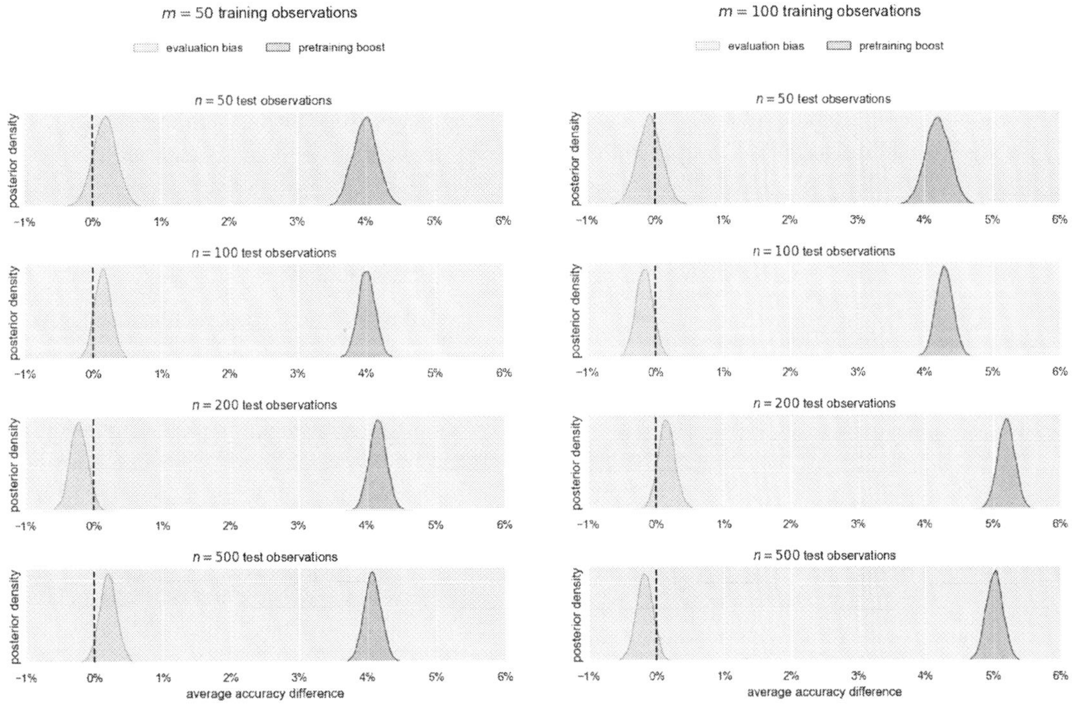

Figure 3: Distributions of average accuracy differences (11). The evaluation bias is akin to $\text{acc}_{\text{test}} - \text{acc}_{\text{extra}}$. The pretraining boost is akin to $\text{acc}_{\text{extra}} - \text{acc}_{\text{base}}$.

The model is fit using Markov Chain Monte Carlo, using the interface provided by the `bambi` package (Capretto et al., 2022).

To analyze the pretraining boost, the control, Y_{ijk0}, is $n \cdot \text{acc}_{\text{base}}$, and the treatment, Y_{ijk1}, is $n \cdot \text{acc}_{\text{extra}}$. Here, the intervention refers to pretraining on unlabeled independent text versus not pretraining at all.

To analyze the evaluation bias, the control, Y_{ijk0}, is $n \cdot \text{acc}_{\text{extra}}$, and the treatment, Y_{ijk1}, is $n \cdot \text{acc}_{\text{test}}$. Here, the intervention refers to pretraining on unlabeled text from the test set instead of on unlabeled independent text.

4,000 samples from the posterior predictive, $\hat{Y}_{ijkl}$, are drawn. Appendix E.1 includes a simulation demonstrating the model's ability to correctly recover null and non-null effects.

6.2 Overall effects

Benchmarks assess methods by taking their average performance across tasks. To place the results in this context, samples from the posterior predictive distribution of $Y_{ijk1} - Y_{ijk0}$ (6.1) are taken, then averaged across i (the 2 LM types—BERT and GPT-2), j (the 25 classification tasks), and k (their subsamples), and divided by n to obtain the distribution of the average accuracy difference (expressed in dot notation, where dots are used as placeholders for indices that have been averaged over):

$$\frac{\bar{\hat{Y}}_{\cdots 1} - \bar{\hat{Y}}_{\cdots 0}}{n}. \tag{11}$$

Each distribution is that of the marginal effect of the modeling intervention: pretraining versus not pretraining (the pretraining boost), or pretraining on unlabeled test set text instead of on unlabeled independent text (the evaluation bias).

6.3 Task-level effects

While taking an average across tasks provides a concise summary, it cannot be used to rule out the existence of an evaluation bias. If the direction of the bias depends on latent properties of the task, averaging may cancel out real, positive biases with real, negative ones. Alternatively, it may dilute the few real, positive biases with many null ones.

Jin et al. (2021) argue and demonstrate that the benefit of task-adaptive pretraining depends on the task's causal direction. If the principle of independent causal mechanisms is also relevant to the fairness of pretraining on test set features, then our accuracy data may contain (for the sake of argument) positive evaluation biases for anti-causal tasks, and null biases for causal tasks.[3]

One way to analyze tasks is to sample from the posterior predictive distribution of the accuracy difference, and only average across subsamples:

$$\frac{\bar{\hat{Y}}_{ij\cdot 1} - \bar{\hat{Y}}_{ij\cdot 0}}{n}. \tag{12}$$

A more concise way is to perform a hypothesis test for each setting of m, n, and the LM type:

$$H_0 : \mathrm{E}[\mathrm{acc}_{\mathrm{test}} - \mathrm{acc}_{\mathrm{extra}}] = 0 \tag{13}$$
$$H_1 : \mathrm{E}[\mathrm{acc}_{\mathrm{test}} - \mathrm{acc}_{\mathrm{extra}}] > 0. \tag{14}$$

The p-value is estimated via permutation testing. It is then adjusted to control the false discovery rate (Benjamini and Hochberg, 1995).

7 Discussion

Figure 3 demonstrates that the average pretraining boost is significant in every configuration of the experiment. This finding replicates that from Gururangan et al. (2020). After averaging across settings for m, n, and the 2 LM types, only two of the 25 classification tasks had a pretraining boost less than 0, and both were greater than -1%. [4] Task-adaptive pretraining had the intended effect.

As shown in Figure 3, the evaluation bias bounces inconsistently and insignificantly around 0. After averaging, 12 of the 25 classification tasks had a positive evaluation bias, 13 had a negative evaluation bias, and all tasks had an average evaluation bias less than 1% in absolute value.

To avoid excessive averaging, we lemon-picked tasks which reported a bias of at least +3% in any experiment configuration. All tasks matching this criterion were from experiments with BERT, as BERT had greater training variance. If there were a task-dependent evaluation bias, one could expect that the bias is consistent across m or n within a task, or there is a consistent pattern with how the bias changes with m or n across tasks. Figure 4 does not clearly support either of these hypotheses.

Moscovich and Rosset (2022) found that the evaluation bias caused by unsupervised methods for tabular data converges to 0 as n increases. This finding is not confirmed by this experiment. Figure 3 shows that within $m = 50$ and $m = 100$, distributions of the evaluation bias hover around 0 across n. Figure 4 also does not support a relationship between n and the evaluation bias for lemon-picked tasks. But far more experiments varying n are needed to thoroughly assess this insensitivity.

8 Overtraining

§7 rules out undertraining on unlabeled text as the cause of a null evaluation bias. What if we overtrain? Overtraining on labeled test data trivially increases test set performance. Perhaps overtraining on unlabeled test set text has a similar effect. To test this hypothesis for text classification, GPT-2 is intentionally overtrained on unlabeled text for 2 epochs instead of 1.

For each of the 25 classification tasks and their subsamples, pretraining for 2 epochs instead of 1 resulted in a lower pretraining loss. The final pretraining loss is 20% lower on average, and the pretraining boost is negative, which indicates overfitting, as intended. Figure 5 demonstrates that, despite overtraining, the evaluation bias hovers around 0. All 50 p-values from the test in (13) are greater than 0.5.[5] Overtraining on unlabeled test set text causes test set performance to degrade to the same degree that overfitting on unlabeled independent text does.

9 Zero-shot text classification

Prompting an LLM is a popular choice for solving NLP problems. These prompts can be pretrained on. For example, Gemma 2 (Team et al., 2024) is intentionally pretrained on prompts from the LMSYS benchmark (Zheng et al., 2023).

To study a more modern prompting approach, the experiment in §4 is repeated with two modifications. First, task-adaptive pretraining is done on prompts—unlabeled texts with instructions for solving the task. Second, classification training is not performed; `train` is unused. The further-pretrained LLM is immediately prompted to do the task on `test`.

More specifically, pretraining is performed by adding a QLoRA adapter layer (Dettmers et al.,

[3] We will not assess any particular hypothesis about the role of causality. We are only motivating task-level analysis.

[4] The tasks were `blog_authorship_corpus` and `movie_rationales`.

[5] Note that all p-values from the test in (13) are adjusted to control the false discovery rate.

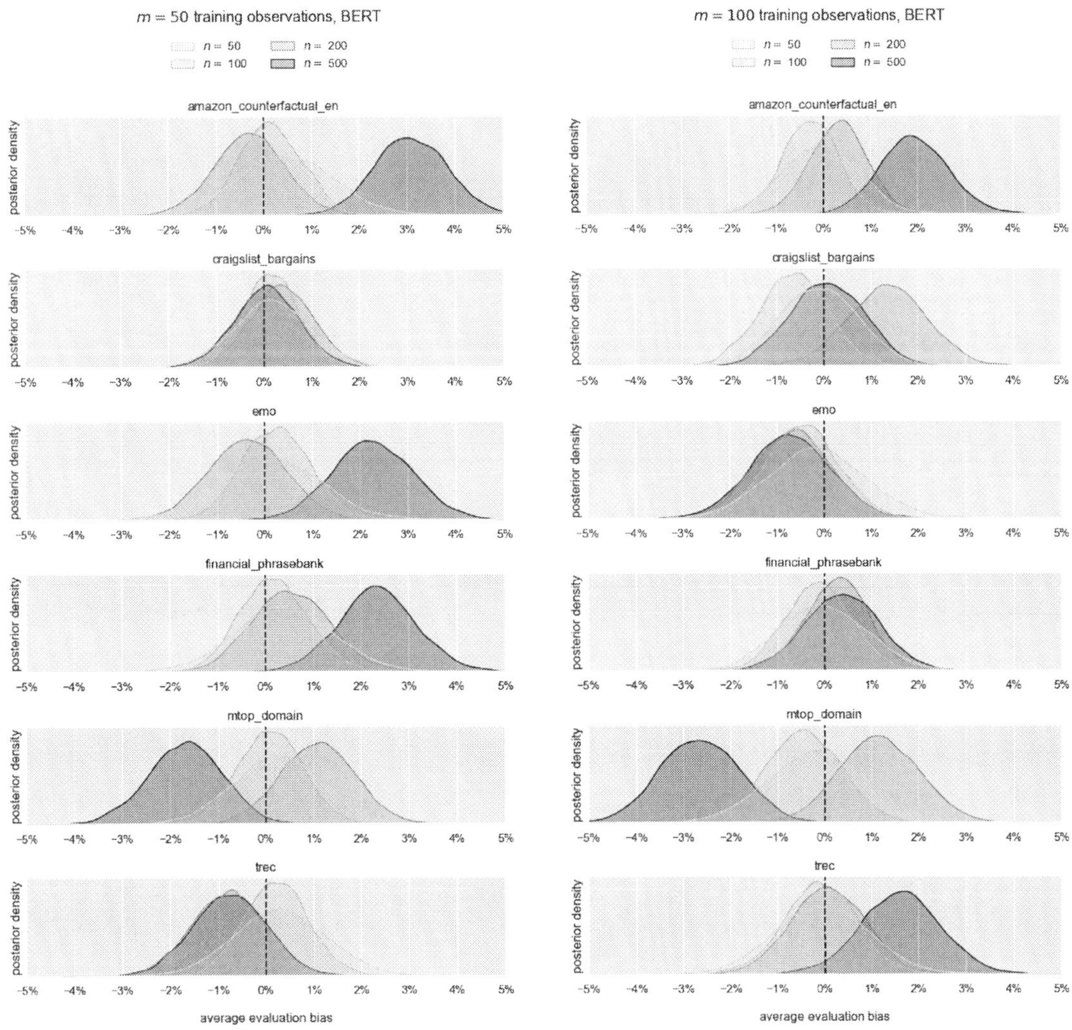

Figure 4: Distributions of average evaluation biases (12) for the subset of tasks which reported an average evaluation bias of at least +3% accuracy in any configuration of the experiment.

2024) to every linear layer in Mistral 7B (Jiang et al., 2023). Perhaps notably, instructions mention the set of possible answers—the class names.

Figure 6 (left) shows that, while pretraining on prompts improves accuracy, pretraining on test set prompts does not increase test set accuracy compared to pretraining on independently drawn prompts. 12 of the 25 tasks had a positive evaluation bias and 13 had a negative evaluation bias. All 25 p-values from (13) are greater than 0.5; there is no evidence of a task-level evaluation bias.

A limitation of this experiment is that it does not account for contamination. If Mistral 7B's pretraining data included labeled or unlabeled parts of the datasets used here, the pretraining boost and evaluation bias may be diluted.

9.1 Packing instead of padding

Experiments so far passed pretraining texts independently, adding and masking pad tokens to enable batching. Packing instead combines texts into a single sequence of tokens whose length is the model's context length. Packing is often used during the initial pretraining of an LLM, where the model is trained on continuous streams of text to increase throughput (Brown et al., 2020).

Does packing impact evaluation bias differently than padding? One hypothesis is that, without special handling of the attention mask, packing causes the model to attend to previous texts, so the transformer has greater flexibility in modeling unlabeled text. To study the effects of packing, the zero-shot experiment in §9 is repeated with packing instead

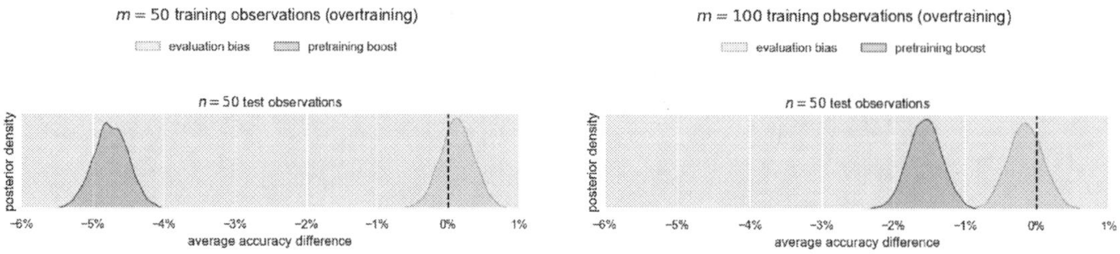

Figure 5: Average accuracy differences (11) after pretraining GPT-2 for 2 epochs instead of 1 (§8).

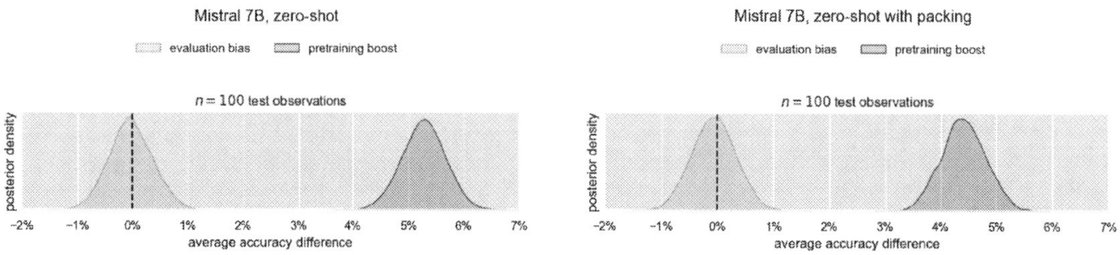

Figure 6: Average accuracy differences (11) for zero-shot classification (§9) with padding (left) and packing (right). For each of the 25 classification tasks, 20 subsamples were taken.

of padding. Figure 6 (right) shows that there is a pretraining boost, but no evaluation bias. All 25 p-values from (13) are greater than 0.5.

9.2 On testing test set contamination

Contamination detectors aim to flag overoptimistic LLM evaluations. An LLM is contaminated if it was pretrained and evaluated on the same set of labeled data, as this procedure results in an evaluation bias. In contrast, the result from §9.1 implies that contamination of *unlabeled* test set text does not result in an evaluation bias. Do contamination detectors pick up this nuance?

The experiment in §9.1 is run for the `ag_news` task and $n = 500$. Next, text-label pairs from `test` are passed to the contamination hypothesis test in Oren et al. (2024). The p-value for the model pretrained on unlabeled text from `extra` is 0.33. The p-value for the model pretrained on unlabeled text from `test` is 0.015, which indicates contamination. However, the observed evaluation bias for this task is statistically indistinguishable from 0.

Detectors need to be able to differentiate the contamination of labeled text from the contamination of unlabeled text. For those that do not, contamination flags should be interpreted with care. Even if such a detector never raises false flags, a contamination flag may not indicate an overoptimistic evaluation.

10 Meta-analysis

§4.4 briefly argues for subsampling multiple datasets from the full classification dataset. To assess this argument, the analysis was repeated on 500 random slices of the $m = 100, n = 500$ dataset of accuracies such that exactly 1 ($\text{acc}_{\text{extra}}$, acc_{test}, acc_{base}) triple per classification task (instead of 20 triples) is included. This de-replicated data is often all one gets from benchmarks.

Figure 7 (left) displays the cumulative distribution of the posterior mean of the evaluation bias for $m = 100, n = 500$ under this de-replicated experimental design. The distribution is quite variant. There is a 47% chance that the posterior mean of β—the average increase in the log-odds of a correct prediction by pretraining on unlabeled test set text instead of on unlabeled independent text—is outside the interval $(-0.04, 0.04)$, which would indicate a significant negative or positive bias.[6] For the zero-shot experiment in §9, there is a 50% chance that that the posterior mean of β is outside $(-0.08, 0.08)$. Without repeated subsampling, one may as well flip a coin to decide whether pretraining on unlabeled test set text is fair.

[6]For 0.04, the odds ratio is $e^{0.04} \approx 1.04$. For context, the average odds ratio between adjacent submissions in the RAFT leaderboard is 1.03. For posterior means outside $(-0.04, 0.04)$, all of their 89% credible intervals exclude 0, which evidences a non-null effect.

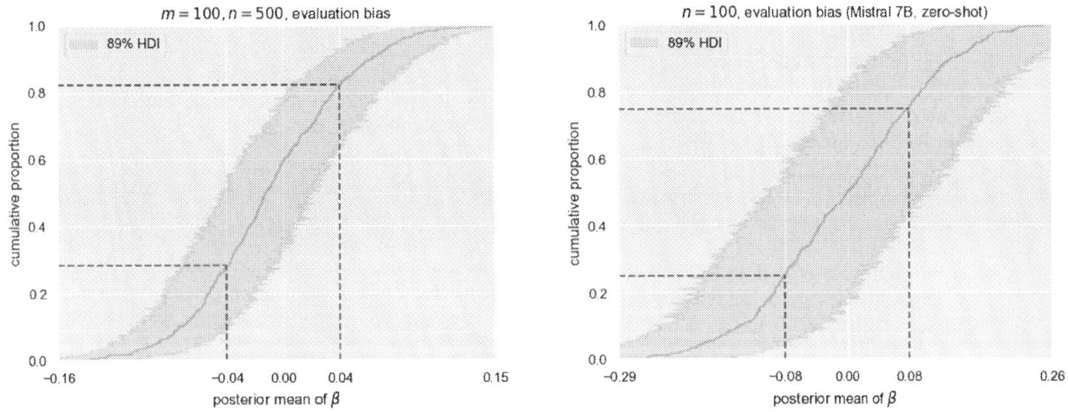

Figure 7: Distributions of conclusions had there been no technical replication (§10).

11 Conclusion

Task-adaptive pretraining on unlabeled test set text—instead of on unlabeled independent text—did not result in a consistent or significant evaluation bias. This appears to be the case when pretraining helps, when it hurts, and when pretraining is done on texts with instructions.

For benchmarks which release unlabeled text from the test set, this finding does not completely absolve LLM evaluations from scrutiny. The reason is that the boost from pretraining on unlabeled text—which is often significant—could be viewed as a type of evaluation bias, depending on how LLMs generalize. More concretely, suppose there is a benchmark and two LLMs, A and B. A was *not* pretrained on the benchmark's unlabeled test set text, while B was. With the perspective that LLM benchmarks supply scores which are correlates of performance on real-world tasks—instead of indicators of performance solely on the benchmark's tasks—then B scoring higher on the benchmark than A may be a misleading signal. If pretraining on the benchmark's unlabeled text causes B to generalize better only *within* the distribution of the benchmark, then B's edge on this benchmark does not signal an edge in real-world tasks. Knowing whether an LLM was pretrained on unlabeled test set text is still important.

One recommendation for designing few-shot benchmarks, which expands on the principle about robustness from Bragg et al. (2021), is based on the meta-analysis in §10: empirical studies of few-shot learning should consider including multiple, independent subsamples of training data. While a single training set combined with a large test set is sufficient for precise, unbiased estimation of out-of-sample performance, this estimator is conditional on the training set. In few-shot learning, the training set is, by definition, minimal. The estimator hides two sources of variance—that from the randomly drawn training set, and that from randomness inherent in the training procedure. Figure 7 shows that this variance is large-enough to turn a methodology into a coin flip for two different training procedures. In-context learning with LLMs is also sensitive to the selection of few-shot examples (Lu et al., 2022, Alzahrani et al., 2024). Benchmarks which require training on multiple, independent subsamples would expose training variance.

Limitations

This paper does not study semi-supervised methods like Pattern-Exploiting Training, or hand-inspecting the test set text and targeting interventions accordingly. We also do not study the effect of including unlabeled test set texts in the initial pretraining stage of an LLM.

The results are empirical. There may be tasks where an evaluation bias exists, and these were not part of the 25 classification tasks we collected. The results do not theoretically or universally establish that pretraining on unlabeled test set text is fair.

Acknowledgements

The author is grateful to Eilon Reisin-Tzur for valuable feedback and insightful discussions, and for motivating the question addressed in Appendix F. The author is also grateful to his family for the continued provision of sustenance, shelter, and crossword puzzles.

References

Neel Alex, Eli Lifland, Lewis Tunstall, Abhishek Thakur, Pegah Maham, C. Riedel, Emmie Hine, Carolyn Ashurst, Paul Sedille, Alexis Carlier, Michael Noetel, and Andreas Stuhlmüller. 2021. Raft: A real-world few-shot text classification benchmark. In *Proceedings of the Neural Information Processing Systems Track on Datasets and Benchmarks*, volume 1.

Norah Alzahrani, Hisham Abdullah Alyahya, Yazeed Alnumay, Sultan Alrashed, Shaykhah Alsubaie, Yusef Almushaykeh, Faisal Mirza, Nouf Alotaibi, Nora Altwairesh, Areeb Alowisheq, et al. 2024. When benchmarks are targets: Revealing the sensitivity of large language model leaderboards. *arXiv preprint arXiv:2402.01781*.

Yoav Benjamini and Yosef Hochberg. 1995. Controlling the false discovery rate: a practical and powerful approach to multiple testing. *Journal of the Royal statistical society: series B (Methodological)*, 57(1):289–300.

Jonathan Bragg, Arman Cohan, Kyle Lo, and Iz Beltagy. 2021. Flex: Unifying evaluation for few-shot nlp. *Advances in Neural Information Processing Systems*, 34:15787–15800.

Tom Brown, Benjamin Mann, Nick Ryder, Melanie Subbiah, Jared D Kaplan, Prafulla Dhariwal, Arvind Neelakantan, Pranav Shyam, Girish Sastry, Amanda Askell, et al. 2020. Language models are few-shot learners. *Advances in neural information processing systems*, 33:1877–1901.

Tomás Capretto, Camen Piho, Ravin Kumar, Jacob Westfall, Tal Yarkoni, and Osvaldo A Martin. 2022. Bambi: A simple interface for fitting bayesian linear models in python. *Journal of Statistical Software*, 103(15):1–29.

Emile Chapuis, Pierre Colombo, Matteo Manica, Matthieu Labeau, and Chloé Clavel. 2020. Hierarchical pre-training for sequence labelling in spoken dialog. In *Findings of the Association for Computational Linguistics: EMNLP 2020*, pages 2636–2648, Online. Association for Computational Linguistics.

Ankush Chatterjee, Kedhar Nath Narahari, Meghana Joshi, and Puneet Agrawal. 2019. SemEval-2019 task 3: EmoContext contextual emotion detection in text. In *Proceedings of the 13th International Workshop on Semantic Evaluation*, pages 39–48, Minneapolis, Minnesota, USA. Association for Computational Linguistics.

Tim Dettmers, Artidoro Pagnoni, Ari Holtzman, and Luke Zettlemoyer. 2024. Qlora: Efficient finetuning of quantized llms. *Advances in Neural Information Processing Systems*, 36.

Jacob Devlin, Ming-Wei Chang, Kenton Lee, and Kristina Toutanova. 2019. BERT: Pre-training of deep bidirectional transformers for language understanding. In *Proceedings of the 2019 Conference of the North American Chapter of the Association for Computational Linguistics: Human Language Technologies, Volume 1 (Long and Short Papers)*, pages 4171–4186, Minneapolis, Minnesota. Association for Computational Linguistics.

Jay DeYoung, Sarthak Jain, Nazneen Fatema Rajani, Eric Lehman, Caiming Xiong, Richard Socher, and Byron C. Wallace. 2020. ERASER: A benchmark to evaluate rationalized NLP models. In *Proceedings of the 58th Annual Meeting of the Association for Computational Linguistics*, pages 4443–4458, Online. Association for Computational Linguistics.

Thomas Diggelmann, Jordan Boyd-Graber, Jannis Bulian, Massimiliano Ciaramita, and Markus Leippold. 2020. Climate-fever: A dataset for verification of real-world climate claims.

Jack FitzGerald, Christopher Hench, Charith Peris, Scott Mackie, Kay Rottmann, Ana Sanchez, Aaron Nash, Liam Urbach, Vishesh Kakarala, Richa Singh, Swetha Ranganath, Laurie Crist, Misha Britan, Wouter Leeuwis, Gokhan Tur, and Prem Natarajan. 2023. MASSIVE: A 1M-example multilingual natural language understanding dataset with 51 typologically-diverse languages. In *Proceedings of the 61st Annual Meeting of the Association for Computational Linguistics (Volume 1: Long Papers)*, pages 4277–4302, Toronto, Canada. Association for Computational Linguistics.

Giovanni Grano, Andrea Di Sorbo, Francesco Mercaldo, Corrado A Visaggio, Gerardo Canfora, and Sebastiano Panichella. 2017. Android apps and user feedback: a dataset for software evolution and quality improvement. In *Proceedings of the 2nd ACM SIGSOFT international workshop on app market analytics*, pages 8–11.

Yuxian Gu, Xu Han, Zhiyuan Liu, and Minlie Huang. 2022. PPT: Pre-trained prompt tuning for few-shot learning. In *Proceedings of the 60th Annual Meeting of the Association for Computational Linguistics (Volume 1: Long Papers)*, pages 8410–8423, Dublin, Ireland. Association for Computational Linguistics.

Neel Guha, Julian Nyarko, Daniel Ho, Christopher Ré, Adam Chilton, Alex Chohlas-Wood, Austin Peters, Brandon Waldon, Daniel Rockmore, Diego Zambrano, et al. 2024. Legalbench: A collaboratively built benchmark for measuring legal reasoning in large language models. *Advances in Neural Information Processing Systems*, 36.

Suchin Gururangan, Ana Marasović, Swabha Swayamdipta, Kyle Lo, Iz Beltagy, Doug Downey, and Noah A. Smith. 2020. Don't stop pretraining: Adapt language models to domains and tasks. In *Proceedings of the 58th Annual Meeting of the Association for Computational Linguistics*, pages 8342–8360, Online. Association for Computational Linguistics.

Trevor Hastie, Robert Tibshirani, Jerome H Friedman, and Jerome H Friedman. 2009. *The elements of statistical learning: data mining, inference, and prediction*, volume 2. Springer.

He He, Derek Chen, Anusha Balakrishnan, and Percy Liang. 2018. Decoupling strategy and generation in negotiation dialogues. In *Proceedings of the 2018 Conference on Empirical Methods in Natural Language Processing*, pages 2333–2343, Brussels, Belgium. Association for Computational Linguistics.

Zhang Huangzhao. 2018. Yahoo-answers-topic-classification-dataset. `https://github.com/LC-John/Yahoo-Answers-Topic-Classification-Dataset`.

Alon Jacovi, Avi Caciularu, Omer Goldman, and Yoav Goldberg. 2023. Stop uploading test data in plain text: Practical strategies for mitigating data contamination by evaluation benchmarks. In *Proceedings of the 2023 Conference on Empirical Methods in Natural Language Processing*, pages 5075–5084, Singapore. Association for Computational Linguistics.

Albert Q Jiang, Alexandre Sablayrolles, Arthur Mensch, Chris Bamford, Devendra Singh Chaplot, Diego de las Casas, Florian Bressand, Gianna Lengyel, Guillaume Lample, Lucile Saulnier, et al. 2023. Mistral 7b. *arXiv preprint arXiv:2310.06825*.

Zhijing Jin, Julius von Kügelgen, Jingwei Ni, Tejas Vaidhya, Ayush Kaushal, Mrinmaya Sachan, and Bernhard Schoelkopf. 2021. Causal direction of data collection matters: Implications of causal and anticausal learning for NLP. In *Proceedings of the 2021 Conference on Empirical Methods in Natural Language Processing*, pages 9499–9513, Online and Punta Cana, Dominican Republic. Association for Computational Linguistics.

Johannes Kiesel, Maria Mestre, Rishabh Shukla, Emmanuel Vincent, Payam Adineh, David Corney, Benno Stein, and Martin Potthast. 2019. SemEval-2019 task 4: Hyperpartisan news detection. In *Proceedings of the 13th International Workshop on Semantic Evaluation*, pages 829–839, Minneapolis, Minnesota, USA. Association for Computational Linguistics.

Ravin Kumar, Colin Carroll, Ari Hartikainen, and Osvaldo Martin. 2019. Arviz a unified library for exploratory analysis of bayesian models in python. *Journal of Open Source Software*, 4(33):1143.

Nikola Ljubešić, Darja Fišer, and Tomaž Erjavec. 2019. The frenk datasets of socially unacceptable discourse in slovene and english.

Yao Lu, Max Bartolo, Alastair Moore, Sebastian Riedel, and Pontus Stenetorp. 2022. Fantastically ordered prompts and where to find them: Overcoming few-shot prompt order sensitivity. In *Proceedings of the 60th Annual Meeting of the Association for Computational Linguistics (Volume 1: Long Papers)*, pages 8086–8098, Dublin, Ireland. Association for Computational Linguistics.

P. Malo, A. Sinha, P. Korhonen, J. Wallenius, and P. Takala. 2014. Good debt or bad debt: Detecting semantic orientations in economic texts. *Journal of the Association for Information Science and Technology*, 65.

Irene Manotas, Ngoc Phuoc An Vo, and Vadim Sheinin. 2020. LiMiT: The literal motion in text dataset. In *Findings of the Association for Computational Linguistics: EMNLP 2020*, pages 991–1000, Online. Association for Computational Linguistics.

Richard McElreath. 2018. *Statistical rethinking: A Bayesian course with examples in R and Stan*. Chapman and Hall/CRC.

Vangelis Metsis, Ion Androutsopoulos, and Georgios Paliouras. 2006. Spam filtering with naive bayes-which naive bayes? In *CEAS*, volume 17, pages 28–69. Mountain View, CA.

Tomas Mikolov, Ilya Sutskever, Kai Chen, Greg S Corrado, and Jeff Dean. 2013. Distributed representations of words and phrases and their compositionality. *Advances in neural information processing systems*, 26.

Richard D Morey, Rink Hoekstra, Jeffrey N Rouder, Michael D Lee, and Eric-Jan Wagenmakers. 2016. The fallacy of placing confidence in confidence intervals. *Psychonomic bulletin & review*, 23:103–123.

Amit Moscovich and Saharon Rosset. 2022. On the cross-validation bias due to unsupervised preprocessing. *Journal of the Royal Statistical Society Series B: Statistical Methodology*, 84(4):1474–1502.

Niklas Muennighoff, Nouamane Tazi, Loic Magne, and Nils Reimers. 2023. MTEB: Massive text embedding benchmark. In *Proceedings of the 17th Conference of the European Chapter of the Association for Computational Linguistics*, pages 2014–2037, Dubrovnik, Croatia. Association for Computational Linguistics.

James O'Neill, Polina Rozenshtein, Ryuichi Kiryo, Motoko Kubota, and Danushka Bollegala. 2021. I wish I would have loved this one, but I didn't – a multilingual dataset for counterfactual detection in product review. In *Proceedings of the 2021 Conference on Empirical Methods in Natural Language Processing*, pages 7092–7108, Online and Punta Cana, Dominican Republic. Association for Computational Linguistics.

Yonatan Oren, Nicole Meister, Niladri S. Chatterji, Faisal Ladhak, and Tatsunori Hashimoto. 2024. Proving test set contamination in black-box language models. In *The Twelfth International Conference on Learning Representations, ICLR 2024, Vienna, Austria, May 7-11, 2024*. OpenReview.net.

Bo Pang and Lillian Lee. 2005. Seeing stars: Exploiting class relationships for sentiment categorization with respect to rating scales. In *Proceedings of the 43rd Annual Meeting of the Association for Computational Linguistics (ACL'05)*, pages 115–124, Ann

Arbor, Michigan. Association for Computational Linguistics.

Alec Radford, Jeffrey Wu, Rewon Child, David Luan, Dario Amodei, Ilya Sutskever, et al. 2019. Language models are unsupervised multitask learners. *OpenAI blog*, 1(8):9.

Elvis Saravia, Hsien-Chi Toby Liu, Yen-Hao Huang, Junlin Wu, and Yi-Shin Chen. 2018. CARER: Contextualized affect representations for emotion recognition. In *Proceedings of the 2018 Conference on Empirical Methods in Natural Language Processing*, pages 3687–3697, Brussels, Belgium. Association for Computational Linguistics.

Timo Schick and Hinrich Schütze. 2021. Exploiting cloze-questions for few-shot text classification and natural language inference. In *Proceedings of the 16th Conference of the European Chapter of the Association for Computational Linguistics: Main Volume*, pages 255–269, Online. Association for Computational Linguistics.

Jonathan Schler, Moshe Koppel, Shlomo Argamon, and James W Pennebaker. 2006. Effects of age and gender on blogging. In *AAAI spring symposium: Computational approaches to analyzing weblogs*, volume 6, pages 199–205.

Eva Sharma, Chen Li, and Lu Wang. 2019. BIGPATENT: A large-scale dataset for abstractive and coherent summarization. In *Proceedings of the 57th Annual Meeting of the Association for Computational Linguistics*, pages 2204–2213, Florence, Italy. Association for Computational Linguistics.

Roshan Sharma. 2019. Twitter-sentiment-analysis. `https://github.com/sharmaroshan/Twitter-Sentiment-Analysis`.

Gemma Team, Morgane Riviere, Shreya Pathak, Pier Giuseppe Sessa, Cassidy Hardin, Surya Bhupatiraju, Léonard Hussenot, Thomas Mesnard, Bobak Shahriari, Alexandre Ramé, et al. 2024. Gemma 2: Improving open language models at a practical size. *arXiv preprint arXiv:2408.00118*.

Tan Thongtan and Tanasanee Phienthrakul. 2019. Sentiment classification using document embeddings trained with cosine similarity. In *Proceedings of the 57th Annual Meeting of the Association for Computational Linguistics: Student Research Workshop*, pages 407–414, Florence, Italy. Association for Computational Linguistics.

Lewis Tunstall, Nils Reimers, Unso Eun Seo Jo, Luke Bates, Daniel Korat, Moshe Wasserblat, and Oren Pereg. 2022. Efficient few-shot learning without prompts. *arXiv preprint arXiv:2209.11055*.

Mengqiu Wang, Noah A. Smith, and Teruko Mitamura. 2007. What is the Jeopardy model? a quasi-synchronous grammar for QA. In *Proceedings of the 2007 Joint Conference on Empirical Methods in Natural Language Processing and Computational Natural Language Learning (EMNLP-CoNLL)*, pages 22–32, Prague, Czech Republic. Association for Computational Linguistics.

Thomas Wolf, Lysandre Debut, Victor Sanh, Julien Chaumond, Clement Delangue, Anthony Moi, Pierric Cistac, Tim Rault, Remi Louf, Morgan Funtowicz, Joe Davison, Sam Shleifer, Patrick von Platen, Clara Ma, Yacine Jernite, Julien Plu, Canwen Xu, Teven Le Scao, Sylvain Gugger, Mariama Drame, Quentin Lhoest, and Alexander Rush. 2020. Transformers: State-of-the-art natural language processing. In *Proceedings of the 2020 Conference on Empirical Methods in Natural Language Processing: System Demonstrations*, pages 38–45, Online. Association for Computational Linguistics.

Tianyi Zhang, Felix Wu, Arzoo Katiyar, Kilian Q Weinberger, and Yoav Artzi. 2021. Revisiting few-sample bert fine-tuning. In *International Conference on Learning Representations*.

Xiang Zhang, Junbo Zhao, and Yann LeCun. 2015. Character-level convolutional networks for text classification. *Advances in neural information processing systems*, 28.

Lianmin Zheng, Wei-Lin Chiang, Ying Sheng, Tianle Li, Siyuan Zhuang, Zhanghao Wu, Yonghao Zhuang, Zhuohan Li, Zi Lin, Eric Xing, et al. 2023. Lmsys-chat-1m: A large-scale real-world llm conversation dataset. *arXiv preprint arXiv:2309.11998*.

A Classification tasks

The experiment was ran on 25 publicly available text classification tasks found in `https://huggingface.co/datasets`. Inclusion criteria:

1. All text is in English.
2. The number of classes is not greater than 25, because only 50 or 100 observations are used for training the classifier.
3. The task is to classify one text, not a pair as in, e.g., textual entailment tasks.
4. Texts are not so long that too much useful signal is dropped when text is truncated to fit in BERT/GPT-2's context window, which is set to 256 tokens.
5. Based on our best judgment, it is likely that BERT/GPT-2 can do better than guessing.

Table 2 lists the exact tasks.

B Other experiment choices

This section expands on §4.

First, we clarify how classification training is performed. For BERT, the linear layer transforms

Hugging Face dataset	**Author(s)**	**Number of classes**	**Text length (25, 75) percentiles**
ag_news	Zhang et al. (2015)	4	(196, 266)
SetFit/amazon_counterfactual_en	O'Neill et al. (2021)	2	(60, 125)
app_reviews	Grano et al. (2017)	5	(10, 77)
blog_authorship_corpus	Schler et al. (2006)	2	(92, 556)
christinacdl/clickbait_notclickbait_dataset		2	(46, 69)
climate_fever	Diggelmann et al. (2020)	4	(80, 156)
aladar/craigslist_bargains	He et al. (2018)	6	(346, 713)
disaster_response_messages		3	(74, 178)
emo	Chatterjee et al. (2019)	4	(44, 83)
dair-ai/emotion	Saravia et al. (2018)	6	(53, 129)
SetFit/enron_spam	Metsis et al. (2006)	2	(342, 1553)
financial_phrasebank	Malo et al. (2014)	3	(79, 157)
classla/FRENK-hate-en	Ljubešić et al. (2019)	2	(34, 160)
hyperpartisan_news_detection	Kiesel et al. (2019)	2	(39, 63)
limit	Manotas et al. (2020)	2	(53, 123)
AmazonScience/massive	FitzGerald et al. (2023)	18	(24, 44)
movie_rationales	DeYoung et al. (2020)	2	(2721, 4659)
mteb/mtop_domain	Muennighoff et al. (2023)	11	(26, 44)
ccdv/patent-classification	Sharma et al. (2019)	9	(441, 775)
rotten_tomatoes	Pang and Lee (2005)	2	(76, 149)
silicone	Chapuis et al. (2020)	4	(29, 75)
trec	Wang et al. (2007)	6	(36, 61)
tweets_hate_speech_detection	Sharma (2019)	2	(62, 107)
yahoo_answers_topics	Huangzhao (2018)	10	(58, 213)
yelp_review_full	Zhang et al. (2015)	5	(287, 957)

Table 2: Brief descriptions of the 25 classification tasks used in this experiment. Click the link in the cell to be taken to the dataset homepage in `https://huggingface.co/datasets`. The dataset subset (or config) and the chosen prediction task are specified in code in `src/pretrain_on_test/data.py`.

the [CLS] token embedding. For GPT-2, the linear layer transforms the last token's embedding. The output dimension of the linear layer is the number of classes in the classification task. This layer, along with the rest of the weights in the LM, are finetuned to minimize classification cross entropy loss on train.

The BERT model used here is bert-base-uncased. The GPT-2 model used here is gpt2 (small), with 124M parameters.

train is stratify-sampled by the class to ensure every class is represented, and to reduce the variance of accuracy estimators. test is not stratify-sampled. We are only interested in the *difference* between accuracies, which is a function of the difference between model likelihoods because the priors are uniform. So even if accuracies are worse than the majority vote, differences are still meaningful for the purposes of this experiment.

train text is not included during pretraining to eliminate the overlap of pretraining data between $\text{acc}_{\text{extra}}$ and acc_{test}. This choice was made in an effort to widen any gap between them.

train contains $m = 50$ or $m = 100$ observations. $m = 50$ is inspired by the RAFT benchmark. $m = 100$ stretches the intention of "few" in few-shot learning, but was tested in an attempt to make lower-variance comparisons. BERT is quite sensitive—see Appendix D.2.

C Hyperparameters and reproducibility

This paper's experiment and analysis code, and data, is available here: https://github.com/kddubey/pretrain-on-test.

experiment.sh lists hyperparameters used for each classification task and experiment configuration. For the experiment in §4, BERT was pretrained for 2 epochs, and GPT-2 was pretrained for 1 epoch. Classification hyperparameters were pre-specified based on Zhang et al. (2021), with batch sizes set to avoid out-of-memory errors. Run the script on a GPU with at least 15 GB RAM to reproduce results in §5. It takes about 5 days on a T4 GPU. Training is performed using the transformers package (Wolf et al., 2020).

D Results

D.1 Task-level analysis

The notebook analysis/dataset.ipynb can be run to (1) produce visualizations of the distributions of $\text{acc}_{\text{extra}}$, acc_{test}, and acc_{base} (for each classification task and experiment configuration), and (2) compute p-values for the hypothesis test specified in (13). For all settings of m and n, no p-values were statistically significant at the 0.05 level.

In Figure 4, amazon_counterfactual_en and mtop_domain have a consistent evaluation bias across m for $n = 500$ and $n = 200$, respectively. But these tasks did not result in an evaluation bias in any other experiment configuration, including those with GPT-2 and Mistral 7B.

Care has to be taken when attempting to analyze or interpret $\text{acc}_{\text{extra}} - \text{acc}_{\text{base}}$ and $\text{acc}_{\text{test}} - \text{acc}_{\text{extra}}$ *together*. That's because these differences are not independent: if $\text{acc}_{\text{extra}}$ is high, then $\text{acc}_{\text{extra}} - \text{acc}_{\text{base}}$ increases and $\text{acc}_{\text{test}} - \text{acc}_{\text{extra}}$ decreases. This paper does not analyze the scores together, per se. We care about $\text{acc}_{\text{test}} - \text{acc}_{\text{extra}}$. $\text{acc}_{\text{extra}} - \text{acc}_{\text{base}}$ only exists to sanity check that the pretraining code works; there may be an effect to detect.

D.2 Difference distributions

Figures 13 - 20 visualize the distributions of the paired differences—$\text{acc}_{\text{extra}} - \text{acc}_{\text{base}}$ and $\text{acc}_{\text{test}} - \text{acc}_{\text{extra}}$—for each configuration of the experiment.

E Analysis

The analysis in §6 can be reproduced by running all of the notebooks in analysis/fit_posteriors/. Figure 3 can be reproduced by running the notebook analysis/results/posterior_pred.ipynb. Figure 4 can be reproduced by running the notebook analysis/results/posterior_pred_conditional.ipynb. Changing the threshold for the bias to +2% accuracy instead of +3% did not change conclusions.

Posterior samples of β (which were used to draw posterior predictive samples) were taken from four chains with 1,000 draws each, after 500 steps of tuning.

E.1 Hierarchical model checks

Hierarchical models require some basic checks to have faith in their results (McElreath, 2018).

For each of the 24 hierarchical models (16 in §7, 4 in §8, and 4 in §9), no divergences were observed during the fitting procedure. All trace plots were healthy.

Figure 11 contains prior predictive distributions for $m = 100, n = 200$, demonstrating that priors are not unreasonable. Using default priors from the bambi package (Capretto et al., 2022), while scientifically unreasonable (because they result in wide, basin-like accuracy distributions), did not change the conclusions of this paper.

Figure 12 contains posterior distributions of β for $m = 100, n = 200$, demonstrating the hierarchical model's ability to recover both null and non-null effects. This test can be reproduced by running the notebook analysis/test.ipynb.

Figure 9 checks that posterior predictions for the average task accuracies are calibrated. Figure 10 demonstrates the importance of including the W_{jl} term. These figures can be reproduced by running the notebook analysis/results/posterior_pred_conditional.ipynb.

F Meta-analysis

The meta-analysis in §10 can be reproduced by running the script, analysis/meta/meta.py, and then the notebook analysis/meta/meta.ipynb. No divergences were observed.

Another question is whether the subsample causes a consistent evaluation bias. §10 establishes that picking a single subsample causes the comparison between acc_{test} and $\text{acc}_{\text{extra}}$ to be a coin flip. But is the result of the coin flip explained by the specific subsample that was drawn? If so, comparing models using a single subsample may not be so noisy, because the effect of pretraining on unlabeled test set text would be consistent across models.

One way to answer this question is to measure the correlation between the evaluation bias of BERT and GPT-2 for each setting of m and n, and each of the 25 tasks. A positive correlation suggests that the subsample causes the evaluation bias. Spearman's rank correlation coefficient is used because we are only interested in the consistency of the relationship, not its linearity.

The observed distributions of correlations across m, n, and the tasks are plotted in Figure 8 (a). For context, 10 distributions of randomly permuted pairs of subsample-level biases are plotted in Figure 8 (b) and (c). These correlations are theoretically 0, and are positive or negative by chance alone. The observed distributions are qualitatively indistinguishable from the null ones. Notably, the variance is consistent. A deeper dive into the correlations did not find any consistently positive (or negative) correlations at the task level. This result further evidences the importance of repeated subsampling. Taking a single subsample does not result in a consistent pretraining boost or evaluation bias between BERT and GPT-2. This analysis can be reproduced by running the notebook analysis/dataset_level.ipynb.

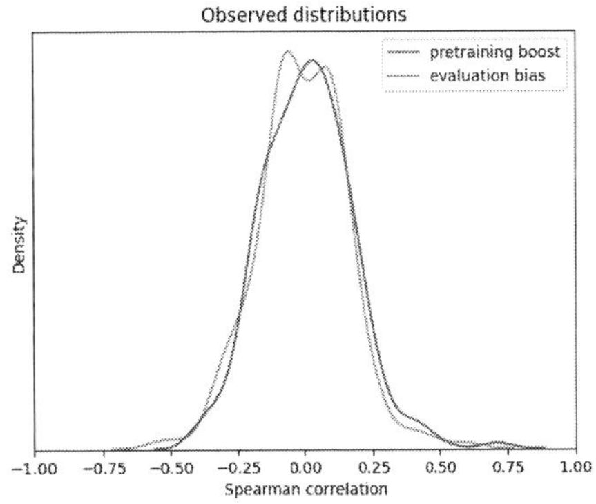

(a) Observed

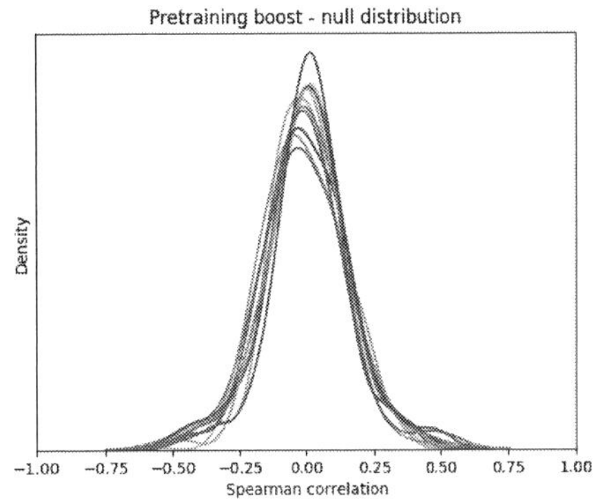

(b) Randomly permuted

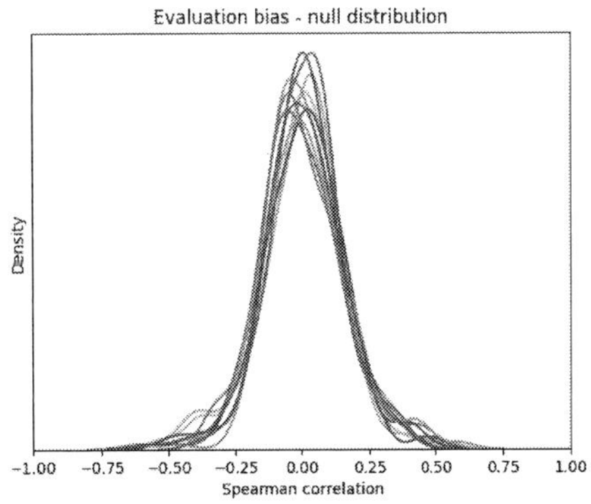

(c) Randomly permuted

Figure 8: Distribution of correlation between BERT and GPT-2 across all m, n, and the 25 classification tasks.

G Zero-shot text classification

Here is an example of a prompt for the ag_news task (Zhang et al., 2015):

```
Your task is to classify a given text as
one of these categories:
World
Sports
Business
Sci/Tech

The text is a news article. Answer with its topic.

### Text: Bombardier CEO Quits, Shares
Dive Paul Tellier stepped down on Monday
as president and chief executive of
Bombardier Inc. (BBDsvb.TO: Quote,
Profile, Research) (BBDb.
### Answer:
```

For packing (§9.1), the prompts at inference are in the same format as above. For training, 8 texts were packed. Here is an example of an input sequence for ag_news, where 4 texts are packed:

```
Your task is to classify a given text as
one of these categories:
World
Sports
Business
Sci/Tech

The text is a news article. Answer with its topic.

### Text: US Electoral College withstands critics
... so far (AFP) AFP - Lambasted as antiquated
and anti-democratic, the Electoral College that
decides the US presidency has survived for
centuries as an unmovable albeit creaky pillar
of the American political system.


### Text: Voters in Hungary decide referenda
Voters in Hungary went to the polls Sunday to
decide a double referendum on citizenship
rights and their nation #39;s health care
system.


### Text: White House: Trying to Confirm Terror
Group #39;s Allegiance to bin
&lt;b&gt;...&lt;/b&gt; The Bush administration
says it #39;s trying to confirm the latest
declaration from the most feared militant group
in Iraq. In a statement posted on a Web site
Sunday, the group led by terror mastermind Abu
Musab


### Text: Fans rush to create mods for
long-awaited #39;Doom 3 #39; Activision #39;s
Doom 3, which launched earlier this month,
wasn #39;t on store shelves for three days
before players started creating their own
modifications - known as mods -o the game.
```

The zero-shot experiment files are in `cloud_scripts/gcp/experiments/zero_shot/` and `cloud_scripts/gcp/experiments/zero_shot_packing/`. Batch sizes are set to run on a GPU with at least 20 GB RAM. The GPU must support the data types needed for QLoRA, e.g., an L4 GPU. Figure 6 can be reproduced by running the notebooks in `analysis/fit_posteriors/zero_shot` and `analysis/fit_posteriors/zero_shot_packing` and then the notebook, `analysis/results/posterior_pred.ipynb`.

The Mistral 7B model is Mistral-7B-v0.3, the non-instruction-trained model.

We only study $n = 100$ in an initial effort to provide evidence of an evaluation bias (due to the relatively small test set), and take 20 repeated subsamples instead of 50. While $n = 100$ is quite small, benchmarks such as LegalBench (Guha et al., 2024) have test data in this range. And the analysis transparently exposes variance.

QLoRA hyperparameters were pre-specified: every adapter has rank 16 with $\alpha = 32$ (LoRA scaling factor), a 0.05 dropout rate, and no bias parameters. The adapter layers introduce $41,943,040$ new, trainable parameters to Mistral 7B, whose parameters are frozen. Pretraining was done for 1 epoch.

To increase the power of the contamination hypothesis test run in §9.2, shards were formed to be similar to the sequences passed in during pretraining. Here is an example of what the first 2 text-label pairs in the dataset passed to the contamination test looks like:

```
### Text: Customers bemoan changes in Quicken
2005 The new version of the personal finance
program drops support for a widely used file
format.
### Answer: Sci/Tech

### Text: Blair gives partial Iraq apology Tony
Blair has offered his Labour party a partial
apology for waging war in Iraq, striving to pull
angry supporters behind him ahead of an election
next year.
### Answer: World
```

The 2 p-values in §9.2 can be obtained by running the notebook `analysis/contamination/test.ipynb` on an L4 GPU.

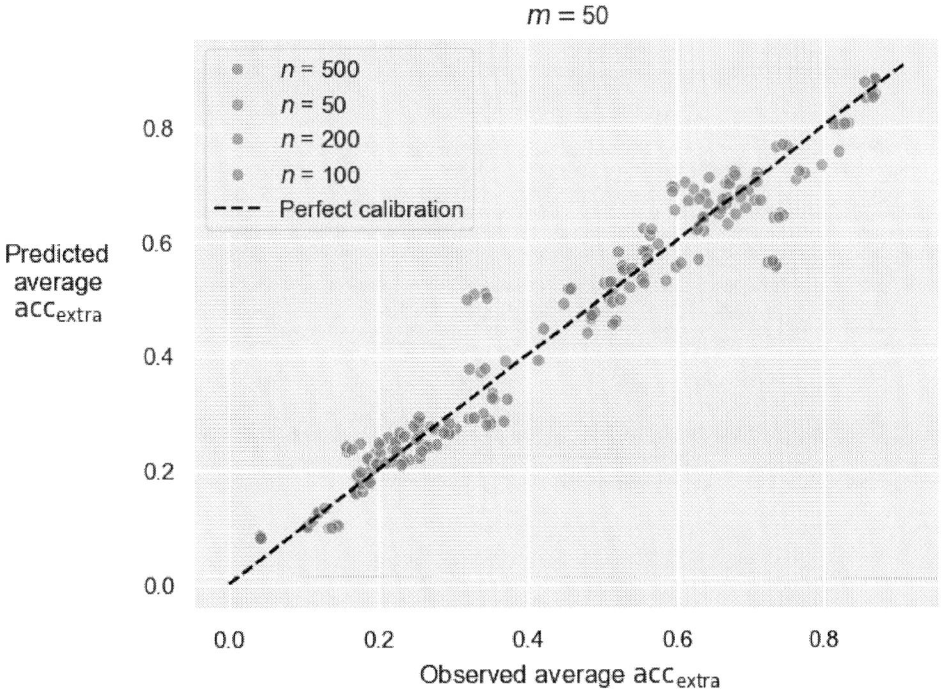

Figure 9: Each of the points represents a task and an LM type (BERT or GPT-2).

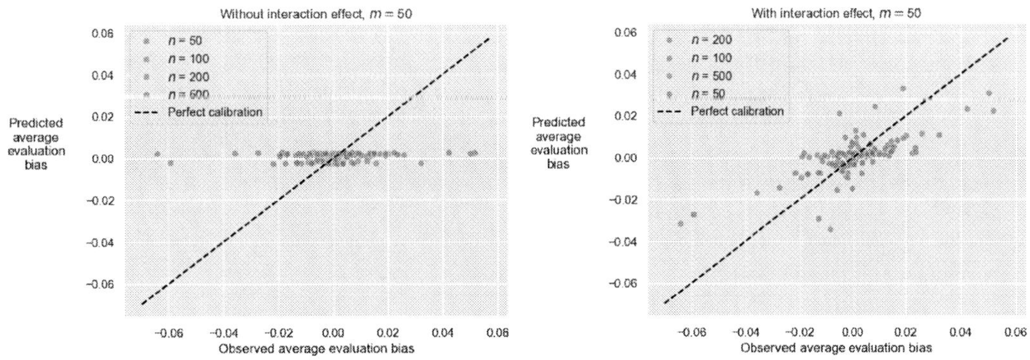

Figure 10: Omitting the interaction effect causes underfitting. Note that the prior causes effects to shrink towards 0. Each of the points represents a task and an LM type (BERT or GPT-2).

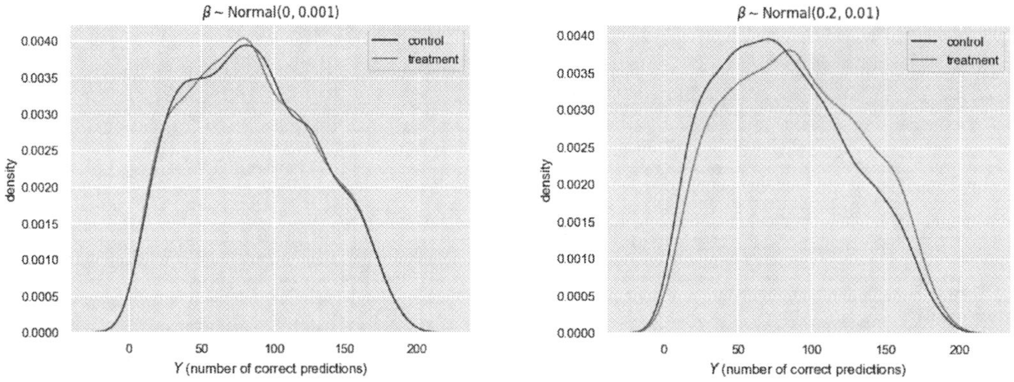

(a) Null effect

(b) Non-null, positive effect

Figure 11: Prior predictive distributions for $m = 100, n = 200$ from two different priors for β—the expected increase in the log-odds of a correct prediction resulting from an intervention/treatment.

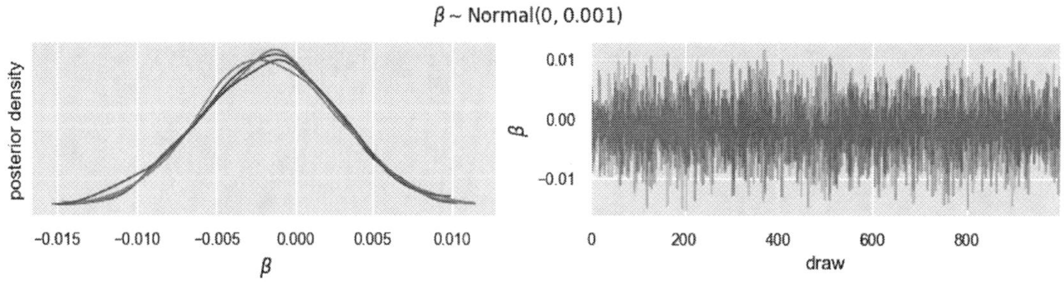

(a) Null effect is recovered.

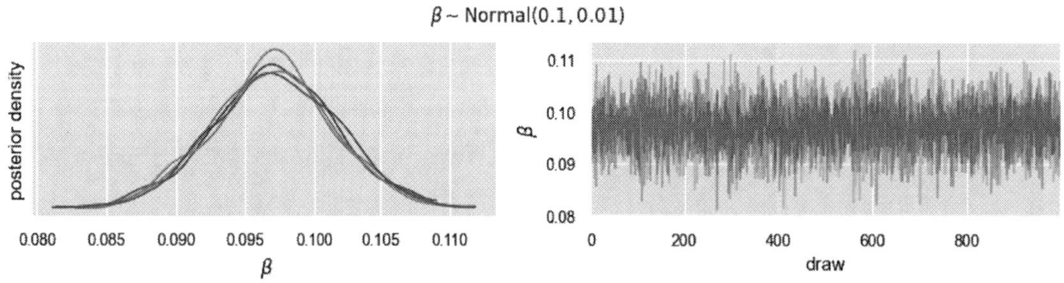

(b) Non-null, positive effect is recovered.

Figure 12: Posterior distributions and trace plots for null and non-null effects **from simulated data** where $m = 100, n = 200$, approximated by four chains with 1,000 draws each, after 500 steps of tuning. For each model, no divergences were observed during the fitting procedure. Visualizations were produced by the `arviz` package (Kumar et al., 2019).

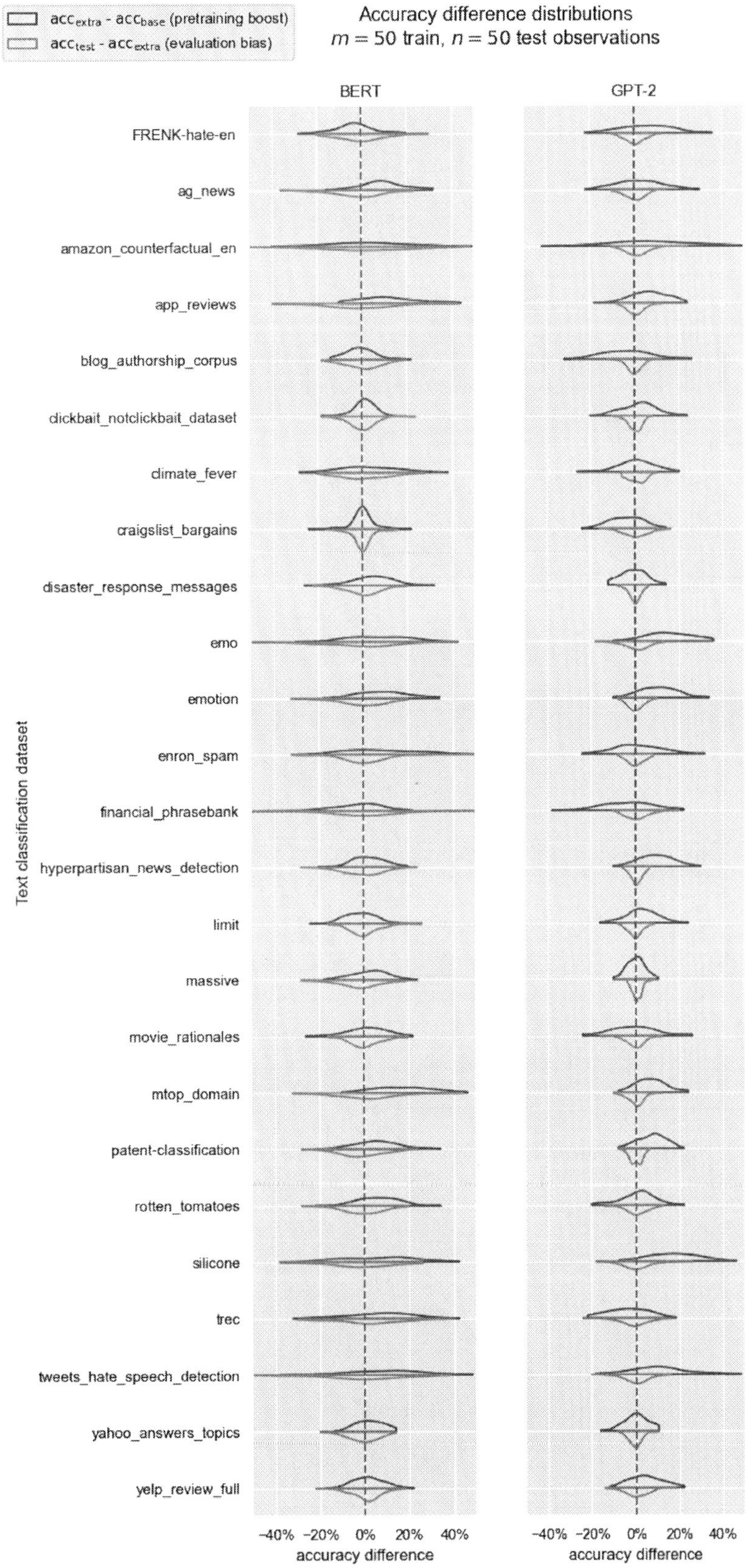

acc$_{extra}$ - acc$_{base}$ (pretraining boost)
acc$_{test}$ - acc$_{extra}$ (evaluation bias)
Accuracy difference distributions
$m = 50$ train, $n = 50$ test observations
BERT
GPT-2
Text classification dataset
FRENK-hate-en
ag_news
amazon_counterfactual_en
app_reviews
blog_authorship_corpus
clickbait_notclickbait_dataset
climate_fever
craigslist_bargains
disaster_response_messages
emo
emotion
enron_spam
financial_phrasebank
hyperpartisan_news_detection
limit
massive
movie_rationales
mtop_domain
patent-classification
rotten_tomatoes
silicone
trec
tweets_hate_speech_detection
yahoo_answers_topics
yelp_review_full
-40% -20% 0% 20% 40%
accuracy difference
-40% -20% 0% 20% 40%
accuracy difference

Figure 13

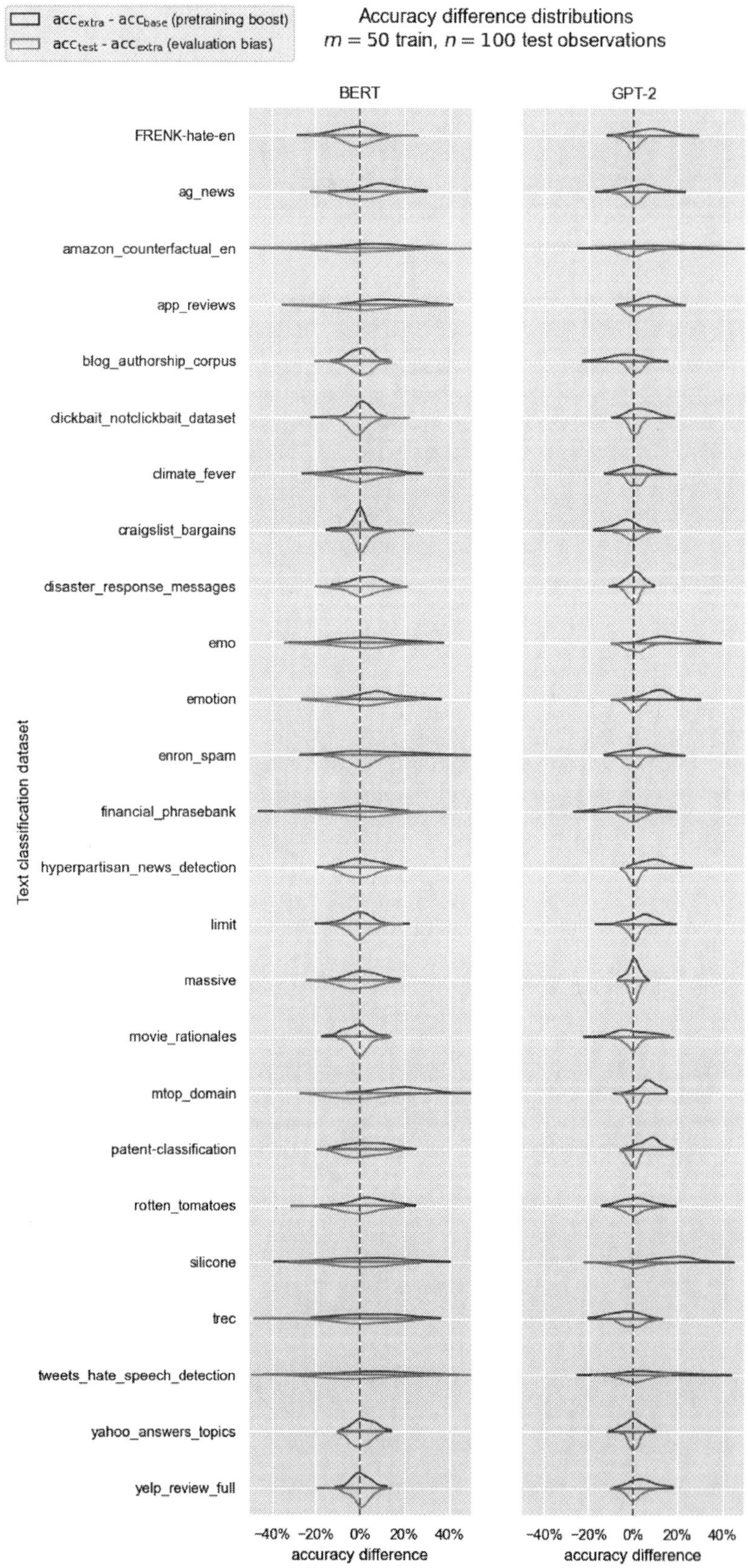

acc_{extra} - acc_{base} (pretraining boost)
acc_{test} - acc_{extra} (evaluation bias)
Accuracy difference distributions
$m = 50$ train, $n = 100$ test observations
BERT
GPT-2
FRENK-hate-en
ag_news
amazon_counterfactual_en
app_reviews
blog_authorship_corpus
clickbait_notclickbait_dataset
climate_fever
craigslist_bargains
disaster_response_messages
emo
emotion
enron_spam
financial_phrasebank
hyperpartisan_news_detection
limit
massive
movie_rationales
mtop_domain
patent-classification
rotten_tomatoes
silicone
trec
tweets_hate_speech_detection
yahoo_answers_topics
yelp_review_full
Text classification dataset
−40% −20% 0% 20% 40%
accuracy difference
−40% −20% 0% 20% 40%
accuracy difference

Figure 14

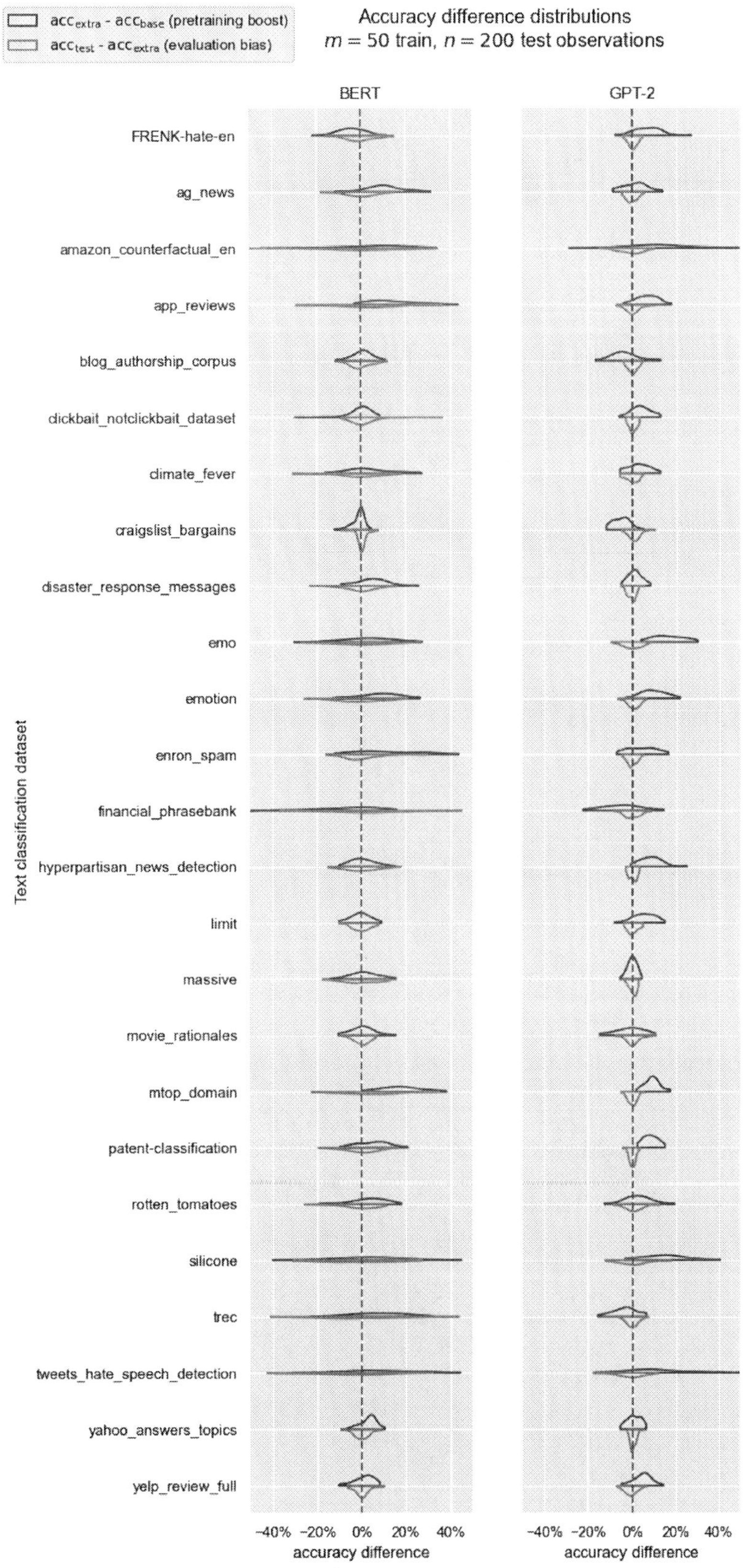
acc_extra - acc_base (pretraining boost)
acc_test - acc_extra (evaluation bias)
Accuracy difference distributions
m = 50 train, n = 200 test observations
BERT
GPT-2
FRENK-hate-en
ag_news
amazon_counterfactual_en
app_reviews
blog_authorship_corpus
clickbait_notclickbait_dataset
climate_fever
craigslist_bargains
disaster_response_messages
emo
emotion
enron_spam
financial_phrasebank
hyperpartisan_news_detection
limit
massive
movie_rationales
mtop_domain
patent-classification
rotten_tomatoes
silicone
trec
tweets_hate_speech_detection
yahoo_answers_topics
yelp_review_full
Text classification dataset
−40% −20% 0% 20% 40%
accuracy difference

Figure 15

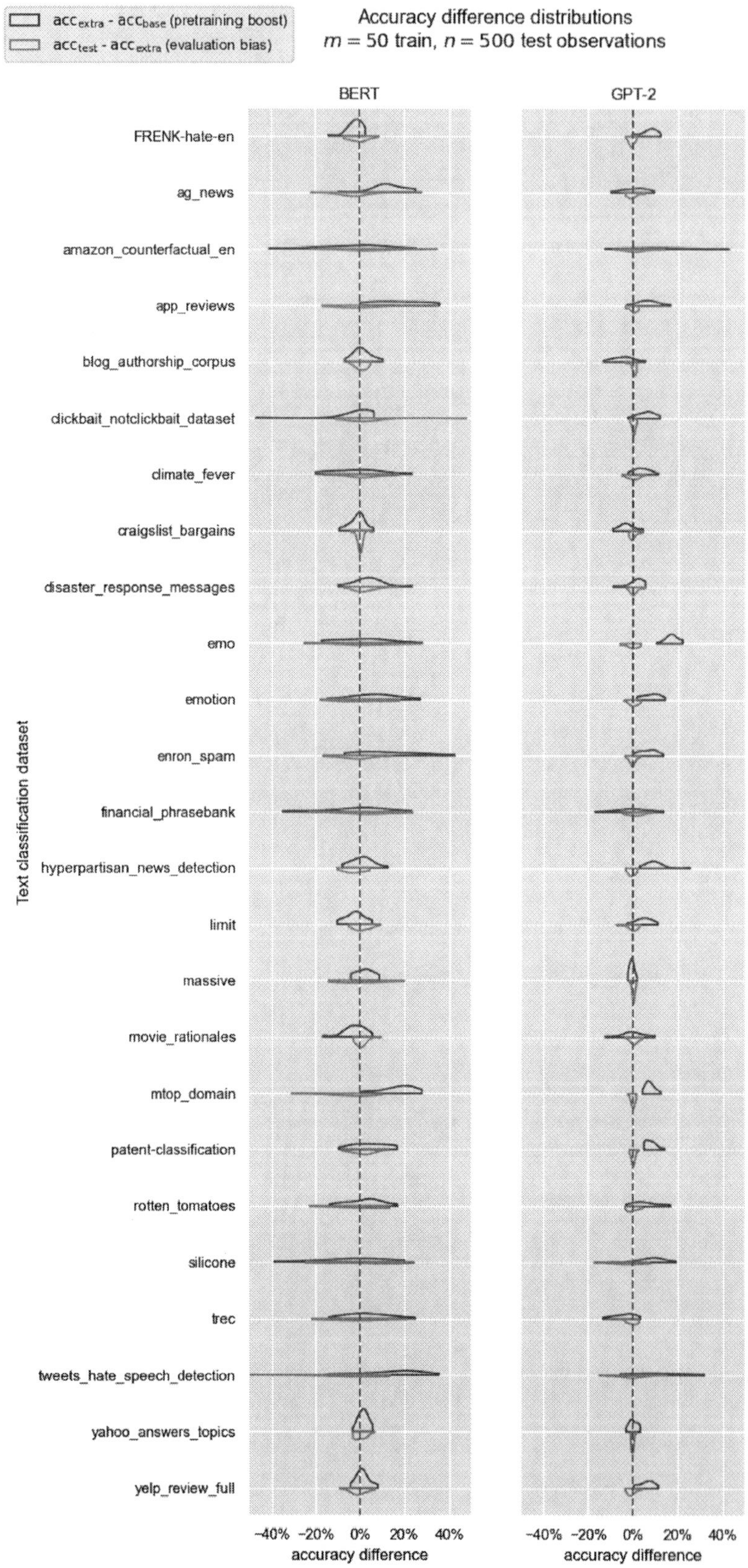
acc_extra - acc_base (pretraining boost)
acc_test - acc_extra (evaluation bias)
Accuracy difference distributions
m = 50 train, n = 500 test observations
BERT
GPT-2
Text classification dataset
FRENK-hate-en
ag_news
amazon_counterfactual_en
app_reviews
blog_authorship_corpus
clickbait_notclickbait_dataset
climate_fever
craigslist_bargains
disaster_response_messages
emo
emotion
enron_spam
financial_phrasebank
hyperpartisan_news_detection
limit
massive
movie_rationales
mtop_domain
patent-classification
rotten_tomatoes
silicone
trec
tweets_hate_speech_detection
yahoo_answers_topics
yelp_review_full
-40% -20% 0% 20% 40%
accuracy difference

Figure 16

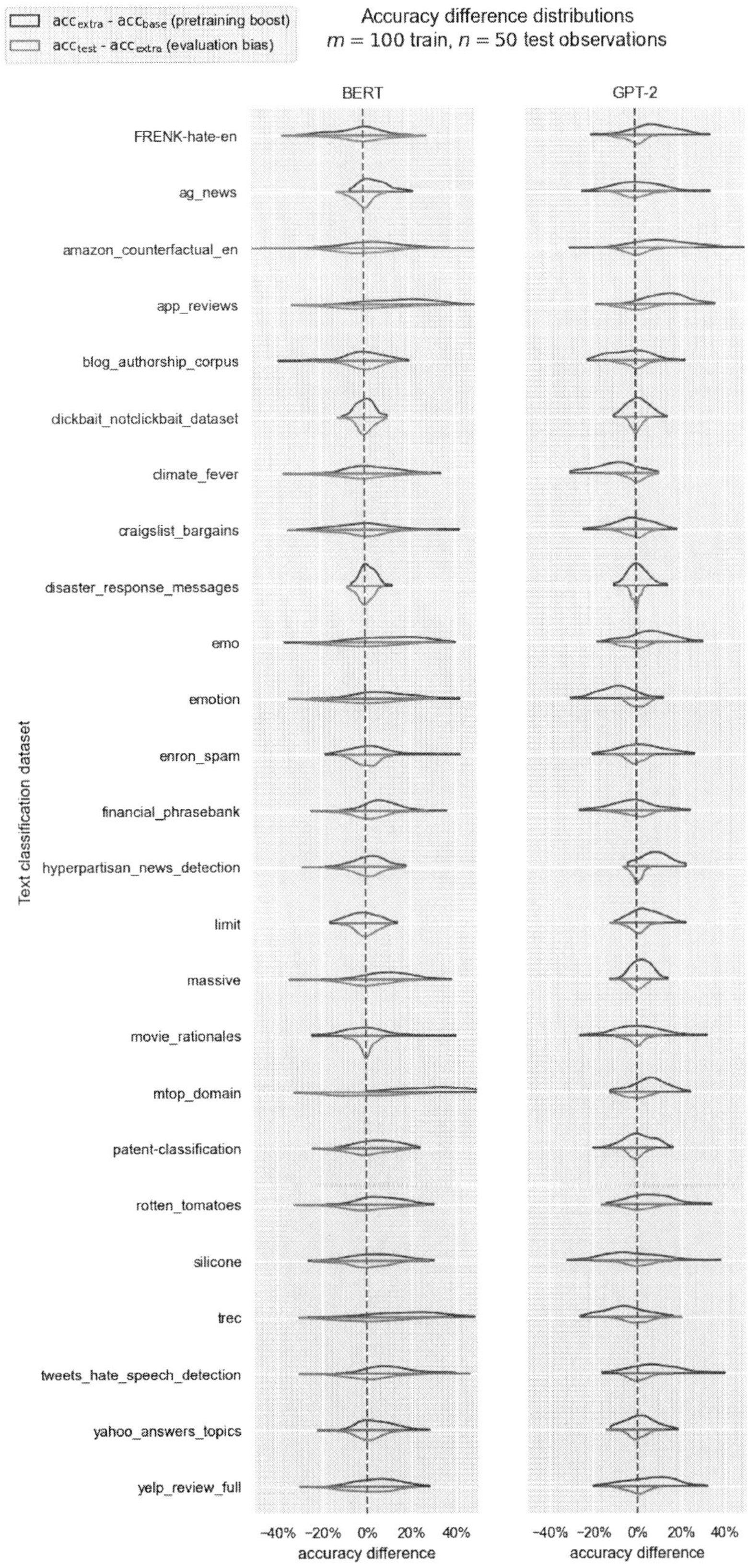

acc_extra - acc_base (pretraining boost)
acc_test - acc_extra (evaluation bias)
Accuracy difference distributions
m = 100 train, n = 50 test observations
BERT
GPT-2
FRENK-hate-en
ag_news
amazon_counterfactual_en
app_reviews
blog_authorship_corpus
clickbait_notclickbait_dataset
climate_fever
craigslist_bargains
disaster_response_messages
emo
emotion
enron_spam
financial_phrasebank
hyperpartisan_news_detection
limit
massive
movie_rationales
mtop_domain
patent-classification
rotten_tomatoes
silicone
trec
tweets_hate_speech_detection
yahoo_answers_topics
yelp_review_full
Text classification dataset
-40% -20% 0% 20% 40%
accuracy difference
-40% -20% 0% 20% 40%
accuracy difference

Figure 17

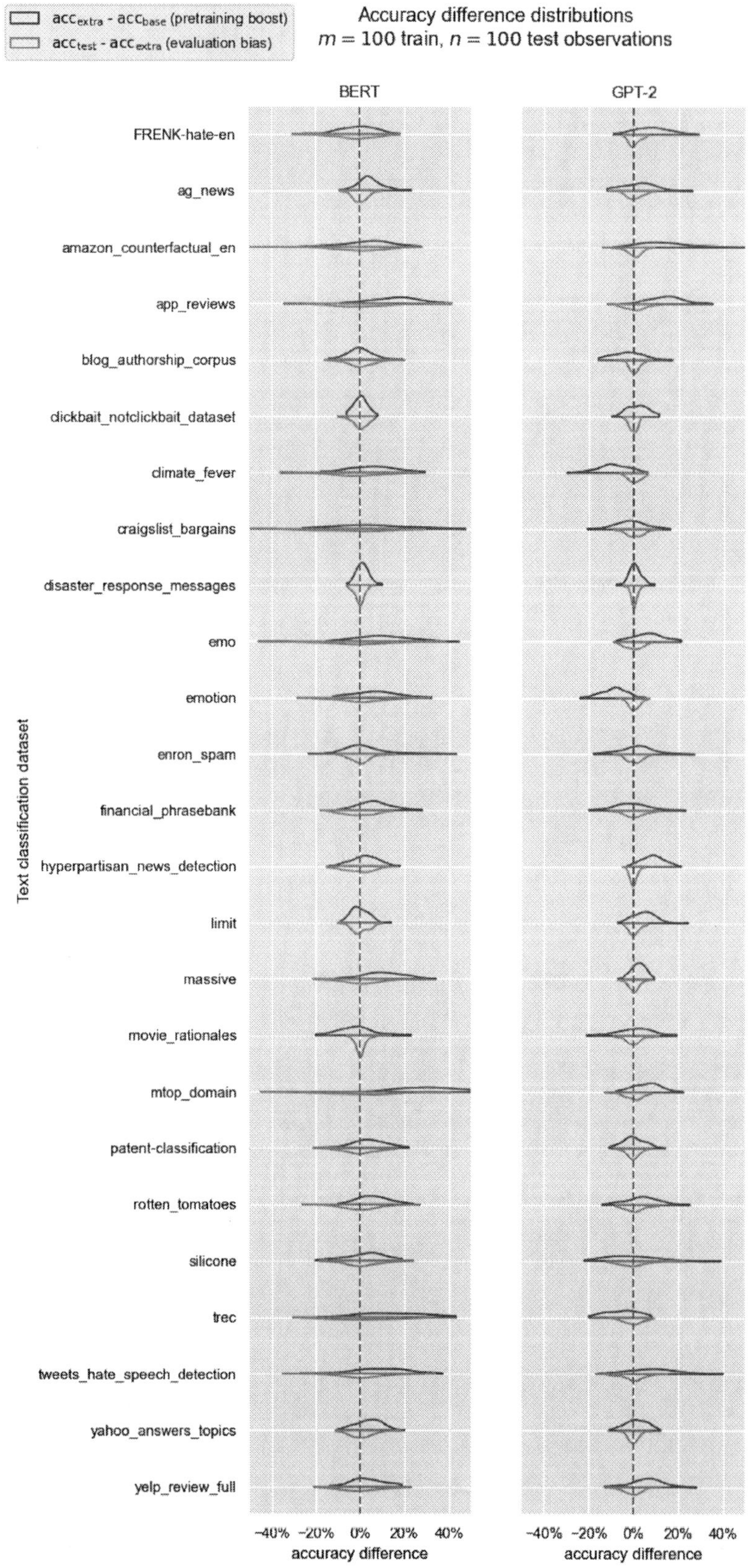

acc_extra - acc_base (pretraining boost)
acc_test - acc_extra (evaluation bias)
Accuracy difference distributions
m = 100 train, n = 100 test observations
BERT
GPT-2
Text classification dataset
FRENK-hate-en
ag_news
amazon_counterfactual_en
app_reviews
blog_authorship_corpus
clickbait_notclickbait_dataset
climate_fever
craigslist_bargains
disaster_response_messages
emo
emotion
enron_spam
financial_phrasebank
hyperpartisan_news_detection
limit
massive
movie_rationales
mtop_domain
patent-classification
rotten_tomatoes
silicone
trec
tweets_hate_speech_detection
yahoo_answers_topics
yelp_review_full
−40% −20% 0% 20% 40%
accuracy difference
−40% −20% 0% 20% 40%
accuracy difference

Figure 18

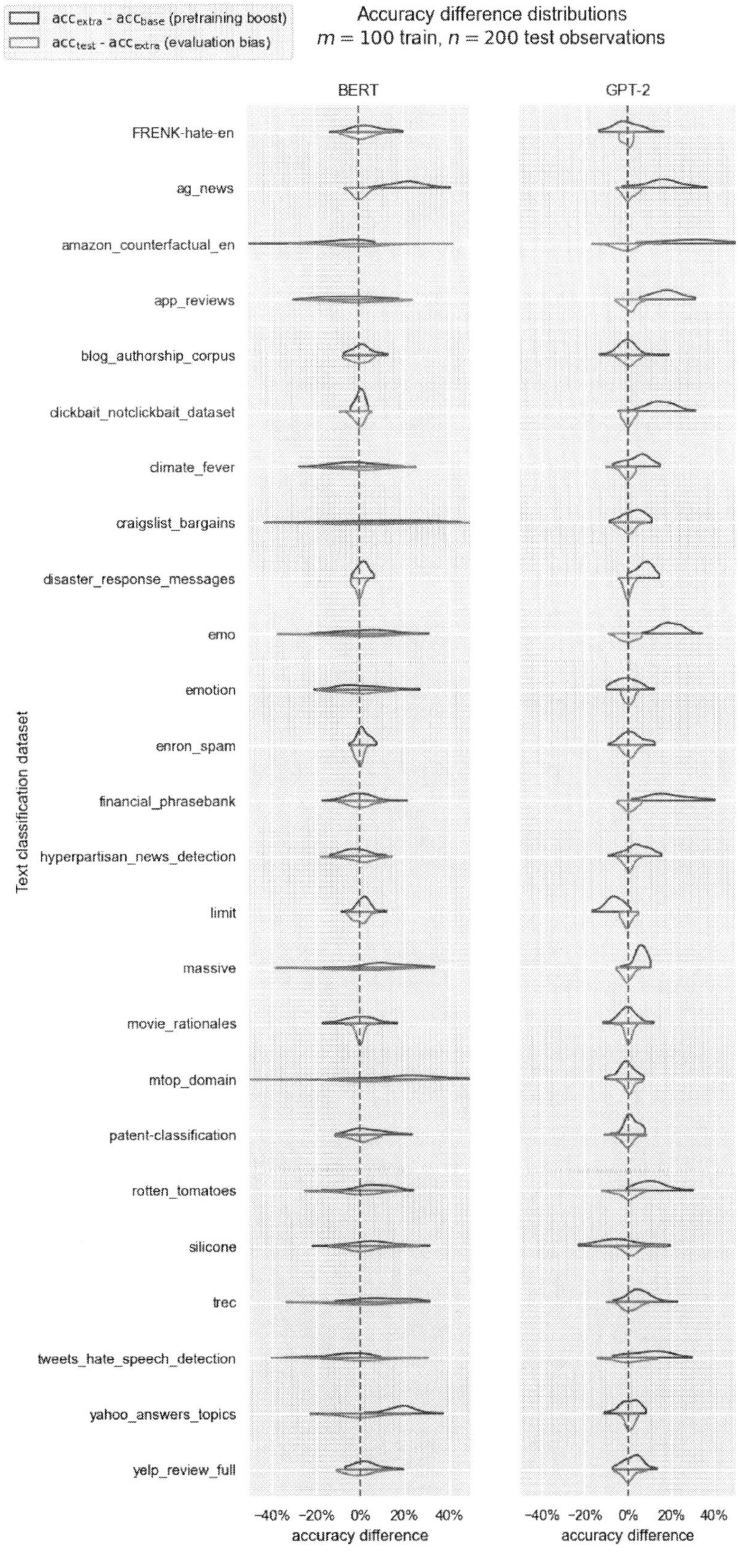

acc_{extra} - acc_{base} (pretraining boost)
acc_{test} - acc_{extra} (evaluation bias)
Accuracy difference distributions
$m = 100$ train, $n = 200$ test observations
BERT
GPT-2
Text classification dataset
FRENK-hate-en
ag_news
amazon_counterfactual_en
app_reviews
blog_authorship_corpus
clickbait_notclickbait_dataset
climate_fever
craigslist_bargains
disaster_response_messages
emo
emotion
enron_spam
financial_phrasebank
hyperpartisan_news_detection
limit
massive
movie_rationales
mtop_domain
patent-classification
rotten_tomatoes
silicone
trec
tweets_hate_speech_detection
yahoo_answers_topics
yelp_review_full
−40% −20% 0% 20% 40%
accuracy difference
−40% −20% 0% 20% 40%
accuracy difference

Figure 19

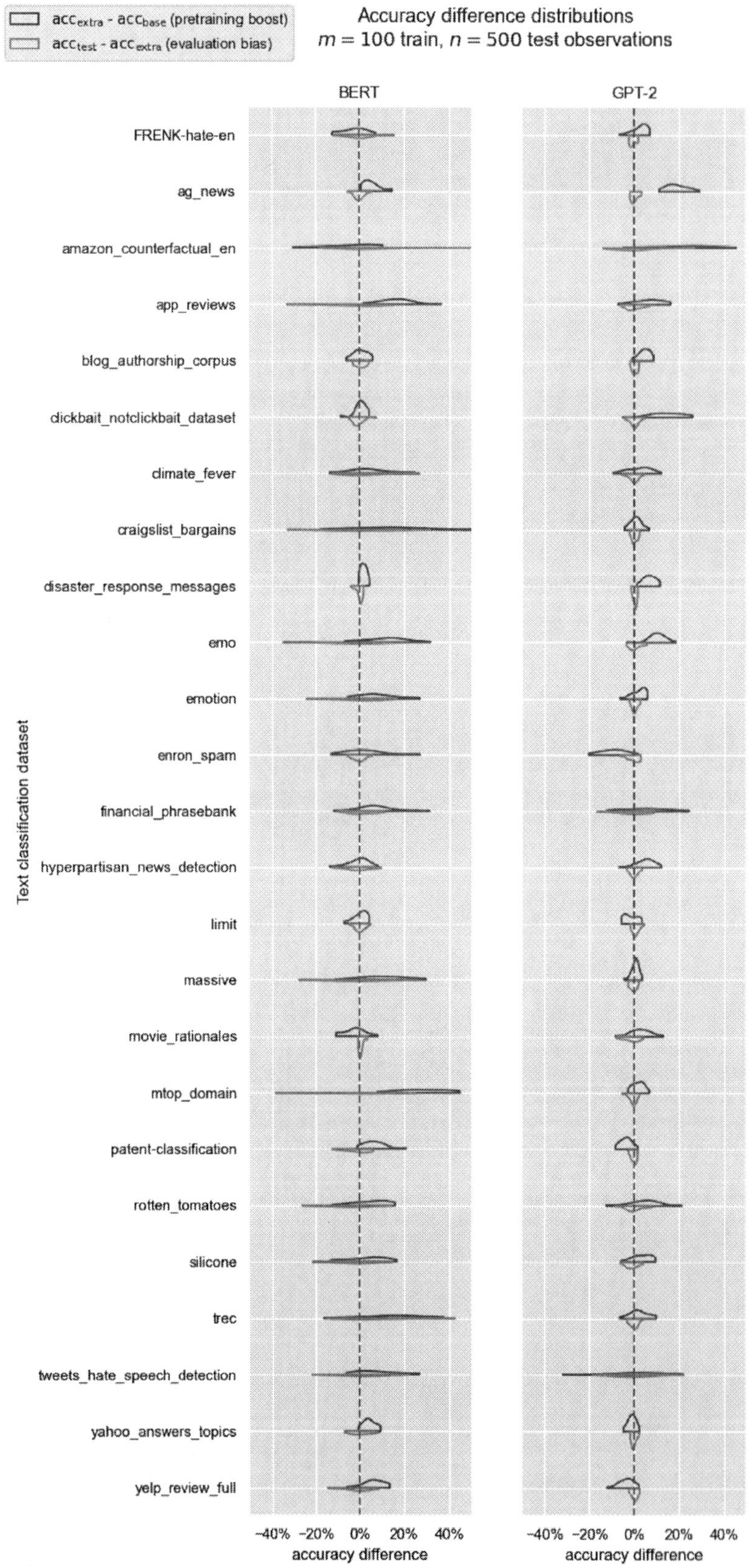

acc_{extra} - acc_{base} (pretraining boost)
acc_{test} - acc_{extra} (evaluation bias)
Accuracy difference distributions
m = 100 train, n = 500 test observations
BERT
GPT-2
Text classification dataset
FRENK-hate-en
ag_news
amazon_counterfactual_en
app_reviews
blog_authorship_corpus
clickbait_notclickbait_dataset
climate_fever
craigslist_bargains
disaster_response_messages
emo
emotion
enron_spam
financial_phrasebank
hyperpartisan_news_detection
limit
massive
movie_rationales
mtop_domain
patent-classification
rotten_tomatoes
silicone
trec
tweets_hate_speech_detection
yahoo_answers_topics
yelp_review_full
−40% −20% 0% 20% 40%
accuracy difference

Figure 20

From Language to Pixels: Task Recognition and Task Learning in LLMs

Janek Falkenstein, Carolin Schuster, Alex Berger and **Georg Groh**
Technical University of Munich, Germany
{j.falkenstein, carolin.schuster, a.berger}@tum.de
grohg@in.tum.de

Abstract

Large language models (LLMs) can perform unseen tasks by learning from a few in-context examples. How in-context learning works is still uncertain. We investigate the mechanisms of in-context learning on a challenging non-language task. The task requires the LLM to generate pixel matrices representing images of basic shapes. We introduce a framework to analyze if this task is solved by recognizing similar formats from the training data (task recognition) or by understanding the instructions and learning the skill de novo during inference (task learning). Our experiments demonstrate that LLMs generate meaningful pixel matrices with task recognition and fail to learn such tasks when encountering unfamiliar formats. Our findings offer insights into LLMs' learning mechanisms to guide future research on their seemingly human-like behavior.

1 Introduction

The rapid development of LLMs increases the chance of misinterpreting their capabilities. It is crucial to explore the potential of LLMs and research their underlying mechanisms. This helps in interpreting LLMs outputs, guides future research to improve language models, and informs their use and regulation.

Since Brown et al. (2020) demonstrated the abilities of GPT-3, there has been a growing interest in researching LLMs' potential to generalize to other tasks. Many studies demonstrated LLMs' abilities in solving reasoning tasks (Li et al., 2021; Srivastava et al., 2023; Huang and Chang, 2023). Contrary, it has been shown that LLMs still struggle to reason about seemingly simple tasks where humans perform superior (Valmeekam et al., 2022; Binz and Schulz, 2023; Huang and Chang, 2023). These findings demonstrate ambiguity in LLMs' general abilities and the need to further probe challenging tasks.

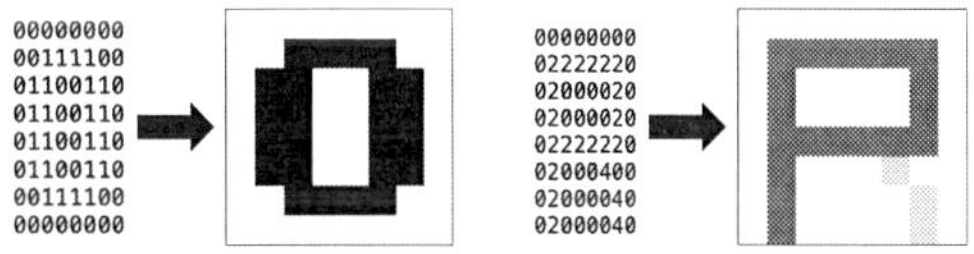

Figure 1: Two 8×8 pixel matrices representing simple images generated by an LLM using in-context learning.

In addition to the ambiguity about general capabilities, it is also unclear how and why LLMs benefit from in-context learning, i.e., how they can learn from instructions and demonstrations in the prompt. Brown et al. (2020) suggest that in-context learning could stem from genuinely learning new tasks, identifying tasks learned during training, or a mix of both approaches. However, the mechanisms of in-context learning remain uncertain.

On one hand, the inner workings (e.g., attention patterns) are too vast and complex to analyze directly. On the other hand, finding a higher-level abstraction to describe the model's internal processes is challenging. It is crucial to differentiate LLMs' achievements from human-like comprehension and reasoning as their training misses critical contexts, such as communicative intent (Bender and Koller, 2020; Asher et al., 2023). Especially terms like "learning" and "understanding" should be used cautiously (Bender et al., 2021; Shanahan, 2022). However, higher-level frameworks can help to explain LLM behaviors and assess LLMs' potential (Shanahan et al., 2023).

We adopt the abstraction level from Brown et al. (2020) and the terminology proposed by Pan et al. (2023) and distinguish between **task learning** (TL) and **task recognition** (TR). TR assesses how well LLMs can identify tasks through demonstrations and apply their pre-trained priors. TL describes the ability to learn new input-label mappings not encountered during training. Building on this, we introduce a framework that involves breaking tasks into subtasks and analyzing each for TL and TR to thoroughly investigate in-context learning.

Proceedings of the 2nd GenBench Workshop on Generalisation (Benchmarking) in NLP, pages 27–41
November 16, 2024

We instruct a model to generate pixel art as 8×8 pixel matrices (see Figure 1). The experiments solely use the model's inherent tokens without additional fine-tuning or incorporating image models. While investigating this task, we demonstrate unique capabilities, pinpoint where the pixel matrix task falls along the spectrum between TL and TR, and establish and validate a straightforward framework of breaking complex tasks into subtasks to clarify how LLMs achieve the observed capabilities.

Our main contributions are summarized as follows:

- We show that LLMs can create pixel matrices of digits, letters, and simple everyday objects.
- We find that LLMs rely on task recognition to generate meaningful pixel matrices, which indicates strong task recognition but limited task learning abilities for uncommon non-language tasks.
- We propose a framework to break tasks into subtasks to better explain the capabilities of LLMs and separate the effects of TL and TR.

2 Related Work

Text-to-image models The success of LLMs has influenced the research on multi-modal models for vision and language. Many text-to-image models use text encoders from LLM transformers and combine them with an image encoder (e.g., Radford et al., 2021; Alayrac et al., 2022; Saharia et al., 2022). Others adhere closer to the LLM architecture. Koh et al. (2023) have used visual encoders to ground an LLM in the visual domain, enabling image captioning and text-to-image tasks. Similarly, Pourreza et al. (2023) generates images represented as brush strokes. They add an image feature extractor and cross-attention blocks to provide visual feedback during stroke generation. These studies demonstrate that LLMs possess implicit knowledge about images and the visual domain. Our task is distinct in that it generated images without extra image encoders or training.

Pure LLMs on image generation Probing the ability of LLMs to create images without fine-tuning or adding layers has been done by benchmarks that assemble tasks to assess LLM performances. BIG-bench (Srivastava et al., 2023) includes some tasks that involve ASCII art and Bang et al. (2023) let ChatGPT draw country flags with Scalable Vector Graphics (SVG) code. Chalamalasetti et al. (2023) benchmark LLMs on describing 5×5 grids filled with two different symbols and following such descriptions. In addition, some blog posts explore ChatGPT's ability to draw images with SVG (Pu, 2022; Shahir, 2023 Shiryaev, 2022). To our knowledge, no comprehensive study has explored LLMs' capacity for generating visuals, and we are the first to assess the pixel matrix image format.

In-context learning How in-context learning works is still disputed. Some recent studies compared in-context learning to implicit fine-tuning or Bayesian inference (Dai et al., 2023; Von Oswald et al., 2023; Xie et al., 2022). Whether this capability arises from comprehending the instruction or recognizing the task from the training data is still an open research question. Pan et al. (2023) introduced the terminology employed in our paper and distinguished cases where TL and TR were applied. Other studies experimented with modifying the prompt or comparing tasks, aiming to ascertain whether LLMs employ TR or TL (Reynolds and McDonell, 2021; Min et al., 2022). We diverge in our approach by closely examining one particular task concerning TL or TR to contribute insights to the broader understanding of in-context learning and to provide a framework for future task evaluations.

Decomposing Tasks Letting the model explain each reasoning step (Chain-of-Thought) has been shown to improve results (Lampinen et al., 2022; Kojima et al., 2022; Wei et al., 2022). Other studies have shown that explicitly decomposing complex tasks and solving the subtasks enhances performance (Zhou et al., 2022; Khot et al., 2022; Prasad et al., 2023; Radhakrishnan et al., 2023). Our experiments do not focus on prompting or explicitly breaking down tasks to improve performance. However, these results support our proposed framework: when analyzing LLMs, it is useful to consider subtasks, as models likely implicitly decompose tasks and solve subtasks through either TL or TR.

3 Method

Our experimental setup aims to assess LLMs' general capabilities on the challenging pixel-matrix task and determine whether it is addressed through

TR or TL. Simultaneously, we demonstrate our framework's utility in explaining LLMs' capabilities and differentiating between TL and TR.

We choose the pixel matrix task because it is particularly challenging. It requires the model to translate instructions and visual knowledge into a new format. The task's complexity helps to clearly distinguish between TR and TL and assess our framework. Simpler tasks can be solved in many different ways, and the likelihood that the model recognizes or learns arbitrary parts increases, complicating the decision between TR and TL.

By thoroughly examining a single task, we provide evidence contributing to a broader understanding of in-context learning and the differentiation between TR and TL.

3.1 Prompt Structures and Dataset

The prompts for the pixel matrix experiments consist of a task description and four demonstrations. The description introduces the concept of pixels and pixel matrices. The demonstrations show example pixel matrices with labels. These 8×8 pixel matrices are depicted with 8 rows, each containing 8 pixel symbols (e.g., 0 and 1, or G and K). After the four examples, another label specifying the object to be sketched is added. See Figure 2 for the prompt structure. The model is expected to generate a corresponding pixel matrix.

We evaluate the performance of creating pixel matrices across four categories: *digits*, *letters*, *punctuation symbols*, and *real-world objects*. The *real-world objects* are simple enough to be displayable on an 8×8 pixel canvas (e.g., chess board, padlock, or sun). Appendix C includes a complete enumeration of the objects. In total, we have 93 different objects. We generate ten instances for each object. We test each of the four object categories separately.

3.2 Experimental Setup

For the experiments, we modified the pixel symbols, the few-shot examples, and the task description of the prompt. We used the *gpt-3.5-turbo-0613* model accessed through the OpenAI API. Other open-source models, such as Bloom (Scao et al., 2022), GPT-Neox20B (Black et al., 2022), and Starcoder (Li et al., 2023), cannot generate meaningful pixel matrices (see Appendix E.3). Therefore, we focus our analysis on GPT-3.5.

```
Images displayed on a computer screen are a
collection of color dots, called pixels. [...]
We can represent different objects by creating a
pixel matrix which consists of 0s and 1s. [...]

Here is an example of an 8 by 8 pixel matrix
showing  three:
00000000
00111110
00000110
00111100
00001110
00000110
00111100
00000000
###

[... three more examples ...]

This is an example of a grid of pixels that
form an image of [object]:
```

Figure 2: Prompt structure used for generating pixel matrices in the experiments. The descriptions and examples were adjusted according to each experiment.

General capabilities We conducted a *Baseline* experiment that shows the model's general capabilities and acts as a baseline for the other experiments. The pixel symbols are 0 and 1 and represent white and black. Furthermore, we conducted experiments with color representations to evaluate advanced capabilities and determine the limits of the pixel matrix task. The *Color Digits* experiment added four additional digits for red, blue, yellow, and green, while the *Color RGB* experiment used RGB code values as pixel symbols.

Task recognition vs. task learning These experiments aim to understand whether GPT-3.5 approaches the pixel matrix task through TR or TL. We follow three hypotheses as indicators for TL:

- Performance should be independent of the frequency in the training data and equal across tasks of the same difficulty.
- Performance should deteriorate when providing misleading instructions.
- Performance should improve when making the task easier.

Following these hypotheses, we designed three experiments.

The first experiment, (*GK Pixels*), substitutes the pixel values 0 and 1 with two letters chosen uniformly at random from the Latin alphabet. Black-and-white pixel matrices with 0s and 1s are prevalent in the training data, while matrices with values

G and K are not. Simple objects like digits and letters represented as matrices are likely well represented and learned during training, enabling TR. In contrast, the GK Pixel matrix format must be recognized or learned from the context.

The second experiment, *Wrong Labels*, uses mislabeled examples in the prompt. We hypothesize that a deteriorating performance would indicate TL because misleading examples make the instructions of the task unclear. However, a constant performance in this experiment means that in-context learning helps to identify a given task rather than learning it (Min et al., 2022; Pan et al., 2023). We conducted the *Wrong Labels* experiment by mislabeling each of the four prompt examples. We also experimented without any examples (zero-shot) to test if the model could learn from the instruction of the prompt alone.

GPT-3.5's tokenizer[1] combines multiple pixel symbols of our baseline matrix format into one token (see Figure 7). Consequently, a single pixel matrix can be represented by various tokens, expanding the token vocabulary from two to more than ten. Hence, learning the task becomes more challenging because it is necessary to understand the meaning of each potential token. For the third experiment (*One Token*), we inserted spaces between pixel symbols to ensure one token corresponds to a single pixel symbol and make the task easier to learn. Such adjustment enhanced results for straightforward pattern completion tasks (Mirchandani et al., 2023). In the case of TL, we anticipate improved results for our task.

In addition to these three experiments, we use the *baseline* results to compare objects similarly challenging to sketch but unevenly represented in the training data or of different difficulty but evenly represented in the training data. If the results align with the assumed difficulty, it suggests TL without relying on pixel matrices in the training data. For TR, only the training data is relevant. Consequently, when two similarly challenging objects have uneven representation, the one more prevalent during training should yield more accurate results.

Breaking tasks into subtasks With this set of experiments, we demonstrate how manually decomposing tasks can help distinguish between TL and TR. If the model fails to complete the subtasks, we infer that the main task is solved by TR. When the model succeeds in difficult tasks not seen during training, we do not immediately attribute this to TL but instead examine the subtasks. Labeling the process as TL is inappropriate if the model simply combines subtasks it solved using TR.

To test one subtask explicitly, we generated textual descriptions of objects' shapes and visuals using a simple prompt. For the GK task, we tested the subtasks of translating 01 pixel matrices to GK pixel matrices. For the specific prompts, see Appendix A. If LLMs can generate GK pixel matrices correctly, one could assume they first recognize the 01 pixel matrices from training data and then use the prompt to translate 01 pixel matrices to GK pixel matrices, solving two subtasks and combining the results.

We also tested our pixel matrix task using a different image format by having the model generate SVG code instead. This format allows for a more straightforward combination of different shapes because overlapping shapes do not affect each other. Examining the generation of *real-world objects* can reveal whether the model predominantly replicates SVG code for the specific object or decomposes the object into subparts and combines them.

3.3 Evaluation

We converted each pixel matrix to an image with a simple Python script. Then, we conducted a classification study with three annotators. Each annotator described the generated images by specifying the *digits*, *letters*, and *punctuation symbols* they observed without knowing the possible set of characters. For *real-world objects*, we provided the correct answer. We let the annotator decide whether the respective object is recognizable because even a good image on an 8×8 pixel canvas is challenging to recognize without context. We counted the percentage of generations correctly classified or marked as recognizable for each experiment.

4 Results

This section presents the results of our experiments. The quantitative results are summarized in Table 1.

4.1 General Capabilities

We demonstrate the general capabilities of GPT-3.5 to create pixel matrices, including colorful images.

[1] https://platform.openai.com/tokenizer

[2] The objects of the mislabeled demonstrations are also generated and evaluated for *digits* and *letters*, potentially adversely impacting the displayed score by about 20%.

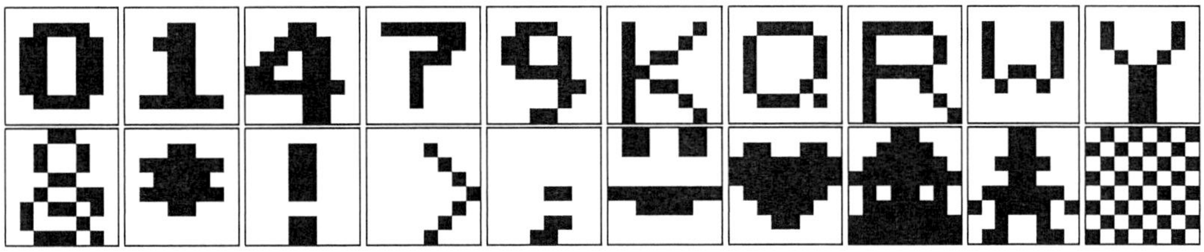

Figure 3: Selected positive examples of the baseline experiment: digits 0, 1, 4, 7, and 9; letters K, Q, R, W, and Y; the symbols ampersand, asterisk, exclamation point, and semi-colon; the objects sad face, heart, house, stick figure, and chess board.

Experiments	Digits	Letters	Punct.	Objs.
Baseline	73%	76%	45%	14%
Color Digits	56%	65%	32%	3%
Color RGB	15%	6%	10%	6%
GK Symbols	36%	37%	21%	2%
One Token	72%	72%	36%	12%
Wrong Label [2]	50%	67%	35%	12%

Table 1: Comparing experiment results: Percentage of recognizable images across generation tasks and image categories. Results obtained by human evaluation.

Basic experiment For *digits*, 73 % were correctly identified by the annotators, with the only exception being the number 4, which is only recognizable in three out of ten instances. For two-digit numbers (10 and 32), none of the generated examples accurately display the number. Instead, some pixel matrices represent other meaningful objects, like the letters A or H, or the number 9.

Almost all *letters* are consistently generated correctly and recognizable. Exceptions occurred with more complex letters. The letter E often features more than three horizontal lines, and W and M are occasionally wrong. Surprisingly, the letter V consistently appears as an X in the pixel matrix. The German umlauts Ä, Ö, and Ü fail to show corresponding vowels, often resulting in seemingly random pixel matrices.

Except for the percent and dollar signs, most *punctuation symbols* are generated correctly at least once in ten instances. Even complex symbols like the ampersand are successfully abstracted and generated on an 8×8 pixel matrix. More common symbols like the comma and exclamation marks are consistently generated. Left closing symbols yield good results, while not a single right closing symbol is generated correctly (see Figure 8). The output typically corresponds to the left symbol when requesting a right closing symbol.

Simple and common everyday items like the heart, sad face, and house yield mostly recognizable images. For the stick figure and cat, some instances are of high quality, while others seem completely random. Results for the remaining objects appear mostly random. Compare Figure 3 for selected positive examples.

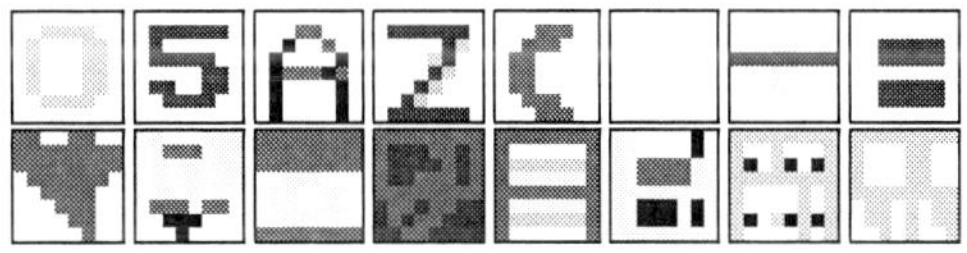

Figure 4: Images generated with pixel values for color: *digits*, *letters*, and *punctuation symbols* (top row); two hearts, suns, windows, and cacti (bottom row).

Adding color Results for *digits*, *letters*, and *punctuation symbols* show slightly lower accuracy than simple black-and-white images. Complex letters such as W and M become even less recognizable than in the basic experiment. Certain letters comprised multiple colors.

The quality of the generated pixel matrices in the *real-world object* category declines. The images display vibrant colors, but the colors lack an association with the specified objects. The images for the star and sun do not contain more yellow, and those for a window or glass do not contain more blue. Only the cactus images consistently appear green. Compare Figure 4 for selected images from these experiments.

For the experiment with RGB color codes as pixel symbols, the model more often did not adhere to the format, i.e., generating an output that is not a pixel matrix. Only 15 % of the digits were recognized compared to 56 % with a pixel matrix of 5 color values.

4.2 Task Recognition vs. Task Learning

The results demonstrated in this section reveal insights into where the pixel matrix task lies on the spectrum between TR and TL. The corresponding discussion can be found in Section 5.2.

```
- The fundamental shape is a vertical line
positioned in the center of the 8x8 grid.
- At the top of the line, there is a small
horizontal line extending towards the right
side of the grid, connected to the vertical
line's midsection.
- The bottom part of the vertical line extends
slightly below the grid's baseline, forming a
slight curve.
```

Figure 5: Excerpt from a generated description for the digit 7 with incorrect shapes and inconsistencies.

```
The simplified 8x8 pixel representation of a
house consists of a square shape measuring 6
pixels in height and 6 pixels in width,
representing the main body of the house. On top
of the square, centered horizontally, there is
a triangle shape measuring 4 pixels in height
and 6 pixels in width, representing the roof.
The top row of the triangle is aligned with the
top row of the square.
```

Figure 6: Excerpt from a generated description for a real-world object, illustrating the ability to describe individual components accurately, yet assembling them incohesive.

Different pixel symbols When substituting 0 and 1 with the letters G and K the model generates pixel matrices in the correct format. Some instances are generated correctly. Still, overall, the results are significantly worse across all four categories (see Table 1).

Wrong labels The performance remains largely unchanged compared to the baseline when the labels of the demonstrations are wrong. The numbers in Table 1 for *digits*, *letters*, and *punctuation* are lower for this experiment because these datasets test objects that were wrongly labeled. Nevertheless, occasionally the model ignores the incorrect labels and produces correct pixel matrices. The zero-shot experiment outputs do not adhere to the format and reveal that the model needs examples to recognize the format.

One token per pixel symbol We observe slightly lower accuracy than the basic experiment, particularly for *punctuation symbols*. The output more often does not conform to the correct format, generating a message stating it is a language model and cannot generate images.

4.3 Breaking Tasks into Subtasks

Translating 01 pixel matrices to GK pixel matrices is successful in most instances (51 out of 60). Generated textual descriptions often lack coherence for

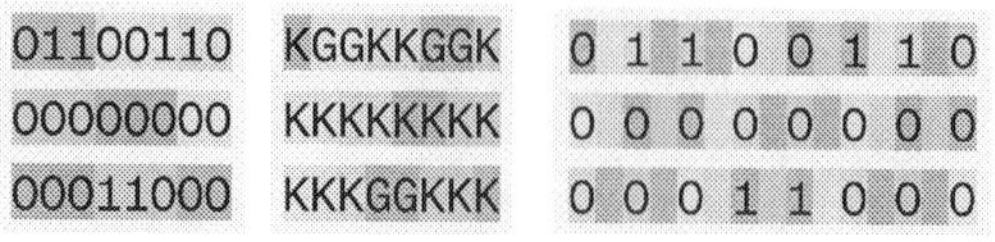

Figure 7: Comparing tokenization of different image formats: each color-coded sequence represents symbols combined into a single token. Images are screenshots from the OpenAI tokenizer webpage.

digits, *letters*, and most *punctuation symbols*. The described shapes appear random for all numbers except for 0, 1, and 8 (see Figure 5). Some level of abstraction is observed for *real-world objects*, but coherency keeps lacking. The generated texts mention useful shapes for an object but unrealistically combine them (see Figure 6).

According to our evaluation, 35% of SVG images of *real-world objects* are correct, a much higher score than for all other experiments. With only a few exceptions, the resulting images display the colors relevant to the desired object. Inaccurate images frequently present correct parts of objects, but the model fails to assemble the details in a hierarchical, cohesive way (compare Figure 9).

5 Discussion

In this section, we examine our experiment results. We discuss the overall performance in the pixel matrix task, assess if they tackle the task through TL or TR, and evaluate if breaking down the task into subtasks is a valid framework to explain LLM abilities.

5.1 LLMs Pixel Matrix Capabilities

GPT-3.5 showcases a solid ability to generate simple images in the form of pixel matrices without fine-tuning or including an image layer.

The capability of an LLM to use tokens trained to represent text for other purposes, such as representing pixels, highlights its potential beyond language generation (e.g., pattern completion). The results also indicate that language models possess information about different modalities, such as images. While image models rely on explicit images for training, LLMs have the advantage that textual descriptions inherently involve abstraction and the omission of (potentially) unnecessary details. Therefore, LLMs could help to increase the generalizability of image models.

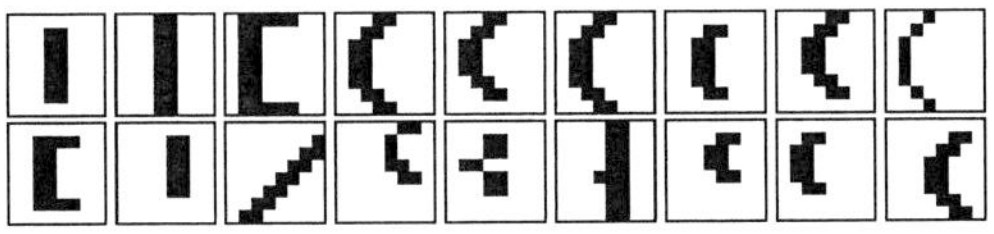

Figure 8: Left (top row) and right (bottom row) closing symbols, emphasizing the discrepancy in image quality for closely related objects.

5.2 Pixel Matrix Task Is Solved by Task Recognition

We found evidence that the pixel matrix task cannot be solved without TR. This evidence includes the deteriorated outcomes with uncommon (GK) pixel values and unaltered results despite incorrect examples in the prompt. Additionally, our zero-shot experiments confirm that relying solely on the instruction part of the prompt is insufficient for the model to learn the task. Altering the format to represent each pixel by one token does not improve the results despite simplifying the task and making it easier to learn.

Further, several pairs of objects with the same difficulty level are solved in only one of two instances. These object pairs include digits vs. number 10, letter A vs. letter Ä, and left closing symbols vs. right closing symbols (see Figure 8). If the model *understands* the tasks (rather than only replicating training instances), it would be able to solve either both or none of the pair's instances. We assume that the former object in each pair is significantly more present during training than the latter. Similarly, drawing the complex shapes of some *digits*, *punctuation symbols*, and *letters* appears more challenging than drawing simple *real-world objects*. For instance, copying an ampersand is challenging, whereas a simple smiley face is not. However, the results are consistently better for such complex shapes than for simple *real-world objects*.

Our findings indicate that the pixel matrix task is solved through TR, not TL. Thus, it shows that LLMs lack human-like understanding and generalization capabilities despite sometimes seeming otherwise. Rather, the large data corpus is extremely powerful and includes samples of uncommon tasks. Given the current architecture, we assert that LLMs will not attain understanding and reasoning. Enhancing current LLMs requires incorporating even more diverse data and improved training.

5.3 What Task Is Recognized?

The results of the baseline experiment show that the pixel matrix task has been learned only to a limiting degree during training. Language models are not extensively trained on text-to-pixel matrix data, making it challenging to generalize this task to new images by combining seen objects and concepts. We conclude that it is more appropriate to say that it recognizes the task of drawing a specific object instead of a general text-to-image task. Therefore, the model cannot generalize to pixel matrices for objects it has not encountered during training, as this ability is neither acquired during training nor inference. In conclusion, it's crucial to pinpoint the exact task that is recognized and solved to not overestimate the capabilities.

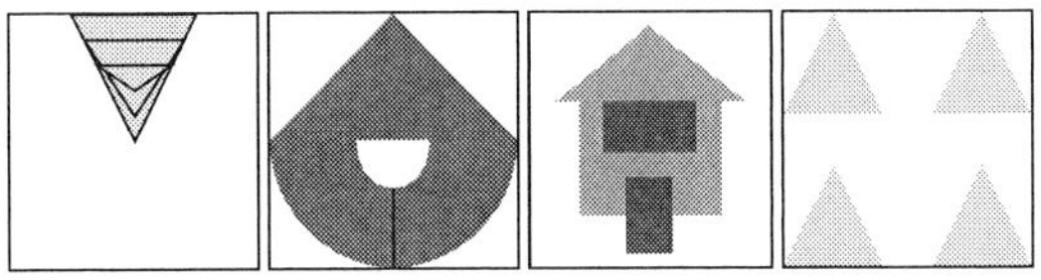

Figure 9: SVG-generated images (crown, wine glass, house, and lightning flash) exhibit a lack of cohesiveness in the arrangement of their components.

5.4 Decomposing Tasks to Evaluate Capabilities of LLMs

The previous results show that the model applies TR to solve the experiments with 01-pixel matrices. The pixel matrix task can be broken down into subtasks, such as accessing visual information about the object, decomposing objects into basic shapes, generating different shapes on a pixel matrix, and combining this information to form a pixel matrix representing a certain object. We show that the generated textual descriptions for *digits*, *letters*, and *punctuation symbols* were inadequate. Also, combining different shapes on a pixel matrix is challenging, as overlapping parts result in new tokens. The model relies on TR because it fails to solve these subtasks sufficiently.

In contrast, the *GK pixel* and the *SVG code* task are solved by solving subtasks. TR alone does not explain the results of the *GK pixel* matrix task because the model likely did not encounter such pixel matrices during training. We believe the model breaks down the task into creating a 01-pixel matrix and exchanging 0s and 1s with Gs and Ks. We show that an LLM can solve both individual subtasks. In the *SVG code* experiments, combining various shapes is accomplished by concatenating corresponding lines of code, which makes combining subtasks easier than for the pixel matrix task. The results show that the model draws different parts of objects but fails to put them together with correct dimensions and spatial correlations (see Figure 9). This suggests that the model decomposes the object into its visual parts, recognizes these from training data, and combines them into one image rather than relying directly on TR.

Our framework of breaking down tasks into subtasks helps to assess TL and TR abilities. On the one hand, as in the case of pixel matrices, it helps to identify difficult subtasks and areas for improvement, such as targeted training data. On the other hand, the SVG and GK experiments demonstrate how our framework helps explain LLM capabilities and distinguish between TL and TR. When examining tasks like the GK pixel matrix, one might mistakenly conclude that the model is learning from scratch. However, decomposing the task reveals that simpler subtasks might be recognized from the training data. This prevents premature conclusions about TL but raises a philosophic question: How much must the model decompose the task, and how simple must the subtasks be to classify it as TL?

6 Conclusion

Our study demonstrates that LLMs can generate pixel matrices representing objects such as digits, letters, and simple real-world items. Our experiments show evidence of strong task recognition and limited task learning ability. We argue that breaking down complex tasks into smaller subtasks is a useful framework for evaluating and explaining LLM capabilities, preventing misleading conclusions when assessing the task's overall performance, and helping to distinguish between TL and TR.

As LLMs improve their ability to recognize tasks, locate relevant training data, and break down complex tasks, distinguishing between task learning and task recognition becomes increasingly complex. Although one might argue that this, at the core, represents task recognition of subtasks, future research is needed to explore how this process compares to human learning.

7 Limitations

Our evaluation captures broader trends, and our discussion is based on conclusions drawn from clear tendencies in the results rather than small differences. More thorough evaluations and comparisons across different models could strengthen the results. We have conducted a short ablation study with different models (see Appendix E.3). As the outputs depend on prompts, more prompt engineering and other prompts could have yielded different results.

We also rely on the generated outputs and general knowledge about LLMs to interpret their results because empirical analysis of the model's internal workings (e.g., evaluating attention patterns) is extremely resource-intensive. Thus, we interpret LLMs, highly complex statistical distributions, using simple human-like concepts (e.g., breaking down tasks).

References

Jean-Baptiste Alayrac, Jeff Donahue, Pauline Luc, Antoine Miech, Iain Barr, Yana Hasson, Karel Lenc, Arthur Mensch, Katherine Millican, Malcolm Reynolds, Roman Ring, Eliza Rutherford, et al. 2022. Flamingo: a visual language model for few-shot learning. In *Advances in Neural Information Processing Systems*.

Nicholas Asher, Swarnadeep Bhar, Akshay Chaturvedi, Julie Hunter, and Soumya Paul. 2023. Limits for learning with language models. In *Proceedings of the 12th Joint Conference on Lexical and Computational Semantics (*SEM 2023)*, pages 236–248, Toronto, Canada. Association for Computational Linguistics.

Yejin Bang, Samuel Cahyawijaya, Nayeon Lee, Wenliang Dai, Dan Su, Bryan Wilie, Holy Lovenia, Ziwei Ji, Tiezheng Yu, Willy Chung, et al. 2023. A multitask, multilingual, multimodal evaluation of chatgpt on reasoning, hallucination, and interactivity. *arXiv preprint arXiv:2302.04023*.

Emily M Bender, Timnit Gebru, Angelina McMillan-Major, and Shmargaret Shmitchell. 2021. On the dangers of stochastic parrots: Can language models be too big? In *Proceedings of the 2021 ACM conference on fairness, accountability, and transparency*, pages 610–623.

Emily M. Bender and Alexander Koller. 2020. Climbing towards NLU: On meaning, form, and understanding in the age of data. In *Proceedings of the 58th Annual Meeting of the Association for Computational Linguistics*, pages 5185–5198, Online. Association for Computational Linguistics.

Marcel Binz and Eric Schulz. 2023. Using cognitive psychology to understand gpt-3. *Proceedings of the National Academy of Sciences*, 120(6):e2218523120.

Sidney Black, Stella Biderman, Eric Hallahan, Quentin Anthony, Leo Gao, Laurence Golding, Horace He, Connor Leahy, Kyle McDonell, Jason Phang, Michael Pieler, Usvsn Sai Prashanth, Shivanshu Purohit, Laria Reynolds, Jonathan Tow, Ben Wang, and Samuel Weinbach. 2022. GPT-NeoX-20B: An open-source autoregressive language model. In *Proceedings of BigScience Episode #5 – Workshop on Challenges & Perspectives in Creating Large Language*

Models, pages 95–136, virtual+Dublin. Association for Computational Linguistics.

Tom Brown, Benjamin Mann, Nick Ryder, Melanie Subbiah, Jared D Kaplan, Prafulla Dhariwal, Arvind Neelakantan, Pranav Shyam, Girish Sastry, Amanda Askell, et al. 2020. Language models are few-shot learners. *Advances in neural information processing systems*, 33:1877–1901.

Kranti Chalamalasetti, Jana Götze, Sherzod Hakimov, Brielen Madureira, Philipp Sadler, and David Schlangen. 2023. clembench: Using game play to evaluate chat-optimized language models as conversational agents. In *Proceedings of the 2023 Conference on Empirical Methods in Natural Language Processing*, pages 11174–11219, Singapore. Association for Computational Linguistics.

Damai Dai, Yutao Sun, Li Dong, Yaru Hao, Shuming Ma, Zhifang Sui, and Furu Wei. 2023. Why can GPT learn in-context? language models secretly perform gradient descent as meta-optimizers. In *Findings of the Association for Computational Linguistics: ACL 2023*, pages 4005–4019, Toronto, Canada. Association for Computational Linguistics.

Jie Huang and Kevin Chen-Chuan Chang. 2023. Towards reasoning in large language models: A survey. In *Findings of the Association for Computational Linguistics: ACL 2023*, pages 1049–1065, Toronto, Canada. Association for Computational Linguistics.

Tushar Khot, Harsh Trivedi, Matthew Finlayson, Yao Fu, Kyle Richardson, Peter Clark, and Ashish Sabharwal. 2022. Decomposed prompting: A modular approach for solving complex tasks. *arXiv preprint arXiv:2210.02406*.

Jing Yu Koh, Ruslan Salakhutdinov, and Daniel Fried. 2023. Grounding language models to images for multimodal generation. *arXiv preprint arXiv:2301.13823*.

Takeshi Kojima, Shixiang Shane Gu, Machel Reid, Yutaka Matsuo, and Yusuke Iwasawa. 2022. Large language models are zero-shot reasoners. *Advances in neural information processing systems*, 35:22199–22213.

Andrew Lampinen, Ishita Dasgupta, Stephanie Chan, Kory Mathewson, Mh Tessler, Antonia Creswell, James McClelland, Jane Wang, and Felix Hill. 2022. Can language models learn from explanations in context? In *Findings of the Association for Computational Linguistics: EMNLP 2022*, pages 537–563, Abu Dhabi, United Arab Emirates. Association for Computational Linguistics.

Belinda Z. Li, Maxwell Nye, and Jacob Andreas. 2021. Implicit representations of meaning in neural language models. In *Proceedings of the 59th Annual Meeting of the Association for Computational Linguistics and the 11th International Joint Conference on Natural Language Processing (Volume 1: Long Papers)*, pages 1813–1827, Online. Association for Computational Linguistics.

Raymond Li, Loubna Ben Allal, Yangtian Zi, Niklas Muennighoff, Denis Kocetkov, Chenghao Mou, Marc Marone, Christopher Akiki, Jia Li, Jenny Chim, et al. 2023. Starcoder: may the source be with you! *arXiv preprint arXiv:2305.06161*.

Sewon Min, Xinxi Lyu, Ari Holtzman, Mikel Artetxe, Mike Lewis, Hannaneh Hajishirzi, and Luke Zettlemoyer. 2022. Rethinking the role of demonstrations: What makes in-context learning work? In *Proceedings of the 2022 Conference on Empirical Methods in Natural Language Processing*, pages 11048–11064, Abu Dhabi, United Arab Emirates. Association for Computational Linguistics.

Suvir Mirchandani, Fei Xia, Pete Florence, brian ichter, Danny Driess, Montserrat Gonzalez Arenas, Kanishka Rao, Dorsa Sadigh, and Andy Zeng. 2023. Large language models as general pattern machines. In *7th Annual Conference on Robot Learning*.

Jane Pan, Tianyu Gao, Howard Chen, and Danqi Chen. 2023. What in-context learning "learns" in-context: Disentangling task recognition and task learning. In *Findings of the Association for Computational Linguistics: ACL 2023*, pages 8298–8319, Toronto, Canada. Association for Computational Linguistics.

Reza Pourreza, Apratim Bhattacharyya, Sunny Panchal, Mingu Lee, Pulkit Madan, and Roland Memisevic. 2023. Painter: Teaching auto-regressive language models to draw sketches. In *Proceedings of the IEEE/CVF International Conference on Computer Vision*, pages 305–314.

Archiki Prasad, Alexander Koller, Mareike Hartmann, Peter Clark, Ashish Sabharwal, Mohit Bansal, and Tushar Khot. 2023. Adapt: As-needed decomposition and planning with language models. *arXiv preprint arXiv:2311.05772*.

Evan Pu. 2022. Probing compositional understanding of chatgpt with svg. `https://evanthebouncy.medium.com/probing-compositional-understanding-of-chatgpt-with-svg-74ec9ca106b4` accessed 12/10/2023.

Alec Radford, Jong Wook Kim, Chris Hallacy, Aditya Ramesh, Gabriel Goh, Sandhini Agarwal, Girish Sastry, Amanda Askell, Pamela Mishkin, Jack Clark, et al. 2021. Learning transferable visual models from natural language supervision. In *International conference on machine learning*, pages 8748–8763. PMLR.

Ansh Radhakrishnan, Karina Nguyen, Anna Chen, Carol Chen, Carson Denison, Danny Hernandez, Esin Durmus, Evan Hubinger, Jackson Kernion, Kamilė Lukošiūtė, et al. 2023. Question decomposition improves the faithfulness of model-generated reasoning. *arXiv preprint arXiv:2307.11768*.

Laria Reynolds and Kyle McDonell. 2021. Prompt programming for large language models: Beyond the few-shot paradigm. In *Extended Abstracts of the 2021 CHI Conference on Human Factors in Computing Systems*, CHI EA '21, New York, NY, USA. Association for Computing Machinery.

Chitwan Saharia, William Chan, Saurabh Saxena, Lala Li, Jay Whang, Emily L Denton, Kamyar Ghasemipour, Raphael Gontijo Lopes, Burcu Karagol Ayan, Tim Salimans, et al. 2022. Photorealistic text-to-image diffusion models with deep language understanding. *Advances in Neural Information Processing Systems*, 35:36479–36494.

Teven Le Scao, Angela Fan, Christopher Akiki, Ellie Pavlick, Suzana Ilić, Daniel Hesslow, Roman Castagné, Alexandra Sasha Luccioni, François Yvon, Matthias Gallé, et al. 2022. Bloom: A 176b-parameter open-access multilingual language model. *arXiv preprint arXiv:2211.05100*.

Jamshaid Shahir. 2023. Writing code to produce images with chatgpt. `https://towardsdatascience.com/image-generation-with-chatgpt-68c98a061bec` accessed 12/10/2023.

Murray Shanahan. 2022. Talking about large language models. *arXiv preprint arXiv:2212.03551*.

Murray Shanahan, Kyle McDonell, and Laria Reynolds. 2023. Role play with large language models. *Nature*, pages 1–6.

Denis Shiryaev. 2022. Drawing mona lisa with chatgpt. `https://neural.love/blog/chatgpt-svg` accessed 12/10/2023.

Aarohi Srivastava, Abhinav Rastogi, Abhishek Rao, Abu Awal Md Shoeb, Abubakar Abid, Adam Fisch, Adam R Brown, Adam Santoro, Aditya Gupta, Adrià Garriga-Alonso, et al. 2023. Beyond the imitation game: Quantifying and extrapolating the capabilities of language models. *Transactions on Machine Learning Research*.

Karthik Valmeekam, Alberto Olmo, Sarath Sreedharan, and Subbarao Kambhampati. 2022. Large language models still can't plan (a benchmark for LLMs on planning and reasoning about change). In *NeurIPS 2022 Foundation Models for Decision Making Workshop*.

Johannes Von Oswald, Eyvind Niklasson, Ettore Randazzo, Joao Sacramento, Alexander Mordvintsev, Andrey Zhmoginov, and Max Vladymyrov. 2023. Transformers learn in-context by gradient descent. In *Proceedings of the 40th International Conference on Machine Learning*, volume 202 of *Proceedings of Machine Learning Research*, pages 35151–35174. PMLR.

Jason Wei, Xuezhi Wang, Dale Schuurmans, Maarten Bosma, Fei Xia, Ed Chi, Quoc V Le, Denny Zhou, et al. 2022. Chain-of-thought prompting elicits reasoning in large language models. *Advances in Neural Information Processing Systems*, 35:24824–24837.

Sang Michael Xie, Aditi Raghunathan, Percy Liang, and Tengyu Ma. 2022. An explanation of in-context learning as implicit bayesian inference. In *International Conference on Learning Representations*.

Denny Zhou, Nathanael Schärli, Le Hou, Jason Wei, Nathan Scales, Xuezhi Wang, Dale Schuurmans, Claire Cui, Olivier Bousquet, Quoc Le, et al. 2022. Least-to-most prompting enables complex reasoning in large language models. *arXiv preprint arXiv:2205.10625*.

A Prompt Details

This section supplements Section 3 by offering additional details and complete examples of the prompts used in our experiments.

A.1 Main Experiments

All prompts consist of one natural language instruction that describes the pixel matrix task by introducing pixels and the concept of pixel matrices and pixel symbols. This part is adjusted if the pixel symbols change. The second part of the prompts contains the demonstrations adapted to the object category and pixel symbols.

Independent of the pixel format, the prompt includes examples of numbers 2, 3, 8, and 6 for digits. The prompt examples for letters are A, F, G, and H. In the category of punctuation symbols, the examples are the forward slash, division sign, question mark, and the dot symbol, and for real-world objects, the examples are the smiley face, umbrella, tree, and deer.

See Figure 10 for a complete prompt for the baseline experiment.

A.2 Generating Descriptions

Refer to Figure 12 for the prompt used to generate descriptions of the objects' shapes and appearances.

A.3 Translating 01 to GK pixel matrices

Refer to Figure 13 for the prompt used to translate 01 pixel matrices to GK pixel matrices.

B Model Configurations

Pre-experiments revealed that a temperature of 1 was a good balance between randomness to ensure differences between each instance while maintaining the required format. We implemented a stop sequence for OpenAI models and restricted generated tokens to 100 for huggingface models. Apart from these modifications, we adhered to the default settings provided by the respective model APIs.

C Enumeration of All Objects

We evaluated the performance of creating pixel matrices across four categories: digits, letters, punctuation symbols, and real-world objects. Digits range from 0 to 9, with additional two-digit numbers, 10 and 32. The letter category comprises all Latin alphabet letters, including German umlauts (Ä, Ü, Ö) and eszett (ß), totaling 30 letters. The punctuation

```
Images displayed on a computer screen are a
collection of color dots, called pixels. If you
look really closely at the screen, you will be
able to see the individual pixels. The
collection of pixels that make up an image are
stored as a matrix.
We can represent different objects (e.g.,
numbers, letters, or shapes) by creating a
pixel matrix which consists of 0s and 1s. The
matrix should be of the size 8 by 8. Each entry
represents a pixel of a black or a white pixel.
That means the image has a display capable of 8
pixels in width and 8 pixels in height. Since
there are only 64 pixels in total the objects
to be displayed are significantly simplified.

Here is an example of an 8 by 8 pixel matrix
showing  three:
00000000
00111110
00000110
00111100
00001110
00000110
00111100
00000000
###
Here is an example of a grid of pixels that
form an image of  two:
00000000
00111100
01100110
00001100
00011000
00110000
01111110
00000000
###
Here is an example of a grid of pixels that
form an image of  eight:
00000000
00111100
01100110
00111100
01100110
00110100
00011000
00000000
###
Here is an example of a grid of pixels that
form an image of  six:
00000000
00111100
01100000
01100000
00111100
01100110
00111100
00000000
###
This is an example of a grid of pixels that
form an image of [object]:
```

Figure 10: The full prompt used to generate digits for the baseline experiments, with a placeholder for the requested digit.

```
Images displayed on a computer screen are
actually a collection of dots of color, called
pixels. If you look really closely at the
screen, you will be able to see the individual
pixels. The collection of pixels that make up
an image are stored as a matrix. Each pixel can
represent a different color.
We can represent different objects (e.g.,
numbers, letters, or shapes) by creating a
pixel matrix which consists different symbols
and each symbol stands for a different color.
In our 8x8 pixel matrix, we use the following
symbols to encode color: white (represented by
"0"), black ("1"), red ("2"), yellow ("3), green
("4"), and blue ("5"). This means each entry of
the matrix is either a 0, a 1, a 2, a 3, a 4, or
a 5. The matrix should be of the size 8 by 8.

Here is an example of an 8 by 8 pixel matrix
showing a smiley face:
31133113
31133113
33333333
33313333
13333331
31333313
33111133
33333333
###

Here is an example of a grid of pixels that
form an image of a tree:
00444400
04444440
44444444
44444444
44444444
00011000
00011000
00011000
###

Here is an example of a grid of pixels that
form an image of an umbrella:
00555500
05555550
55555555
00001000
00001000
00001000
00101000
00011000
###

Here is an example of a grid of pixels that
form an image of a deer:
10001000
11111000
01010000
11110001
01111111
01111111
01010101
01010101
###
```

Figure 11: Complete prompt used for experiments with new symbols representing different colors for the real-world object category. The first part and the demonstrations are adjusted.

```
Describe a simplified visual representation of
[object] which can be used to create an 8x8
pixel artwork of [object]. Emphasize only the
essential features for recognition, omitting
intricate details due to space constraints.
Deliver a concise description of the
fundamental shape and distinctive traits and if
necessary mention proportions, alignments, and
spatial relationships in a simplified rendition
of [object].
```

Figure 12: Prompt for generating descriptions of objects shapes which were added to pixel matrix prompt with the idea to enhance the outputs.

```
I want you to translate a 01 pixel matrix to a
GK pixel matrix. Replace every 0 with a G and
every 1 with a K.
Here is an example of a 01 pixel matrix:
00000000
00111100
01100000
01100000
00111100
01100110
00111100
00000000
###
Translation:
GGGGGGGG
GGKKKKGG
GKKGGGGG
GKKGGGGG
GGKKKKGG
GKKGGKKG
GGKKKKGG
GGGGGGGG
###

[...three more examples...]

Here is an example of a 01 pixel matrix:
[Exmaple 01 pixel matrix]
Translation:
```

Figure 13: Prompt for generating descriptions of objects shapes which were added to pixel matrix prompt with the idea to enhance the outputs.

digits	0, 1, 2, 3, 4, 5, 6, 7, 8, 9, 10, 32
letters	A, B, C, D, E, F, G, H, I, J, K, L, M, N, O, P, Q, R, S, T, U, V, W, X, Y, Z, Ä, Ö, Ü, ß
punct.	comma, semicolon, exclamation point, equal sign, plus sign, hashtag, dollar sign, percent sign, ampersand, asterisk, left parenthesis, right parenthesis, left bracket, right bracket, left curly brace, right curly brace, less than sign, greater than sign, backslash, underscore, colon, single quote, double quote, at sign, caret
objs.	sad face, cup, heart, wine glass half full, cactus, key, skull, mouse, crown, lightning flash, padlock, cat, crab, a chess board, a house, coffee, car, window, chair, star, mountain, sun, boat, stick figure, fly

Table 2: Enumeration of all generated objects in our experiments.

symbol category encompasses 25 different symbols, while real-world objects consist of 26 diverse items. All objects are enumerated in Table C.

D Evaluation

We recruited 3 students from our university to annotate the images generated in our experiments. Figure 14 shows our whole set of instructions.

Image Classification Annotation Task

Introduction

Thank you for participating in our image classification research project! Your assistance in classifying a set of nearly 8000 images is vital for the success of our study. Before you start, please read the following instructions carefully.

In this annotation task, you will classify small 8x8 pixel images that display simple objects falling into four categories: digits, letters, punctuation, and real-world objects. The task is expected to take up to 4 hours to complete.

Instructions

Classification Guidelines:

The first set of images includes digits, letters, and punctuation. Here, you must give an answer to what you see in the image. Do not name the category but the concrete object (e.g., number 3, letter H, or plus symbol). The second set of images includes real world images, and here we provide you with the corresponding object. Your task is to verify if the object is recognizable. What you interpret as recognizable is up to you.

We will provide you with the image folders and an Excel table. The table has one sheet for the first set of images and a second for the real-world object with the corresponding object that is supposed to be displayed on the image.

Feedback:

If you have any feedback, suggestions, or concerns about the classification process, feel free to communicate with us.

Contact Information

If you have any questions or need assistance, please contact [contact information].

Data Use

Your classification of the images will be saved and used to conduct a study on how LLMs are able to generate such images. This study will use the average of multiple annotators and can become public. By finishing the annotation task, you consent to us using your annotation data accordingly. We do not save any private information.

Thank you! Your dedication to this image classification task is greatly appreciated. Your efforts contribute significantly to the success of our research. Thank you for your time and commitment!

Figure 14: The complete instructions given to the human annotators.

E Complementary Results

Some figures showin images resulting from our experiments.

E.1 GPT-4 Color RGB

See Figure 16 for selected images generated by GPT-4 with RGB color codes as pixel symbols.

E.2 Images with Scalable Vector Graphics

Compare Figure 17 for images generated with SVG code.

E.3 Model Comparison

By default, we employed *gpt-3.5-turbo-0613* accessed through the OpenAI API. We further compared various models (Bloom (Scao et al., 2022), GPT-Neox20B (Black et al., 2022), Starcoder (Li et al., 2023)) on the pixel matrix task. Our primary aim is to contrast models fine-tuned on code with instruction-tuned LLMs based on our hypothesis that with TL, the performance should be independent of the frequency in the training data. Anticipating a higher occurrence of pixel matrices in code-based data and better instruction comprehension by classic LLMs, we hypothesize that the traditional models will excel if TL is applied. Conversely, with TR, the code models should demonstrate better performance.

GPT-3.5, with 175 billion parameters, demonstrates the best performance. In contrast, Bloom, also equipped with 175 billion parameters, adheres to the format but fails to solve any pixel matrix correctly. Gpt-Neox with 20 billion parameters does not generate any meaningful pixel matrix. The smallest model (15.5 billion parameters), Stracoder, fine-tuned specifically for code-related tasks, displays the best performance besides GPT-3.5. Its outputs for digits and letters are nearly as good as GPT-3.5, but it struggles with punctuation symbols and real-world objects.

GPT-4 shows significant improvements compared to GPT-3.5. It creates much more meaningful real-world objects on an 8x8 canvas (e.g., padlock, flash, key, or cactus), and it consistently creates colorful digits with RGB codes as pixel values, which GPT-3.5 cannot generate (see Figure 16).

E.4 16×16 pixel matrices

One thought was that an 8×8 pixel canvas might be too limiting, hindering the LLM from generating meaningful images of real-world objects like a cat

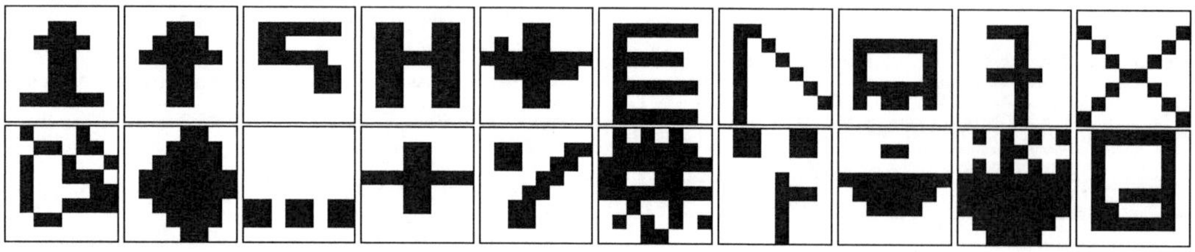

Figure 15: Negative examples from the baseline experiment: digits 1, 4, 5, 10, and 32; letters E, N, Ö, T, and V; the symbols at-sign, dollar sign, double quote, equal sign, and percent sign; the objects boat, cup, fly, star and wine glass.

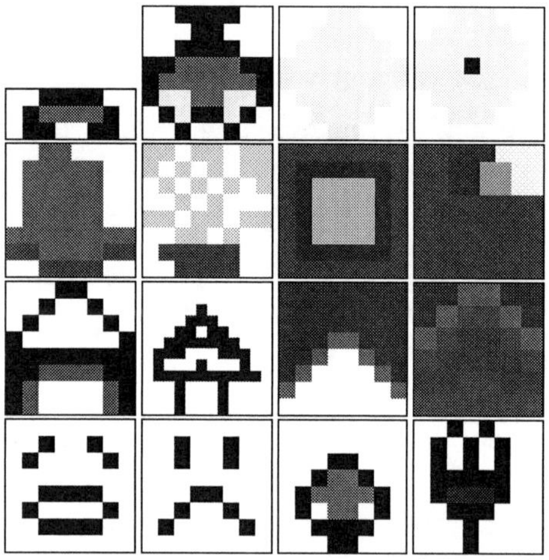

Figure 16: Selected instances of images generated by GPT-4 on an 8 by 8 pixel matrix with RGB values as pixel symbols showing two instances of each object: car, sun, cactus, coffe, house, mountain, sad face, wine glass. The magenta stripes resulting from translating slightly off output textual format to images.

or a boat. We conducted experiments with a pixel matrix of size 16×16. However, the overall results showed a slight degradation, and we did not see any improvements for specific objects where a larger canvas may be beneficial.

F Supplementary Discussion

We attributed some observed behavior to the autoregressive architecture of GPT-like models. For example, the letter V was never correctly generated and always resulted in the letter X. We assume that after correctly generating the first line of the matrix according to V, the subsequent generations favored a pixel matrix showing the letter X due to its higher frequency in training compared to that of a V. If the prompt would be truly "understood", the attention to the previous pixels should not overshadow the requested object.

In the *One Token* Experiment, overall results

Figure 17: Example results from experiments with SVG code as image format showing two instances of each object: house, car, sun, crown, mountain, heart, cactus, window, wine glass, and lightning flash.

showed a slight decline, but notable improvements were observed with the new matrix format, especially for the object 'chess board'. An additional experiment with the chess board showed that while 42 out of 60 generations were correct with the basic matrix format, all 60 chess board generations were correct with the new format. We assume this might be because this object resembles a pattern completion task, which is less error-prone with fewer tokens Mirchandani et al. (2023).

We have conducted most of our experiments with a format that used more than ten different tokens to represent a pixel matrix as the tokenizer combines sequences of 0s and 1s. During our experiments with G and K as symbols, we assume that it translated in 01-matrices to the new format even though the tokens are different and the number of tokens changes (see Figure 7). Thus, the token embeddings represent even uncommon non-semantic similarities.

The SlayQA Benchmark of Social Reasoning: Testing Gender-inclusive Generalization with Neopronouns

Bastian Bunzeck and **Sina Zarrieß**
Computational Linguistics, Department of Linguistics
Bielefeld University, Germany
{bastian.bunzeck, sina.zarriess}@uni-bielefeld.de

Abstract

We introduce SlayQA, a novel benchmark data set designed to evaluate language models' ability to handle gender-inclusive language, specifically the use of neopronouns, in a question-answering setting. Derived from the Social IQa data set, SlayQA modifies context-question-answer triples to include gender-neutral pronouns, creating a significant linguistic distribution shift in comparison to common pretraining corpora like C4 or Dolma. Our results show that state-of-the-art language models struggle with the challenge, exhibiting small, but noticeable performance drops when answering question containing neopronouns compared to those without.

1 Introduction

Currently, the recognition of the importance of inclusivity and representation in NLP is growing (Sun et al., 2019; Stanczak and Augenstein, 2021; Lauscher et al., 2022). Traditional data sets often reflect and perpetuate binary gender norms, which can marginalize non-binary and gender non-conforming individuals and cause harm (Ansara and Hegarty, 2013). This lack of inclusivity highlights a critical need for resources that better represent the full spectrum of gender identities. One aspect of gender-inclusive language use that is gaining more and more acceptance is the usage of neopronouns like *xe/xyr* or *ze/zir*. Neopronouns are novel pronouns that people who do not identify themselves as belonging to the polar extremes of the gender spectrum can choose to use for reference to themselves instead of the classical, gendered pronouns: *he/him* and *she/her*. Current benchmarks that assess this kind of linguistic inclusivity mostly focus on the generation of correct neopronouns in context or similar tasks (Ovalle et al., 2023; Hossain et al., 2023). On the other hand, resources that simply implement established LM benchmarks in a more inclusive way are rare.

Figure 1: Visualization of the conversion process that turns Social IQa data into SlayQA data

To address this gap, we present SlayQA: **S**ocial **l**inguistics **a**nalytics **y**ielding **Q**ueer **A**gents, a novel benchmark set derived from the existing Social IQa (SIQa) data set (Sap et al., 2019b). It contains a situation description (the context), social reasoning questions and three prospective answers, where all context-question-answer pairs include at least two acts of pronoun-based reference and gender-neutral pronouns. Because SlayQA systematically replaces established, gendered pronouns with gender-affirming neopronouns, it is a more inclusive data set that better reflects the diversity of human identities. Although neo-pronouns are commonly rated less grammatical than their established counterparts (Hekanaho, 2021; Rose et al., 2023), they are beginning to be adopted in various social circles. Here, the key word is *beginning* – they are still infrequent in discourse and and also in common pretraining corpora like C4 (Raffel et al., 2020), Dolma (Soldaini et al., 2024), and

Proceedings of the 2nd GenBench Workshop on Generalisation (Benchmarking) in NLP, pages 42–53
November 16, 2024 ©2024 Association for Computational Linguistics

RedPajama-Data-1T (Together Computer, 2023). As such, our pronoun-altered benchmark marks a significant pronoun distribution shift in comparison to these pretraining corpora. Consequentially, SlayQA helps to assess how well language models are able to generalize to novel linguistic structures.

2 Related work

Dev et al. (2021) conduct a survey on harms involving gender-neutral speech and neopronouns in general purpose NLP systems. Replies included, for example, the non-detection of hate-speech or automatic educational assessments marking gender-inclusive language as wrong. Furthermore they show that from skewed training data, bias in word embeddings arises. For GLoVe embeddings (Pennington et al., 2014), gendered pronouns appear in close proximity in their vector space, whereas neopronouns hardly cluster with them. Similarly, in the original BERT model (Devlin et al., 2019), neopronouns are out-of-vocabulary items. In a more applied setting, Lauscher et al. (2023) show that machine translation systems are able to translate gendered pronouns well, but not neopronouns. They are either plainly copied or the included agents are misgendered. Furthermore, for sentences with gender-neutral or neopronouns, overall translation quality (e.g. syntactic, semantic) diminishes.

The most prominent NLP benchmarks for gender-inclusivity are TANGO (Ovalle et al., 2023) and MISGENDERED (Hossain et al., 2023). While TANGO contains sentences with names and neopronouns to be completed by generative models, MISGENDERED also includes an explicit statement of the agents' preferred pronouns. Their goals are therefore almost identical: to assess whether language models can correctly produce text with neo pronouns when prompted with them. Evaluations on these data sets show similar results: errors rarely occur with gendered pronouns, but correct continuation scores drop with the gender-neutral singular *they*. Worst scores (accuracy below 10%) are found for neopronouns. A possible explanation can be found in Ovalle et al. (2024), who show that the BPE algorithm (Gage, 1994) commonly used in state-of-the-art LLMs dissects neopronouns into smaller parts, which never happens to established pronouns. This is caused by data scarcity – common pre-training data sets lack examples of neopronouns in use. As the BPE algorithm leaves lexical tokens intact if and only if they occur with a high enough frequency, neopronouns are usually split.

	C4	Dolma
he	144.202.977	965.297.366
she	92.421.725	544.245.250
they	260.126.090	1.705.400.768
thon	872.654	992.499
e	213.797.769	240.457.628
ae	3.910.812	4.135.288
co	83.935.707	199.206.147
vi	10.139.390	12.534.070
xe	1.148.568	2.134.212
ey	869.765	1.691.904
ze	1.618.896	1.793.116

Table 1: Frequencies for established subject pronouns and subject neopronouns in C4 and Dolma

Current data sets that are used to measure the question answering abilities of NLP systems are not concerned with gender-inclusivity. While Rogers et al. (2023) present a large taxonomy including many different kinds of tasks, domains and data formats, 'fairness' seems to be only an afterthought in contemporary QA evaluation, e.g. by only referring to the inclusion of multilingual data.

3 (Neo)pronouns in pre-training corpora and evaluation data sets

3.1 (Neo)pronouns in C4 and Dolma

We argue that our benchmark introduces a significant distribution shift between the pretraining corpora and the evaluation data with regard to pronouns. To assess this proposed distribution shift, we determine the frequencies of established and neopronouns in these corpora through the n-gram lookup function of *What's In My Big Data?* (WIMBD) (Elazar et al., 2024) – if the neopronouns occur less frequently in pretraining corpora than established pronouns, then our neopronoun benchmark introduces a drastic distribution shift in its pronoun distribution compared to these corpora.

We adapt our list of pronouns from the seminal study by Hossain et al. (2023). For the sake of brevity, we do not include further gender-affirming pronoun variations like nounself, emojiself, numberself or nameself pronouns (Lauscher et al., 2022).

We search C4 (Raffel et al., 2020) and Dolma (Soldaini et al., 2024) for the subject, object, possessive (pronoun and determiner) and reflexive

	context	question	answerA	answerB	answerC
he	10.238	146	2.020	2.066	2.060
she	13.291	221	2.759	2.716	2.715
they	14.178	150	2.996	2.993	3.007
thon	0	0	0	0	0
e	1	0	0	0	0
ae	0	0	0	0	0
co	0	0	0	0	0
vi	0	0	0	0	0
xe	0	0	0	0	0
ey	0	0	0	0	0
ze	0	0	0	0	0

Table 2: Token frequencies for morphological paradigms of gendered and gender-neutral pronouns in Social IQa data

forms of the neopronouns from Hossain et al. (2023), as we evaluate models trained on these corpora. While we also evaluate models trained on RedPajama-Data-1T (Together Computer, 2023), no n-gram frequencies for this data set are available through WIMBD. C4 is based on CommonCrawl web dumps that were then cleaned, filtered and deduplicated to certain degrees. RedPajama-Data-1T and Dolma also contain considerable portions of CommonCrawl enriched with data from diverse sources, such as GitHub code, Reddit posts, academic papers from SemanticScholar and Arxiv, etc., which were then also cleaned, filtered and deduplicated. They were explicitly created as open data sets that mirror the data that commercial/closed models like Anthropic's Claude, OpenAI's ChatGPT or Meta's Llama models are trained on. Therefore, they can be seen as somewhat exemplary for the data that commercial models are trained on, and the overall frequency distributions found in them should be generally similar to those in not publicly available pre-training corpora.

The frequencies for subject pronouns in both corpora are found in Table 1, all other results are listed in Appendix A. In comparison to the established pronouns, neopronouns occur with reduced frequencies. The neopronouns *e* and *co* are exceptions, but as *e* is a highly frequent letter in the English language and *co* also serves as a productive morpheme, it is reasonable to assume that the vast majority of these instances are not representative of pronoun usage. The neopronouns that do not constitute such widely used building blocks of ordinary English, e.g. *thon*, *xe* or *ey*, occur much less throughout the training data. For example, *he* occurs one thousand times more than *thon* in Dolma. These distributions are stable across all morphological forms (see Tables 5, 6, 7 and 8). Although the possesive and reflexive pronouns are overall less frequent, all forms are still found across all training corpora. The only exception is the reflexive *virself*, which is completely absent from the C4 data. Yet, the presence of all other forms in the data, and especially the presence of the reflexives, which should not be accidental n-gram matches, confirms that pronoun use of these neopronouns is indeed included in these pre-training data sets, just to a much lesser degree than the usage of established pronouns.

Although no n-gram frequency results are available for RedPajama-Data-1T, we assume that the underlying distribution should be mostly equal to the two examined corpora – all three corpora are mainly based on CommonCrawl web dumps, so it is reasonable to expect a large lexical overlap between them.

A final indicator for the different pronoun distributions can be found in Table 9, where we show the number of sub-word tokens which the different grammatical forms of our investigated (neo)pronouns are split into by the tokenizers of our tested models. Here, we find generally higher numbers for the neopronouns, especially for the reflexive forms. Because the standard BPE tokenization algorithm keeps highly frequent forms intact as one token, this split of lexical words into several sub-words is another display of their infrequency compared to established pronouns.

3.2 (Neo)pronouns in SIQa

While the mentioned pre-training corpora contain very little neopronouns, the numbers are even more extreme for the SIQa data set (Sap et al., 2019b). The original SIQa contains 37.588 triples of context, question and three prospective answers. It is based on the Atomic data set (Sap et al., 2019a), which contains commonsense if-then statements for machine learning. These were then manually rewritten into context, question and right answer triples. False answers were added manually and by sampling randomly from correct answers to different questions. As gender fairness was not a concern in the compilation of this data set, the distributions of gendered pronouns and gender-neutral neopronouns deviate strongly. Table 2 shows the absolute token counts (aggregating over the complete morphological paradigms) for SIQa. Gendered pronouns occur quite frequently – mostly in the context, less so in the answers, rarely in the questions. Neopronouns are not featured at all in any form (the one *e* is likely to be a typo).

Nevertheless, SIQa exhibits some gender-inclusive tendencies. The gender-neutral singular reflexive *themself* occurs 74 times across the whole data set, indicating that more usage of gender-neutral *they* is likely to be featured more prominently. Besides, also the choice of included names appears to be fairly inclusive after a cursory qualitative inspection, because many of the named agents in SIQa feature gender-neutral names like *Alex* or *Kai*. Yet, it is still rather conservative and does not feature any neopronouns.

4 Benchmark creation

4.1 Neopronouns and (co)reference

Pronouns usually either substitute for a noun (phrase) or are used to signal reference to something that can be inferred from the situational context (Quirk et al., 1985). As such, they are ubiquitous in everyday language, but generally do not attract new lexemes because they constitute a closed word class. Novel items are only slowly introduced via grammaticalization (Heine and Song, 2011). Neopronouns, then, present a unique case; some of them developed organically within specific social groups to promote gender inclusivity, others were deliberately created for that purpose (e.g., *ey* in 1975, *thon* in the late 19th century, see McGaughey, 2020). While neopronouns are gaining traction in some communities, they remain less widely adopted, with gender-neutral *they* being the notable exception.

For SlayQA, we specifically filter out examples that do not include at least two coreference chains with named entities. This filtering is crucial because without multiple entities in the text, the replacement of pronouns with neopronouns does not significantly alter the amount of generalization measured by the task. When only one entity is present, changed pronouns do not pose an insurmountable challenge to a model's understanding of the situation – there are no options for interpreting the neopronoun in/correctly. However, when multiple named entities are involved, the task becomes much more demanding, as the model must accurately track and resolve these coreferences across texts. This ensures that SlayQA actually tests the ability to handle neopronouns *in use*.

4.2 Creating the distribution shift

To create the envisioned distribution shift, we first parsed all examples in the SIQa training and development data sets as a combined `context + question + answers` string with `spacy` (Honnibal et al., 2020) and performed coreference resolution with `coreferee` (Hudson, 2023). For the following data modification step, we included all sentences that feature at least two coreference chains which resolve to proper nouns, i.e. names in the case of the SIQa data set. Sentences without any pronouns or with coreference that resolves to a singular entity were therefore discarded. From the original 35.364 entries in the training data, 1.985 examples were left after this procedure.

In a second step, we then iterated over all leftover examples and filtered out those that did not contain any male or female gendered pronoun. After this step, 1.388 examples were left. For each context-question-answers entry in the filtered data, we then replaced all forms of established male pronouns (forms of *he*) and established female pronouns (forms of *she*) with one randomly chosen set of corresponding neopronoun forms. We decided not to alter forms of *they* as they are a) already used in a gender-neutral fashion in several examples in SIQa, and b) proved to be hard to correctly parse into singular or plural forms, where replacement of the plural form with a singular neopronoun might create illogical examples.

Finally, we noticed that a minority of data points in SIQa feature incorrect or mixed pronoun use. In the following example, *Kai* is first referred to with

Motivation					
Practical	*Cognitive*	*Intrinsic*	*Fairness*		
	□		□		
Generalisation type					
Compositional	*Structural*	*Cross Task*	*Cross Language*	*Cross Domain*	*Robustness*
□					
Shift type					
Covariate	*Label*	*Full*	*Assumed*		
□					
Shift source					
Naturally occuring	*Partitioned natural*	*Generated shift*	*Fully generated*		
		□			
Shift locus					
Train–test	*Finetune train–test*	*Pretrain–train*	*Pretrain–test*		
			□		

Table 3: GenBench Evaluation Card for SlayQA

male pronouns (*himself*, *him*) in the context, but then with the gender-neutral singular *they* in the first answer:

- `context: Tracy saw Kai standing there by himself and decided to go talk to him.`
- `question: How would Kai feel as a result?`
  - `answerA: upset they had to deal with someone`
  - `answerB: they want to be left alone`
  - `answerC: happy to not be lonely anymore`

We acknowledge this haphazard noise in the original data but due to the rarity of its occurrence, we do not further attempt to clean the data from it.

5 SlayQA in the generalisation taxonomy

Table 3 shows where SlayQA is located in the generalisation hierarchy by Hupkes et al. (2023).

Motivation SlayQA is both cognitively and fairness-motivated. Humans are generally able to use neopronouns correctly and productively. Consequently, if language models are indeed good models of human language (usage), they should not struggle with social reasoning that includes neopronouns. Additionally, the inclusion and correct processing of neopronouns also relates to fairness of language technologies – they should be applicable to all potential users, even in the light of a changing linguistic and societal landscape (cf. also related work in Section 2).

Generalisation type SlayQA assesses whether language models can interpret novel, highly infrequent pronoun forms in social reasoning contexts. This is a test for compositional generalisation, as neopronouns are systematic, productively used, substitutive with regard to the referents they replace, and localist in the sense of only depending on context, question and answer sentences. As such, our benchmark fulfils the criteria essential for compositional generalisation, as laid out by Hupkes et al. (2020).

Shift type Our benchmark constitutes a covariate shift. We assume that social reasoning of the kind that SIQa tests is somehow implicitly, if not explicitly, included in the pre-training data. By changing the pronouns in the complete data sets (context, questions and answers), we do not alter the nature of the task or the correctness patterns of the answers. While the test distribution now differs more strongly from the training distribution: $p(x_{tst}) \neq p(x_{tr})$, the conditional probabilities still stay the same: $p(y_{tst}|x_{tst}) = p(y_{tr}|x_{tr})$.

Shift source Our benchmark includes a generated shift. As the original SIQa data set is crowdsourced, it is reasonable to assume that it still follows a somewhat *representative*, if not completely *authentic* (in the sense of Stefanowitsch, 2020) linguistic distribution, comparable to common pre-training corpora without synthetic data. This representative distribution is explicitly altered for SlayQA by including a much higher proportion of neopronouns than classical corpora.

Shift locus The data shift is localized between pre-training and testing. We explicitly do not fine-tune the models on social reasoning with neopronouns, as we are interested in the compositional abilities of LLMs *as is* and do not want to skew them with additional training on data that reflects the fairness generalization we aim to assess.

6 Evaluation

6.1 Methodology

Models We evaluate five different, autoregressive models: OLMo-1B (Groeneveld et al., 2024) as a representative model for the Dolma pre-training corpus (Soldaini et al., 2024), three RedPajama-INCITE-7B models (base, chat-tuned and instruction-tuned) for the RedPajama-Data-1T data (Together Computer, 2023) and a quantized version of the instruction-tuned Llama-3.1 8B (Team, 2024) for C4 (Raffel et al., 2020). Because the original Llama-1 was provably trained on C4 (among other data sets, see Touvron et al., 2023a), we assume that this data set is still fully present in the training data of Llama-3. However, it is not clear whether this is actually the case, since the most recent Llama paper (Team, 2024) does not reveal any information about the concrete make-up of the pre-training data.

Due to the exorbitant resource demands of so-called small state-of-the-art models like OlMo-7B or Llama-3.1-8B, their evaluation on this proposed benchmark was, unfortunately, beyond the capabilities of our available GPU resources. Therefore, we opted to only evaluate smaller (OLMo-1B) or quantized models. For the Llama-3.1 model, we had to resort to a version working with lower number precision (quantized from FP16 down to INT4 with `AutoAWQ`, based on Lin et al., 2024). Unfortunately, this specific configuration is only available for the instruction-tuned model, so we do not provide scores for the base model.

Data We evaluate our models on three data sets: our distribution-shifted benchmark, the original 1.388 unaltered data points with at least two coreference chains, and a random selection of 1.388 examples sampled from Social IQa that were not restricted with regard to coreference. For reproducibility reasons, we host SlayQA[1], the randomly sampled Social IQa set[2] and the unaltered data points, NoSlayQA[3], on the Hugging Face hub.

Scoring To assess the preference of the individual models, we use the Hugging Face `transformers` library (Wolf et al., 2020) and its evaluation metrics. In line with Brown et al. (2020), we measured the language models' preference for a specific answer by calculating its probability conditioned on the context and question. To do so, we chose a perplexity-based (Jelinek et al., 1977) approach.[4] We calculated the perplexities of concatenated context + question + answer strings for all three choices in each example and then selected the answer with the lowest perplexity as the one preferred by the model. As such, we perform zero-shot evaluation on models not explicitly fine-tuned for this task. Performance is measured as accuracy against the gold standard labels in the data.

6.2 Results

The results of the zero-shot evaluation are displayed in Table 4. Across all models and evaluation data sets, the results lie between 7% and 13% above the baseline. This indicates that all models have acquired some generalization capabilities in the social reasoning domain, at least as instantiated by the SIQa/SlayQA question patterns. The differences between the models and between the data sets for the various models are comparatively small, but still exhibit somewhat systematic patterns.

From a model-centric viewpoint, the Llama-3.1-8B model in particular outperforms the other models, achieving the highest scores on all three data sets – 46.97% on the SIQa subset, 46.4% on NoSlayQA, and 44.16% on SlayQA. This quantized model consistently outpaces the RedPajama series and the OLMo-1B model by three to four percentage points. The RedPajama models demonstrate slightly varying performance, with the Base variant surpassing the others on the SIQa subset and the instruction-tuned version achieving the worst performance. The scores for OLMo-1B are comparable to the best RedPajama scores.

[1] `https://huggingface.co/datasets/bbunzeck/slayqa`

[2] `https://huggingface.co/datasets/bbunzeck/minisiqa`

[3] `https://huggingface.co/datasets/bbunzeck/noslayqa`

[4] Original experiments with the `outlines` library (Willard and Louf, 2023) and constrained generation showed similar tendencies, but generally resulted in lower accuracy scores.

Model	SIQa subset	NoSlayQA	SlayQA
Random baseline	33.33%	33.33%	33.33%
allenai/OLMo-1B	43.88%	42.87%	42.21%
togethercomputer/RedPajama-INCITE-Base-3B-v1	42.87%	43.3%	40.99%
togethercomputer/RedPajama-INCITE-Instruct-3B-v1	40.71%	41.35%	40.78%
togethercomputer/RedPajama-INCITE-Chat-3B-v1	41.5%	43.95%	41.93%
hugging-quants/Meta-Llama-3.1-8B-Instruct-AWQ-INT4	46.97%	46.4%	44.16%

Table 4: Results for different models

When comparing the data sets, it is striking that scores for SlayQA are consistently lower than the scores the unaltered NoSlayQA. Despite the differences being fairly marginal, this pattern is stable across all five models. Interestingly, performance on the (presumably easier) SIQa subset, which was not filtered for two coreference chains, is not always higher than the performance on (No)SlayQA. While this is the case for OLMo-1b and Llama-3.1-8B, the RedPajama models always perform better on NoSlayQA than on the SIQa subset.

7 Discussion and conclusion

We created SlayQA as a more inclusive benchmark for evaluating question answering and social reasoning in LMs. A key motivation was to test how well these models can generalize in this domain, particularly under the significant distribution shift between pre-training and test data that we created by replacing gendered pronouns with neopronouns that occur much less frequently in the investigated pre-training corpora.

The results indicate that we have succeeded in our objectives. The scores on SlayQA are consistently lower than those on the parallel NoSlayQA data set, which suggests that the models struggle more with the challenges SlayQA presents. Interestingly, however, the scores on SlayQA are not always below our random selection SIQa data. This finding is intriguing because we expected questions requiring the tracking of two coreference chains to be more challenging than those without such demands. It is quite possible that questions without two coreference chains introduce different, perhaps equally complex, challenges. Moreover it should also be noted that the relatively small differences between models could be due to training noise – for an even more comprehensive evaluation of neopronouns' influence, several comparable models that differ in their random initializations would be needed. As these are not readily available and costly to train, we have to leave this direction to future work.

From a model-centric standpoint, the largest model (Llama-3.1-8B) consistently outperforms the smaller models, even though it was drastically quantized to much lower number precision. Among the smaller models, the performance differences are minimal, with no substantial gap between the 1B OLMo and 2B RedPajama models. Additionally, there are no significant differences between the base RedPajama model and those fine-tuned for instruction-following or conversational tasks, which is surprising given the assumption that fine-tuning should improve performance on question answering tasks compared to vanilla models.

Although we were not able to evaluate larger models, our accuracies do not deviate drastically from comparable zero-shot evaluations for much larger models. In the the Llama-1 paper, Touvron et al. (2023a) report scores between 48.5% for Llama-1-7B and 52.3% for Llama-1-65B. For Llama-2 (Touvron et al., 2023b), scores align as well (48.3% for the 7B model, 50.7% for the 70B model). Even the largest Llama-3 model with 405B parameters only achieves 53.7% on SIQa, as reported in Team (2024). Judging from these meagre scaling effects, we assume that evaluations of larger models on SlayQA should not deviate drastically.

While we decided to employ a zero-shot evaluation approach for comparability, it would also be interesting to see how models fare in multi-shot reasoning or fine-tuning contexts. The AllenAI leader board for SIQa[5] reports the best fine-tuned model with a score of 84.31%. Furthermore, prompting has started to replace more technical evaluation ap-

[5] https://leaderboard.allenai.org/socialiqa/submissions/public

proaches (although it remains debated, see Hu and Levy, 2023) – as such it would be also interesting to see how commercial and open models work in SIQa in prompting settings with chain-of-thought or different reasoning approaches.

Future research similar to SlayQA should definitely aim to include even more novel and linguistically interesting forms, e.g. the aforementioned nounself, emojiself, numberself or nameself pronouns (Lauscher et al., 2022). Their unique structure and usage should be even rarer than neopronouns and could pose even more veritable challenges to the generalization capabilities of modern LMs. Additionally, the SlayQA paradigm could be expanded to other benchmarks that test different capabilities. For example, it would be interesting whether performance on the grammatical benchmark BLiMP (Warstadt et al., 2020) deteriorates with the inclusion of neopronouns. Finally, the influence of different language modeling choices, e.g. tokenization, deserves further scrutiny. As our tested models did not drastically differ in subword tokenization for the tested (neo)pronouns, we cannot draw definite conclusions. Evaluation on a wider range of models could illuminate this further.

Limitations

As this study is the first of its kind, it is still limited in various ways. As previously mentioned, evaluations of extremely large LMs were impossible due to limited resources. Yet, the comparison of our results with those of contemporary model reports showed similar scores, so we assume that this limitation did not impact the current study in a major way. Another limiting factor lies in the focus on neopronouns. As mentioned in the previous paragraph, further ways of gender-inclusive pronoun usage exist. Each one of them is deserving of recognition in inclusive NLP research, but for the sake of brevity, we focused on neopronouns only. As a final limitation, we question the quality of SIQa as a benchmark of social reasoning. We include one example in section 4.2, but our manual inspection of SIQa yielded many more such examples with confusing or borderline nonsensical "correct" answers. While we chose it as the base of SlayQA due to its widespread use in evaluation of SOTA models, its quality for the kind of reasoning it aim to evaluate is fairly questionable.

Acknowledgements

We thank Clara Lachenmaier and Judith Sieker for their helpful comments and remarks on earlier drafts of this paper.

This research has been funded by the Deutsche Forschungsgemeinschaft (DFG, German Research Foundation) – CRC-1646, project number 512393437, project A02.

References

Y Gavriel Ansara and Peter Hegarty. 2013. Misgendering in English language contexts: Applying non-cisgenderist methods to feminist research. *International Journal of Multiple Research Approaches*, 7(2):160–177.

Tom Brown, Benjamin Mann, Nick Ryder, Melanie Subbiah, Jared D Kaplan, Prafulla Dhariwal, Arvind Neelakantan, Pranav Shyam, Girish Sastry, Amanda Askell, Sandhini Agarwal, Ariel Herbert-Voss, Gretchen Krueger, Tom Henighan, Rewon Child, Aditya Ramesh, Daniel Ziegler, Jeffrey Wu, Clemens Winter, Chris Hesse, Mark Chen, Eric Sigler, Mateusz Litwin, Scott Gray, Benjamin Chess, Jack Clark, Christopher Berner, Sam McCandlish, Alec Radford, Ilya Sutskever, and Dario Amodei. 2020. Language models are few-shot learners. In *Advances in Neural Information Processing Systems*, volume 33, pages 1877–1901. Curran Associates, Inc.

Sunipa Dev, Masoud Monajatipoor, Anaelia Ovalle, Arjun Subramonian, Jeff Phillips, and Kai-Wei Chang. 2021. Harms of Gender Exclusivity and Challenges in Non-Binary Representation in Language Technologies. In *Proceedings of the 2021 Conference on Empirical Methods in Natural Language Processing*, pages 1968–1994, Online and Punta Cana, Dominican Republic. Association for Computational Linguistics.

Jacob Devlin, Ming-Wei Chang, Kenton Lee, and Kristina Toutanova. 2019. BERT: Pre-training of Deep Bidirectional Transformers for Language Understanding. In *Proceedings of the 2019 Conference of the North*, pages 4171–4186, Minneapolis, Minnesota. Association for Computational Linguistics.

Yanai Elazar, Akshita Bhagia, Ian Magnusson, Abhilasha Ravichander, Dustin Schwenk, Alane Suhr, Pete Walsh, Dirk Groeneveld, Luca Soldaini, Sameer Singh, Hanna Hajishirzi, Noah A. Smith, and Jesse Dodge. 2024. What's In My Big Data? *Preprint*, arXiv:2310.20707.

Philip Gage. 1994. A new algorithm for data compression. *C Users J.*, 12(2):23–38.

Dirk Groeneveld, Iz Beltagy, Pete Walsh, Akshita Bhagia, Rodney Kinney, Oyvind Tafjord, Ananya Harsh Jha, Hamish Ivison, Ian Magnusson, Yizhong Wang,

Shane Arora, David Atkinson, Russell Authur, Khyathi Raghavi Chandu, Arman Cohan, Jennifer Dumas, Yanai Elazar, Yuling Gu, Jack Hessel, Tushar Khot, William Merrill, Jacob Morrison, Niklas Muennighoff, Aakanksha Naik, Crystal Nam, Matthew E. Peters, Valentina Pyatkin, Abhilasha Ravichander, Dustin Schwenk, Saurabh Shah, Will Smith, Emma Strubell, Nishant Subramani, Mitchell Wortsman, Pradeep Dasigi, Nathan Lambert, Kyle Richardson, Luke Zettlemoyer, Jesse Dodge, Kyle Lo, Luca Soldaini, Noah A. Smith, and Hannaneh Hajishirzi. 2024. OLMo: Accelerating the Science of Language Models. *Preprint*, arXiv:2402.00838.

Bernd Heine and Kyung-An Song. 2011. On the grammaticalization of personal pronouns. *Journal of Linguistics*, 47(3):587–630.

Laura Hekanaho. 2021. Generic and Nonbinary Pronouns: Usage, acceptability and attitudes. *Neuphilologische Mitteilungen*, 121(2):498–509.

Matthew Honnibal, Ines Montani, Sofie Van Landeghem, and Adriane Boyd. 2020. spaCy: Industrial-strength natural language processing in python.

Tamanna Hossain, Sunipa Dev, and Sameer Singh. 2023. MISGENDERED: Limits of Large Language Models in Understanding Pronouns. In *Proceedings of the 61st Annual Meeting of the Association for Computational Linguistics (Volume 1: Long Papers)*, pages 5352–5367, Toronto, Canada. Association for Computational Linguistics.

Jennifer Hu and Roger Levy. 2023. Prompting is not a substitute for probability measurements in large language models. In *Proceedings of the 2023 Conference on Empirical Methods in Natural Language Processing*, pages 5040–5060, Singapore. Association for Computational Linguistics.

Richard Paul Hudson. 2023. Coreferee.

Dieuwke Hupkes, Verna Dankers, Mathijs Mul, and Elia Bruni. 2020. Compositionality Decomposed: How do Neural Networks Generalise? *Journal of Artificial Intelligence Research*, 67:757–795.

Dieuwke Hupkes, Mario Giulianelli, Verna Dankers, Mikel Artetxe, Yanai Elazar, Tiago Pimentel, Christos Christodoulopoulos, Karim Lasri, Naomi Saphra, Arabella Sinclair, Dennis Ulmer, Florian Schottmann, Khuyagbaatar Batsuren, Kaiser Sun, Koustuv Sinha, Leila Khalatbari, Maria Ryskina, Rita Frieske, Ryan Cotterell, and Zhijing Jin. 2023. A taxonomy and review of generalization research in NLP. *Nature Machine Intelligence*, 5(10):1161–1174.

Fred Jelinek, Robert L Mercer, Lalit R Bahl, and James K Baker. 1977. Perplexity—a measure of the difficulty of speech recognition tasks. *The Journal of the Acoustical Society of America*, 62(S1):S63–S63.

Anne Lauscher, Archie Crowley, and Dirk Hovy. 2022. Welcome to the modern world of pronouns: Identity-inclusive natural language processing beyond gender. In *Proceedings of the 29th International Conference on Computational Linguistics*, pages 1221–1232, Gyeongju, Republic of Korea. International Committee on Computational Linguistics.

Anne Lauscher, Debora Nozza, Ehm Miltersen, Archie Crowley, and Dirk Hovy. 2023. What about "em"? How Commercial Machine Translation Fails to Handle (Neo-)Pronouns. In *Proceedings of the 61st Annual Meeting of the Association for Computational Linguistics (Volume 1: Long Papers)*, pages 377–392, Toronto, Canada. Association for Computational Linguistics.

Ji Lin, Jiaming Tang, Haotian Tang, Shang Yang, Wei-Ming Chen, Wei-Chen Wang, Guangxuan Xiao, Xingyu Dang, Chuang Gan, and Song Han. 2024. AWQ: Activation-aware weight quantization for on-device LLM compression and acceleration. In *Proceedings of Machine Learning and Systems*, volume 6, pages 87–100.

Sebastian McGaughey. 2020. Understanding Neopronouns. *The Gay & Lesbian Review Worldwide*, 27(2).

Anaelia Ovalle, Palash Goyal, Jwala Dhamala, Zachary Jaggers, Kai-Wei Chang, Aram Galstyan, Richard Zemel, and Rahul Gupta. 2023. "I'm fully who I am": Towards Centering Transgender and Non-Binary Voices to Measure Biases in Open Language Generation. In *2023 ACM Conference on Fairness, Accountability, and Transparency*, pages 1246–1266, Chicago IL USA. ACM.

Anaelia Ovalle, Ninareh Mehrabi, Palash Goyal, Jwala Dhamala, Kai-Wei Chang, Richard Zemel, Aram Galstyan, Yuval Pinter, and Rahul Gupta. 2024. Tokenization matters: Navigating data-scarce tokenization for gender inclusive language technologies. In *Findings of the Association for Computational Linguistics: NAACL 2024*, pages 1739–1756, Mexico City, Mexico. Association for Computational Linguistics.

Jeffrey Pennington, Richard Socher, and Christopher Manning. 2014. Glove: Global Vectors for Word Representation. In *Proceedings of the 2014 Conference on Empirical Methods in Natural Language Processing (EMNLP)*, pages 1532–1543, Doha, Qatar. Association for Computational Linguistics.

Randolph Quirk, Sidney Greenbaum, Geoffrey Leech, and Jan Svartvik. 1985. *A Comprehensive Grammar of the English Language*. Longman, London.

Colin Raffel, Noam Shazeer, Adam Roberts, Katherine Lee, Sharan Narang, Michael Matena, Yanqi Zhou, Wei Li, and Peter J. Liu. 2020. Exploring the limits of transfer learning with a unified text-to-text transformer. *Journal of Machine Learning Research*, 21(140):1–67.

Anna Rogers, Matt Gardner, and Isabelle Augenstein. 2023. QA Dataset Explosion: A Taxonomy of NLP Resources for Question Answering and Reading Comprehension. *ACM Computing Surveys*, 55(10):1–45.

Ell Rose, Max Winig, Jasper Nash, Kyra Roepke, and Kirby Conrod. 2023. Variation in acceptability of neologistic English pronouns. *Proceedings of the Linguistic Society of America*, 8(1):5526.

Maarten Sap, Ronan Le Bras, Emily Allaway, Chandra Bhagavatula, Nicholas Lourie, Hannah Rashkin, Brendan Roof, Noah A. Smith, and Yejin Choi. 2019a. ATOMIC: An Atlas of Machine Commonsense for If-Then Reasoning. *Proceedings of the AAAI Conference on Artificial Intelligence*, 33(01):3027–3035.

Maarten Sap, Hannah Rashkin, Derek Chen, Ronan Le Bras, and Yejin Choi. 2019b. Social IQa: Commonsense Reasoning about Social Interactions. In *Proceedings of the 2019 Conference on Empirical Methods in Natural Language Processing and the 9th International Joint Conference on Natural Language Processing (EMNLP-IJCNLP)*, pages 4462–4472, Hong Kong, China. Association for Computational Linguistics.

Luca Soldaini, Rodney Kinney, Akshita Bhagia, Dustin Schwenk, David Atkinson, Russell Authur, Ben Bogin, Khyathi Chandu, Jennifer Dumas, Yanai Elazar, Valentin Hofmann, Ananya Harsh Jha, Sachin Kumar, Li Lucy, Xinxi Lyu, Nathan Lambert, Ian Magnusson, Jacob Morrison, Niklas Muennighoff, Aakanksha Naik, Crystal Nam, Matthew E. Peters, Abhilasha Ravichander, Kyle Richardson, Zejiang Shen, Emma Strubell, Nishant Subramani, Oyvind Tafjord, Pete Walsh, Luke Zettlemoyer, Noah A. Smith, Hannaneh Hajishirzi, Iz Beltagy, Dirk Groeneveld, Jesse Dodge, and Kyle Lo. 2024. Dolma: An Open Corpus of Three Trillion Tokens for Language Model Pretraining Research. *Preprint*, arXiv:2402.00159.

Karolina Stanczak and Isabelle Augenstein. 2021. A Survey on Gender Bias in Natural Language Processing. *Preprint*, arXiv:2112.14168.

Anatol Stefanowitsch. 2020. *Corpus Linguistics: A Guide to the Methodology*. Language Science Press, Berlin.

Tony Sun, Andrew Gaut, Shirlyn Tang, Yuxin Huang, Mai ElSherief, Jieyu Zhao, Diba Mirza, Elizabeth Belding, Kai-Wei Chang, and William Yang Wang. 2019. Mitigating Gender Bias in Natural Language Processing: Literature Review. In *Proceedings of the 57th Annual Meeting of the Association for Computational Linguistics*, pages 1630–1640, Florence, Italy. Association for Computational Linguistics.

Llama Team. 2024. The Llama 3 Herd of Models. Technical report.

Together Computer. 2023. RedPajama: An open dataset for training large language models.

Hugo Touvron, Thibaut Lavril, Gautier Izacard, Xavier Martinet, Marie-Anne Lachaux, Timothée Lacroix, Baptiste Rozière, Naman Goyal, Eric Hambro, Faisal Azhar, Aurelien Rodriguez, Armand Joulin, Edouard Grave, and Guillaume Lample. 2023a. LLaMA: Open and Efficient Foundation Language Models. *Preprint*, arXiv:2302.13971.

Hugo Touvron, Louis Martin, Kevin Stone, Peter Albert, Amjad Almahairi, Yasmine Babaei, Nikolay Bashlykov, Soumya Batra, Prajjwal Bhargava, Shruti Bhosale, Dan Bikel, Lukas Blecher, Cristian Canton Ferrer, Moya Chen, Guillem Cucurull, David Esiobu, Jude Fernandes, Jeremy Fu, Wenyin Fu, Brian Fuller, Cynthia Gao, Vedanuj Goswami, Naman Goyal, Anthony Hartshorn, Saghar Hosseini, Rui Hou, Hakan Inan, Marcin Kardas, Viktor Kerkez, Madian Khabsa, Isabel Kloumann, Artem Korenev, Punit Singh Koura, Marie-Anne Lachaux, Thibaut Lavril, Jenya Lee, Diana Liskovich, Yinghai Lu, Yuning Mao, Xavier Martinet, Todor Mihaylov, Pushkar Mishra, Igor Molybog, Yixin Nie, Andrew Poulton, Jeremy Reizenstein, Rashi Rungta, Kalyan Saladi, Alan Schelten, Ruan Silva, Eric Michael Smith, Ranjan Subramanian, Xiaoqing Ellen Tan, Binh Tang, Ross Taylor, Adina Williams, Jian Xiang Kuan, Puxin Xu, Zheng Yan, Iliyan Zarov, Yuchen Zhang, Angela Fan, Melanie Kambadur, Sharan Narang, Aurelien Rodriguez, Robert Stojnic, Sergey Edunov, and Thomas Scialom. 2023b. LLaMA 2: Open Foundation and Fine-Tuned Chat Models. *Preprint*, arXiv:2307.09288.

Alex Warstadt, Alicia Parrish, Haokun Liu, Anhad Mohananey, Wei Peng, Sheng-Fu Wang, and Samuel R. Bowman. 2020. BLiMP: The Benchmark of Linguistic Minimal Pairs for English. *Transactions of the Association for Computational Linguistics*, 8:377–392.

Brandon T. Willard and Rémi Louf. 2023. Efficient Guided Generation for Large Language Models. *Preprint*, arXiv:2307.09702.

Thomas Wolf, Lysandre Debut, Victor Sanh, Julien Chaumond, Clement Delangue, Anthony Moi, Pierric Cistac, Tim Rault, Remi Louf, Morgan Funtowicz, Joe Davison, Sam Shleifer, Patrick Von Platen, Clara Ma, Yacine Jernite, Julien Plu, Canwen Xu, Teven Le Scao, Sylvain Gugger, Mariama Drame, Quentin Lhoest, and Alexander Rush. 2020. Transformers: State-of-the-Art Natural Language Processing. In *Proceedings of the 2020 Conference on Empirical Methods in Natural Language Processing: System Demonstrations*, pages 38–45, Online. Association for Computational Linguistics.

A Pronoun frequencies in pre-training corpora

The following tables contain the absolute token frequencies of all non-subject forms of the established gendered pronouns *he* and *she*, the gender-neutral *they* (which is more commonly used in the plural form, except the explicitly singular *themself*), and eight neopronouns from Hossain et al. (2023). Frequencies are reported for C4 (Raffel et al., 2020) and Dolma (Soldaini et al., 2024), and were calculated with WIMBD (Elazar et al., 2024).

	C4	Dolma
him	76.642.827	466.261.554
her	120.502.480	610.920.325
them	206.400.522	1.224.786.435
thon	872.654	992.499
em	14.687.464	25.071.924
aer	607.125	638.705
co	83.935.707	199.206.147
vir	456.939	645.878
xem	285.577	357.204
em	14.687.464	25.071.924
zir	22.433	40.578

Table 5: Frequencies for established object pronouns and object neopronouns in C4 and Dolma

	C4	Dolma
his	154.746.745	932.171.598
her	120.502.480	610.920.325
their	300.195.337	1.677.918.677
thons	54.734	90.213
es	17.287.828	20.223.489
aer	607.125	638.705
cos	2.040.163	5.310.600
vis	2.335.366	4.775.286
xyr	3.579	10.039
eir	201.341	375.303
zir	22.433	40.578

Table 6: Frequencies for established possessive determiners and neo-determiners in C4 and Dolma

	C4	Dolma
his	154.746.745	932.171.598
hers	2.652.526	10.223.659
theirs	2.429.259	12.494.222
thons	54.734	90.213
ems	2.938.663	4.043.142
aers	20.147	24.815
cos	2.040.163	5.310.600
virs	4.374	11.125
xyrs	1.912	1.977
eirs	20.911	24.996
zirs	681	2.317

Table 7: Frequencies for established possessive pronouns and possessive neopronouns in C4 and Dolma

	C4	Dolma
himself	22.378.650	134.674.595
herself	11.941.936	63.594.961
themself	158.315	1.289.078
thonself	36	248
emself	1.017	2.341
aerself	28	161
coself	51	193
virself	0	49
xemself	155	626
emself	1.017	2.341
zirself	387	1.695

Table 8: Frequencies for established reflexive pronouns and reflexive neopronouns in C4 and Dolma

B Token numbers for (neo)pronouns

	OLMo					RedPajama-INCITE					Llama-3.1-8B				
	Subj.	Obj.	Det.	Poss.	Reflex.	Subj.	Obj.	Det.	Poss.	Reflex.	Subj.	Obj.	Det.	Poss.	Reflex.
he	1	1	1	1	1	1	1	1	1	1	1	1	1	1	2
she	1	1	1	1	2	1	1	1	1	2	1	1	1	2	3
they	1	1	1	2	2	1	1	1	2	2	1	1	1	2	2
thon	1	1	2	2	3	1	1	2	2	3	1	1	2	2	2
e	1	1	1	1	2	1	1	1	1	2	1	1	1	1	2
ae	1	2	2	2	3	1	2	2	2	3	1	2	2	2	3
co	1	1	1	1	2	1	1	1	1	2	1	1	1	1	2
vi	1	1	1	2	2	1	1	1	2	2	1	1	1	2	2
xe	1	2	2	2	3	1	2	2	2	3	1	2	2	2	3
ey	1	1	2	2	2	1	1	2	2	2	1	1	2	2	2
ze	1	2	2	2	3	1	2	2	2	3	1	2	2	2	3

Table 9: Number of sub-word tokens that a form of a (neo)pronoun is split into by a specific model

Automated test generation to evaluate tool-augmented LLMs as conversational AI agents

Samuel Arcadinho
samuel.arcadinho@zendesk.com

David Aparício
david.aparicio@zendesk.com

Mariana S. C. Almeida
mariana.almeida@zendesk.com

Abstract

Tool-augmented LLMs are a promising approach to create AI agents that can have realistic conversations, follow procedures, and call appropriate functions. However, evaluating them is challenging due to the diversity of possible conversations, and existing datasets focus only on single interactions and function-calling. We present a test generation pipeline to evaluate LLMs as conversational AI agents. Our framework uses LLMs to generate diverse tests grounded on user-defined procedures. For that, we use intermediate graphs to limit the LLM test generator's tendency to hallucinate content that is not grounded on input procedures, and enforces high coverage of the possible conversations. Additionally, we put forward ALMITA, a manually curated dataset for evaluating AI agents in customer support, and use it to evaluate existing LLMs. Our results show that while tool-augmented LLMs perform well in single interactions, they often struggle to handle complete conversations. While our focus is on customer support, our method is general and capable of AI agents for different domains.

1 Introduction

Large language models (LLMs) are revolutionizing AI agents and have demonstrated remarkable generalization capabilities across various domains (Wu et al., 2023; Lan and Chen, 2024; Li et al., 2024). In particular, LLMs have made a profound impact as chatbots and as AI agents in customer support systems (Dam et al., 2024; Katragadda, 2024).

Nevertheless, carelessly deploying an LLM as an AI agent, and allowing them to interact with real users and APIs, can lead to misinformation, reputational damage and costs to the company. Thus, it is critical to evaluate AI agents beforehand. Despite this need, evaluating the performance of LLMs in real-world scenarios remains a significant challenge. This is specially true in a conversational context, which is more complex than answering single-interaction requests. Most current approaches to evaluate LLMs focus primarily on specific tasks such as multi-QA (Zhuang et al., 2024; Kamalloo et al., 2024) or code generation (Liu et al., 2024b,a), which do not fully evaluate the broader set of capabilities that LLMs are expected to possess to truly function as an effective conversational AI agents.

Focusing on customer support, an effective AI agent is should be capable of interacting with tools and the customer in order to resolve customer issues, while stricly adhering to procedures described by customer support admins. In order to assess the AI agent's performance, it is crucial to measure its ability to follow a given set of procedures and their resilience against potential customer manipulations. For that, it is key to have a comprehensive evaluation dataset, which can lead to valuable insights into the agent's abilities and limitations.

We propose a method to generate evaluation datasets for tool-augmented LLMs as conversational AI agents. Our method automates dataset generation using an LLM to create conversations based on procedures, which are then transformed into tests. We use intermediate graph structures to improve the quality of the generated dataset (i.e., tests follow user-defined procedures) and make it more comprehensive (i.e., tests cover most relevant cases). To assess the AI agent's ability to handle attacks, we incorporate red teaming in our examples.

Our generation pipeline, illustrated in Figure 1, builds diverse datasets autonomously by using synthetically generated intents as seeds for procedures. Additionally, our pipeline also allows for the inclusion of real data where available, such as actual procedures or APIs used by a company to generate synthetic conversations. While datasets can be created fully automatically, we also put forward ALMITA (**A**utomated benchmark of **L**anguage **M**odels for **I**ntelligent **T**ool-augmented **A**gents), a manually curated dataset. We use this high-quality dataset to benchmark LLMs as conversational tool-augmented AI agents.

Proceedings of the 2nd GenBench Workshop on Generalisation (Benchmarking) in NLP, pages 54–68
November 16, 2024 ©2024 Association for Computational Linguistics

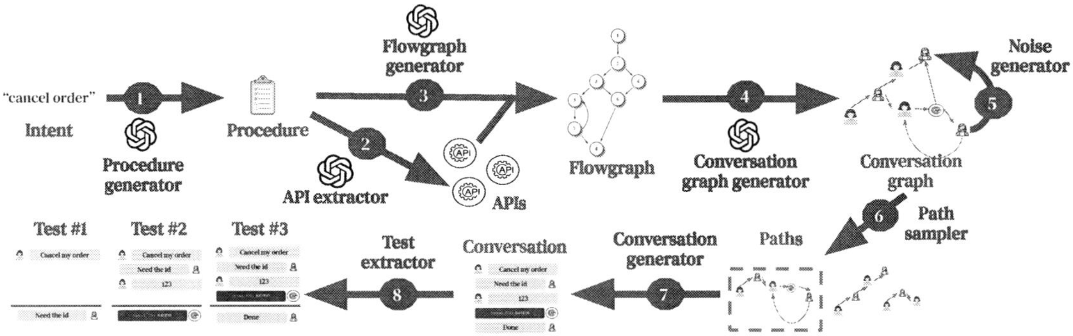

Figure 1: Automated test generation pipeline. For a given intent (e.g., cancel order) (1) we use an LLM to generate a corresponding procedure. Then, (2) an LLM extracts relevant APIs from the procedure, and (3) generates a flowgraph from the procedure and its APIs. Next, (4) an LLM generates a conversation graph from the flowgraph and (5) adds noise to the graph (e.g., users going out of the expected procedure), to make the graph more realistic. To obtain conversations from the graph, (6) we sample paths from it, which correspond to different interactions. Finally, (7) an LLM generates conversations from the paths and (8) we extract tests from the sampled conversations.

Our main contributions are:

- A method that generates datasets to evaluate tool-augmented LLMs as AI conversational agents, reducing manual effort needed to obtain such datasets. Our method provides an holistic evaluation of AI agents, with realistic and diverse conversations, use of tools (e.g., functions/APIs), and grounded on user-defined procedures.
- `ALMITA`, the first conversational dataset that can be used to evaluate customer support AI agents, including both tooling (i.e., functions) and conversation reply to follow company user-defined procedures. `ALMITA` contains 1420 synthetic tests that were manually curated to ensure high-quality samples[1].
- Benchmarking of multiple LLMs on the proposed dataset. Our results indicate that current LLMs have high performance regarding single message accuracy and in calling the correct functions, but have limited accuracy when the complete conversation is considered, which might indicate that they would not be successful if deployed as fully autonomous customer support AI agents.

We also note that, while our evaluation focuses on customer support, the same method could be applied, with some changes, to other domains.

[1] `ALMITA`, along with all other datasets generated using our pipeline and referenced in the paper, are available in `https://github.com/zendesk/almita-dataset`.

2 Related work

With the increasing use of LLMs as AI agents, significant efforts have been made to develop benchmarks to evaluate their ability to correctly answer customer requests in conversational settings. GAIA proposes 466 human-annotated questions covering tasks like general knowledge, daily tasks, and data analysis (Mialon et al., 2023). Recently, AgentInstruct introduced a framework for generating synthetic data from diverse sources, such as code, web articles, and textbook chapters, to help agents generate and refine instruction sets (Mitra et al., 2024). Unlike our work, these datasets do not assess tool-augmented AI agents.

Datasets to evaluate tool-augmented LLMs have been proposed. Zeng et al. (2023) propose AgentTuning and compile multiple agent datasets to create sequences of API calls. AgentBench features multi-step interactions between an agent and the environment, using various tools to solve user requests (Liu et al., 2023). Patil et al. (2023) and Qin et al. (2023) build datasets of APIs from sources like TorchHub, TensorHub, and rapidAI, prompting an LLM to generate instructions solvable by these APIs. Basu et al. (2024) combine multiple datasets to convert user instructions into API calls. APIGen introduced an automatic method to generate synthetic datasets for tool function calling (Liu et al., 2024c). Unlike our work, these datasets are not conversational and just focus on mapping utterances to API calls, and they do not use intermediate structures (i.e., graphs) to ensure coverage and reduce hallucinations in generated tests.

Other relevant work focuses on graph learning and on using different intermediate structures to reducing hallucinations. Ye et al. (2023) propose InstructGLM, which uses natural language to describe node features used to tune an LLM for inference on graphs. Wang et al. (2024) introduce NLGraph, a benchmark for graph-based problems written in natural language, demonstrating that LLMs can perform structured operations on textual descriptions of graphs. Additionally, Narayan et al. (2023) propose using question-answer blueprints as intermediate representations to reduce hallucinations. These works do not fully encompass our problem setting of generating conversations in dialog format, calling APIs, and extracting tests.

3 Method

Our automated test generation pipeline, illustrated in Figure 1, begins by generating textual procedures from input intents. While one could use an LLM to directly generate conversations from procedures, our approach converts the procedures into a flowgraph and then into a conversation graph. Our assumption is that using these intermediate structured representations makes the task of creating the conversations grounded on the procedures more accurate; see Section 4.2 for supporting evidence. Additionally, the graphs allow us to introduce noise into the conversations, making conversations more realistic and challenging, and enable us to sample paths, ensuring path coverage and conversation diversity. We then generate conversations from the sampled paths. Finally, we extract tests from these conversations by breaking down the conversation at each user message, storing the context, and recording the generated response as the correct reply.

3.1 Intent generator

Intents (or *issues*, e.g., cancel order) serve as the seeds for our automated test generation method. Intents can be generated by an LLM (as is the case in this work), sourced from predefined domain-specific intents, or a mix of both. The prompt used to generate intents is shown in Appendix A.1.

3.2 Procedure generator

A procedure describes how a given issue/intent should be solved by an agent. We use an LLM to generate a procedure for each input intent by asking it to provide a list of instructions that helps an agent fulfill a given task. We enforce in the prompt to avoid outputting general statements (e.g., "cancelling policies might depend on the company" or "explain the company's policy") since our goal is to generate specific and unambiguous procedures with precise and granular steps. We also enforce that conditionals are possible but that they need to have a clear solution in the steps of the procedure. Finally, steps might contain actions based on APIs (e.g., search a database, escalate an issue) but they cannot be browsing actions (e.g., click on the login page). The full prompt is shown in Appendix A.2. Similarly to what we described for intents, existing procedures (e.g., of a company) can be included as input for our method. Moreover, procedures can be generated based on existing knowledge, namely existing tickets or help center articles.

Consider the intent *"order not received"*: a simple procedure could be *"If the customer did not receive their order, allow the customer to cancel or refund their order given that they provide a correct order id"*. We use this procedure as an illustrative example throughout the paper (see Figures 2 to 4.)

3.3 API extractor

Our target use-case is tool-augmented AI agents. We use an LLM to generate APIs that are useful for an input procedure. We enforce in the prompt that the extracted APIs are agent APIs and not customer facing APIs. Generated APIs include not only the API name, but also their input output parameters, as well as a small description. The full prompt is shown in Appendix A.3. These APIs should be explicitly called by the agent to fulfill the procedure. Similarly to intents and procedures, existing APIs can be easily included in our pipeline.

3.4 Flowgraph generator

The flowgraph generator receives as input a procedure and relevant APIs and generates a directed graph encapsulating the logic of the procedure from the agent's perspective: nodes are agent actions and edges are customer replies or API outputs. Nodes are of 4 different types: (i) a single `start_message` node is the initial message sent by the agent to the customer, (ii) `message` nodes are additional messages sent by the agent to the customer, (iii) `api` nodes are API calls performed by the agent, and (iv) `end_message` nodes are messages by the agent that end the interaction. To reduce hallucinations and increase completeness, we enforce in the prompt (Appendix A.4) that every detail from the procedure needs to be in `message` nodes.

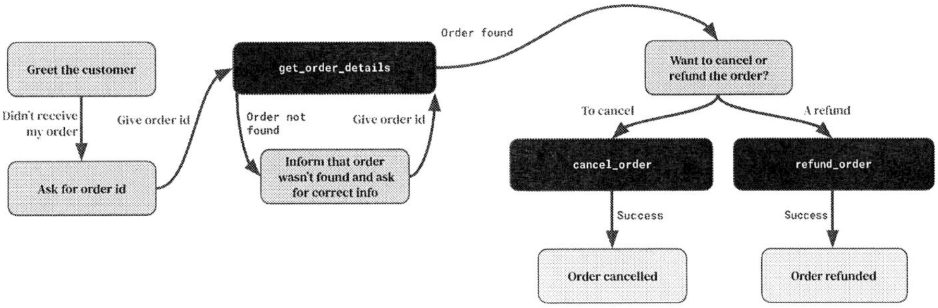

Figure 2: Flowgraph for intent *Order not received* and procedure *"If the customer did not receive their order, allow the customer to cancel or refund their order given that they provide a correct order id"*. Blue nodes are message nodes, black nodes are API call nodes, orange nodes are end nodes. Edge labels are user messages or API outputs.

An example of a flowgraph is given in Figure 2. Nodes in the flowgraph have a `node_id` (e.g., "N1"), a `node_type` (one of the four described above), and a `node_description`, which should be related to a step in the procedure (e.g., "Tell the user the order was not found") or an API call (e.g., "`refund_order`"). Edges in the graph are either the user interaction (e.g., "Gives order id and email") or the result of an API call (e.g., "Found order"). Edges in the flowgraph have an `edge_id` (e.g., "E1"), a tuple with the source node and the target node (e.g., "(N1, N2)"), and an edge description, as described previously. We do one-shot prompting, providing an example to the LLM; thus, a complete flowgraph can be seen in flowgraph prompt in Appendix A.4.

To try to guarantee correct flowgraphs, we instruct the LLM to generate graphs with only one root node with type `start_message`, to always have concrete messages in the node and edge descriptions, and to provide API outputs in the outgoing edges of `api` nodes. To try to limit hallucinations and ensure that the graph encapsulates the entire procedure, we instruct the LLM to follow strictly what is in the procedure and to include all content from it. At the end of the generation step, we convert the graph into a `networkx` graph and, if parsing succeeds, we pragmatically verify if all the rules described previously are followed; if they are not followed, we discard the generated flowgraph.

3.5 Conversation graph generator

A flowgraph represents a sequence of agent steps to fulfill a procedure. The flowgraph's structure does not directly map to a conversation, which can make the task of creating a conversation from a flowgraph hard. Thus, the goal of the conversation graph generator is to convert the flowgraph into a a conversation graph, which is a structure that is more akin to a dialogue. The generated conversation graph is a directed graph that is expected to have nodes of three different types: (i) `agent` nodes are messages sent by the agent, (ii) `customer` nodes are messages sent by the customer, and (iii) `api` nodes are API calls by the agent.

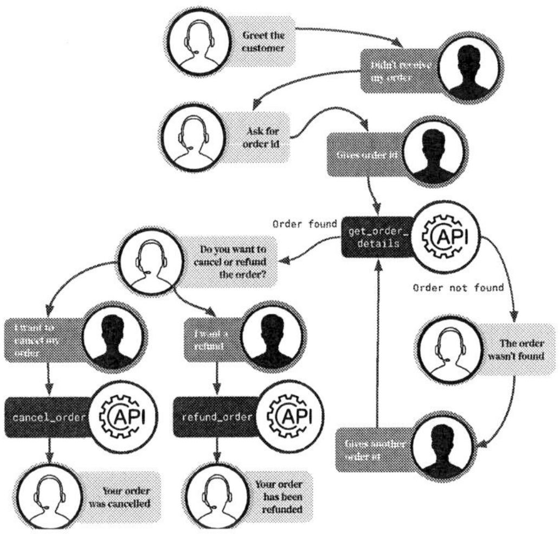

Figure 3: Conversation graph for flowgraph from Fig. 2 for intent *Order not received*. Blue nodes are agent nodes, green are user nodes, and black are API nodes.

An example of a conversation graph is given in Figure 3. Nodes in the conversation graph have a `node_id` (e.g., "N1"), a `node_type` (one of the three described above), and a `node_description`, which is a message for `agent` and `customer` nodes, and an API call for `api` nodes. Edges in the conversation graph connect consecutive messages/api calls. Some conversation paths have conditions, such as an API call returning that the order was found or not; in these cases, edges have an edge description, otherwise the edge description is empty.

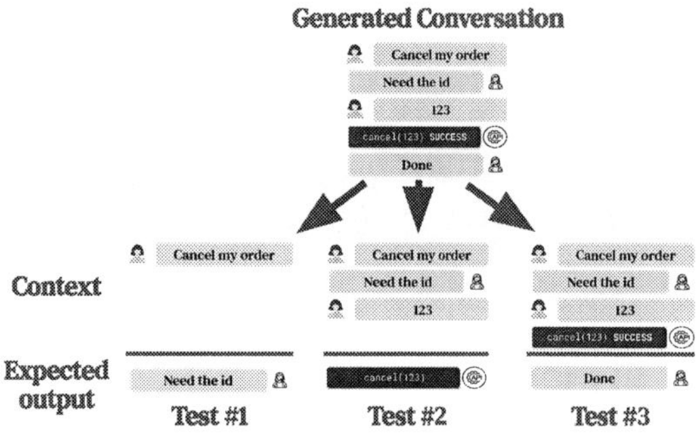

Figure 4: Tests extracted from one conversation.

Edges in the flowgraph have an `edge_id` (e.g., "E1"), a tuple with the source node and the target node (e.g., "(N1, N2)"), and an edge description.

In an effort to mitigate incorrect conversation graphs, we provide the LLM with additional graph construction rules, e.g., `customer` nodes should be followed by either `agent` or `api` nodes, leaf nodes should be `assistant` nodes. We use one-shot prompting by giving the LLM as input an example of a flowgraph and the corresponding conversation graph, as shown in Appendix A.5. Similarly to flowgraphs, we load the generated graph into `networkx` and verify if the required conditions are met, otherwise the graph is discarded.

3.6 Noise generator

Conversation graphs are built from agent procedures, thus they are expected to only contain *good* behaviour by both the agent and the customer (i.e., happy paths). To make AI agents more resilient to unexpected customer behaviour, which might be malicious or not, we augment the conversation graphs with behaviour outside of the procedure.

The noise generator traverses the `agent` nodes in the conversation graph and, with a certain probability (e.g., 20%), inserts an edge to a new `customer` node with a `node_description` message which can either be an "out-of-procedure" message or an "attack" message. These messages are generated beforehand by an LLM. Additionally, we add an edge from the noisy `customer` node to a new `agent` node with `node_description` as "Say you're only here to help with the original issue."

3.7 Path sampler

We extract conversations between a customer and an agent by sampling paths from the conversation graph. Given a conversation graph $\mathcal{G}$ with N nodes and a desired number of conversations M, we employ a weighted random walks algorithm to sample paths, Algorithm 1, which is an enhanced version of vanilla random walks, designed to improve node coverage. For that, we use a weighting vector $\mathbf{w}$ with N elements initialized with ones (line 3). Each path p is built by iteratively sampling nodes using $sample\_node$ (line 7). A node n, which is a child of the last node in the current path p, is sampled with a probability inversely proportional to its weight w_i, where w_i is the number of times node n was visited plus one (line 9). The index i of node n in graph $\mathcal{G}$ is provided by $node\_index$ (line 8). Path construction terminates when a leaf node is reached (lines 11–13).

Algorithm 1 Conversation path sampling

1: **Inputs:** $\mathcal{G}, M$
2: $\mathcal{P} \leftarrow \emptyset$
3: $\mathbf{w} \leftarrow \mathbf{1}_N$
4: **while** $|\mathcal{P}| < M$ **do**
5:     $p \leftarrow \emptyset$
6:     **while** True **do**
7:         $n \leftarrow sample\_node(\mathcal{G}, p, \mathbf{w})$
8:         $i \leftarrow node\_index(\mathcal{G}, n)$
9:         $w_i \leftarrow w_i + 1$
10:         $p \leftarrow p \mid n$
11:         **if** n is EndNode **then**
12:             $\mathcal{P} \leftarrow \mathcal{P} \mid p$
13:             **break**

3.8 Conversation generator

The conversation generator creates synthetic conversations from an input conversation graph, a sampled path, and relevant APIs. We provide the LLM with context about the conversation graph structure and the APIs. Using one-shot prompting, we present the LLM with an example triplet consisting of a conversation graph, a list of APIs, and a sampled path, as well as a possible conversation based on these conditions (see Appendix A.6). In an effort to generate valid conversations, we include conditions in the prompt, such as always generating a message with the API output following an API message, alternating customer and assistant messages, ensuring agents act on API output messages, and verifying API input and output types.

3.9 Test extractor

The test extractor converts a single conversation into one or more tests. It iteratively breaks down

	Intents	Proc.	Proc. w/ APIs	Flowgraphs	Conv.Graphs	Conversations	Tests
Generated	84	168	132	70	49	217	1,420
+ auto. filters	–	–	98	55	33	–	–
+ man. filters	–	132	70	49	33	192	–
ALMITA	**14**	**18**	**18**	**18**	**18**	**192**	**1,420**
auto-ALMITA	**52**	**63**	**63**	**63**	**63**	**407**	**2,696**

Table 1: Statistics while bootstrapping ALMITA's dataset from 84 intents. We show the number of samples after (i) generation, (ii) automatic filtering, and (iii) human filtering annotations. "–" indicates no filtering. auto-ALMITA was created using the same 84 seed intents as ALMITA, but using the same pipeline without any human filtering, so that we can assess the capabilities of our test generation pipeline when no human annotators are available.

the conversation into sub-conversations (or contexts), each ending with a customer message (e.g., "Cancel my order") or an API output (e.g., "success" following a cancel function call). The rationale is that since the generated conversations exemplify correct flows, we can construct contexts using the preceding messages, with the expected output being the next non-customer message, whether it's an agent response or an API call. Figure 4 illustrates an example of three tests extracted from a generated conversation. Tests are used to evaluate an AI agent by providing it with the context and comparing its response with the expected output.

4 Results

In Section 4.1 we detail the creation of ALMITA, a manually curated dataset for evaluating LLMs as AI customer support agents. Two annotators independently review each datapoint to identify incorrect instances, followed by a discussion to align their assessments and minimize disagreements. Any datapoint deemed incorrect by at least one annotator is then removed. GPT-4 is used for all generation steps (see Figure 1). To assess the benefits of the graph intermediate structures, we conduct an ablation study comparing conversations generated directly from procedures to those using the intermediate structures, with manual curation for quality assessment (Section 4.2). In Section 4.3, we evaluate various AI agents on ALMITA. Finally, in Section 4.4, we assess the effectiveness of our pipeline in generating high-quality test sets automatically. We do this by comparing the AI agents' performance on ALMITA with those on its fully automated counterpart, auto-ALMITA.

4.1 Dataset generation: ALMITA

We begin by asking the LLM to generate intents using the prompt from Appendix A.1, resulting in 84 intents. Using them as input, we prompt the model to generate two procedures per intent, for a total of 168 procedures. After manual annotation, we remove 36 procedures that did not comply with the rules from Section 3.2. The valid procedures average 315 words (ranging from 171 to 535) and 11 steps (ranging from 6 to 19). Next, we extract APIs for each procedure as outlined in Section 3.3. APIs not in the correct JSON format are automatically filtered out, along with procedures with invalid APIs, resulting in 70 valid procedures. Each of these procedures, on average, includes 4 APIs (ranging from 2 to 9). For each of the 70 procedures with APIs, we generate the corresponding flowgraph. We automatically filter out 15 flowgraphs and manually filter 6 more that do not adhere to the rules discussed in Section 3.4. The valid flowgraphs average 15 nodes (ranging from 10 to 20) and 17 edges (ranging from 10 to 25). For each of the remaining 49 valid flowgraphs, we generate the corresponding conversation graph. We automatically exclude 16 conversation graphs and manually exclude 7 more based on adherence to rules (Section 3.5). The valid conversation graphs average 23 nodes (ranging from 16 to 37) and 24 edges (ranging from 15 to 37). From these conversation graphs, we generate 217 conversations after path sampling (Section 3.7). We manually filter out 25 conversations for not following the rules (Section 3.8). Thus, from the original 84 intents, we obtain 192 valid conversations. Each conversation traverses an average of 12 nodes (ranging from 3 to 24). Finally, tests are extracted from these conversations as detailed in Section 3.9, resulting in 1420 generated tests. Table 1 summarizes the dataset statistics. In the end, the ALMITA dataset comprises 14 intents, 18 procedures, 18 flowgraphs, 18 conversations graphs, 192 conversations and 1420 tests.

LLM	Reply		API			Test	Conversation
	Recall	Correct	Recall	Correct	Correct params.	Correct	Correct
GPT-4o	92.7	75.2	96.7	**99.8**	92.2	**88.9**	14.1
Mistral-NeMo-I	92.0	65.0	89.8	99.5	92.1	84.7	7.3
Claude3-s	88.0	60.3	96.2	**99.8**	90.5	83.3	10.4
GPT-4	53.2	**77.7**	**98.1**	**99.8**	**93.0**	76.9	4.2
Llama3.1-8b-I	74.8	53.5	72.1	90.8	85.9	73.1	1.6
GPT-4o w/ F	**92.9**	74.8	97.2	99.0	86.6	88.0	**15.6**

Table 2: AI agents evaluated on their capacity to produce correct replies with correct API calls. We test different LLMs using the same prompt. Additionally, we evaluate LLMs using function calling (with the "w/ F" suffix). The versions of the closed source models are *gpt-4-0613*, *gpt-4o-2024-05-13*, *anthropic.claude-3-sonnet-20240229-v1:0*. The "-I" suffix indicates that it is an instruction model. All results are percentages, with the highest value in **bold**.

4.2 Ablation study: conversations from procedures

We conduct an ablation study to validate the effectiveness of our intermediate graph representations in generating correct conversations. We remove the flowgraph generator, conversation graph generator, noise generator, and path sampler, and generate conversations directly from the procedures and APIs using the prompt from Appendix A.7. Annotating conversations directly generated from procedures showed to be a much more complex and time-consuming than annotating conversations generated from graphs. For this reason we only annotate 50 conversations. All 50 conversations are generated from the same 70 input procedures as ALMITA, and they are curated by the same two annotators, following the same annotation strategy. K The simplified pipeline results in $\approx 68\%$ (34/50) valid conversations, as evaluated by the same annotators that curated ALMITA. In contrast, the original pipeline with intermediate graph representations yields $\approx 88\%$ $(192/217)$ valid conversations. This indicates that graph representations improve the validity of generated conversations. Even when considering the cumulative impact of curating flowgraphs, the original pipeline would automatically generate $\approx 78\%$ $(192/217 \times 49/55)$ valid conversations, which is above $\approx 68\%$.

Moreover, while the prompt used in the simplified pipeline could potentially be improved, the simplified pipeline intrinsically does not ensure that all branching paths from the procedure are explored. This highlights the benefit of intermediate graph representations in covering all possible conversation paths.

4.3 Evaluation of LLM AI agents

We use ALMITA to evaluate LLMs serving as customer support AI agents. The dataset allows us to evaluate the following dimensions, which we report in Table 2: (i) *reply recall*: when the correct action is to reply, the agent correctly sends a reply message instead of calling an unnecessary API, (ii) *correct reply*: when both the correct and the predicted action is to reply, the agent's reply matches the expected reply (we use BERTScore with a similarity threshold of 0.55 after inspecting of some examples), (iii) *API recall*: when the correct action is to do an API call, the agent correctly detects that it needed to perform an API call instead of replying, (iv) *correct API*: when both the correct and the predicted action is to perform an API call, the agent calls the correct API; (v) *correct API parameters*: when both the correct and the predicted action are the same API call, the agents calls the API with the correct parameter values, (vi) *test correctness (or test accuracy)*: whether the test is fully correct (i.e., call the correct reply/API and, if the correct action is an API, call the correct API and use the correct parameters, or if the correct action is a reply, provide a correct reply), (vii) *conversation correctness (or conversation accuracy)*: whether the sequence of all tests from the conversation where all correct.

We evaluate 5 different LLMs: GPT4-o, GPT-4, Claude3-sonnet, Mistral-NeMo-Instruct, and Llama3.1-8b-Instruct. To ensure fairness, we use a uniform prompt for all models (details in Appendix A.8). Our prompt aims to be general, avoiding any favoritism towards a specific model, although we acknowledge that different models may excel with different prompting styles. Since the dataset includes API calling, we also test GPT4-o with function calling, denoted as GPT-4o w/F.

We observe that all LLMs demonstrate high accuracy when responding with an API, achieving over 85% correctness in both the *correct API* and *correct API parameters* dimensions. With the exception of Llama3.1-8b-I, which performs considerably worse, the other models correctly determine when an API should be called, with an *API recall* exceeding 90%. However, performance in other dimensions is notably lower, suggesting that datasets focused solely on API calls do not comprehensively evaluate an AI agent's capabilities.

Interestingly, GPT-4 tends to call APIs even when unnecessary, resulting in a lower *reply recall* compared to other models. In terms of *correct reply*, GPT models outperform the others, though this may be biased by the use of GPT-4 for test generation. For *test correctness*, GPT-4o, Claude3-s, and Mistral-NeMo-Instruct show the highest performance, while GPT-4 and Llama3.1-8b-Instruct rank among the lowest.

Most critically, we see that all models have very low performance regarding *correct conversation*. In practice, this would mean that these AI agents would very likely fail at some step of a conversation with a user. This showcases that current LLMs have some limitations that require either better models or very engineered prompts to suitably serve as fully autonomous customer support AI agents.

Our dataset could, potentially, be useful to evaluate future models and/or strategies on their AI agent capabilities. Furthermore, since the pipeline is automated, the dataset could be updated to include more (and harder) tests, as well as adapted to new or more specific domains.

4.4 Fully automated tests: auto-ALMITA

In this section, we analyze the results obtained by AI agents on auto-ALMITA, the fully automated version of the ALMITA dataset. This dataset was created using the same seed intents from the ALMITA dataset, described in section 4.1. Then we run the same pipeline without the manual filtering steps. Auto-ALMITA retains more data points and greater diversity (see Table 1), albeit with some reduction in quality. Being fully automatically generated, auto-ALMITA can also be easily extended without additional curation efforts.

We evaluate the same LLM agents from Table 2 and compare the global metric *test correct* obtained by the AI agents both auto-ALMITA and ALMITA in Figure 5. Both datasets rank the LLMs in the same order, with a high correlation value of 0.98 (detailed results are provided in Supplementary Table 1). These findings suggest that the proposed pipeline can generate evaluation datasets for AI agents entirely automatically, which lead to conclusions similar to those derived from curated datasets.

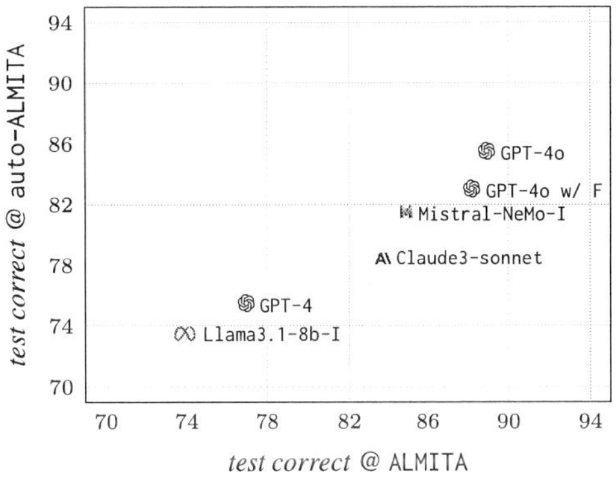

Figure 5: *test correct* value for different LLM Agents on the auto-ALMITA and ALMITA datasets.

5 Conclusions

LLMs are being used as customer support AI agents. However, existing evaluation datasets are limited in their scope. We propose an automated test generation pipeline to evaluate tool-augmented conversational AI agents. Our proposed method uses LLMs to generate intermediate graph structures that help limit hallucinations and improve diversity in the generated tests. We evaluate different LLMs to analyze the current capabilities of LLMs implemented as AI agents.

To facilitate this, we developed the ALMITA dataset, which we used to thoroughly evaluate these AI agents and identify their limitations. ALMITA allows for a multifaceted evaluation across several key dimensions, such as reply accuracy, API call correctness, and overall conversation integrity. Our findings highlighted significant limitations in current LLMs, particularly in maintaining correct conversations throughout a user interaction.

Importantly, the ALMITA dataset can be used by other researchers to evaluate AI agents, providing a comprehensive benchmark for assessing various aspects of their performance, possibly in other target domains. Additionally, since our test generation pipeline is fully automated, we have the capability to create new, more challenging versions of the dataset. This adaptability ensures that our framework can be continually updated to reflect more complex and realistic scenarios, further enhancing its utility for ongoing research and development of AI agents in customer support and beyond.

6 Limitations

Our evaluation has some limitations. Namely, we did not evaluate the diversity of the generated tests quantitatively. We performed human annotation, to verify correctness at each step, but the number of annotations and of annotators was small. Our test generation pipeline only used a single LLM as the generator, namely GPT4 and this might influence evaluation. A possible mitigation for this is to repeat the test generation pipeline for other LLMs and aggregate the tests. We evaluated multiple LLMs but only using a single prompt. Our goal was to test different models on the generated dataset, but more advanced AI agents could be considered.

Additionally, we acknowledge that some metrics may be too strict. As a future direction, we would like to consider the severity of the errors of an AI agent in a conversation. Conversations are relatively fluid and we may have other replies/actions that are somehow acceptable for a given procedure besides of the most obvious and direct one that was annotated in the dataset. There is still to be develop more advanced and more semantic conversational metrics allowing for some path variations, similarly to what has been happening for the comparison of two sentences where different words and order of words can lead to similar meanings.

References

Kinjal Basu, Ibrahim Abdelaziz, Subhajit Chaudhury, Soham Dan, Maxwell Crouse, Asim Munawar, Sadhana Kumaravel, Vinod Muthusamy, Pavan Kapanipathi, and Luis A Lastras. 2024. Api-blend: A comprehensive corpora for training and benchmarking api llms. *arXiv preprint arXiv:2402.15491*.

Sumit Kumar Dam, Choong Seon Hong, Yu Qiao, and Chaoning Zhang. 2024. A complete survey on llm-based ai chatbots. *arXiv preprint arXiv:2406.16937*.

Ehsan Kamalloo, Shivani Upadhyay, and Jimmy Lin. 2024. Towards robust qa evaluation via open llms. In *Proceedings of the 47th International ACM SIGIR Conference on Research and Development in Information Retrieval*, pages 2811–2816.

Vamsi Katragadda. 2024. Leveraging intent detection and generative ai for enhanced customer support. *Journal of Artificial Intelligence General science (JAIGS) ISSN: 3006-4023*, 5(1):109–114.

Yu-Ju Lan and Nian-Shing Chen. 2024. Teachers' agency in the era of llm and generative ai. *Educational Technology & Society*, 27(1):I–XVIII.

Yuanchun Li, Hao Wen, Weijun Wang, Xiangyu Li, Yizhen Yuan, Guohong Liu, Jiacheng Liu, Wenxing Xu, Xiang Wang, Yi Sun, et al. 2024. Personal llm agents: Insights and survey about the capability, efficiency and security. *arXiv preprint arXiv:2401.05459*.

Fang Liu, Yang Liu, Lin Shi, Houkun Huang, Ruifeng Wang, Zhen Yang, and Li Zhang. 2024a. Exploring and evaluating hallucinations in llm-powered code generation. *arXiv preprint arXiv:2404.00971*.

Jiawei Liu, Chunqiu Steven Xia, Yuyao Wang, and Lingming Zhang. 2024b. Is your code generated by chatgpt really correct? rigorous evaluation of large language models for code generation. *Advances in Neural Information Processing Systems*, 36.

Xiao Liu, Hao Yu, Hanchen Zhang, Yifan Xu, Xuanyu Lei, Hanyu Lai, Yu Gu, Yuxian Gu, Hangliang Ding, Kai Men, Kejuan Yang, Shudan Zhang, Xiang Deng, Aohan Zeng, Zhengxiao Du, Chenhui Zhang, Shengqi Shen, Tianjun Zhang, Yu Su, Huan Sun, Minlie Huang, Yuxiao Dong, and Jie Tang. 2023. Agentbench: Evaluating llms as agents. *ArXiv*, abs/2308.03688.

Zuxin Liu, Thai Hoang, Jianguo Zhang, Ming Zhu, Tian Lan, Shirley Kokane, Juntao Tan, Weiran Yao, Zhiwei Liu, Yihao Feng, et al. 2024c. Apigen: Automated pipeline for generating verifiable and diverse function-calling datasets. *arXiv preprint arXiv:2406.18518*.

Grégoire Mialon, Clémentine Fourrier, Craig Swift, Thomas Wolf, Yann André LeCun, and Thomas Scialom. 2023. Gaia: a benchmark for general ai assistants. *ArXiv*, abs/2311.12983.

Arindam Mitra, Luciano Del Corro, Guoqing Zheng, Shweti Mahajan, Dany Rouhana, Andres Codas, Yadong Lu, Wei ge Chen, Olga Vrousgos, Corby Rosset, Fillipe Silva, Hamed Khanpour, Yash Lara, and Ahmed Awadallah. 2024. Agentinstruct: Toward generative teaching with agentic flows.

Shashi Narayan, Joshua Maynez, Reinald Kim Amplayo, Kuzman Ganchev, Annie Louis, Fantine Huot, Anders Sandholm, Dipanjan Das, and Mirella Lapata. 2023. Conditional generation with a question-answering blueprint. *Transactions of the Association for Computational Linguistics*, 11:974–996.

Shishir G Patil, Tianjun Zhang, Xin Wang, and Joseph E Gonzalez. 2023. Gorilla: Large language model connected with massive apis. *arXiv preprint arXiv:2305.15334*.

Yujia Qin, Shihao Liang, Yining Ye, Kunlun Zhu, Lan Yan, Yaxi Lu, Yankai Lin, Xin Cong, Xiangru Tang, Bill Qian, et al. 2023. Toolllm: Facilitating large language models to master 16000+ real-world apis. *arXiv preprint arXiv:2307.16789*.

Heng Wang, Shangbin Feng, Tianxing He, Zhaoxuan Tan, Xiaochuang Han, and Yulia Tsvetkov. 2024. Can language models solve graph problems in natural language? *Advances in Neural Information Processing Systems*, 36.

Qingyun Wu, Gagan Bansal, Jieyu Zhang, Yiran Wu, Shaokun Zhang, Erkang Zhu, Beibin Li, Li Jiang, Xiaoyun Zhang, and Chi Wang. 2023. Autogen: Enabling next-gen llm applications via multi-agent conversation framework. *arXiv preprint arXiv:2308.08155*.

Ruosong Ye, Caiqi Zhang, Runhui Wang, Shuyuan Xu, Yongfeng Zhang, et al. 2023. Natural language is all a graph needs. *arXiv preprint arXiv:2308.07134*, 4(5):7.

Aohan Zeng, Mingdao Liu, Rui Lu, Bowen Wang, Xiao Liu, Yuxiao Dong, and Jie Tang. 2023. Agenttuning: Enabling generalized agent abilities for llms. *ArXiv*, abs/2310.12823.

Yuchen Zhuang, Yue Yu, Kuan Wang, Haotian Sun, and Chao Zhang. 2024. Toolqa: A dataset for llm question answering with external tools. *Advances in Neural Information Processing Systems*, 36.

A Prompts

A.1 Intent generation

System prompt

You are <REDACTED>, a platform providing customer support. You serve clients from numerous different industries: internet providers, financial institutions, e-commerce platforms, entertainment websites, etc. All these clients have customer that can contact customer support to obtain information, complain about something, or other reasons to contact the customer support team.

User prompt

Your task is to generate a list of problems that can lead to a customer contacting support. Think of the type of client for which the issue is relevant, a description of the detailed issue, and a short name for the error.
Generate {{ number_issues }} issues from a diverse pool of clients. Format your answer as a json with the following structure:

```
[{
    "client": e.g., a bank, internet provider, etc.
         Do not limit yourself to these examples!,
    "issue": description of the error, be specific!,
    "name": a short name for the issue
}]
```

A.2 Procedure generation

System prompt

You are <REDACTED>, a platform providing customer support. You serve clients from numerous different industries: internet providers, financial institutions, e-commerce platforms, entertainment websites, etc. All these clients have customer that can contact customer support to obtain information, complain about something, or other reasons to contact the customer support team.
Your task is to generate a procedure that helps an agent to fulfil a task. The agent can take actions or they can ask the customer for data (e.g., email address). You can include branching in the procedure.

Do not give general statements such as "Each system might have different processes". Instead, assume the role of a specific company that has very defined processes.
Do not give general steps such as "Explain the company's policy". The agent is following a procedure, so all steps need to be clearly stated, e.g., state precisely what is the policy. Do not leave room for ambiguity nor lack of information.
Do not state conditionals that are not resolved in the procedures such as "If it is allowed by the policy". Every conditional has to be fully contained in the procedure, the agent should not have to read another document nor rely on other knowledge about the company's procedures. Your role is to make up reasonable scenarios that are unambiguous.
Steps should be precise and granular.
Avoid giving examples, we want a concise procedure.
Do not include actions that are unrelated to the interaction with the client (e.g., document the interaction, monitor the process). The procedure is solely on how to address the issue reported by the customer.
Assume that you don't have a browser. Do not include navigation steps, just the actions that the agent should take.

User prompt

```
# Issue
{{ issue }}
```

A.3 API extraction

System prompt

You are a programming assistant working for a customer experience company. Given a procedure an agent should follow to solve a customer problem, your job is to extract ALL possible APIs used by the agent.
Never generate an API call that asks for passwords. The APIs should be as specific as possible to what is in the procedure and not general methods. All the API parameters should have type different than None. When representing structured output follow python convention like list[str] or dict[str, float]. Optional parameters should follow the python convetion of Optional[str]. If the procedure doesn't have any action an agent should solve, return an empty JSON.

```
# Output
Respond only in JSON format with the following
      schema. The name of the api should be written
      in snake case.
{"apis": [{"name": str, "desc": str, "params":
      [{"name": str}], "output": {"name": str,
      "type": str}}]}
```

User prompt

```
# Procedure
```
{{ procedure }}
```
```

A.4 Flowgraph generation

System prompt

You are and experienced flowchart creator. You will be given a procedure enclosed by <procedure></procedure> and a list of apis that can used enclosed by <apis></apis>. Your job is to extract the flowchart used to solve the problem. Your flowchart will be used by an assistant to know how to solve the problem. The agent has no access to the procedure, so all the information has to be contained in this flowchart!!
You are and experienced flowchart creator. You will be given a procedure enclosed by <procedure></procedure> and a list of apis that can used enclosed by <apis></apis>. Your job is to extract the flowchart used to solve the problem. Your flowchart will be used by an assistant to know how to solve the problem. The agent has no access to the procedure, so all the information has to be contained in this flowchart!!

The flowchart is constituted by nodes and edges in the following format:

```
[node_id](node_type){node_description}
[edge_id](parent_node_id,
      child_node_id){edge_description}
```

Node ids should always be N followed by an integer. Edge ids should always be E followed by an integer.
You can use nodes of the type start_message, message, api and end_message.
- start_message: initial message sent by the assistant to the customer, taken from the procedure. It doesn't have a parent node.
- message: node with a message sent by an assistant to the customer. this message should have all the details found in the procedure.
- api: api call the assistant should perform.
- end_message: node to send a message and finish execution.

Graph construction rules
- The graph only have one root node of type 'start_message'.
- An outgoing edge from a message node is the reply of the customer. Customer messages have to be specific.
- An outgoing edge from an api node is the output of the api.
- End nodes cannot have outgoing edges and should be of type end_message.
- End nodes have the node type 'end_message'.
- Never have an edge going back to the start node N0.

Details
The messages by the agent and the customer should follow stricly what is in the procedure. ALL the details in the procedure need to be in the flowchat! Don't assume that the agent will ever see the procedure, so it is critical that the details are here, such as reasons for something to fail, or information that needs to be collected.
Make sure all steps are nodes. Some procedures might have branching paths.
Always use the APIs when appropriate.
The flowchart must be enclosed by <flow></flow>.

```
Example of a flow:
<flow>
[N0](start_message){Greet the customer}
[E0](N0, N1){Didn't receive my order}
[N1](message){Ask customer for order id, the email
    or phone number}
[E2](N1, N2){Gives order id and email}
[E3](N1, N3){Gives order id and phone number}
[N2](api){get_order_details_by_email}
[N3](api){get_order_details_by_phone_number}
[N4](message){Do you want to cancel or refund the
    order?}
[E3](N2, N4){Found order}
[E5](N3, N4){Found order}
[N5](message){Tell the user the order wasn't found
    and ask for correct information}
[E5](N2, N5){Order not Found}
[E6](N3, N5){Order not Found}
[E6](N5, N2){User provides another email or order
    id}
[E7](N5, N3){User provides another phone number or
    order id}
[N6](api){cancel_order}
[E8](N4, N6){I want to cancel the order}
[N7](end_message){Order cancelled}
[E9](N6, N7){Success}
[N8](api){refund_order}
[E9](N4, N8){I want a refund}
[N9](end_message){Order refunded}
[E10](N8, N9){Success}
</flow>

<apis>
{{ apis }}
</apis>
```

User prompt

```
<procedure>
{{ procedure }}
</procedure>
```

A.5 Conversation graph generation

System prompt

Your task is to convert a flowchart into a conversation graph.
The flowchart will be given in between <flowchart></flowchart>.
The flowchart is constituted by nodes and edges in the following format:

```
[node_id](node_type){node_description}
[edge_id](parent_node_id,
    child_node_id){edge_description}
```

Nodes are of the following types:
- start_message: initial message sent by the assistant to the customer, taken from the procedure.
- message: node with a message sent by an assistant to the customer.
- api: api call the assistant should perform.
- end_message: node to send an assistant message and finish execution. You need to convert it into a conversation graph where:

```
[node_id](node_type){node_description}
[edge_id](parent_node_id,
    child_node_id){edge_description}
```

Nodes are of the following types:
- assistant: message sent by the agent.
- user: message sent by the user.
- api: api call the agent should perform.

Graph construction rules:
- api nodes have outgoing edges with labels
- api nodes are followed by api or assistant nodes
- user nodes are followed by api or assistant nodes
- assistant nodes **can be only followed by** user nodes
- leaf nodes are assistant nodes

Edges connect user nodes to either assistant or api nodes. Only edges from API calls can have descriptions.
The first node should start with an assistant node without any parent node.
For instance, consider the following flow graph:

```
<flow>
[N0](start_message){Greet the customer}
[E0](N0, N1){Didn't receive my order}
[N1](message){Ask customer for order id}
[E2](N1, N2){Gives order id}
[N2](api){get_order_details}
[N3](message){Do you want to cancel or refund the
    order?}
[E3](N2, N3){Found order}
[N4](message){Tell the user the order wasn't found}
[E4](N2, N4){Order not Found}
[E5](N4, N2){User gives another order id}
[N5](api){cancel_order}
[E6](N3, N5){I want to cancel the order}
[N6](end_message){Order cancelled}
[E7](N5, N6){Success}
[N7](api){refund_order}
[E8](N3, N7){I want a refund}
[N8](end_message){Order refunded}
[E9](N7, N8){Success}
</flow>
```

The correct output is:

```
<flow>
[N0](assistant){Greet the customer}
[N1](user){Didn't receive my order}
[E0](N0, N1){}
[N2](assistant){Ask customer for order id}
[E1](N1, N2){}
[N3](user){Gives order id}
[E2](N2, N3){}
[N4](api){get_order_details}
[E3](N3, N4){}
[N5](assistant){Do you want to cancel or refund the
    order?}
[E4](N4, N5){Found order}
[N6](assistant){Tell the user the order wasn't
    found}
[E4](N4, N6){Order not Found}
[N7](user){User gives another order id}
[E5](N6, N7){}
[E6](N7, N4){}
[N8](user){I want to cancel the order}
[E7](N5, N8){}
[N9](api){cancel_order}
[E8](N8, N9){}
[N10](assistant){Order cancelled}
[E9](N9, N10){Success}
[N11](user){I want a refund}
[E10](N5, N11){}
[N12](api){refund_order}
[E11](N11, N12){}
[N13](assistant){Your order has been refunded}
[E12](N12, N13){Success}
</flow>
```

User prompt

```
{{ flowgraph }}
```

A.6 Conversations generation

System prompt

You will receive a conversation graph with nodes and edges in the following format:
-`[Ni](assistant){message}`: Agent nodes with the corresponding message.
-`[Nj](user){message}`: User nodes with the corresponding message.
-`[Nk](api){message}`: API nodes with the corresponding message.

The graph also has edges with the following format:
-`[Ei](Ni,Nj){}`: Message Ni happens before Nj.
-`[Ej](Ni,Nj){api_output}`: Only applicable when Ni is an API node.
Message Ni happens before Nj and has api outputs api_output.
The flowchart is given inside <flow></flow>. The initial node is [N1]. The agent is guiding the user throughout the process. Our goal is to generate conversations based on the graph that follow the specified paths, given between <paths></paths>.

For instance, consider the following flow graph:

```
<flow>
[N1](assistant){Greet the customer}
[N2](user){Didn't receive my order}
[E1](N1, N2){}
[N3](assistant){Ask customer for order id}
[E2](N2, N3){}
[N4](user){Gives order id}
[E3](N3, N4){}
[N5](api){get_order_details}
[E4](N4, N5){}
[N6](assistant){Want to cancel or refund the order?}
[E5](N5, N6){Found order}
[N7](assistant){Tell user the order wasn't found}
[E5](N5, N7){Order not Found}
[N8](user){User gives another order id}
[E6](N7, N8){}
[E7](N8, N5){}
[N9](user){I want to cancel the order}
[E8](N6, N9){}
[N10](api){cancel_order}
[E9](N9, N10){}
[N11](assistant){Order cancelled}
[E10](N10, N11){Success}
[N12](user){I want a refund}
[E11](N6, N12){}
[N13](api){refund_order}
[E12](N12, N13){}
[N14](assistant){Order refunded}
[E13](N13, N14){Success}
</flow>
```

And the apis are:

```
<apis>
[
    {
        "name": "get_order_details",
        "params": [{"order_id": "int"}],
        "output": {'name': 'sent_status', 'type':
            'list[dict[str, str]]'}
    }
]
</apis>
```

If the given path is: [N1, N2, N3, N4, N5, N7], one possible conversation is the following:

```
[
    {
        "role": "user",
        "content": "I didn't receive my order"
    },
    {
        "role": "assistant",
        "content": "Can you give me the order ID?"
    },
        {
        "role": "user",
        "content": "The order ID is #812"
    },
    {
        "role": "api",
        "content": "get_order_details(order_id=812)"
    },
    {
        "role": "api_output",
        "content": "{"sent_status": [{"item":
            "Product1", "status": "shipped"}]}"
    },
    {
        "role": "assistant",
        "content": "I couldn't find your order."
    },
]
```

Generate the conversation in the format specified above. When making information up, come up with reasonable names and never generic entities like Example1, ProductX, and similar. For example, if talking about products, mention existing products.
Only use the given APIs and make sure all the parameters are defined.
The conversations should follow the following rules:
- After a message with api role always include a message with api_output role.
- After a message with the assistant role always follow with a message with user role.
- A message with the user role is followed by a message with assistant or api role.
- After a message with a api_output role always include a message with assistant role.
- The API output should be in the format specified in the API definition. That is always in JSON format.
Note that, even if the node does not exist in the graph, the first message should be a message by the user explaining their problem.

User prompt

```
{{ conversation_graph }}
<apis>{{ apis }}</apis>
path: {{ path }}
```

A.7 Conversations from procedures

System prompt

You are an experienced customer service agent. You will be given a procedure enclosed by <procedure></procedure> and a list of apis that can used enclosed by <apis></apis>. Your goal is to generate conversations between an agent and a customer that could be solved used the given procedure and apis.
For instance, consider the following procedure:

```
<procedure>
# Handling a Customer Who Didn't Receive Their Order

Start Interaction:
1.1. Greet the customer courteously.

Identify the Issue:
2.1. Confirm the customer didn't receive the order.

Obtain Order Information:
3.1. Ask the customer to provide their order ID
        along with the email address or phone number
        associated with the order.

Retrieve Order Details:
4.1. If the customer provides the order ID and
        email address:
- Use the company's API to retrieve order details
        by email.
4.2. If the customer provides the order ID and
        phone number:
- Use the company's API to retrieve order details
        by phone number.

Check if Order is Found:
5.1. If the order is found, proceed to Step 6.
5.2. If the order is not found:
- Inform the customer that the order wasn't found.
- Ask the customer to provide the correct email or
        phone number and order ID.
- Repeat Step 3 based on the new information.

Determine Customer's Request:
6.1. Ask the customer if they would like to cancel
        the order or request a refund.

Processing Customer's Request:
7.1. Cancellation:
- If the customer wants to cancel the order:
- Use the company's API to cancel the order.
- Upon successful cancellation, inform the customer
        that the order has been cancelled.
7.2. Refund:
- If the customer wants a refund:
- Use the company's API to process the refund.
- Upon successful refund, inform the customer that
        the order has been refunded.

End Interaction:
8.1. Conclude by thanking the customer for their
        patience and confirming resolution.
```

And the apis are:

```
<apis>
[
    {
        "name": "get_order_details",
        "params": [{"order_id": "int"}],
        "output": "bool"
    }
]
</apis>
```

One possible conversation is the following:

```
[
    {
        "role": "assistant",
        "content": "Hello, how can I assist you?"
    },
    {
        "role": "user",
        "content": "I didn't receive my order"
    },
    {
        "role": "assistant",
        "content": "Can you give me the order ID?"
    },
    {
        "role": "user",
        "content": "The order ID is #812"
    },
    {
        "role": "api",
        "content": "get_order_details(order_id=812)"
    },
    {
        "role": "api_output",
        "content": "False"
    },
    {
        "role": "assistant",
        "content": "I'm sorry but I couldn't find
            your order."
    },
]
```

Generate the conversation in the format specified above. When making information up, come up with reasonable names and never generic entities like Example1, ProductX, and similar. For example, if talking about products, mention existing products.
Only use the given APIs and make sure all the parameters are defined.
The conversations should follow the following rules:

```
- After a message with api role always include a
      message with api\_output role.
- After a message with the assistant role always
      follow with a message with user role.
- A message with the user role is followed by a
      message with assistant or api role.
- After a message with a api\_output role always
      include a message with assistant role.
```

Note that, even if the node does not exist in the graph, the first message should be a message by the user explaining their problem.

User prompt

```
<procedure>{{ procedure }}</procedure>
<apis>{{ apis }}</apis>
```

A.8 Tool-augmented AI agent

System prompt

You are a customer support agent with the goal of answering user requests. You will be given the following information:

```
- conversation: Messages exchanged between the end
      user and you, and the executed actions with
      their
outputs.
```

This is the procedure you know about:

```
<procedure>
{{ procedure }}
</procedure>
```

You only know answers about this procedure! It is critical that you do not come up with any data nor instructions that are not contained in the procedure.
This is the list of available actions.

```
<actions>
{{ available_actions }}
</actions>
```

Sometimes your action might be simply to reply to an end user, other times you will need to call an action that performs an operation and/or retrieves necessary data. Some actions require information/-parameters in order to be callable. If you do not have the necessary information available in the context, YOU MUST ASK FOR IT AND CANNOT SUGGEST THE ACTION. Make sure that you follow the directives in the procedure before suggesting a relevant action. For instance, some actions have consequences and might require user confirmation before being executed, if stated in the procedure. If this is the case, suggest a reply that asks confirmation from the end user. Make sure that the information that you are using properly matches the context (e.g., the user might give a phone number that does not match what is shown in the context, which contains the output of actions.)
You MUST reply with a JSON object as follows:

```
{
     'type': name of the function to call,
     'parameters': parameters to pass to the
          function,
}
```

User prompt

```
<conversation>
{{ conversation }}
</conversation>
```

B auto-ALMITA: Detailed evaluation

Supplementary Table 1 provides detailed results obtained with the auto-ALMITA dataset, considering the 6 LLM agents and all the evaluation metrics from Section 4.3.

LLM	Reply		API			Test	Conversation
	Recall	Correct	Recall	Correct	Correct params.	Correct	Correct
GPT-4o	91.1	77.1	89.5	95.1	84,4	**85.4**	**14.7**
Mistral-NeMo-I	89.2	67.5	89.5	93.8	80.7	81.3	10.3
Claude3-s	79.9	67.1	92.9	**95.9**	84.1	78.9	6.9
GPT-4	60.5	**82.9**	92.6	94.6	**84.5**	75.5	6.4
Llama3.1-8b-I	79.4	61.8	64.3	95.7	83.8	73.4	3.2
GPT-4o w/ F	**89.6**	75.3	**93.0**	93.8	72.2	82.9	11.5

Supplementary Table 1: LLM AI agents evaluated on auto-ALMITA. For each LLM, the highest value in shown in **bold**. All results are percentages.

MMLU-SR: A Benchmark for Stress-Testing Reasoning Capability of Large Language Models

Wentian Wang*
USC

Sarthak Jain Rutgers
Paul Kantor Rutgers & UW-Madison
Jacob Feldman Rutgers
Lazaros Gallos Rutgers
Hao Wang Rutgers

Abstract

We propose MMLU-SR, a novel dataset designed to measure the true comprehension abilities of Large Language Models (LLMs) by challenging their performance in question-answering tasks with modified terms. We reasoned that an agent that "truly" understands a concept can still evaluate it when key terms are replaced by suitably defined alternate terms, and sought to differentiate such comprehension from mere text replacement. In our study, we modified standardized test questions by replacing a key term with a dummy word along with its definition. The key term could be in the context of questions, answers, or both questions and answers. Notwithstanding the high scores achieved by recent popular LLMs on the MMLU leaderboard, we found a substantial reduction in model performance after such replacement, suggesting poor comprehension. This new benchmark provides a rigorous benchmark for testing true model comprehension, and poses a challenge to the broader scientific community.

1 Introduction

Large Language Models (LLMs) have achieved impressive quantitative performance on a wide range of benchmarks, natural language processing (Zellers et al., 2019; Wang et al., 2019), general knowledge question-answering(Hendrycks et al., 2021; Clark et al., 2018), and coding (Chen et al., 2021; others, 2021). Additionally, by integrating with some advanced prompting techniques, such as Chain-of-Thought (CoT) (Wei et al., 2023) and its variants (Yao et al., 2023; Trivedi et al., 2023; Zhang et al., 2023), LLMs seem to exhibit a certain level of reasoning abilities including mathematics (Zhang et al., 2024) and even causal inference/discovery (Vashishtha et al., 2023; Wang et al., 2020; Mao et al., 2022; Gupta et al., 2021). However, some studies (Oren et al., 2023) have raised concerns about data leakage (i.e., training models on the test sets), potentially rendering these results unreliable. These seemingly contradictory findings prompt the question of whether LLMs are genuinely performing reasoning tasks or merely predicting the next token. If LLMs are truly capable of reasoning, they should remain unaffected by the replacement of key symbols within the test set.

A hallmark of human intelligence is the ability to handle abstract concepts and to associate them with arbitrary terms (Penn et al., 2008). With a few exceptions such as onomatopoeia, the connection between particular words and particular meanings is arbitrary, and identical concepts are invoked by different words in different human languages (e.g. *dog* vs *chien*). Similarly, human reasoners are capable of analogizing structural relationships from one domain to another, meaning that conceptual equivalence can be retained even when details change (Gentner and Medina, 1998). It follows that true human-like comprehension should be unimpaired when terms are substituted for synonymous terms, as long as the substitution is comprehensibly defined.

We wondered whether LLM peformance reflects true human-like comprehension in this sense, or whether it relies heavily on the specific terms used on training corpora. To assess this, we propose MMLU-SR, a new benchmark dataset that uses symbol replacement to remove some important terms from the questions and answers as shown in Figure 1. Instead of relying on memorized terms, this approach tests whether LLMs can reason using the definitions and concepts of those terms, ensuring a more robust evaluation of their understanding.

Our evaluations on GPT-3.5/4, Gemini, and Llama3 families showed significantly lower performance on MMLU-SR compared to the original MMLU, demonstrating the effectiveness of our approach in preventing models from exploiting memorized data. MMLU-SR thus provides a more chal-

*Visiting student at Rutgers ML Lab.

Proceedings of the 2nd GenBench Workshop on Generalisation (Benchmarking) in NLP, pages 69–85
November 16, 2024 ©2024 Association for Computational Linguistics

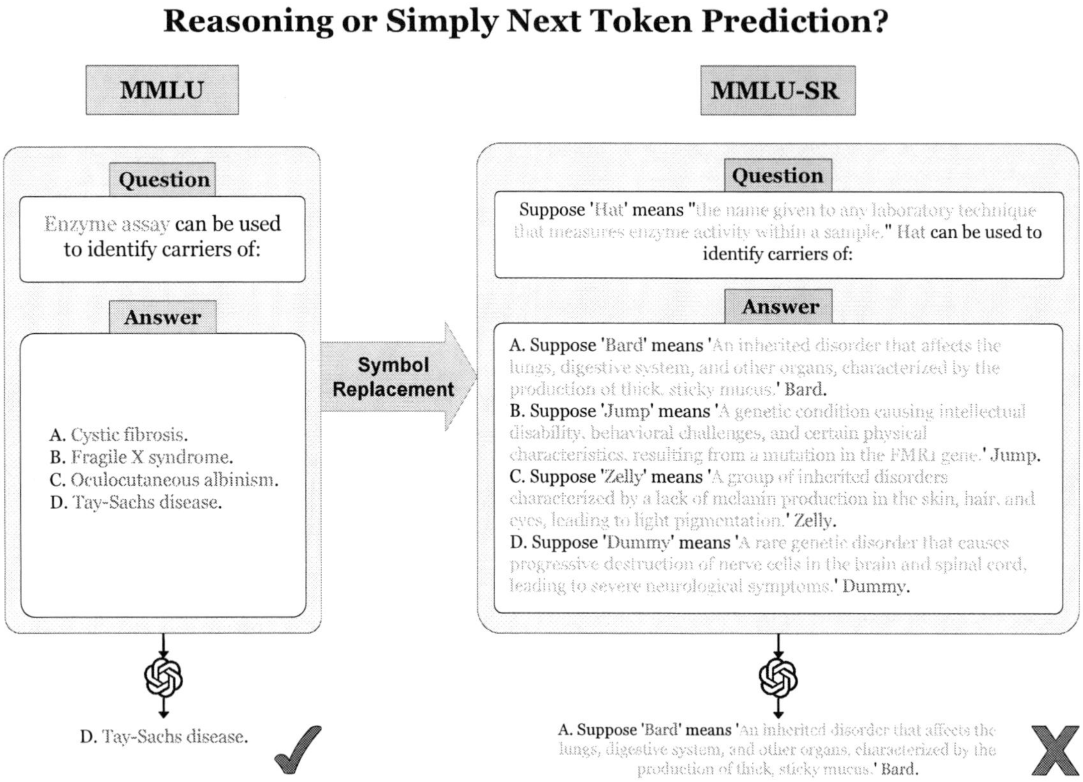

Figure 1: Illustration of our MMLU-SR testing scenarios. The red-colored and green-colored words represent the original symbols in the MMLU dataset showing in answers and questions, which are replaced in the MMLU-SR dataset with random words followed by their definitions, shown in orange text. The example question from the MMLU dataset is correctly answered by both GPT-3.5-turbo and ChatGPT-4. However, the modified question from the MMLU-SR "Question and Answer" dataset is answered incorrectly by both models.

lenging and revealing test of LLMs' true reasoning abilities and understanding.

Our findings indicate that while current LLMs excel on traditional benchmarks, they face substantial difficulties when key terms are replaced, highlighting the need for benchmarks like MMLU-SR to ensure robust and comprehensive evaluation of language models.

2 Related Works

MMLU Variants Benchmarks. MMLU Variants such as CMMLU (Li et al., 2024) and TMMLU+ (Tam et al., 2024) are adaptations of the MMLU benchmark for non-English languages; they translate the original MMLU questions and answers into other languages, providing a way to evaluate language models' performance in non-English contexts. These benchmarks are crucial for assessing the generalizability and robustness of models across different languages and cultural settings. They preserve the original structure and intent of MMLU while enabling a broader examination of multilingual capabilities.

Reasoning Capabilities Benchmarks. Several advanced reasoning benchmarks have been developed to evaluate the reasoning capabilities of language models. AGIEval (Zhong et al., 2023) includes standardized tests and civil service exams to assess reasoning and problem-solving skills in academic and professional scenarios. BoolQ (Clark et al., 2019) comprises over 15,000 real yes/no questions paired with Wikipedia passages to test the ability of models to infer answers from contextual information. GSM8K (Cobbe et al., 2021) features 8.5K grade-school math problems requiring multistep operations, targeting the evaluation of basic to intermediate mathematical problem-solving abilities. DROP (Dua et al., 2019), an adversarially-created reading comprehension benchmark, challenges models to navigate references and perform

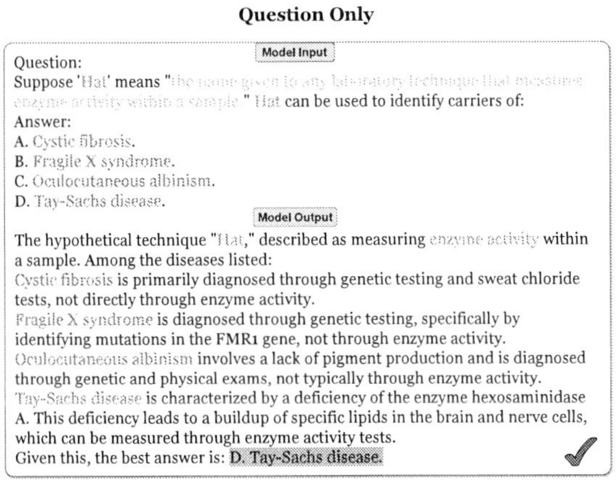

Figure 2: Example ChatGPT-4 output of MMLU-SR 'Question Only".

discrete operations such as addition and sorting, thus evaluating their capacity to understand complex texts and execute logical reasoning tasks. Beyond purely language-based evaluation, on the multimodal front, MMNeedle (Wang et al., 2024) introduced one of the first multimodal benchmarks to evaluate long-context multimodal reasoning capabilities of multimodal LLMs.

Unlike advanced reasoning benchmarks and MMLU variants for language extension (e.g., CMMLU and TMMLU+), our MMLU-SR benchmark introduces a novel approach. It enhances the challenge by replacing key words within the questions with random words, each paired with its definition, to differentiate from other benchmarks. This approach targets the models' reasoning abilities by preventing reliance on memorized terms or vocabularies. By altering key symbols, MMLU-SR ensures that the evaluation focuses on the models' understanding and reasoning, rather than their recognition of specific vocabulary, thus providing a more robust assessment of their true cognitive capabilities. We build our benchmark on the MMLU dataset because it encompasses a wide range of subjects across various domains, including Humanities, Social Sciences, STEM, and Other fields. This diverse subject matter ensures a comprehensive evaluation of language models' reasoning capabilities, in contrast to other reasoning benchmarks that often focus exclusively on specific STEM subjects.

3 MMLU-SR Dataset

3.1 Dataset Construction

We have developed the MMLU-SR benchmark to rigorously evaluate the reasoning and understanding capabilities of LLMs. Inspired by ObjectNet (Borji, 2020), our benchmark contains three subsets: "Question Only", "Answer Only", and "Question and Answer", each offering a unique perspective on the data to comprehensively assess LLM performance. To reduce human efforts in some redundant tasks, we proposed an automatic process to generate our dataset.

1. **Term Extraction and Definition Generation**: We extracted key terms from the questions and answers across all 57 subjects using the assistance of `gpt-3.5-turbo`. The process involved careful few-shot prompting, and we separately extracted the contexts of questions or answers alone to ensure the model focused on extracting terms rather than solving the questions. We also retrieved appropriate definitions within the specific subject for each extracted term. For terms where the automated process provided irrelevant or inaccurate definitions, we manually reviewed and corrected these entries (see Appendix F for details on the extent of manual modifications).

2. **Dictionary Creation**: Once the terms and their definitions were extracted for each subject, we created JSON files where the terms served as keys and the definitions as values. This dictionary served as the basis for replacing terms in the questions and answers.

3. **Data Replacement**: Using the created dictionaries, we replaced the key terms in the questions with random dummy words followed by their definitions to create the "Question Only" dataset. Similarly, we did this for the answers to form the "Answer Only" dataset. This ensured that the context remained human-readable but required reasoning to infer the replaced terms. Some definitions and replacements required manual adjustments to ensure clarity and accuracy.

4. **Combining Question and Answer Sets**: After creating the "Question Only" and "Answer Only" datasets, we combined them to form the "Question and Answer" dataset. This step

involved ensuring that the terms were consistently replaced across both questions and answers, maintaining the coherence of the dataset.

5. **Final Adjustments**: All CSV sheets were encoded in UTF-8 without headers. We manually fixed any typos that existed in the original MMLU dataset to ensure the quality and readability of the MMLU-SR dataset.

The MMLU-SR dataset was created using these meticulous steps. We formed both development and test sets, with the development set used for few-shot learning and the test set reserved for evaluation. This structured approach ensured that the dataset effectively tested the reasoning abilities of LLMs, differentiating between simple pattern recognition and genuine understanding. To effectively demonstrate how our MMLU-SR dataset can challenge more sophisticated models, we use Figure 2, Figure 3, and Figure 4 that feature responses from ChatGPT-4. For comparative insights, example responses of ChatGPT-3.5 are available from Table 8, Table 9, and Table 10 in Appendix B.

3.2 "Question Only" Dataset

Our "Question Only" dataset replaces key symbols with dummy words in most questions from the original MMLU dataset and keeps the answer choices unchanged. However, some straightforward questions, such as those involving only mathematical operations and numbers or simple questions like "Which of the following statements is true?", remain unmodified. Generally, we changed at least one important term in the context, replacing it with a random dummy word followed by its definition; sometimes, multiple terms are replaced in the question to further test the model's reasoning capabilities.

Figure 2 illustrates an example where the dummy word 'Hat' is used to replace term 'enzyme assay' and is defined as "the name given to any laboratory technique that measures enzyme activity within a sample." In this case, ChatGPT-4 successfully recognized 'Hat' and understood that the critical aspect was whether the diseases listed in the answer choices could be identified through enzyme activity. The model systematically eliminated each answer option, except for the last one, as it was the only choice that could be measured through enzyme activity tests. This setup effectively tests the model's ability to comprehend and reason based on the provided definitions, rather than relying on pre-trained knowledge of the term 'enzyme assay'.

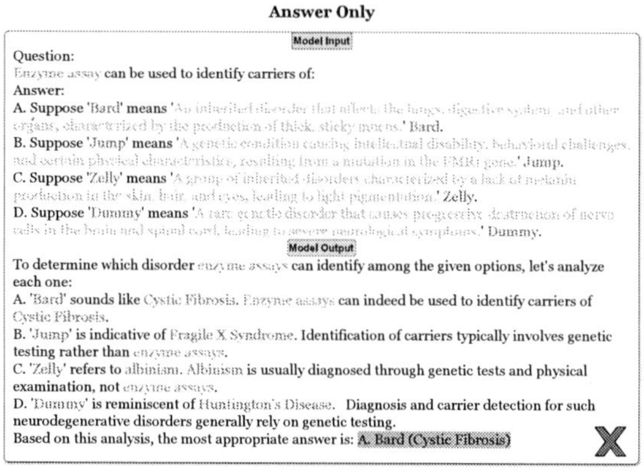

Figure 3: Example ChatGPT-4 output of MMLU-SR "Answer Only".

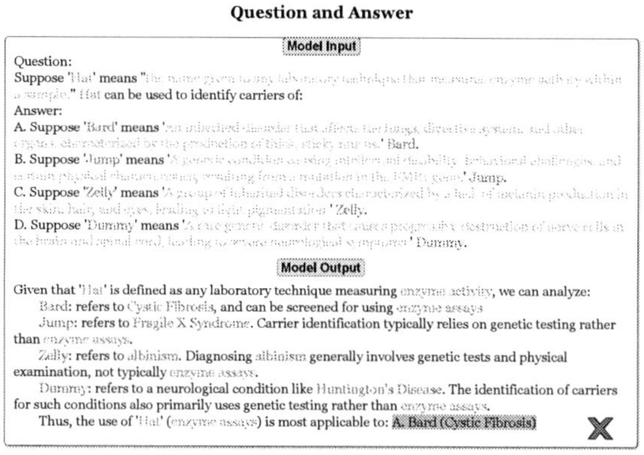

Figure 4: Example ChatGPT-4 output of MMLU-SR "Question and Answer".

3.3 "Answer Only" Dataset

Our "Answer Only" dataset modifies the answer choices in most text from the original MMLU dataset similarly to the "Question Only" dataset and keeps the questions unchanged. We ensure that at least one answer choice is modified among all four choices. In specific cases, such as "moral scenarios" where the answers are simple TRUE or FALSE choices, we make substitutions like "Suppose 'Jack' means 'True'." and "Suppose 'Luck' means 'False'." Despite these modifications, Table 3 still shows the accuracy drops among all models compared to the original "moral scenarios" sheet from MMLU. This underscores the challenge posed to models in adapting to these symbolic substitutions. Figure 3 demonstrates that ChatGPT-4 was able to recognize the replaced terms in answer choices A, B, and C, identifying 'Bard' as 'Cystic

Table 1: Performance of `gpt-4o-mini`,`gpt-4o`, `gemini-1.5-pro`, and `llama3-70b`.

Dataset	Humanities	Social Sciences	STEM	Other	Average
		GPT-4o-mini			
MMLU (5-shot)	0.793	0.858	**0.689**	0.782	0.771
Question Only (5-shot)	0.744	0.792	**0.621**	0.724	0.710
Answer Only (5-shot)	0.659	0.738	**0.602**	0.651	0.655
Question and Answer (5-shot)	0.588	0.666	**0.531**	0.585	0.585
		GPT-4o			
MMLU (5-shot)	0.880	0.906	**0.771**	0.854	0.845
Question Only (5-shot)	0.838	0.856	**0.702**	0.811	0.792
Answer Only (5-shot)	0.764	0.824	**0.705**	0.760	0.757
Question and Answer (5-shot)	0.708	0.754	**0.635**	0.712	0.695
		Gemini-1.5-pro			
MMLU (5-shot)	0.849	0.881	**0.802**	0.815	0.832
Question Only (5-shot)	0.795	0.836	**0.700**	0.754	0.764
Answer Only (5-shot)	0.741	0.816	0.747	**0.739**	0.758
Question and Answer (5-shot)	0.690	0.752	**0.670**	0.681	0.694
		Llama3-70B			
MMLU (5-shot)	**0.681**	0.868	0.697	0.814	0.765
Question Only (5-shot)	0.635	0.812	**0.631**	0.770	0.712
Answer Only (5-shot)	**0.539**	0.683	0.565	0.622	0.602
Question and Answer (5-shot)	**0.523**	0.653	0.536	0.591	0.576

Table 2: Relative percentage drop of accuracy in MMLU-SR compared to MMLU.

Dataset	Humanities	Social Sciences	STEM	Other	Average
		GPT-4o-mini			
Question Only (5-shot)	6.18%	7.69%	**9.87%**	7.42%	7.91%
Answer Only (5-shot)	**16.90%**	13.99%	12.63%	16.75%	15.05%
Question and Answer (5-shot)	**25.85%**	22.38%	22.93%	25.19%	24.12%
		GPT-4o			
Question Only (5-shot)	4.77%	5.52%	**8.95%**	5.03%	6.27%
Answer Only (5-shot)	**13.18%**	9.05%	8.56%	11.01%	10.41%
Question and Answer (5-shot)	**19.55%**	16.78%	17.64%	16.63%	17.75%
		Gemini-1.5-pro			
Question Only (5-shot)	6.36%	5.11%	**12.72%**	7.48%	8.17%
Answer Only (5-shot)	**12.72%**	7.38%	6.86%	9.33%	8.89%
Question and Answer (5-shot)	**18.73%**	14.64%	16.46%	16.44%	16.59%
		Llama3-70B			
Question Only (5-shot)	6.75%	6.45%	**9.47%**	5.41%	6.93%
Answer Only (5-shot)	20.85%	21.31%	18.94%	**23.59%**	21.31%
Question and Answer (5-shot)	23.20%	24.77%	23.10%	**27.40%**	24.71%

Fibrosis', 'Jump' as 'Fragile X Syndrome', and 'Zelly' as 'Albinism'. The model incorrectly identified the term 'Dummy' as 'Huntington's Disease', while the correct term is 'Tay-Sachs Disease'. Both disorders are indeed genetic, but they are distinct in their genetic causes and manifestations. It appears that ChatGPT-4, focusing on the broader category of 'genetic disorder' from the provided definition, inadvertently linked the description to the wrong disease. Such misidentification led the model to persist in incorrectly affirming that choice A ('Bard' as 'Cystic Fibrosis') was the correct answer (it is not).

3.4 "Question and Answer" Dataset

Our "Question and Answer" dataset integrates elements from both the "Question Only" and "Answer Only" datasets, replacing fundamental terms in both the questions and answer choices with dummy

Table 3: Detailed accuracy for different Humanities subjects across different models.

Subject	MMLU			Question Only			Answer Only			Question and Answer		
	GPT	Gemini	Llama3	GPT	Gemini	Llama3	GPT	Gemini	Llama3	GPT	Gemini	Llama3
Formal Logic	0.730	0.698	**0.532**	0.603	0.500	**0.484**	0.643	0.579	**0.516**	0.556	0.500	**0.460**
Logical Fallacies	0.902	0.902	**0.853**	0.883	0.834	**0.810**	0.853	0.847	**0.663**	0.834	0.841	**0.564**
Moral Disputes	0.882	**0.832**	0.847	0.832	0.806	**0.769**	0.777	0.830	**0.630**	0.711	0.749	**0.653**
Moral Scenarios	0.813	0.760	**0.318**	0.830	0.774	**0.289**	**0.143**	0.199	0.318	0.177	**0.167**	0.253
Philosophy	0.891	0.865	**0.865**	0.778	**0.724**	0.772	0.698	0.756	**0.598**	0.582	0.611	**0.582**
World Religions	0.901	**0.895**	0.906	0.895	**0.836**	0.895	0.842	0.813	**0.696**	0.825	0.772	**0.684**
High School European History	0.903	0.885	**0.848**	0.885	0.855	**0.830**	0.897	0.849	**0.721**	0.861	0.818	**0.739**
High School Us History	0.946	**0.922**	0.946	0.917	0.902	**0.887**	0.897	0.863	**0.799**	0.863	0.819	**0.799**
High School World History	0.937	**0.920**	0.945	0.924	0.920	**0.916**	0.907	0.865	**0.806**	0.882	**0.827**	0.840
Prehistory	0.948	**0.901**	0.910	0.904	0.836	**0.793**	0.843	0.803	**0.670**	0.790	0.769	**0.670**
International Law	0.942	0.926	**0.868**	0.901	**0.860**	0.868	0.934	0.843	**0.769**	0.835	0.802	**0.760**
Jurisprudence	0.898	0.861	**0.852**	0.852	0.861	**0.806**	0.861	0.806	**0.602**	0.722	0.750	**0.556**
Professional Law	0.749	0.666	**0.616**	0.683	0.627	**0.583**	0.641	0.585	**0.461**	0.563	0.544	**0.461**

Table 4: Detailed accuracy for different Social Science subjects across different models.

Subject	MMLU			Question Only			Answer Only			Question and Answer		
	GPT	Gemini	Llama3	GPT	Gemini	Llama3	GPT	Gemini	Llama3	GPT	Gemini	Llama3
Econometrics	0.711	0.702	**0.693**	0.588	0.579	**0.570**	0.640	0.614	**0.561**	0.535	0.535	**0.421**
High School Macroeconomics	0.921	0.880	**0.821**	0.849	0.785	**0.779**	0.813	0.785	**0.628**	0.721	0.715	**0.572**
High School Microeconomics	0.971	0.929	**0.870**	0.903	0.870	**0.773**	0.857	0.815	**0.664**	0.769	0.744	**0.571**
High School Government And Politics	0.984	0.974	**0.969**	0.979	0.943	**0.938**	0.943	0.922	**0.798**	0.922	0.845	**0.782**
Public Relations	0.836	**0.746**	0.755	0.755	0.755	**0.736**	0.664	0.682	**0.600**	0.627	0.646	**0.555**
Security Studies	0.824	0.841	**0.824**	0.788	0.792	**0.767**	0.731	0.796	**0.673**	0.633	0.714	**0.624**
Us Foreign Policy	0.930	0.940	**0.930**	0.920	0.930	**0.890**	0.870	0.880	**0.740**	0.810	0.810	**0.780**
Human Sexuality	0.931	0.893	**0.855**	0.924	0.855	**0.840**	0.863	0.847	**0.710**	0.802	0.756	**0.756**
Sociology	0.935	**0.891**	0.920	0.900	0.896	**0.841**	0.881	0.881	**0.806**	0.831	0.851	**0.786**
High School Geography	0.955	0.939	**0.924**	0.894	0.909	**0.833**	0.884	0.864	**0.737**	0.813	0.813	**0.662**
High School Psychology	0.965	0.938	**0.921**	0.923	0.917	**0.884**	0.927	0.912	**0.719**	0.872	0.859	**0.739**
Professional Psychology	0.908	0.895	**0.845**	0.845	0.801	**0.788**	0.817	0.791	**0.627**	0.719	0.737	**0.601**

words followed by their definitions. As illustrated in Figure 4, ChatGPT-4 successfully interpreted the original terms for each replaced term in answer choices A through C. However, similar to the results seen in Figure 3, the model incorrectly recognized the term in the last answer choice D ('Dummy' for Huntington's Disease), leading to an incorrect answer. This outcome contrasts with Figure 2, where ChatGPT-4 correctly answered the questions when only the questions were modified. This illustrates that as complexity in context increases, with terms being replaced in both questions and answers, the model struggles to accurately identify the correct original term, consequently leading to an incorrect answer choice.

4 Experiments

4.1 Evaluation Protocol

We evaluated seven models across OpenAI, Gemini, Llama families: `gpt-3.5-turbo`, `gpt-4o-mini`, `gpt-4o`, `gemini-1.0-pro`, `gemini-1.5-pro`, `llama3-8b`, and `llama3-70b`. The evaluation for GPT and Gemini models was conducted using the Gemini-benchmark pipeline (Akter et al., 2023). For these models, we set the temperature parameter to 0 and utilized carefully crafted prompts that required responses in the format of "Answer: Letter of Choice." This approach ensures that the generated responses are directly comparable and suitable for evaluation. Additionally, both models were evaluated in the 5-shot setting, using examples from our development dataset to enhance their contextual understanding. Llama3 was evaluated using the lm-evaluation-harness framework (Gao et al., 2023). This model employed a different evaluation strategy; it uses log likelihood to determine the model's responses. Consistent with the other models, Llama3 also uses the same 5-shot setting, ensuring a standardized comparison across all tests. The complete results of all seven models are available in Appendix E.

Table 5: Detailed accuracy for different STEM subjects across different models.

Subject	MMLU			Question Only			Answer Only			Question and Answer		
	GPT	Gemini	Llama3	GPT	Gemini	Llama3	GPT	Gemini	Llama3	GPT	Gemini	Llama3
Abstract Algebra	0.660	0.690	**0.380**	0.470	0.550	**0.370**	0.640	0.730	**0.400**	0.460	0.520	**0.400**
College Mathematics	**0.490**	0.680	0.510	**0.420**	0.630	0.490	**0.440**	0.650	0.460	**0.410**	0.610	0.480
High School Statistics	0.769	0.866	**0.699**	0.708	0.708	**0.657**	0.750	0.829	**0.620**	0.644	0.662	**0.597**
Elementary Mathematics	0.735	0.921	**0.606**	0.675	0.786	**0.521**	0.706	0.900	**0.561**	0.661	0.825	**0.497**
High School Mathematics	0.541	0.700	**0.422**	0.537	0.504	**0.356**	0.541	0.615	**0.426**	0.511	0.526	**0.367**
Astronomy	0.947	**0.901**	0.921	0.908	**0.829**	0.849	0.888	0.849	**0.697**	0.855	0.796	**0.684**
College Physics	0.686	0.716	**0.559**	0.559	0.647	**0.451**	0.618	0.745	**0.431**	0.480	0.608	**0.422**
Conceptual Physics	0.911	0.932	**0.783**	0.804	0.757	**0.677**	0.791	0.843	**0.494**	0.685	0.698	**0.447**
High School Physics	0.748	0.782	**0.563**	0.649	0.556	**0.530**	0.589	0.616	**0.477**	0.543	0.596	**0.450**
College Chemistry	**0.570**	0.610	0.580	**0.540**	0.550	0.570	0.550	0.530	**0.480**	**0.480**	0.560	0.470
High School Chemistry	0.759	0.788	**0.734**	0.709	**0.685**	0.631	0.670	0.680	**0.537**	0.586	0.626	**0.468**
College Biology	0.951	**0.868**	0.931	0.938	0.882	**0.854**	0.924	0.861	**0.708**	0.833	0.826	**0.625**
High School Biology	0.958	0.929	**0.903**	0.932	0.893	**0.858**	0.884	0.858	**0.713**	0.858	0.829	**0.729**
College Computer Science	0.790	0.790	**0.670**	0.690	**0.610**	0.650	0.760	0.730	**0.610**	0.670	0.660	**0.570**
Computer Security	0.840	**0.820**	0.830	0.830	0.770	**0.750**	0.760	0.730	**0.660**	0.760	**0.610**	0.720
High School Computer Science	0.910	0.920	**0.870**	0.860	0.880	**0.790**	0.880	0.910	**0.820**	0.850	0.870	**0.740**
Machine Learning	0.777	0.714	**0.652**	0.661	0.643	**0.589**	0.643	0.661	**0.527**	0.580	0.580	**0.509**
Electrical Engineering	0.841	0.807	**0.745**	0.752	0.724	**0.655**	0.655	0.710	**0.510**	0.566	0.655	**0.490**

Table 6: Detailed accuracy for different Other subjects across different models.

Subject	MMLU			Question Only			Answer Only			Question and Answer		
	GPT	Gemini	Llama3	GPT	Gemini	Llama3	GPT	Gemini	Llama3	GPT	Gemini	Llama3
Anatomy	0.911	**0.793**	0.807	0.874	0.733	**0.726**	0.815	0.667	**0.563**	0.726	0.659	**0.578**
Clinical Knowledge	0.898	**0.838**	0.849	0.811	0.785	**0.740**	0.796	0.755	**0.638**	0.713	0.709	**0.608**
College Medicine	0.832	0.844	**0.757**	0.780	0.786	**0.740**	0.798	0.763	**0.647**	0.717	0.740	**0.659**
Human Aging	0.830	**0.807**	0.807	0.794	**0.744**	0.758	0.704	0.740	**0.457**	0.632	0.691	**0.471**
Medical Genetics	0.960	0.910	**0.830**	0.900	0.850	**0.820**	0.840	0.780	**0.570**	0.830	0.740	**0.550**
Nutrition	0.899	0.876	**0.853**	0.863	**0.758**	0.804	0.798	0.784	**0.663**	0.699	0.703	**0.647**
Professional Medicine	0.956	**0.864**	0.868	0.919	**0.776**	0.868	0.901	0.783	**0.754**	0.842	**0.735**	0.754
Virology	0.578	0.578	**0.536**	0.548	0.506	**0.488**	0.524	0.542	**0.452**	0.524	0.494	**0.404**
Business Ethics	0.860	0.850	**0.750**	0.890	0.780	**0.720**	0.750	0.670	**0.500**	0.710	0.640	**0.480**
Management	0.913	**0.893**	0.913	0.883	**0.816**	0.903	**0.757**	0.835	0.728	0.767	0.767	**0.650**
Marketing	0.949	0.940	**0.923**	0.906	0.927	**0.880**	0.838	0.846	**0.615**	0.808	0.803	**0.662**
Global Facts	0.650	0.600	**0.530**	0.540	0.540	**0.430**	**0.580**	0.690	0.540	0.520	0.470	**0.410**
Miscellaneous	0.955	0.955	**0.903**	0.932	0.877	**0.860**	0.861	0.847	**0.692**	0.840	0.791	**0.616**
Professional Accounting	0.766	0.663	**0.638**	0.716	0.674	**0.596**	0.681	0.638	**0.514**	0.631	0.596	**0.489**

4.2 Results and Analysis

General Trend. Table 1 shows the accuracy of the four models `gpt-4o-mini`, `gpt-4o`, `gemini-1.5-pro`, and `llama3-70b` evaluated in both MMLU and our MMLU-SR. The data highlights how each model performs in the Humanities, Social Sciences, STEM, and Other academic fields, providing average scores for each subset. We observe consistent drop in model performance across all subsets when transitioning from the standard MMLU dataset to the more challenging MMLU-SR dataset, as evidenced by the decline in average accuracy from 0.771 on the MMLU dataset to 0.710, 0.655, and 0.585, on our MMLU-SR's "Question Only", "Answer Only", and "Question and Answer" subsets, respectively, for the `gpt-4o-mini` model. This trend of decreased performance is similarly observed in the other models.

We observe a crucial trend in decreasing accuracy across datasets: The "Question Only" dataset experiences the least drop, followed by the "Answer Only" dataset, with the most significant decline occurring in the "Question and Answer" dataset. This trend can be primarily attributed to two major reasons: (1) When only the question is modified, the model retains the original answer choices, facilitating the inference of the modified question's meaning; in contrast, altering the answer choices removes this contextual aid, challenging the model's ability to correctly match the question with the appropriate answer. (2) Answer choices are typically more concise and therefore lack the extensive context found in questions; consequently, replacing terms in the answers not only introduces ambiguity but also demands more complex inferential reasoning, disrupting the model's learned pattern-recognition strategies and resulting in a greater accuracy drop. The observations above also *justify the design of our MMLU-SR* on three variants (i.e., "Question Only", "Answer Only", and "Question and Answer").

Accuracy Drop in Each Category. Table 2 shows several aspects in the relative percentage drop of accuracy in MMLU-SR compared to that in MMLU across different categories for `gpt-4o-mini`, `gpt-4o`, `gemini-1.5-pro`, and `llama3-70b`:

1. **Humanities and Social Sciences.** For `gpt-4o-mini` and `gpt-4o`, the accuracy drops significantly in the Humanities category, with a slightly lower drop in Social Sciences. The `gemini-1.5-pro` shows the smallest performance decline in the Humanities and Social Science categories compared to the other two models evaluated. `llama3-70b` exhibits a pattern similar to `gpt-4o-mini`, with the Humanities and Social Sciences categories showing a moderate percentage drop, though slightly higher than `gpt-4o-mini`, in the "Answer Only" and "Question and Answer" dataset.

2. **STEM.** For `gemini-1.5-pro` and `llama3-70b`, the STEM category shows a relatively moderate decrease in accuracy across the MMLU-SR datasets. Notably, `gemini-1.5-pro` experiences the highest drop of 12.72% in the "Question Only" dataset, indicating some sensitivity in this area. `llama3-70b` demonstrates a similar trend, with the highest drop of 9.47% in the STEM category, suggesting both models retain some robustness in STEM but are still impacted by symbol replacement. On the other hand, `gpt-4o-mini` experiences a higher drop in the "Answer Only" and "Question and Answer" datasets, particularly with a 22.93% drop in the latter, highlighting its relative vulnerability in this domain compared to `gemini-1.5-pro` and `llama3-70b`.

3. **Other.** The Other category generally shows a significant drop across all models and datasets, with the highest drops often observed in the "Question and Answer" dataset. For example, `gpt-4o-mini` experiences a notable drop of 25.19%, the highest among all categories and models, indicating a high sensitivity to contextual changes in this area. Similarly, `llama3-70b` follows closely with a 27.40% drop, which is the highest in the Other category for this model. `gemini-1.5-pro` also shows a substantial drop of 16.44%, though slightly less compared to the other models, suggesting that the "Other" category, like Humanities, might be more context-dependent and hence more susceptible to performance degradation when symbols are replaced.

Detailed Accuracy Drop in Each Subject. Table 3 shows a detailed comparison of accuracy scores across different models evaluated on various subjects in the Humanities category. The MMLU scores serve as a baseline for comparison. `gpt-4o` demonstrates exceptional performance across most subjects in this category, often leading in accuracy, particularly in complex subjects like Philosophy and International Law. `gemini-1.5-pro` also shows strong performance, but `gpt-4o` frequently matches or exceeds its accuracy. Notably, `gpt-4o` performs particularly well in subjects like High School World History and Jurisprudence. However, all models continue to struggle with Moral Scenarios, where the accuracy score drops significantly, particularly for `llama3-70b`, which shows a drastic decrease, reflecting a higher sensitivity to the challenges posed by the MMLU-SR datasets

Table 4 shows a detailed comparison of accuracy across different models evaluated on various subjects in the Social Science category. We observe that all models perform exceptionally well in Social Science on MMLU, particularly in High School Government and Politics, where `gpt-4o` achieves an impressive accuracy of 0.984. While there is still a drop in accuracy from MMLU to MMLU-SR's "Question and Answer" dataset, `gpt-4o` demonstrates remarkable resilience, maintaining accuracy levels around 0.7∼0.9 across most subjects. This performance significantly outpaces the other models, particularly in subjects like High School Psychology and Sociology. The drop in accuracy, though less pronounced for `gpt-4o`, still illustrates how our symbol replacement method increases difficulty, effectively stress-testing the models' reasoning capabilities versus mere memorization of pre-trained terms.

Table 5 shows a detailed comparison of accuracy across various STEM subjects for different models. Each model demonstrated varying degrees of success across the subjects, with notable difficulties in some areas. College Mathematics and High School Mathematics remain challenging for all models, including `gpt-4o`, with accuracy dropping to around 0.4 to 0.5 in MMLU-SR's "Question and Answer" dataset. However, `gpt-4o` shows marked improvement in subjects like Astronomy, College Biology, and High School Biology, maintaining high accuracy even in the more challenging MMLU-SR datasets. The subject with the lowest accuracies among all models is still High School Mathematics, where `llama3-70b` struggles the most, especially in the Answer Only" and "Question and Answer" datasets. Similarly, College Physics and Abstract Algebra also show significant drops in accuracy across all models, highlighting the persistent challenges in subjects involving extensive calculations and complex problem-solving.

Table 6 shows a detailed comparison of accuracy scores across different models evaluated on various subjects in the Other category. We observe that `gpt-4o` performs exceptionally well in MMLU, with accuracy consistently above 0.9 in most subjects, significantly outperforming other models. Marketing stands out with a particularly high accuracy of 0.949 for `gpt-4o`, indicating outstanding performance in this subject. Professional Accounting shows improved performance with `gpt-4o`, achieving an accuracy of 0.766 in MMLU. Virology remains challenging, but `gpt-4o` shows improvement with an accuracy of 0.578. While there is still a drop in accuracy from MMLU to MMLU-SR's "Question and Answer" dataset, `gpt-4o` maintains relatively high performance, with accuracy generally staying above 0.7 for most subjects. Even in challenging areas like Virology and Global Facts, `gpt-4o` demonstrates resilience, maintaining accuracy levels significantly higher than other models.

CoT and System Instruction. We developed a simple baseline to test our MMLU-SR dataset on more recent and sophisticated models like GPT-4. This involves adding the instruction "Let's think step by step" at the end of answer choices to enable zero-shot CoT prompting. As shown in Table 7 from Appendix A, we also included a system instruction informing ChatGPT-4 that the following questions would involve symbol replacement with arbitrary definitions. However, the example demonstrates that despite applying (zero-shot) CoT, the model still incorrectly interprets the term 'Dummy' in choice D as 'neurodegenerative disorder,' leading to the wrong answer, choice A. We applied this system instruction across the entire MMLU-SR dataset as well, with results shown in Table 11 from Appendix C. The results indicate that while the system instruction slightly improves accuracy in the "Question Only" and "Answer Only" datasets, the model still struggles with the increased complexity in the "Question and Answer" dataset.

5 Conclusion

We introduced MMLU-SR, a novel benchmark that challenges LLMs by replacing key terms in questions with random words followed by their definitions, aiming to test the models' reasoning and comprehension abilities rather than their memorization skills. Our evaluation across multiple domains revealed that popular LLMs suffer from significant drops in performance with these modifications, highlighting their reliance on memorized terms. MMLU-SR's unique approach addresses concerns about overfitting to traditional benchmarks and provides a more rigorous measure of true language understanding. This dataset will enable researchers to better identify and address the reasoning limitations of current LLMs, fostering the development of more robust and genuinely intelligent models.

6 Acknowledgements

We thank the anonymous reviewers for their thoughtful feedback and for recognizing the significance and contributions of our research. This research is based on work partially supported by DARPA Grant HR00112420363, NSF Grant IIS-2127918, and NSF CAREER Award IIS-2340125.

References

S. N. Akter, Z. Yu, A. Muhamed, T. Ou, A. Bäuerle, Á. A. Cabrera, K. Dholakia, C. Xiong, and G. Neubig. 2023. An in-depth look at gemini's language abilities. *arXiv preprint arXiv:2312.11444*.

Ali Borji. 2020. Objectnet dataset: Reanalysis and correction. *Preprint*, arXiv:2004.02042.

Mark Chen et al. 2021. Evaluating large language models trained on code. *Preprint*, arXiv:2107.03374.

Christopher Clark, Kenton Lee, Ming-Wei Chang, Tom Kwiatkowski, Michael Collins, and Kristina Toutanova. 2019. Boolq: Exploring the surprising difficulty of natural yes/no questions. *Preprint*, arXiv:1905.10044.

Peter Clark, Isaac Cowhey, Oren Etzioni, Tushar Khot, Ashish Sabharwal, Carissa Schoenick, and Oyvind

Tafjord. 2018. Think you have solved question answering? try arc, the ai2 reasoning challenge. *ArXiv*, abs/1803.05457.

Karl Cobbe, Vineet Kosaraju, Mohammad Bavarian, Mark Chen, Heewoo Jun, Lukasz Kaiser, Matthias Plappert, Jerry Tworek, Jacob Hilton, Reiichiro Nakano, Christopher Hesse, and John Schulman. 2021. Training verifiers to solve math word problems. *Preprint*, arXiv:2110.14168.

Dheeru Dua, Yizhong Wang, Pradeep Dasigi, Gabriel Stanovsky, Sameer Singh, and Matt Gardner. 2019. Drop: A reading comprehension benchmark requiring discrete reasoning over paragraphs. *Preprint*, arXiv:1903.00161.

Leo Gao, Jonathan Tow, Baber Abbasi, Stella Biderman, Sid Black, Anthony DiPofi, Charles Foster, Laurence Golding, Jeffrey Hsu, Alain Le Noac'h, Haonan Li, Kyle McDonell, Niklas Muennighoff, Chris Ociepa, Jason Phang, Laria Reynolds, Hailey Schoelkopf, Aviya Skowron, Lintang Sutawika, Eric Tang, Anish Thite, Ben Wang, Kevin Wang, and Andy Zou. 2023. A framework for few-shot language model evaluation.

D. Gentner and J. Medina. 1998. Similarity and the development of rules. *Cognition*, 65(2/3):263–297.

Shantanu Gupta, Hao Wang, Zachary Lipton, and Yuyang Wang. 2021. Correcting exposure bias for link recommendation. In *ICML*.

Dan Hendrycks, Collin Burns, Steven Basart, Andy Zou, Mantas Mazeika, Dawn Song, and Jacob Steinhardt. 2021. Measuring massive multitask language understanding. In *Proceedings of the International Conference on Learning Representations (ICLR)*.

H. Li, Y. Zhang, F. Koto, Y. Yang, H. Zhao, Y. Gong, N. Duan, and T. Baldwin. 2024. Cmmlu: Measuring massive multitask language understanding in chinese. *arXiv preprint arXiv:2306.09212*.

Chengzhi Mao, Kevin Xia, James Wang, Hao Wang, Junfeng Yang, Elias Bareinboim, and Carl Vondrick. 2022. Causal transportability for visual recognition. In *CVPR*.

Y. Oren, N. Meister, N. Chatterji, F. Ladhak, and T. B. Hashimoto. 2023. Proving test set contamination in black box language models. *arXiv preprint arXiv:2310.17623*.

Shuai Lu others. 2021. Codexglue: A machine learning benchmark dataset for code understanding and generation. *CoRR*, abs/2102.04664.

D. C. Penn, K. J. Holyoak, and D. J. Povinelli. 2008. Darwin's mistake: explaining the discontinuity between human and nonhuman minds. *Behavioral and Brain Sciences*, 31(2):109–130.

Z.-R. Tam, Y.-T. Pai, Y.-W. Lee, S. Cheng, and H.-H. Shuai. 2024. An improved traditional chinese evaluation suite for foundation model. *arXiv preprint arXiv:2403.01858*.

Harsh Trivedi, Niranjan Balasubramanian, Tushar Khot, and Ashish Sabharwal. 2023. Interleaving retrieval with chain-of-thought reasoning for knowledge-intensive multi-step questions. *Preprint*, arXiv:2212.10509.

Aniket Vashishtha, Abbavaram Gowtham Reddy, Abhinav Kumar, Saketh Bachu, Vineeth N Balasubramanian, and Amit Sharma. 2023. Causal inference using llm-guided discovery. *arXiv preprint arXiv:2310.15117*.

Alex Wang, Amanpreet Singh, Julian Michael, Felix Hill, Omer Levy, and Samuel R. Bowman. 2019. Glue: A multi-task benchmark and analysis platform for natural language understanding. *Preprint*, arXiv:1804.07461.

Hengyi Wang, Haizhou Shi, Shiwei Tan, Weiyi Qin, Wenyuan Wang, Tunyu Zhang, Akshay Nambi, Tanuja Ganu, and Hao Wang. 2024. Multimodal needle in a haystack: Benchmarking long-context capability of multimodal large language models. *arXiv preprint arXiv:2406.11230*.

Yuhao Wang, Vlado Menkovski, Hao Wang, Xin Du, and Mykola Pechenizkiy. 2020. Causal discovery from incomplete data: A deep learning approach. In *AAAI StarAI Workshop*.

J. Wei, X. Wang, D. Schuurmans, M. Bosma, B. Ichter, F. Xia, E. Chi, Q. Le, and D. Zhou. 2023. Chain-of-thought prompting elicits reasoning in large language models. *arXiv preprint arXiv:2201.11903*.

Shunyu Yao, Dian Yu, Jeffrey Zhao, Izhak Shafran, Thomas L. Griffiths, Yuan Cao, and Karthik Narasimhan. 2023. Tree of thoughts: Deliberate problem solving with large language models. *Preprint*, arXiv:2305.10601.

Rowan Zellers, Ari Holtzman, Yonatan Bisk, Ali Farhadi, and Yejin Choi. 2019. Hellaswag: Can a machine really finish your sentence? *Preprint*, arXiv:1905.07830.

Boning Zhang, Chengxi Li, and Kai Fan. 2024. Mario eval: Evaluate your math llm with your math llm–a mathematical dataset evaluation toolkit. *arXiv preprint arXiv:2404.13925*.

Zhuosheng Zhang, Aston Zhang, Mu Li, and Alex Smola. 2023. Automatic chain of thought prompting in large language models. In *The Eleventh International Conference on Learning Representations (ICLR 2023)*.

Wanjun Zhong, Ruixiang Cui, Yiduo Guo, Yaobo Liang, Shuai Lu, Yanlin Wang, Amin Saied, Weizhu Chen, and Nan Duan. 2023. Agieval: A human-centric benchmark for evaluating foundation models. *Preprint*, arXiv:2304.06364.

A CoT Examples

Table 7 shows an example of incorrect answer using zero-shot CoT with a system instruction produced by the ChatGPT-4 on MMLU-SR's "Question and Answer" dataset. The correct answer is choice D, but ChatGPT-4 responded with choice A.

B Examples of ChatGPT-3.5 Response

Table 8 shows an example of incorrect answer produced by the ChatGPT-3.5 on MMLU-SR's "Question and Answer" dataset. Table 9 shows an example of incorrect answer produced by the ChatGPT-3.5 on MMLU-SR's "Question and Answer" dataset. Table 10 shows an example of incorrect answer produced by the ChatGPT-3.5 on MMLU-SR's "Question and Answer" dataset.

C System Instruction Example

Table 11 shows the performance comparison of `gemini-1.0-pro` with and without using the system instruction "In each of the questions that I ask, I will replace some of the words that you might know with a word that is arbitrarily assigned a specific meaning just for this test. The meaning of these arbitrary definition may change with every question."

D Hard MMLU-SR Example

Table 12 illustrates a challenging example mentioned in the "Question and Answer" section in the main paper. In the question, we substituted "enzyme assay" with a synonym, "protein", and used the original terms from the MMLU dataset as placeholders in the answer choices, each paired with a definition. ChatGPT-4 correctly identified the term "Tay-Sachs Disease" but associated it with the incorrect answer choice and definition, which was meant for "Fragile X syndrome." This example demonstrates that ChatGPT-4 can be misled by the complexity of the dataset, tending to rely on pre-existing knowledge rather than engaging in substantive reasoning to align terms with their definitions.

E Complete Experiment Results

Table 13 shows our complete experiment results of different LLMs including `gpt-3.5-turbo`, `gpt-4o-mini`, `gemini-1.0-pro`, `gemini-1.5-pro`, `llama3-8b` and `llama3-70b`. The percentage drop of each model is shown in Table 14.

F Numbers of Human Modified Terms

Figure 5 shows the number of manually modified term definitions across 41 subject glossaries. These glossaries were created by consolidating related topics from the original 57 subjects in the MMLU dataset. Of the 28,676 terms initially generated by `gpt-3.5-turbo` for these 41 subjects, approximately 1,197 (4.2%) required human modification.

Table 7: Example of incorrect output using zero-shot CoT with system instruction.

System Prompt	In each of the questions that I ask, I will replace some of the words that you might know with a word that is arbitrarily assigned a specific meaning just for this test. The meaning of these arbitrary definition may change with every question.
Input	Suppose 'Hat' means 'the name given to any laboratory technique that measures enzyme activity within a sample.' Hat can be used to identify carriers of: A. Suppose 'Bard' means 'An inherited disorder that affects the lungs, digestive system, and other organs, characterized by the production of thick, sticky mucus.' Bard. B. Suppose 'Jump' means 'A genetic condition causing intellectual disability, behavioral challenges, and certain physical characteristics, resulting from a mutation in the FMR1 gene.' Jump. C. Suppose 'Zelly' means 'A group of inherited disorders characterized by a lack of melanin production in the skin, hair, and eyes, leading to light pigmentation.' Zelly. D. Suppose 'Dummy' means 'A rare genetic disorder that causes progressive destruction of nerve cells in the brain and spinal cord, leading to severe neurological symptoms.' Dummy. Let's think step by step.
Output	In this scenario, Hat is used to detect variations or abnormalities in enzyme levels that might be indicative of certain genetic disorders. A: Bard refers to cystic fibrosis. Areas of land (Jack) often have boundaries (Winky) that separate them from other areas. B: Jump refers to Fragile X syndrome, primarily involves genetic testing to detect the specific mutation rather than enzyme activity measurements. C: Zelly refers to conditions such as albinism, which are typically diagnosed based on pigment absence rather than enzyme activity, although some biochemical tests can be relevant in specific contexts. D: Dummy could be referring to several neurodegenerative disorders, which might be associated with enzyme activities related to nerve cell function or metabolic processes, but generally, such disorders are diagnosed through genetic markers and neuroimaging rather than enzyme activity alone. Given these explanations, the best match for 'Hat' in terms of being a technique to measure enzyme activity useful for diagnosis would be A, 'Bard' as cystic fibrosis, due to its direct relationship with enzyme dysfunction and measurement. ✗

Table 8: Example of incorrect response generated by ChatGPT-3.5 in "Question Only" dataset.

Input	Suppose 'Hat' means "the name given to any laboratory technique that measures enzyme activity within a sample." Hat can be used to identify carriers of: A. Cystic fibrosis. B. Fragile X syndrome. C. Oculocutaneous albinism. D. Tay-Sachs disease
Output	"Hat" in this context refers to an enzyme assay technique rather than a genetic condition or disease. Therefore, it wouldn't be used to identify carriers of genetic disorders like cystic fibrosis, Fragile X syndrome, oculocutaneous albinism, or Tay-Sachs disease. It's essential to keep in mind the specific context in which terms are used in scientific fields! ✗

Table 9: Example of incorrect response generated by ChatGPT-3.5 in "Answer Only" dataset.

Input	Enzyme assay can be used to identify carriers of: A. Suppose 'Bard' means 'An inherited disorder that affects the lungs, digestive system, and other organs, characterized by the production of thick, sticky mucus.' Bard. B. Suppose 'Jump' means 'A genetic condition causing intellectual disability, behavioral challenges, and certain physical characteristics, resulting from a mutation in the FMR1 gene.' Jump. C. Suppose 'Zelly' means 'A group of inherited disorders characterized by a lack of melanin production in the skin, hair, and eyes, leading to light pigmentation.' Zelly. D. Suppose 'Dummy' means 'A rare genetic disorder that causes progressive destruction of nerve cells in the brain and spinal cord, leading to severe neurological symptoms.' Dummy.
Output	An enzyme assay could be used to identify carriers of Bard, Jump, Zelly, or Dummy if the specific enzyme associated with each disorder is known and can be tested for. Enzyme assays are commonly used in genetic testing to detect the presence or absence of specific enzymes or their activity levels, which can provide information about an individual's genetic makeup and potential carrier status for certain genetic disorders. ✗

Table 10: Example of incorrect response generated by ChatGPT-3.5 in "Question and Answer" dataset.

Input	Suppose 'Hat' means "the name given to any laboratory technique that measures enzyme activity within a sample." Hat can be used to identify carriers of A. Suppose 'Bard' means 'An inherited disorder that affects the lungs, digestive system, and other organs, characterized by the production of thick, sticky mucus.' Bard. B. Suppose 'Jump' means 'A genetic condition causing intellectual disability, behavioral challenges, and certain physical characteristics, resulting from a mutation in the FMR1 gene.' Jump. C. Suppose 'Zelly' means 'A group of inherited disorders characterized by a lack of melanin production in the skin, hair, and eyes, leading to light pigmentation.' Zelly. D. Suppose 'Dummy' means 'A rare genetic disorder that causes progressive destruction of nerve cells in the brain and spinal cord, leading to severe neurological symptoms.' Dummy.
Output	Based on the provided definitions: A. Hat (enzyme activity measurement) can be used to identify carriers of Zelly (lack of melanin production disorders). Explanation: Enzyme activity measurements are often used in medical diagnostics to identify various conditions, including genetic disorders. In this case, the lack of melanin production, as seen in Zelly disorders, can be identified using enzyme activity tests. ✗

Table 11: Performance comparison of the `gemini-1.0-pro` model with and without the system instruction.

Dataset	Humanities	Social Sciences	STEM	Other	Average
Gemini-1.0-pro					
Question Only (5-shot)	0.687	0.744	**0.539**	0.658	0.645
Answer Only (5-shot)	0.619	0.670	**0.504**	0.591	0.586
Question and Answer (5-shot)	0.582	0.622	**0.472**	0.544	0.546
Gemini-1.0-pro with System Instruction					
Question Only	0.688	0.735	**0.535**	0.650	0.652
Answer Only	0.619	0.661	**0.502**	0.576	0.590
Question and Answer	0.570	0.612	**0.460**	0.537	0.545

Table 12: Example of a hard version of MMLU-SR.

Input	Suppose 'Protein' means 'the name given to any laboratory technique that measures enzyme activity within a sample.' Protein can be used to identify carriers of: A. Suppose 'Oculocutaneous albini' means 'An inherited disorder that affects the lungs, digestive system, and other organs, characterized by the production of thick, sticky mucus.' Oculocutaneous albini. B. Suppose 'Tay-Sachs diseas' means 'A genetic condition causing intellectual disability, behavioral challenges, and certain physical characteristics, resulting from a mutation in the FMR1 gene.' Tay-Sachs diseas. C. Suppose 'Cystic fibrosi' means 'A group of inherited disorders characterized by a lack of melanin production in the skin, hair, and eyes, leading to light pigmentation.' Cystic fibrosi. D. Suppose 'Fragile X syndrom' means 'A rare genetic disorder that causes progressive destruction of nerve cells in the brain and spinal cord, leading to severe neurological symptoms.' Fragile X syndrom.
Output	The given problem seems to involve identifying which condition might be detected through a laboratory technique measuring enzyme activity. From the provided definitions, none of the conditions directly indicate an enzyme-related pathology except for a possible misalignment in the definitions and names: A: Oculocutaneous albini is defined incorrectly and does not relate to the production of enzymes. B: Tay-Sachs disease is a genetic disorder characterized by the destruction of nerve cells in the brain due to a deficiency of a specific enzyme (Hexosaminidase A). This is actually a plausible answer if we correct the name to Tay-Sachs disease, which fits the description of a disease involving enzyme activity. C: Cystic fibrosis and D: Fragile X syndrome are misdefined and do not relate to conditions involving measurable enzyme activity relevant to their actual conditions. Thus, the most likely answer, B. Tay-Sachs disease (with the corrected definition and name). ✗

Table 13: Complete performance of `gpt-3.5-turbo`, `gpt-4o-mini`, `gpt-4o`, `gemini-1.0-pro`, `gemini-1.5-pro`, `llama3-8b`, and `llama3-70b`.

Dataset	Humanities	Social Sciences	STEM	Other	Average
GPT-3.5-turbo					
MMLU (5-shot)	0.723	0.770	**0.554**	0.714	0.677
Question Only (5-shot)	0.661	0.702	**0.506**	0.641	0.616
Answer Only (5-shot)	0.540	0.595	**0.441**	0.538	0.520
Question and Answer (5-shot)	0.469	0.523	**0.396**	0.476	0.459
GPT-4o-mini					
MMLU (5-shot)	0.793	0.858	**0.689**	0.782	0.771
Question Only (5-shot)	0.744	0.792	**0.621**	0.724	0.710
Answer Only (5-shot)	0.659	0.738	**0.602**	0.651	0.655
Question and Answer (5-shot)	0.588	0.666	**0.531**	0.585	0.585
GPT-4o					
MMLU (5-shot)	0.880	0.906	**0.771**	0.854	0.845
Question Only (5-shot)	0.838	0.856	**0.702**	0.811	0.792
Answer Only (5-shot)	0.764	0.824	**0.705**	0.760	0.757
Question and Answer (5-shot)	0.708	0.754	**0.635**	0.712	0.695
Gemini-1.0-pro					
MMLU (5-shot)	0.728	0.758	**0.596**	0.703	0.686
Question Only (5-shot)	0.687	0.744	**0.539**	0.658	0.645
Answer Only (5-shot)	0.619	0.670	**0.504**	0.591	0.586
Question and Answer (5-shot)	0.582	0.622	**0.472**	0.544	0.546
Gemini-1.5-pro					
MMLU (5-shot)	0.849	0.881	**0.802**	0.815	0.832
Question Only (5-shot)	0.795	0.836	**0.700**	0.754	0.764
Answer Only (5-shot)	0.741	0.816	0.747	**0.739**	0.758
Question and Answer (5-shot)	0.690	0.752	**0.670**	0.681	0.694
Llama3-8B					
MMLU (5-shot)	0.593	0.757	**0.557**	0.729	0.651
Question Only (5-shot)	0.546	0.685	**0.507**	0.668	0.595
Answer Only (5-shot)	**0.455**	0.599	0.460	0.557	0.510
Question and Answer (5-shot)	**0.421**	0.538	0.424	0.499	0.465
Llama3-70B					
MMLU (5-shot)	**0.681**	0.868	0.697	0.814	0.765
Question Only (5-shot)	0.635	0.812	**0.631**	0.770	0.712
Answer Only (5-shot)	**0.539**	0.683	0.565	0.622	0.602
Question and Answer (5-shot)	**0.523**	0.653	0.536	0.591	0.576

Table 14: Complete relative percentage drop of accuracy in MMLU-SR compared to MMLU.

Dataset	Humanities	Social Sciences	STEM	Other	Average
		GPT-3.5-turbo			
Question Only (5-shot)	8.58%	8.83%	8.67%	**10.22%**	9.08%
Answer Only (5-shot)	**25.31%**	22.73%	20.40%	24.65%	23.27%
Question and Answer (5-shot)	**35.12%**	32.08%	28.52%	33.30%	32.26%
		GPT-4o-mini			
Question Only (5-shot)	6.18%	7.69%	**9.87%**	7.42%	7.91%
Answer Only (5-shot)	**16.90%**	13.99%	12.63%	16.75%	15.05%
Question and Answer (5-shot)	**25.85%**	22.38%	22.93%	25.19%	24.12%
		GPT-4o			
Question Only (5-shot)	4.77%	5.52%	**8.95%**	5.03%	6.27%
Answer Only (5-shot)	**13.18%**	9.05%	8.56%	11.01%	10.41%
Question and Answer (5-shot)	**19.55%**	16.78%	17.64%	16.63%	17.75%
		Gemini-1.0-pro			
Question Only (5-shot)	5.63%	1.85%	**9.56%**	6.40%	5.86%
Answer Only (5-shot)	14.96%	11.61%	15.44%	**15.91%**	14.48%
Question and Answer (5-shot)	20.05%	17.94%	20.81%	**22.60%**	20.85%
		Gemini-1.5-pro			
Question Only (5-shot)	6.36%	5.11%	**12.72%**	7.48%	8.17%
Answer Only (5-shot)	**12.72%**	7.38%	6.86%	9.33%	8.89%
Question and Answer (5-shot)	**18.73%**	14.64%	16.46%	16.44%	16.59%
		Llama3-8B			
Question Only (5-shot)	7.92%	**9.51%**	8.98%	8.36%	8.69%
Answer Only (5-shot)	23.27%	20.87%	17.41%	**23.56%**	21.28%
Question and Answer (5-shot)	28.16%	28.93%	23.88%	**31.56%**	28.63%
		Llama3-70B			
Question Only (5-shot)	6.75%	6.45%	**9.47%**	5.41%	6.93%
Answer Only (5-shot)	20.85%	21.31%	18.94%	**23.59%**	21.31%
Question and Answer (5-shot)	23.20%	24.77%	23.10%	**27.40%**	24.71%

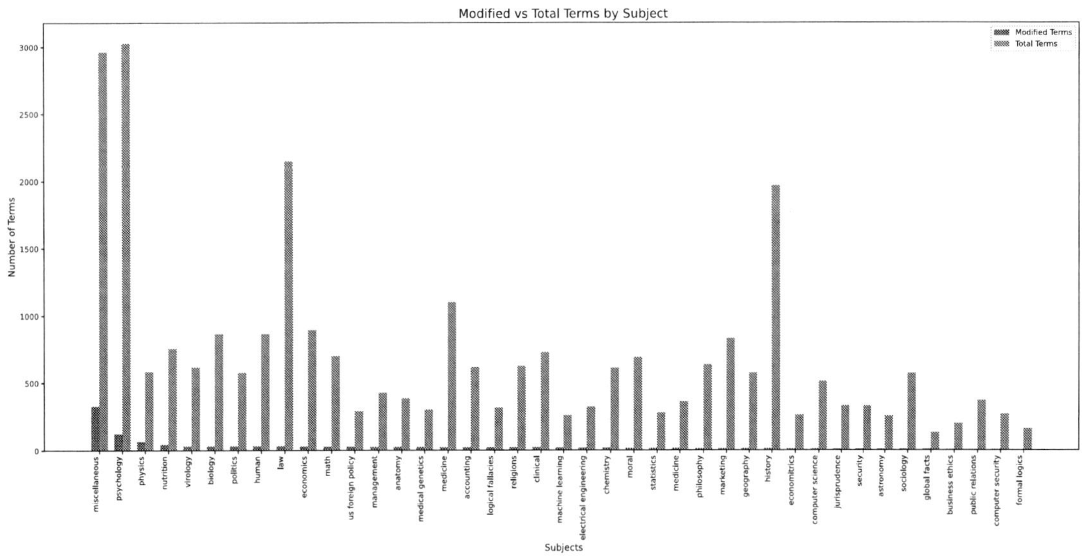

Figure 5: Comparison of total generated terms (red) and human-modified terms (blue) across 41 subject glossaries

MLissard: Multilingual Long and Simple Sequential Reasoning Benchmarks

Mirelle Bueno, Roberto Lotufo, Rodrigo Nogueira

School of Electrical and Computing Engineering,
State University of Campinas (UNICAMP),
m174909@dac.unicamp.br, {lotufo, rfn}@unicamp.br

Abstract

Language models are now capable of solving tasks that require dealing with long sequences consisting of hundreds of thousands of tokens. However, they often fail on tasks that require repetitive use of simple rules, even on sequences that are much shorter than those seen during training. For example, state-of-the-art LLMs can find common items in two lists with up to 20 items but fail when lists have 80 items. In this paper, we introduce MLissard, a multilingual benchmark designed to evaluate models' abilities to process and generate texts of varied lengths and offers a mechanism for controlling sequence complexity.

Our evaluation of open-source and proprietary models show a consistent decline in performance across all models and languages as the complexity of the sequence increases. Surprisingly, the use of in-context examples in languages other than English helps increase extrapolation performance significantly. The datasets and code are available at https://github.com/unicamp-dl/Lissard

1 Introduction

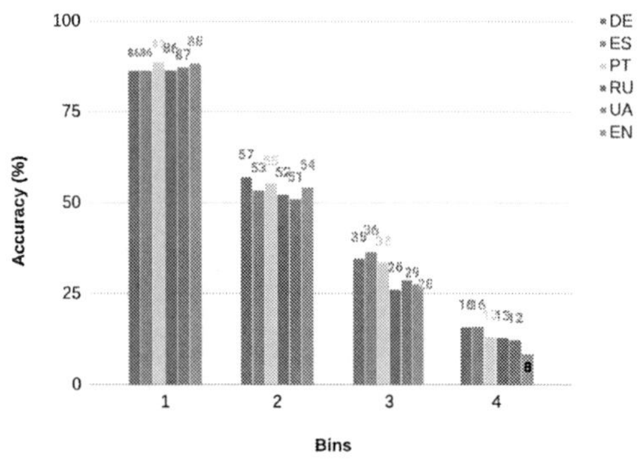

Figure 1: Performance of GPT-4 on the MLissard benchmark. See Table 2 for the definition of the bins.

The efficacy of language models, particularly in reasoning tasks, is significantly impacted by longer text lengths than those seen in training (Li et al., 2023b; Liu et al., 2024; Lake and Baroni, 2018). This phenomenon, referred to as "Length Generalization" or "Length Extrapolation" in the literature (Press et al., 2022; Zhao et al., 2023), is also common in models based on the Transformer architecture (Liška et al., 2018; Lewkowycz et al., 2022; Delétang et al., 2023; Zhou et al., 2023b). Notably, even Large Language Models (LLMs), known for their strong performance in a wide range of tasks and domains, are not immune to this problem (Anil et al., 2022; Chen et al., 2023).

Recent research tried to address this challenge by modifications to the positional embeddings (Press et al., 2022; Chi et al., 2022, 2023; Li et al., 2023b; Ke et al., 2021) or by using prompting strategies such as scratchpad (Nye et al., 2021) and chain-of-thought reasoning (Wei et al., 2022). Nevertheless, there remains a lack of datasets specifically designed for the systematic evaluation of the problem.

While benchmarks such as ZeroSCROLLS (Shaham et al., 2023) and InfiniteBench(Zhang et al., 2024) were designed to evaluate models in natural language tasks that involve long sequences, its effectiveness in monitoring model performance degradation within the context of length generalization may be limited by lack of explicit control of task complexity with respect to sequence length. For example, when using natural language texts there is no guarantee that answering a question about a longer text is harder than responding to one about a shorter text. This limitation highlights the need for benchmarks that can explicitly manipulate and test the impact of sequence length on model performance. In benchmarks pertaining to dialogues (Li et al., 2023a) and multi-document question answering (Liu et al., 2024), techniques like retrieval-augmented generation (RAG) are preva-

Proceedings of the 2nd GenBench Workshop on Generalisation (Benchmarking) in NLP, pages 86–95

lent, and therefore explicitly isolating the length extrapolation issue poses a challenge.

To address these aforementioned problems, we present MLissard, a multilingual benchmark that offer support for 6 languages (English, German, Portuguese, Russian, Spanish and Ukrainian) designed to evaluate the ability of models on tasks that require the use of repetitive simple rules, whose difficulty increases with respect to the sequence length. By incorporating varying degrees of difficulty within the same tasks, MLissard facilitates the identification of a models' breaking points. Given the syntactic nature of the datasets, researchers have the capability to generate new examples and increase the task difficulty, thus making it more challenging for newer and more capable models to be evaluated effectively. This flexibility also mitigates the contamination problem – where models may inadvertently be exposed to test datasets during their training (Ahuja et al., 2023; Li and Flanigan, 2024) – since synthetic datasets can be generated as needed, a advantage over traditional, manually curated datasets. At the time of this research, this is the first multilingual dataset designed to evaluate the quality of models in extrapolation via length.

Our analysis, which includes evaluations on proprietary models such as GPT-4 (OpenAI, 2023), as well as open-source ones like Llama-3 (Dubey et al., 2024), reveals a common trend among them. As illustrated in Figure 1, our findings underscore that irrespective of their architectures and parameter counts, all examined models demonstrate a performance degradation with increasing length, controlled by the number of key entities (see their definition in Table 2), required to solve the tasks. This indicates a common point of failure in generalization for LLMs, even for sequence lengths that are considerably shorter in terms of tokens than those seen during their pretraining or fine-tuning phases.

Our findings further demonstrated that the effect of extrapolation is not isolated; variables such as language and model size significantly influence the outcomes. For instance, despite English being a high-resource language, its performance was only average and was surpassed by other languages such as German. Moreover, ablation tests revealed improvements in extrapolation performance when in-context examples comprised a mixture of languages. This underscores the influence of language selection on the extrapolation capabilities of language models.

2 Related Work

The challenge of length extrapolation in the domain of natural language processing has been a persistent and long-standing issue. An array of studies has demonstrated that neural architectures encounter difficulties when confronted with sequences of longer than those they encountered during their training (Lake and Baroni, 2018; Liška et al., 2018; Keysers et al., 2019; Dubois et al., 2020; Nogueira et al., 2021; Welleck et al., 2022; Lewkowycz et al., 2022; Delétang et al., 2023; Zhou et al., 2023b). Despite efforts to expand the context window in LLMs, this issue persists, particularly when tackling tasks involving complex reasoning (Anil et al., 2022).

Recent endeavors have been undertaken to enhance the general performance of LLMs by employing prompt engineering techniques and by developing novel decoding methods aimed at expanding their capacity to extrapolate effectively over lengthy sequences of tokens. For instance, Nye et al. introduced the concept of a "scratchpad" that enables the model to generate draft responses in natural language before producing the final output. To assess the performance of this method, a range of tasks were employed, including math and coding tasks. Moreover, studies by Wei et al. and Zhou et al. demonstrated improvements by configuring the model to generate explanations for problem-solving and breaking down tasks into multiple interactive steps. These enhancements were particularly noticeable in tasks requiring the ability to extrapolate, such as SCAN (Lake and Baroni, 2018) (compositional generalization), and mathematical reasoning. Additionally, Bueno et al. showed that utilizing markups tokens as position representations help the model to generalize to longer sequences in tasks related to mathematical addition and compositional generalization. Han et al. devised a decoding method to improve generalization over extended sequences.

In addition to techniques for customizing prompts, recent research has explored modifying the position encoding function of the original transformer architecture to enhance its extrapolation capabilities (Press et al., 2022; Chi et al., 2022, 2023; Li et al., 2023b; Qin et al., 2023; Chen et al., 2023). For instance, Kazemnejad et al. conducted an evaluation of commonly used positional encoding methods, finding that omitting positional encoding altogether yielded superior results in downstream tasks.

The studies cited above illustrate multiple methods designed to address the challenge of extrapolation. Nevertheless, there is a notable gap in research concerning the development of diverse and standardized datasets specifically for assessing the generation and synthesis of extended text sequences by neural models. This gap is particularly notable given that many of the traditional datasets may already have been employed in the training of large language models.

3 Datasets Description

Our benchmark incorporates a combination of existing tasks, such as those from BIG-bench (bench authors, 2023), as well as newly developed ones. The criteria for selecting tasks were based on their ease of solution, the ability to expand new examples of varying lengths via scripting, and their effectiveness in exercising reasoning and memorization.

We intentionally excluded classical datasets (e.g., SCAN) from the analysis since their test sets are publicly available and many solutions have been extensively detailed in scientific literature, potentially making them familiar to large language models (LLMs).

In addition to English (EN), the language set includes German (DE), Spanish (ES), Portuguese (PT), Russian (RU), and Ukrainian (UA). We achieved this expansion by integrating automatic translation systems and using Python scripts to generate synthetic data.

The following sections describe the idea of key entities, tasks, and how evaluation was performed.

3.1 Key entities

The notion of key entities functions as an extrapolation factor within the context of a target task. For instance, in a task that seeks to identify common items between two lists, this extrapolation factor is defined by the number of items the model requires to analyze. Utilizing this factor allows for the augmentation of task complexity without modifying its properties. As a result, within specified ranges (bins), we can identify the model's breakpoints.

The choice of bins for each task was designed to reflect different difficulty levels: short, intermediate, long, and super long, for example, Bin 1 consists of sequences of shorter length, while Bin 4 comprises sequences of longer length. Table 2 describes the key entities and the respective lengths in each bin. The values defining the intervals of each bin vary for each task and were empirically determined, inspired by BIG-bench tasks.

3.2 Tasks

In total, four tasks were developed, and Table 1 provides a summary of each one with input and output examples. Due to the high costs of paid APIs, we restricted our tests to 300 examples per task and language. To ensure balanced evaluations across different length partitions, we randomly selected 75 examples for each bin.

3.2.1 Object Counting

The main goal of this task is to assess the proficiency in object counting within sequences, as shown in Table 1. The input to the model is a sequence comprising a list of objects paired with their respective quantities and the expected output is a string with the total count of objects. Diverging from the original BIG-bench task that exclusively encompasses the enumeration of objects from predetermined categories like fruits, vegetables, or musical instruments, our method comprises object counting across different categories.

Automatic translation systems were used to generate the multilingual set, in this case, Google Translate. After this phase, a translation subset was selected for human analysis of the general quality of the translation.

3.2.2 List Intersection

The objective of this task is to find common items in two lists. Items within the lists are composed of words from a designated target language, with both the words and their frequencies sourced from the FrequencyWords[1] repository. For each specific language, stop words and special characters were eliminated. Following this preprocessing phase, a random sampling of words was conducted.

The lists have equal sizes, but the number of overlapping items varies. The target output is the words in common, sorted alphabetically. If there are no items in common, "None" must be returned.

3.2.3 Last Letter Concatenation

The Last Letter Concatenation task, as formulated in the Chain-of-Thought work (Wei et al., 2022), involves concatenating the last letter of each word

[1] https://github.com/hermitdave/FrequencyWords/

Task	Input Example	Output
Last Letter Concatenation	Abil Gaby	l y
Repeat Copy Logic	Repeat 2 times school	school school
Object Counting	I have a chair, and an apple.	2
List Intersection	A: abil,matt / B: matt, gaby	matt

Table 1: Task Summary in the MLissard Benchmark.

Task	Key Entity	Bin 1	Bin 2	Bin 3	Bin 4
LLC	Names	1-8	8-15	15-22	22-30
RCL	Total Repetitions	1-9	9-17	17-25	25-33
OC	Objects	1-7	7-12	12-17	17-23
LI	Items: lists A and B	1-46	46-91	91-136	136-181

Table 2: Key task entities: Last Letter Concatenation (LLC), Repeat Copy Logic (RCL), Object Counting (OC), and List Intersection (LI) and their respective ranges in each bin in Figure 1.

within an input sequence comprised of random names. Table 1 provides an illustrative instance of the dataset, where the input sequence comprises randomly selected names obtained through the target language Name Census[2].

In constructing our dataset, we applied a comparable methodology; however, we sampled the most common names from each target language and expanded the sample length to encompass sequences with an increase of up to thirty names.

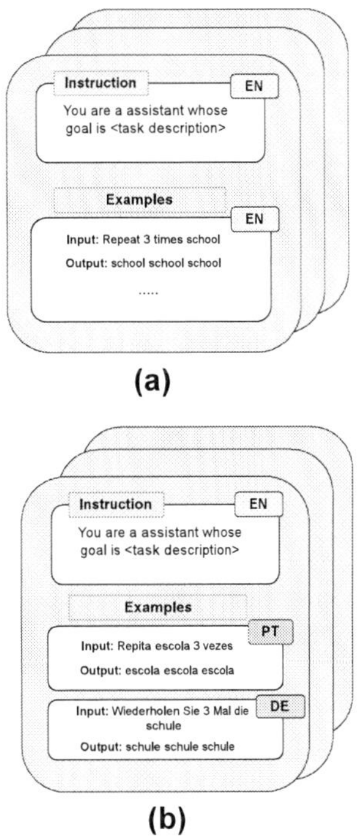

Figure 2: Template for evaluation. Being (a) Instruction and examples of tasks in the target language; (b) Instruction in the target language and multilingual examples.

3.2.4 Repeat Copy Logic

The task proposed by the BIG-bench evaluates language models' ability to comprehend and execute instructions involving repetitions, text-to-copy, basic logic, and conditionals, focusing on their extrapolation capabilities.

Our methodology for creating the dataset includes: i) Collecting responses to all input sequences from the BIG-bench repository[3]; ii) Filtering responses to retain only those correctly an-

[2]Portuguese (PT) - https://censo2010.ibge.gov.br/nomes/#/ranking
Spanish (ES) - https://www.epdata.es/datos/nombres-apellidos-mas-frecuentes-espana-ine/373
English (EN) - https://www.ssa.gov/cgi-bin/popularnames.cgi
German (DE) - http://www.firstnamesgermany.com/
Ukrainian (UA) - https://census.name/ukrainian-name-database/
Russsian (RU) - https://census.name/russian-name-database/

[3]https://github.com/google/BIG-bench/tree/main/bigbench/benchmark_tasks/repeat_copy_logic

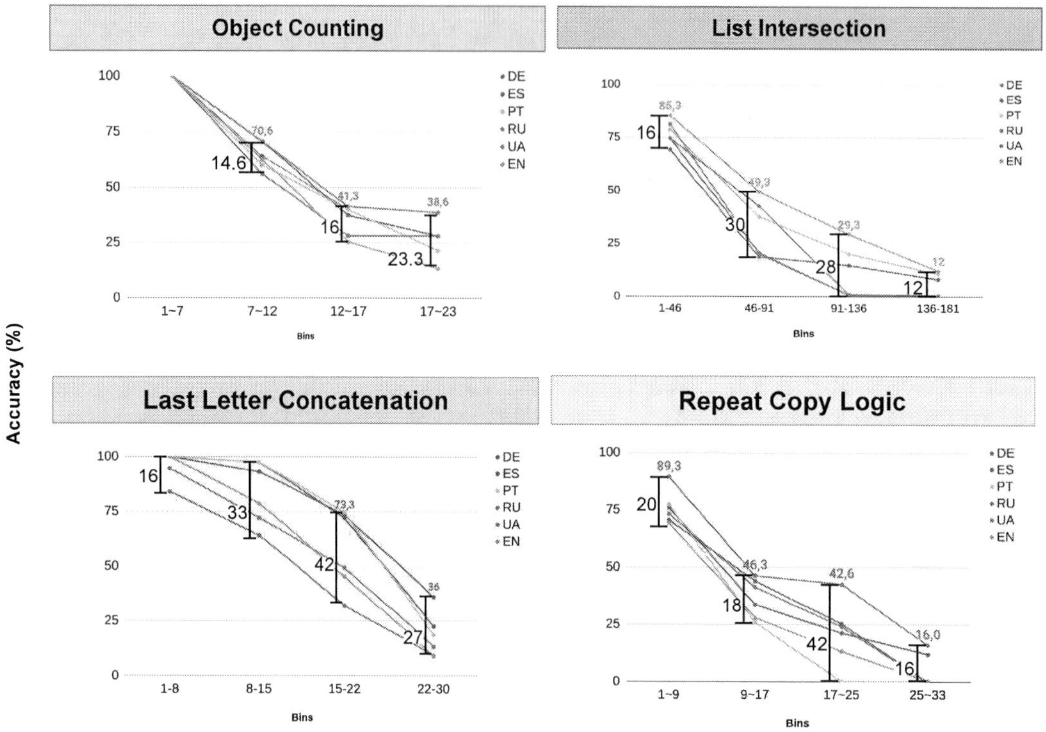

Figure 3: GPT-4 performance in the MLissard.

swered by GPT-4, which correctly answered 17 out of 32 original questions. We adopted this method to scale only the repetition factor; iii) Translating instructions using Google Translate and review the subset for accuracy; iv) Generate extrapolations on selected instructions, varying the repetition factor from 1 to 33 (see Table 1).

We randomly selected 15 of the 17 correctly answered questions for this phase.

4 Baseline Methods

The evaluation of each task involved analyzing responses from GPT-4 (gpt4-0613) and Llama-3 (Llama-3.1-405B-Instruct and Llama-3-instruction-70B) using greedy decoding. We observed no repetition issues. Each task was preceded by a predefined instruction (description of the task) with in-context examples: four for "Object Counting," "Find Intersection," and "Last Letter Concat," and one for "Repeat Copy Logic" because inputs already provided sufficient information to perform the task. Both the instructions and examples were in the target language of the evaluation. For instance, English tasks used English instructions and examples (see Figure 2 (a)). For the in-context examples used during model evaluation, we selected samples contained in the first bin, as these contain the smallest lengths.

We utilized the exact match as the primary metric. This methodology is further modified in section 5.2, where we discuss the impact of cross-language inputs on model performance.

5 Results

Figure 3 presents the results obtained via GPT-4 in the target tasks and languages. Overall, there is a gradual decline in the performance of language models across tasks as complexity increases, as measured by the number of key entities in the input sequence. For instance, in the "Object Counting" task, when presented with inputs containing 1 to 7 objects, the model achieve approximately 100% accuracy. However, their accuracy drops below 50% when confronted with sequences with 12 to 17 objects. This behavior is reflected in the target languages as well, all of which present a loss of more than 50% when dealing with more complex input sequences.

We also observed considerable variability in performance between languages depending on the spe-

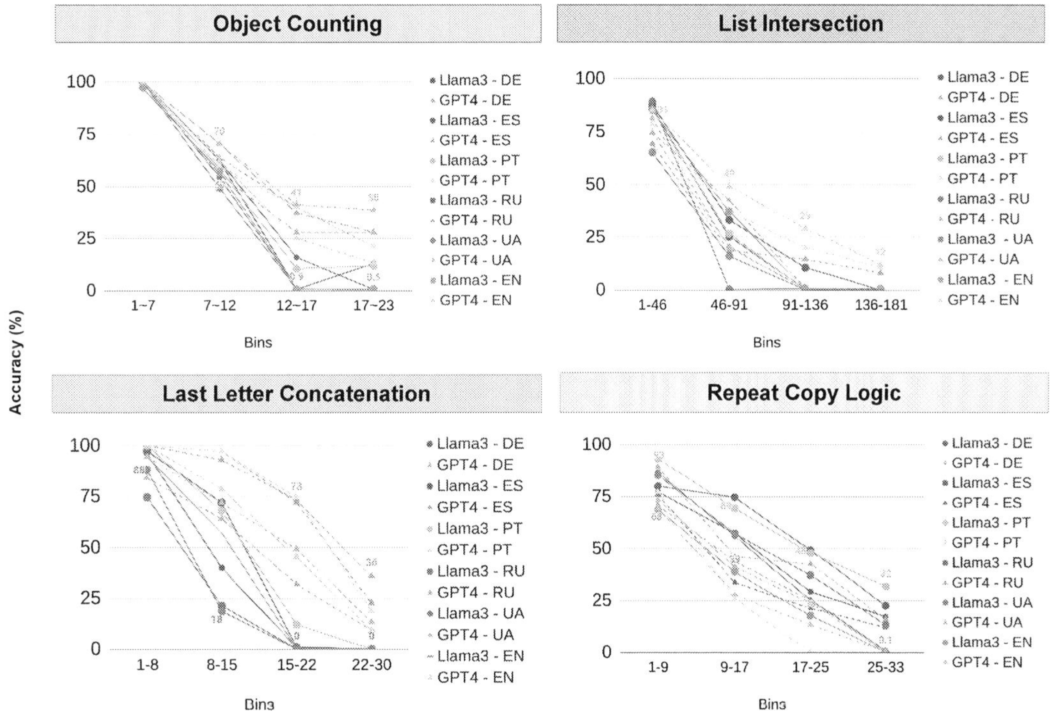

Figure 4: Comparison of Llama-3.1-405B vs. GPT-4 performance in the MLissard Benchmark

cific task. For instance, differences ranging from 2.4 to 42 points are observed in the intermediate bins for tasks such as "Last Letter Concatenation" and "Repeat Copy Logic". These variations are intriguing as there doesn't appear to be a general language preference. For example, in the "Last Letter Concatenation" task, German, Portuguese, and Spanish outperform Russian by a margin of 42.6 points in the 15-22 bin. Conversely, in the "Repeat Copy Logic" task, Russian outperforms Portuguese by 42.5 points.

Contrary to the general trend observed in studies of multilingual models, English did not exhibit exceptional performance when compared to other languages. Except for the "List Intersection" task, English consistently remained at an average or lower accuracy level across bins.

Generalization performance also varies between tasks; as demonstrated in Table 3, GPT-4 has greater difficulty executing the "List Intersection" and "Repeat Copy Logic" tasks. In the "List Intersection" task, the model achieves less than 10% accuracy in bins 3 and 4. In the "Repeat Copy Logic" task, accuracy drops to below 25% in the same bins. Both tasks require extensive memorization and state tracking. We hypothesize that these challenges, along with the increased sentence length, have influenced the observed performance outcomes.

Regarding the performance of open-source models in the MLissard benchmark, Figure 4 illustrates that both models performed similarly in bin 1, with accuracy points ranging between 70 and 100. However, as task complexity increased from bin 2 onwards, differences in performance stood out. Except for the "Repeat Copy Logic" task, GPT-4 outperformed Llama-3.1-405B by 5 to 60 accuracy points (see Table 3).

On the other hand, in the "Repeat Copy Logic" task, there is a reverse comparison, where Llama-3.1-405B outperforms GPT-4 in all bins, with the difference ranging from 9 points to 16 points of accuracy.

In relation to language preference behavior, both the Llama-3.1-405B and GPT-4 models exhibit similar task-dependent variations. Llama-3.1-405B demonstrates more consistent performance across Portuguese, German, and English.

5.1 Impact of model size

The Llama-3.1-405B model achieved state-of-the-art results in general NLP task benchmarks com-

Task	Bin 1		Bin 2		Bin 3		Bin 4	
	Llama	GPT-4	Llama	GPT-4	Llama	GPT-4	Llama	GPT-4
OC	100	100	58	**63**	0.8	**38**	0.7	**24.6**
LI	**86**	76	26	**29**	0.6	**7.7**	0.1	**4**
LLC	95	**100**	48.6	**85.8**	0.4	**60**	0	**16**
RCL	**82**	73.3	**57**	41.3	**33**	24	**15**	0.4
AVG	90.7	87	47.4	54.7	8.7	32.4	3.9	11.7

Table 3: Average accuracy of all languages per bin on tasks Object Counting (OC), List Intersection (LI), Last Letter Concatenation (LLC), and Repeat Copy Logic (RCL). Comparative result between the Llama-3.1-405B and GPT-4 models, highlighting in bold the best system performance in each bin.

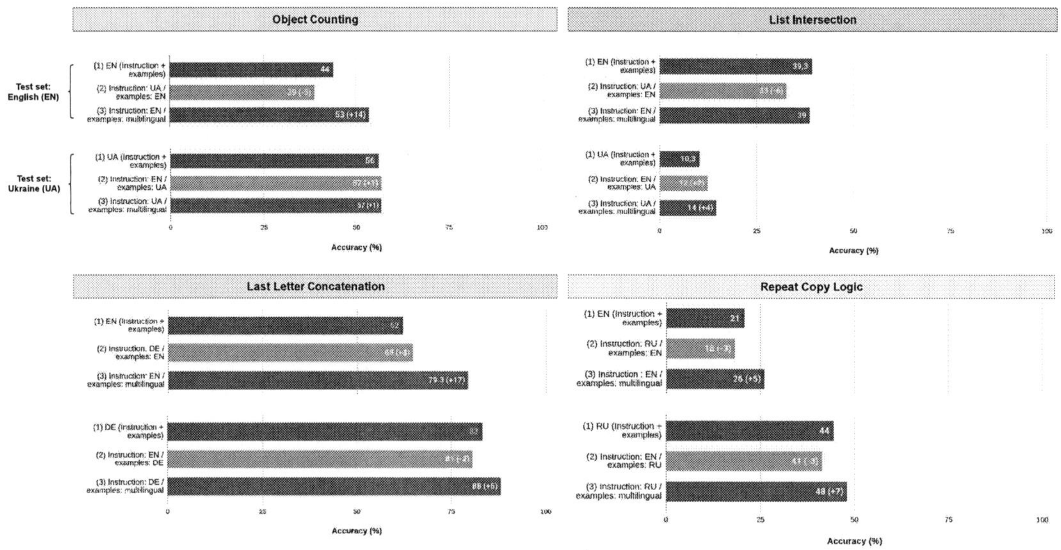

Figure 5: Average accuracy considering all bins. Since (1) Baseline - Both the instruction and the examples derive from the same target language; (2) instruction in the language that performed better or worse and a examples in the target language; (3) Instruction in target language and multilingual examples.

pared to the Llama-3-70B model. We investigated whether this performance trend is also evident in the MLissard benchmarks, especially in relation to the complexity indicated by the bins.

Table 4 compares the average performance of each bin (for all MLissard tasks) using the Llama-3.1-405B and Llama-3-70B models. As expected, Llama-3.1-405B significantly outperforms Llama-3-70B across all languages and complexity bins. The largest differences between the models occur in bins 1 and 2, with performance gaps ranging from 16 to 43 points. In contrast, for bins 3 and 4, which involve more complex tasks, the performance improvement is less pronounced, with variations ranging from 0.3 to 11 points. This suggests that Llama-3.1-405B, like the 70B version, also struggles with long sequences.

5.2 Can cross language improve extrapolation performance?

We aim to examine the impact on extrapolation performance by focusing on two components: 1) providing instructions in a different language than the target language, and 2) using mixed-language few-shot examples (see Figure 2 - (b)). For in-context examples, we used Portuguese, German, Ukrainian, and English. For the "Repeat Copy Logic" task, we provided two contextualized examples (English and Ukrainian), while for the other tasks, we provided four examples.

We conducted ablation tests on all tasks in the MLissard dataset using the GPT-4 model. For com-

Lang	Bin 1		Bin 2		Bin 3		Bin 4	
	70B	**405B**	**70B**	**405B**	**70B**	**405B**	**70B**	**405B**
EN	70.6	90	18.6	48	0.1	0.7	0	0.1
PT	79.3	96.6	24	63.3	0.1	11.3	0	6
ES	74	92.6	16.6	60	0.1	5.7	0	6.5
DE	74.6	91.3	16.8	51.3	0.5	8.3	0	0.3
RU	60.6	88	12.2	38	0	0.8	0	0.6
UA	55.3	86.6	10.7	33.9	0.1	0.5	0	0.4

Table 4: Average accuracy across all MLissard tasks was compared between the Llama-3-70B and Llama-3.1-405B models.

parative purposes, we focused on the languages that achieved the highest and lowest performance in each task. We then compared these results with the baseline (both instructions and examples in the same language).

Figure 5 presents the experimental results for each task. As shown in the results, when we gave prompts in a language different from the test set, accuracy declined by an average of 2.3 percentage points. However, when we kept instructions in the test target language but included paraphrased examples contextualized in multiple languages, performance improved by an average of 6.25 percentage points. This improvement ranged from 2 points in the "List Intersection" task to 17 points in the "Last Letter Concatenation" task and remained consistent across all evaluated languages. These findings indicate that contextual examples in multiple languages can improve the quality of extrapolation.

6 Conclusion

We presented a multilingual benchmark to evaluate the ability of language models to deal with long texts across languages. Our approach distinguishes itself from existing benchmarks through the introduction of a control mechanism, which we refer to as "key entities." This mechanism enables us to systematically increase task complexity in tandem with sequence length. Furthermore, the ability to solve these tasks is predicated on the repeated application of simple rules, providing more control and enabling a detailed analysis of model performance in relation to the frequency of rule application. This contrasts with benchmarks that rely on lengthy natural language texts, where the relationship between text length and task difficulty may become obscured. Despite the apparent simplicity of these tasks, they reveal significant limitations in state-of-the-art LLMs concerning the processing and generation of text as lengths increase. Our findings indicate that language and model size significantly affect extrapolation results. Moreover, including in-context examples in multiple languages improves MLissard's generalization performance.

7 Limitations

Our evaluations were conducted on a set of six languages, therefore, the findings of this work may not necessarily extend to other languages, particularly low-resource ones. Additionally, we solely employed a standard prompt style for our evaluations, and the performance with more sophisticated techniques, such as chain-of-thought (CoT) prompting, remains to be investigated. Finally, given the limitation of our study to two models (GPT-4 and Llama-3), the results may not generalize to other LLMs.

References

Kabir Ahuja, Harshita Diddee, Rishav Hada, Millicent Ochieng, Krithika Ramesh, Prachi Jain, Akshay Nambi, Tanuja Ganu, Sameer Segal, Maxamed Axmed, Kalika Bali, and Sunayana Sitaram. 2023. Mega: Multilingual evaluation of generative ai. *Preprint*, arXiv:2303.12528.

Cem Anil, Yuhuai Wu, Anders Andreassen, Aitor Lewkowycz, Vedant Misra, Vinay Ramasesh, Ambrose Slone, Guy Gur-Ari, Ethan Dyer, and Behnam Neyshabur. 2022. Exploring length generalization in large language models. In *Advances in Neural Information Processing Systems*, volume 35, pages 38546–38556. Curran Associates, Inc.

BIG bench authors. 2023. Beyond the imitation game: Quantifying and extrapolating the capabilities of language models. *Transactions on Machine Learning Research*.

Mirelle Candida Bueno, Carlos Gemmell, Jeff Dalton, Roberto Lotufo, and Rodrigo Nogueira. 2022. Induced natural language rationales and interleaved markup tokens enable extrapolation in large language models. In *Proceedings of the 1st Workshop on Mathematical Natural Language Processing (MathNLP)*, pages 17–24, Abu Dhabi, United Arab Emirates (Hybrid). Association for Computational Linguistics.

Shouyuan Chen, Sherman Wong, Liangjian Chen, and Yuandong Tian. 2023. Extending context window of large language models via positional interpolation. *Preprint*, arXiv:2306.15595.

Ta-Chung Chi, Ting-Han Fan, Peter J Ramadge, and Alexander Rudnicky. 2022. Kerple: Kernelized relative positional embedding for length extrapolation. In *Advances in Neural Information Processing Systems*, volume 35, pages 8386–8399. Curran Associates, Inc.

Ta-Chung Chi, Ting-Han Fan, Alexander Rudnicky, and Peter Ramadge. 2023. Dissecting transformer length extrapolation via the lens of receptive field analysis. In *Proceedings of the 61st Annual Meeting of the Association for Computational Linguistics (Volume 1: Long Papers)*, pages 13522–13537, Toronto, Canada. Association for Computational Linguistics.

Grégoire Delétang, Anian Ruoss, Jordi Grau-Moya, Tim Genewein, Li Kevin Wenliang, Elliot Catt, Chris Cundy, Marcus Hutter, Shane Legg, Joel Veness, and Pedro A. Ortega. 2023. Neural networks and the chomsky hierarchy. *Preprint*, arXiv:2207.02098.

Abhimanyu Dubey, Abhinav Jauhri, Abhinav Pandey, Abhishek Kadian, Ahmad Al-Dahle, Aiesha Letman, Akhil Mathur, Alan Schelten, Amy Yang, Angela Fan, et al. 2024. The llama 3 herd of models. *Preprint*, arXiv:2407.21783.

Yann Dubois, Gautier Dagan, Dieuwke Hupkes, and Elia Bruni. 2020. Location Attention for Extrapolation to Longer Sequences. In *Proceedings of the 58th Annual Meeting of the Association for Computational Linguistics*, pages 403–413, Online. Association for Computational Linguistics.

Chi Han, Qifan Wang, Hao Peng, Wenhan Xiong, Yu Chen, Heng Ji, and Sinong Wang. 2024. LM-infinite: Zero-shot extreme length generalization for large language models. In *Proceedings of the 2024 Conference of the North American Chapter of the Association for Computational Linguistics: Human Language Technologies (Volume 1: Long Papers)*, pages 3991–4008, Mexico City, Mexico. Association for Computational Linguistics.

Amirhossein Kazemnejad, Inkit Padhi, Karthikeyan Natesan Ramamurthy, Payel Das, and Siva Reddy. 2023. The impact of positional encoding on length generalization in transformers. In *Advances in Neural Information Processing Systems*, volume 36, pages 24892–24928. Curran Associates, Inc.

Guolin Ke, Di He, and Tie-Yan Liu. 2021. Rethinking positional encoding in language pre-training. In *International Conference on Learning Representations*.

Daniel Keysers, Nathanael Schärli, Nathan Scales, Hylke Buisman, Daniel Furrer, Sergii Kashubin, Nikola Momchev, Danila Sinopalnikov, Lukasz Stafiniak, Tibor Tihon, et al. 2019. Measuring compositional generalization: A comprehensive method on realistic data. In *International Conference on Learning Representations*.

Brenden Lake and Marco Baroni. 2018. Generalization without systematicity: On the compositional skills of sequence-to-sequence recurrent networks. In *International conference on machine learning*, pages 2873–2882. PMLR.

Aitor Lewkowycz, Anders Andreassen, David Dohan, Ethan Dyer, Henryk Michalewski, Vinay Ramasesh, Ambrose Slone, Cem Anil, Imanol Schlag, Theo Gutman-Solo, Yuhuai Wu, Behnam Neyshabur, Guy Gur-Ari, and Vedant Misra. 2022. Solving quantitative reasoning problems with language models. In *Advances in Neural Information Processing Systems*, volume 35, pages 3843–3857. Curran Associates, Inc.

Changmao Li and Jeffrey Flanigan. 2024. Task contamination: Language models may not be few-shot anymore. *Proceedings of the AAAI Conference on Artificial Intelligence*, 38(16):18471–18480.

Dacheng Li, Rulin Shao, Anze Xie, Ying Sheng, Lianmin Zheng, Joseph E. Gonzalez, Ion Stoica, Xuezhe Ma, and Hao Zhang. 2023a. How long can open-source llms truly promise on context length?

Shanda Li, Chong You, Guru Guruganesh, Joshua Ainslie, Santiago Ontanon, Manzil Zaheer, Sumit Sanghai, Yiming Yang, Sanjiv Kumar, and Srinadh Bhojanapalli. 2023b. Functional interpolation for relative positions improves long context transformers. *Preprint*, arXiv:2310.04418.

Adam Liška, Germán Kruszewski, and Marco Baroni. 2018. Memorize or generalize? searching for a compositional rnn in a haystack. *arXiv preprint arXiv:1802.06467*.

Nelson F. Liu, Kevin Lin, John Hewitt, Ashwin Paranjape, Michele Bevilacqua, Fabio Petroni, and Percy Liang. 2024. Lost in the middle: How language models use long contexts. *Transactions of the Association for Computational Linguistics*, 12:157–173.

Rodrigo Nogueira, Zhiying Jiang, and Jimmy Lin. 2021. Investigating the limitations of transformers with simple arithmetic tasks. *arXiv preprint arXiv:2102.13019*.

Maxwell Nye, Anders Johan Andreassen, Guy Gur-Ari, Henryk Michalewski, Jacob Austin, David Bieber, David Dohan, Aitor Lewkowycz, Maarten Bosma, David Luan, Charles Sutton, and Augustus Odena.

2021. Show your work: Scratchpads for intermediate computation with language models. *Preprint*, arXiv:2112.00114.

OpenAI. 2023. Gpt-4 technical report. *Preprint*, arXiv:2303.08774.

Ofir Press, Noah Smith, and Mike Lewis. 2022. Train short, test long: Attention with linear biases enables input length extrapolation. In *International Conference on Learning Representations*.

Zhen Qin, Yiran Zhong, and Hui Deng. 2023. Exploring transformer extrapolation. *Preprint*, arXiv:2307.10156.

Uri Shaham, Maor Ivgi, Avia Efrat, Jonathan Berant, and Omer Levy. 2023. ZeroSCROLLS: A zero-shot benchmark for long text understanding. In *Findings of the Association for Computational Linguistics: EMNLP 2023*, pages 7977–7989, Singapore. Association for Computational Linguistics.

Jason Wei, Xuezhi Wang, Dale Schuurmans, Maarten Bosma, brian ichter, Fei Xia, Ed Chi, Quoc V Le, and Denny Zhou. 2022. Chain-of-thought prompting elicits reasoning in large language models. In *Advances in Neural Information Processing Systems*, volume 35, pages 24824–24837. Curran Associates, Inc.

Sean Welleck, Peter West, Jize Cao, and Yejin Choi. 2022. Symbolic brittleness in sequence models: on systematic generalization in symbolic mathematics. In *AAAI*.

Xinrong Zhang, Yingfa Chen, Shengding Hu, Zihang Xu, Junhao Chen, Moo Khai Hao, Xu Han, Zhen Leng Thai, Shuo Wang, Zhiyuan Liu, and Maosong Sun. 2024. ∞bench: Extending long context evaluation beyond 100k tokens. *Preprint*, arXiv:2402.13718.

Liang Zhao, Xiaocheng Feng, Xiachong Feng, Bin Qin, and Ting Liu. 2023. Length extrapolation of transformers: A survey from the perspective of position encoding. *Preprint*, arXiv:2312.17044.

Denny Zhou, Nathanael Schärli, Le Hou, Jason Wei, Nathan Scales, Xuezhi Wang, Dale Schuurmans, Claire Cui, Olivier Bousquet, Quoc Le, and Ed Chi. 2023a. Least-to-most prompting enables complex reasoning in large language models. *Preprint*, arXiv:2205.10625.

Hattie Zhou, Arwen Bradley, Etai Littwin, Noam Razin, Omid Saremi, Josh Susskind, Samy Bengio, and Preetum Nakkiran. 2023b. What algorithms can transformers learn? a study in length generalization. In *ICLR, NeurIPS Workshop*.

MultiPragEval: Multilingual Pragmatic Evaluation of Large Language Models

Dojun Park[1*] **Jiwoo Lee**[1*] **Hyeyun Jeong**[1] **Seohyun Park**[1]
Youngeun Koo[2] **Soonha Hwang**[3] **Seonwoo Park**[1] **Sungeun Lee**[1]
[1]Seoul National University, [2]Sungkyunkwan University, [3]Yonsei University
{dojun.parkk, seohyun.parkk88}@gmail.com
{lee9055, tosirihy, su3503, cristlo5}@snu.ac.kr
sarah8835@skku.edu, soonha.hwang@yonsei.ac.kr

Abstract

As the capabilities of Large Language Models (LLMs) expand, it becomes increasingly important to evaluate them beyond basic knowledge assessment, focusing on higher-level language understanding. This study introduces MultiPragEval, the first multilingual pragmatic evaluation of LLMs, designed for English, German, Korean, and Chinese. Comprising 1200 question units categorized according to Grice's Cooperative Principle and its four conversational maxims, MultiPragEval enables an in-depth assessment of LLMs' contextual awareness and their ability to infer implied meanings. Our findings demonstrate that Claude3-Opus significantly outperforms other models in all tested languages, establishing a state-of-the-art in the field. Among open-source models, Solar-10.7B and Qwen1.5-14B emerge as strong competitors. By analyzing pragmatic inference, we provide valuable insights into the capabilities essential for advanced language comprehension in AI systems. The test suite is publicly available on our GitHub repository at `https://github.com/DojunPark/MultiPragEval`.

1 Introduction

Understanding a language involves not only the ability to process explicit information but also an awareness of the context that influences the meaning of each utterance (Sperber and Wilson, 1986). In human communication, context acts as a critical element as it provides a foundation upon which dialogue participants can understand and interact with each other more efficiently. With a shared context, communication becomes more facilitated, allowing subtle nuances to be successfully conveyed, which is essential for engaging in meaningful conversations (Krauss and Fussell, 1996).

With recent advancements in generative AI, current LLMs have demonstrated capabilities that extend far beyond traditional natural language processing (NLP) tasks (Brown et al., 2020; Achiam et al., 2023). These models are increasingly becoming integral to our daily lives as AI assistants, closely engaging with human users in diverse conversational setups that demand a rapid understanding of the users' needs and intentions, far surpassing mere literal interpretation of text (Roller et al., 2021). Given the growing importance of LLMs, accurately evaluating their ability to comprehend context-dependent meanings and demonstrate human-like language comprehension has become crucial (McCoy et al., 2019; Xu et al., 2020).

Aspect	Details
Utterance	*"There's the door."*
Literal Meaning	A door is located over there.
Contextual Implication	***Context:*** An interviewer says it to the interviewee after finishing an interview. ***Implied Meaning:*** The interview has concluded and the interviewee is free to leave the room.

Table 1: Literal and contextual implications of the utterance *"There's the door"* in an interview scenario.

Pragmatics is a branch of linguistics that studies how language is used to achieve specific goals, where the interpretation of utterances depends not only on their literal meaning but also, crucially, on the surrounding context (Grice, 1975). Consider the example in Table 1, which demonstrates both the literal and implied meanings of the utterance, *"There's the door."* Literally, this phrase simply indicates the presence of a door in the specified direction. However, from a pragmatic standpoint, it conveys an additional implied meaning in the context of its usage by an interviewer to an interviewee after an interview has concluded. In this

*These authors contributed equally to this work.

Proceedings of the 2nd GenBench Workshop on Generalisation (Benchmarking) in NLP, pages 96–119
November 16, 2024 ©2024 Association for Computational Linguistics

scenario, the speaker is subtly suggesting that the interviewee is free to leave the room. This example underscores the critical role that context plays in shaping the interpretation of human language.

Despite the clear need for studies analyzing the pragmatic competence of current LLMs, there is not only a lack of systematic evaluation across various models (Chang et al., 2024) but also a strong bias towards English (Guo et al., 2023; Bommasani et al., 2023), leaving the pragmatic abilities of LLMs in other languages largely unexplored and difficult to compare. Such oversight demonstrates a significant gap in current evaluation practices, particularly given the multilingual nature of today's state-of-the-art LLMs (Kwon et al., 2023).

To address these challenges, our study introduces **MultiPragEval**, the first multilingual test suite designed for the pragmatic evaluation of LLMs in English, German, Korean, and Chinese. Our suite comprises 300 question units per language, totaling 1200 units. These questions are divided into five categories based on Grice's Cooperative Principles and the corresponding four conversational maxims: quantity, quality, relation, manner, and an additional category dedicated to assessing mere literal meaning understanding, independent of context.

Our main contributions are as follows:

- **Development of MultiPragEval**: We introduce MultiPragEval, a comprehensive test suite specifically designed to evaluate the pragmatic abilities of LLMs across English, German, Korean, and Chinese.
- **Systematic Evaluation of LLMs**: We conduct a thorough evaluation of 15 state-of-the-art LLMs, including both proprietary and open-source models, assessing their contextual awareness and pragmatic understanding capabilities.
- **In-depth Performance Analysis**: We offer a detailed analysis of LLM performance, systematically categorized according to Grice's Cooperative Principle and its maxims, highlighting critical patterns and implications for further enhancements in LLM capabilities.

2 Related Work

Current Practices in LLM Evaluation. Benchmarks serve as critical tools for standardized evaluation in the field of LLM studies, enabling fair and systematic comparisons across models trained with diverse architectures and strategies (Guo et al., 2023). These benchmarks span a wide range of domains, from general reasoning (Zellers et al., 2019) to specialized fields such as mathematics (Cobbe et al., 2021), coding (Chen et al., 2021), and biomedical sciences (Jin et al., 2019). While comprehensive, they primarily focus on assessing knowledge and logical reasoning, emphasizing explicit semantic meanings over the contextual and implied meanings that can vary in different scenarios (Sileo et al., 2022).

Leaderboards further enhance the field of LLM evaluation by providing a transparent platform where the performance of various models can directly compete with each other. The Open LLM Leaderboard (Beeching et al., 2023), featuring a range of rigorous benchmarks, establishes a venue for open-source models to showcase their capabilities, thereby fostering engagement in LLM development among both individual developers and tech companies. Meanwhile, Chatbot Arena (Chiang et al., 2024) is gaining recognition as a crowdsourced evaluation platform. It leverages real-time feedback from users who vote on outputs from two randomly selected models. Models are then ranked on the leaderboard based on their Elo rating (Elo and Sloan, 1978), thus filling the gaps left by automatic benchmarks.

Recently, efforts have been made to create benchmarks specifically targeted at measuring the capabilities of LLMs in languages such as Chinese (Li et al., 2023) and Korean (Son et al., 2024). This development contributes to advancing a more inclusive multilingual evaluation landscape.

Pragmatic Evaluation of LLMs. As LLMs continue to evolve, it has become crucial to evaluate how effectively they consider context, which crucially shapes meanings beyond their literal interpretations. Bojic et al. (2023) examined multiple LLMs under the framework of Grice's Cooperative Principle and its conversational maxims to assess their capabilities in understanding implicature. The results demonstrated that GPT-4 (Achiam et al., 2023) outperformed other models, including human performance. However, the human participants were not native English speakers but educated individuals from Serbia, which potentially limits the impact of the findings.

di San Pietro et al. (2023) conducted a comparable study focusing on GPT-3.5, leveraging the

Language	Context	Utterance	MCQ
English	While visiting Charlie's house, Emily saw a large pile of oranges in the kitchen and asked why there were so many. Charlie responded:	"My uncle lives in Florida."	Choose the most appropriate meaning of the above utterance from the following options. **(A)** Charlie's uncle sent the oranges. (B) Charlie's uncle resides in Florida. (C) People in Florida do not like oranges. (D) Charlie's uncle lives in a rural house. (E) None of the above.
German	Anna, die Felix besuchte, sah, dass es bei Felix viel Wein gab, und als sie fragte, warum es so viel Wein gab, wie er zu so viel Wein komme, sagte Felix:	"Mein Onkel betreibt ein Weingut in Freiburg."	Wählen Sie die passendste Bedeutung der obigen Äußerung aus den folgenden Aussagen aus. **(A)** Felix hat den Wein von seinem Onkel. (B) Der Onkel von Felix lebt in Freiburg. (C) Freiburger lieben keinen Wein. (D) Der Onkel von Felix wohnt in einem Landhaus. (E) Keine der obigen Aussagen ist richtig.
Korean	철수 집에 놀러 간 영희는 주방에 많은 귤이 쌓여 있는 것을 보고 귤이 왜 이렇게 많은지 물었고 철수는 다음과 같이 말했다.	"우리 작은 아버지께서 제주도에 사셔."	다음 보기에서 위 발화가 갖는 가장 적절한 의미를 고르세요. **(A)** 작은 아버지께서 귤을 보내주었다. (B) 작은 아버지의 거주지는 제주도이다. (C) 제주도 사람들은 귤을 좋아하지 않는다. (D) 작은 아버지께서 전원 주택에 사신다. (E) 정답 없음.
Chinese	王芳去张伟家看到厨房里堆放着几大袋葡萄干，便问为什么有这么多，张伟回答说:	"我叔叔住在新疆。"	请在以下选项中选择最恰当地表达上述话语含义的选项。 **(A)** 叔叔给张伟邮了葡萄干。 (B) 张伟的叔叔住在新疆。 (C) 新疆人不喜欢葡萄干。 (D) 张伟的叔叔住在乡间别墅里。 (E) 没有正确答案。

Table 2: Multilingual test units from the test suite on the maxim of relation, comprising a context, an utterance, and a multiple-choice question (MCQ) to assess the understanding of implied meanings. Charlie's response indirectly addresses Emily's question, thereby violating the maxim of relation. Assuming adherence to the cooperative principle, the most appropriate interpretation is option (A), indicating that Charlie's uncle sent the oranges.

APACS test set (Arcara and Bambini, 2016), which consists of various subtasks such as interviews, descriptions, and narratives. The tests were conducted in both English and Italian, with results reported for Italian due to no notable differences between the two. The findings indicate that GPT-3.5 comes close to human ability but reveals weaknesses in understanding physical metaphors and jokes.

Focusing on Korean, Park et al. (2024) employed 120 test questions aligned with the four Gricean maxims to further probe the capabilities of various LLMs. The findings demonstrate that GPT-4 excelled in both multiple-choice and open-ended question setups, with HyperCLOVA X (Yoo et al., 2024), a Korean-specific LLM, closely following. The study also explored in-context learning, demonstrating that the few-shot learning technique consistently leads to positive outcomes across all tested models.

Sravanthi et al. (2024) introduce a comprehensive pragmatic benchmark that evaluates LLMs across 14 distinct tasks, including implicature, presupposition and deictic detection. Comprising 28k data points, this benchmark aims to provide a nuanced assessment of LLMs' pragmatic abilities, marking a substantial contribution to the field. Yet, there remains a significant need to extend these evaluations to multiple languages to thoroughly assess the multilingual capabilities of LLMs.

3 Methodology

3.1 Theoretical Foundations of Pragmatics

To accurately assess the contextual awareness of LLMs, we primarily focus on implicature, based on Grice's theory (Grice, 1975). Implicature refers to a specific way language is used, in which the literal meaning of an utterance differs from the intended meaning of the speaker, requiring the listener to infer the intended meaning from the surrounding context. This concept is critical for evaluating how well LLMs understand human language, particularly in their ability to capture nuanced meanings beyond the explicit words.

Grice introduced the Cooperative Principle that explains how speakers and listeners cooperate to achieve mutual understanding, and its four conver-

Maxim	Description	Specific Cases Covered
Quantity	Make your contribution as informative as is required.	Tautology, insufficient information, excessive information, and cases where the maxim is abided by.
Quality	Try to make your contribution one that is true.	Irony, hyperbole, and misinformation.
Relation	Ensure that all the information you provide is relevant to the current conversation.	Unrelated information and cases where the maxim is abided by.
Manner	Be perspicuous; Be brief and orderly, and avoid obscurity and ambiguity.	Ambiguity, vagueness, double negation, verbosity, improper order, complicated expressions, and cases where the maxim is abided by.

Table 3: Grice's maxims and their principles with related linguistic phenomena

sational maxims, which suggest how an utterance should desirably be conducted. Detailed in Table 3, the maxim of quantity requires information to be as informative as necessary–neither more nor less. The maxim of quality emphasizes the importance of offering truthful contributions. The maxim of relation ensures all information is pertinent to the current conversation. The maxim of manner demands clarity and brevity, avoiding obscurity and ambiguity.

Considering the critical role of understanding implicated meanings in communication, this study investigates LLMs' comprehension of conversational implicatures. Specifically, we evaluate LLMs' capabilities in inferring implied meanings that arise from either abiding by or violating these maxims.

3.2 Development of the Test Suite

To develop our test suite, we followed a structured process divided into three key phases: describing the initial dataset, expanding its scope, and translating it into the target languages and verifying the translations. Table 2 showcases an example of a test unit focused on the maxim of relation from our complete test suite, presented in English, German, Korean, and Chinese.

Initial Dataset. The development of the MultiPragEval test suite began with the foundational work by (Park et al., 2024), who crafted a set of 120 question units designed to assess LLMs in terms of four conversational maxims. Each maxim was represented by 30 units, which included a structured scenario setting the conversational context, an utterance by a participant, and a set of questions comprising both a multiple-choice question and an open-ended question. We adopted the context, utterance, and multiple-choice question components from this test set as our starting point.

Expansion. Next, we expanded the number of question units from 120 to 300 to encompass a broader range of pragmatic contexts. Each conversational maxim, originally represented by 30 units, was doubled to 60 to deepen the evaluative scope, including more diverse linguistic phenomena as shown in Table 3. Additionally, we introduced a new category specifically designed to assess the understanding of literal meanings, which allows us to explore potential trade-offs between performances in understanding literal versus implied meanings. To further enhance the complexity of our test suite, we included units that do not have a correct answer by adding a 'None of the above' option to the multiple-choice setups.

Translation and Verification. In the subsequent phase, we translated the Korean test set into English, German, and Chinese using DeepL [1] for the initial conversion. Then, Korean-native linguistic experts with CEFR C1 [2] level proficiency in the target languages refined the translations to ensure that these translations preserved the intended meanings and nuances. They also adapted cultural elements by substituting the names of characters and setting details to reflect the local context of each language. Finally, native speakers of each target language, who hold degrees in linguistics and related fields, conducted a thorough verification of the translations. This process confirmed that the quality and accuracy of the translations were on par with the original Korean versions.

3.3 Experimental Setup

Models. Our study includes 15 LLMs, categorized into two types: proprietary LLMs accessed via API, and open-source LLMs where we have direct access to the model weights. As detailed in Table 4, the proprietary models comprise two GPT models (Achiam et al., 2023) by OpenAI,

[1] https://www.deepl.com

[2] https://www.coe.int/en/web/common-european-framework-reference-languages/level-descriptions

Type	Model	Version
Proprietary	GPT-3.5	turbo-0125
	GPT-4	turbo-2024-04-09
	Claude3-Haiku	haiku-20240307
	Claude3-Sonnet	sonnet-20240229
	Claude3-Opus	opus-20240229
	Mistral-small	small-2402
	Mistral-medium	medium-2312
	Mistral-large	large-2402
Open-Src.	Llama-2-13B	chat-hf
	Llama-2-7B	chat-hf
	Llama-3-8B	Instruct
	Gemma-7B	1.1-7b-it
	Solar-10.7B	Instruct-v1.0
	Qwen-14B	1.5-14B-Chat
	Qwen-7B	1.5-7B-Chat

Table 4: Overview of proprietary and open-source LLMs evaluated in the study

along with three different sizes of both Claude3 (Anthropic, 2024) by Anthropic and Mistral by Mistral AI [3]. We exclude Gemini by Google from our analysis due to its limited accessibility via API.

Additionally, we evaluate publicly available open-source models, each with approximately 10 billion parameters. These models were selected based on two criteria: their architecture (Transformer decoder-based models) and their performance on publicly accessible benchmarks. The selected models include three Llama models (Touvron et al., 2023) by Meta, Gemma (Team et al., 2024) by Google, Solar (Kim et al., 2023) by Korean company Upstage, and two Qwen models (Bai et al., 2023) by Chinese firm Alibaba, with consideration also given to the diversity of languages represented in our study.

LLM Response Generation. To generate answers from each LLM, we set the temperature hyperparameter at 0.5 across models to balance coherence and creativity in their responses. For inference on the open-source LLMs, we utilized a single H100-80GB unit. Each model was queried three times to account for the inherent randomness in responses. We then computed the average score for each model across these trials to ensure a robust assessment of performance for each LLM iteration. Scores were calculated based on the ratio of correct answers to the total number of test units across all three trials. The actual prompt for the experiment and inter-rater agreement across three trials are detailed in the Appendix B.

4 Result

4.1 Analysis of LLM Performance

Overall Performance. Table 5 presents the results from the evaluation of the selected LLMs on the MultiPragEval test suite. It demonstrates that Claude3-Opus significantly outperforms all other models across four languages, with GPT-4 trailing by approximately 6-10 points. This performance gap underscores Claude3-Opus's exceptional ability to capture the subtle nuances of language that are highly context-dependent. These findings highlight its position as the most proficient among the current state-of-the-art LLMs across English, German, Korean, and Chinese.

Mistral-Large and Claude3-Sonnet are closely matched for the next tier of performance; Mistral-Large outperforms Claude3-Sonnet in German, Korean, and Chinese. However, Claude3-Sonnet achieves a higher score in English, registering 66.39 compared to Mistral-Large's 61.39. Interestingly, while Mistral-Large generally shows improved scores across languages compared to Mistral-Medium, it scores lower in English, dropping to 61.39 from the medium-sized model's 66.25.

Solar-10.7B demonstrates stable performance, consistently outperforming GPT-3.5 across all four languages. It is the only open-source model that surpasses GPT-3.5 in both English and German. In English, it closely follows Mistral-Large with a score of 59.31 and is just behind Claude3-Sonnet in German, with a score of 55.69.

Qwen-14B also stands out among other open-source LLMs, outperforming its counterparts with scores of 50.00 in Chinese and 49.72 in Korean. In contrast, both Llama2-13B and Llama2-7B demonstrate a strong bias towards literal interpretations yielding poor scores, while Llama3-8B shows enhanced performance compared to its earlier versions. Notably, Llama2-13B achieves a significant leap in Korean, scoring 47.50 compared to Llama2-7B's 3.06, while exhibiting a more gradual increase in other languages.

Performance Gap Across Languages. We observed that the models generally achieve higher per-

[3] https://mistral.ai/

	English					German	Korean	Chinese
	Quan.	Qual.	Rel.	Man.	Avg.	Avg.	Avg.	Avg.
GPT-4	65.00	83.89	82.22	70.00	**75.28**	**72.50**	**81.25**	**68.75**
GPT-3.5	51.11	66.67	52.78	42.89	53.61	52.92	38.89	43.61
Claude3-Opus	81.11	88.89	88.89	81.11	**85.00**	**82.78**	**87.08**	**76.67**
Claude3-Sonnet	62.22	81.67	67.22	54.44	66.39	60.14	63.33	48.61
Claude3-Haiku	56.67	67.78	58.89	43.33	56.67	45.14	38.47	40.83
Mistral-Large	61.11	71.11	61.11	52.22	61.39	63.75	65.56	54.72
Mistral-Medium	61.11	69.44	72.22	62.22	66.25	53.61	52.92	38.89
Mistral-Small	57.22	57.78	54.44	35.00	51.11	51.11	40.42	33.61
Llama3-8B	54.44	68.89	44.44	45.56	53.33	40.00	32.50	46.81
Llama2-13B	26.67	32.22	16.67	32.22	26.94	16.39	**47.50**	8.75
Llama2-7B	31.11	26.67	11.11	18.33	21.81	4.44	3.06	4.17
Gemma-7B	37.78	36.67	35.00	30.56	35.00	27.22	20.83	25.28
Solar-10.7B	58.33	65.56	62.22	51.11	**59.31**	**55.69**	**49.03**	46.39
Qwen-14B	52.22	61.67	56.11	43.33	53.33	43.06	**49.72**	**50.00**
Qwen-7B	53.89	62.22	47.22	37.78	50.28	39.44	35.14	41.11

Table 5: Performance of LLMs on the MultiPragEval test suite: scores across four languages and by maxims with overall averages; Leading scores among proprietary and open-source models are highlighted in bold. The scores for each maxim are color-coded in shades of blue to represent the relative ranking within each model.

formance scores in English than in other languages, likely due to larger English training datasets enhancing reasoning capabilities. Interestingly, flagship proprietary models like GPT-4, Claude-Opus, and Mistral-large show slightly better performance in Korean. We believe there could be two possible reasons for this performance gap. First, it is possible that the initial Korean dataset, from which we extended our test suite (Park et al., 2024), was used in model training, allowing the models to better understand newly created Korean questions that follow the same template. Secondly, the gap could stem from the test suite being initially developed in Korean and then translated into other languages. Cultural nuances and conventions embedded in each language may lead to subtle differences in how the same expressions are interpreted, with the implications being understood differently depending on the language region.

Significant performance discrepancies were also observed across models. Claude-Haiku scored 56.7 in English but only 38.4 in Korean, while Mistral-small dropped from 51.1 in English to 33.6 in Chinese. Llama2-13B showed the largest gap, with scores of 47.5 in Korean versus 8.7 in Chinese. These differences highlight language-specific biases in the models, indicating a need for improvements to boost multilingual capabilities.

Closer Look at Individual Maxims. Table 5 also shows the performance scores of LLMs on individual maxims in the English test suite. We observe a consistent pattern across LLMs where scores for the maxim of quality generally rank highest, while scores for the maxim of manner rank lowest. This pattern is not unique to English but is also observable in other languages, suggesting a universal trend (see Appendix A). This outcome is expected because expressions governed by the maxim of quality, which become untrue statements when interpreted literally, make it easier for LLMs to infer the appropriate implied meanings. Conversely, the maxim of manner, involving verbose or ambiguous expressions, poses more subtle challenges that likewise pose difficulties for humans (Hoffmann, 2010).

Another noteworthy observation is that as the overall performance increases, the scores for the maxim of relation also generally improve. This pattern is more evident among proprietary models, where the maxim of relation mostly ranks second. Similarly, Solar-10.7B and Qwen-14B, which perform comparably to GPT-3.5, achieve higher scores in the maxim of relation compared to those of quantity and manner. Conversely, other open-source models with lower average scores tend to have lower rankings in the maxim of relation, falling

	English			German			Korean			Chinese		
	Avg.	Opt. None	Literal	Avg.	Opt. None	Literal	Avg.	Opt. None	Literal	Avg.	Opt. None	Literal
GPT-4	**75.28**	**90.00**	100.00	**72.50**	**90.56**	97.22	**81.25**	**75.00**	96.67	**68.75**	**79.44**	98.33
GPT-3.5	53.61	55.00	85.56	52.92	69.44	85.56	38.89	31.11	83.33	43.61	62.78	88.33
Claude3-Opus	**85.00**	**92.78**	98.89	**82.78**	**85.00**	93.33	**87.08**	**70.56**	99.44	**76.67**	**83.33**	95.56
Claude3-Sonnet	66.39	81.11	91.67	60.14	67.22	91.67	63.33	28.33	84.44	48.61	34.44	87.78
Claude3-Haiku	56.67	63.89	91.11	45.14	37.22	90.00	38.47	**9.44**	80.00	40.83	**8.33**	80.56
Mistral-Large	61.39	66.11	95.56	63.75	77.22	87.78	65.56	58.33	91.11	54.72	54.44	88.33
Mistral-Medium	66.25	80.56	98.33	53.61	61.11	91.11	52.92	45.00	86.11	38.89	**16.11**	81.11
Mistral-Small	51.11	47.78	92.22	51.11	43.33	87.22	40.42	**31.11**	85.00	33.61	**18.33**	82.78
Llama3-8B	53.33	43.89	85.00	40.00	56.11	87.22	32.50	21.67	80.00	46.81	28.33	89.44
Llama2-13B	26.94	65.00	70.00	16.39	9.44	69.44	47.50	2.22	67.78	8.75	7.78	64.44
Llama2-7B	21.81	13.33	70.56	4.44	**1.11**	<u>45.56</u>	3.06	**0.00**	<u>42.22</u>	4.17	**0.00**	<u>49.44</u>
Gemma-7B	35.00	23.33	77.22	27.22	**7.28**	80.00	20.83	**0.56**	79.44	25.28	**0.00**	80.00
Solar-10.7B	59.31	81.11	97.78	55.69	38.33	86.11	49.03	22.22	78.89	46.39	26.67	88.89
Qwen-14B	53.33	78.33	93.33	43.06	52.78	85.00	49.72	41.67	87.78	50.00	79.44	94.44
Qwen-7B	50.28	31.67	80.00	39.44	**10.00**	76.67	35.14	**0.00**	73.33	41.11	43.33	86.67

Figure 1: Breakdown of LLM scores for 'No Correct Answers' and literal meaning tests across four languages; the heatmap uses two colors–blue indicating higher scores and yellow indicating lower scores.

below the maxim of quantity. This suggests that capturing relevancy within the given context plays a significant role in a more precise interpretation of implied information, contributing to better overall performance.

4.2 Assessing the Stability of Pragmatic Inference

We further explore the stability of LLMs in pragmatic inference under two specific setups. First, we evaluate the models on a subset of each category of maxims, specifically designed where the test questions lack an appropriate answer. This subset is intended to be more challenging as it requires the models to identify incorrect interpretations and select the option '(E) None of the above' without reference to a correct meaning. Secondly, we test the models on additional test units consisting of context, utterance, and question, structured similarly, but where the context is irrelevant to the utterance. This setup is designed to assess whether LLMs can accurately distinguish purely literal meanings from inappropriate interpretations.

Subset of No Correct Answer. Figure 1 illustrates that the scores on the subset without correct answers (Opt. None) generally align with the overall scores, yet they reveal subtle differences in performance details. While Claude3-Opus consistently outperforms GPT-4 by a certain margin in overall scores across all languages, GPT-4 surpasses Claude3-Opus by approximately 5 points in both German and Korean. This result indicates that both models are comparably robust in the challenging setup of pragmatic consideration.

It is evident that models with lower overall scores exhibit significant declines when tested in the setup without a correct answer. Among proprietary LLMs, Claude3-Haiku, along with medium and small-sized models by Mistral, notably drop in scores, indicating their struggles with the task. Similarly, 7-billion parameter models such as Llama2, Gemma, and Qwen also show poor performance, underscoring the complexity of the task for models of this size.

Additional Set of Literal Meaning. The scores on the set asking literal meanings also demonstrate a general increase along with the overall scores. While the flagship models of GPT and Claude show performance close to perfect, GPT-4 demonstrates a slight edge over Claude-3-Opus for English, German, and Chinese. This may suggest a trade-off between pragmatic and literal focus in their infer-

Model	MultiPragEval (Eng.)	MMLU 5-shot	MATH 4-shot	Arena Elo*	ARC 25-shot	HumanEval 0-shot	GSM-8K 8-shot
GPT-4	**75.28**	86.4	**52.9**	1252	96.3	67.0	92.0
GPT-3.5	53.6	70.0	34.1	1110	85.2	48.1	57.1
Claude3-Opus	**85.0**	86.8	**61.0**	1246	96.4	84.9	95.0
Claude3-Sonnet	66.4	79.0	40.5	1199	93.2	73.0	92.3
Claude3-Haiku	56.7	75.2	40.9	1181	89.2	75.9	88.9
Llama3-8B	53.3	68.4	30.0	1154	60.7	62.2	79.6
Llama2-13B	26.9	47.8	6.7	1065	59.4	14.0	77.4
Llama2-7B	21.8	34.1	3.8	1042	53.1	7.9	25.7
Gemma-7B	35.0	66.0	24.3	1091	61.1	32.3	46.4
Qwen-14B	53.3	69.4	24.8	1119	56.6	32.3	61.3
Qwen-7B	50.3	61.7	11.6	1079	54.2	29.9	51.7
Kendall τ	**1.00**	**0.95**	**0.92**	**0.84**	**0.81**	**0.80**	**0.73**

Table 6: Performance scores of LLMs across multiple benchmarks and Kendall's Tau correlation Coefficients Relative to MultiPragEval.
* The Arena Elo scores are as of May 17, 2024.

ences.

The Llama2 models, particularly Llama2-7B, show the lowest scores among the others, with 42.22, 45.56, and 49.44 for Korean, German, and English, respectively. These results generally correlate with lower overall scores in both the pragmatic and no-correct-answer subset questions. We interpret this to mean that these tasks are not independent of each other, but instead mutually influence one another, highlighting the importance of maintaining a good balance between the sub-tasks.

4.3 Comparison with Existing Benchmarks

To further delve into the implications of our findings, we compare the results from our English test suite with existing English-based benchmarks. This analysis encompasses scores from 11 models, for which other benchmark scores were publicly available. We consider seven popular benchmarks: MMLU (Hendrycks et al., 2020) and ARC (Clark et al., 2018) for general reasoning, HumanEval (Chen et al., 2021) for coding, GSM-8K (Cobbe et al., 2021) and MATH (Hendrycks et al., 2021) for mathematics, and Chatbot Arena (Chiang et al., 2024), a crowd-sourced evaluation. We opted to calculate the correlation coefficients using Kendall's Tau (Kendall, 1938) due to its better handling of varying ranges and subtle differences between benchmarks.

The correlations of MultiPragEval with other benchmarks consistently show high values, indicating a general trend toward 'good' performance across different benchmarks. This suggests that improvements in a model's performance on one task generally enhance its performance on other tasks (Raffel et al., 2020).

MMLU and MATH exhibit the highest correlations among other benchmarks, suggesting that the abilities assessed by these benchmarks align closely with those required for pragmatic inference. It is anticipated that MMLU, which evaluates the general language understanding capabilities of LLMs across a broad spectrum of disciplines, reflects the ability to consider contextual information in language, which is a key requirement of MultiPragEval.

However, the high correlation observed with the MATH benchmark is surprising, given its primary focus on mathematical reasoning. Notably, the score gap between Claude3-Opus and GPT-4, which is around 10 points on MultiPragEval, is similarly reflected on MATH but not distinctively on MMLU. This pattern suggests that the sophisticated mathematical problem-solving required by MATH–which demands a higher level of logical reasoning compared to the basic mathematical problems in GSM-8K–may also tap into core capabilities essential for pragmatic inference. This connection between mathematical reasoning and high-level linguistic comprehension indicates an intricate relationship that requires deeper investigation.

5 Conclusion

In this work, we present the first multilingual study of LLMs' capabilities of their pragmatic inference, particularly in the context of Grice's theory of conversational implicature. Our findings demonstrate the usefulness of MultiPragEval test suite in distinguishing the levels of comprehension among various proprietary and open-source models.

The results reveal that among the models evaluated, Claude3-Opus and GPT-4 particularly stand out, with Claude3-Opus consistently outperforming GPT-4 by 6 to 10 points across all languages, affirming its state-of-the-art capability in pragmatic understanding. Top-performing open-source models like Solar-10.7B and Qwen-14B demonstrate superior or comparable performance to lite-size proprietary models such as GPT-3.5, Claude3-Haiku, and Mistral-Small. The performance gaps across languages within models and individual Grice's maxims further highlight language biases and areas for improvement.

Our findings, with the highest correlations with MMLU and MATH, suggest that general language understanding and complex logical reasoning are intricately linked to pragmatic inference abilities. This insight guides us towards further research to empirically demonstrate how these abilities relate to pragmatic reasoning.

Limitations

While our study provides a comprehensive comparison of 15 proprietary and open-source models, it does not include a comparison with human performance. Including human performance would offer deeper insights into how closely LLMs approximate human abilities. Moreover, human performance can vary across languages, which would enrich our understanding of the LLMs' multilingual pragmatic abilities. Recognizing this gap, we aim to incorporate human performance comparisons in our future research.

Another limitation of our study is its exclusive focus on implicature, despite pragmatics encompassing a broader range of phenomena such as speech acts, presupposition, and politeness. This focus was chosen due to the increasing role of LLMs as AI assistants, which often need to interpret human expressions that are frequently conveyed implicitly. The ability of LLMs to capture these subtle nuances directly influences human judgments about the quality of these systems. Furthermore, contextual awareness is critical not only for linguists but also for NLP engineers who aim to provide reliable services to users. We believe that our specific focus on implicature provides valuable insights into how effectively current LLMs manage the complexities inherent in interpreting implied meanings, a crucial aspect of human communication.

Our study set the temperature value to 0.5 to achieve a moderate balance between consistency and creativity in responses. However, it is important to note that the optimal temperature may vary for each LLM, and the effect of temperature settings on pragmatic inference remains unclear. Recognizing the potential influence of temperature on LLMs' pragmatic abilities, we suggest that future studies investigate the relationship between temperature and pragmatic reasoning to gain deeper insights into how LLMs handle nuanced language tasks.

Ethics Statement

In this work, we introduce a test suite designed to evaluate the pragmatic abilities of LLMs. We have ensured that all data created for this study does not infringe on any existing intellectual property rights, while also ensuring it contains no personally identifiable information. Linguistic experts were involved in the creation and translation of the test suite; all contributors were fully informed about the research's purpose and the methods employed. We commit to making the dataset publicly available to foster transparency and further research in the field.

Acknowledgements

This research was supported by Basic Science Research Program through the National Research Foundation of Korea (NRF) funded by the Ministry of Education (RS-2023-00274280). Additionally, this work was supported by Artificial intelligence industrial convergence cluster development project funded by the Ministry of Science and ICT(MSIT, Korea)&Gwangju Metropolitan City.

References

Josh Achiam, Steven Adler, Sandhini Agarwal, Lama Ahmad, Ilge Akkaya, Florencia Leoni Aleman, Diogo Almeida, Janko Altenschmidt, Sam Altman, Shyamal Anadkat, et al. 2023. Gpt-4 technical report. *arXiv preprint arXiv:2303.08774*.

AI Anthropic. 2024. The claude 3 model family: Opus, sonnet, haiku. *Claude-3 Model Card*.

Giorgio Arcara and Valentina Bambini. 2016. A test for the assessment of pragmatic abilities and cognitive substrates (apacs): Normative data and psychometric properties. *Frontiers in psychology*, 7:172889.

Jinze Bai, Shuai Bai, Yunfei Chu, Zeyu Cui, Kai Dang, Xiaodong Deng, Yang Fan, Wenbin Ge, Yu Han, Fei

Huang, et al. 2023. Qwen technical report. *arXiv preprint arXiv:2309.16609*.

Edward Beeching, Clémentine Fourrier, Nathan Habib, Sheon Han, Nathan Lambert, Nazneen Rajani, Omar Sanseviero, Lewis Tunstall, and Thomas Wolf. 2023. Open llm leaderboard. `https://huggingface.co/spaces/HuggingFaceH4/open_llm_leaderboard`.

Ljubisa Bojic, Predrag Kovacevic, and Milan Cabarkapa. 2023. Gpt-4 surpassing human performance in linguistic pragmatics. *arXiv preprint arXiv:2312.09545*.

Rishi Bommasani, Percy Liang, and Tony Lee. 2023. Holistic evaluation of language models. *Annals of the New York Academy of Sciences*, 1525(1):140–146.

Tom Brown, Benjamin Mann, Nick Ryder, Melanie Subbiah, Jared D Kaplan, Prafulla Dhariwal, Arvind Neelakantan, Pranav Shyam, Girish Sastry, Amanda Askell, et al. 2020. Language models are few-shot learners. *Advances in neural information processing systems*, 33:1877–1901.

Yupeng Chang, Xu Wang, Jindong Wang, Yuan Wu, Linyi Yang, Kaijie Zhu, Hao Chen, Xiaoyuan Yi, Cunxiang Wang, Yidong Wang, et al. 2024. A survey on evaluation of large language models. *ACM Transactions on Intelligent Systems and Technology*, 15(3):1–45.

Mark Chen, Jerry Tworek, Heewoo Jun, Qiming Yuan, Henrique Ponde de Oliveira Pinto, Jared Kaplan, Harri Edwards, Yuri Burda, Nicholas Joseph, Greg Brockman, et al. 2021. Evaluating large language models trained on code. *arXiv preprint arXiv:2107.03374*.

Wei-Lin Chiang, Lianmin Zheng, Ying Sheng, Anastasios Nikolas Angelopoulos, Tianle Li, Dacheng Li, Hao Zhang, Banghua Zhu, Michael Jordan, Joseph E. Gonzalez, and Ion Stoica. 2024. Chatbot arena: An open platform for evaluating llms by human preference.

Peter Clark, Isaac Cowhey, Oren Etzioni, Tushar Khot, Ashish Sabharwal, Carissa Schoenick, and Oyvind Tafjord. 2018. Think you have solved question answering? try arc, the ai2 reasoning challenge. *arXiv preprint arXiv:1803.05457*.

Karl Cobbe, Vineet Kosaraju, Mohammad Bavarian, Mark Chen, Heewoo Jun, Lukasz Kaiser, Matthias Plappert, Jerry Tworek, Jacob Hilton, Reiichiro Nakano, et al. 2021. Training verifiers to solve math word problems. *arXiv preprint arXiv:2110.14168*.

Chiara Barattieri di San Pietro, Federico Frau, Veronica Mangiaterra, and Valentina Bambini. 2023. The pragmatic profile of chatgpt: assessing the pragmatic skills of a conversational agent.

Arpad E Elo and Sam Sloan. 1978. The rating of chessplayers: Past and present.

Herbert P Grice. 1975. Logic and conversation. In *Speech acts*, pages 41–58. Brill.

Zishan Guo, Renren Jin, Chuang Liu, Yufei Huang, Dan Shi, Linhao Yu, Yan Liu, Jiaxuan Li, Bojian Xiong, Deyi Xiong, et al. 2023. Evaluating large language models: A comprehensive survey. *arXiv preprint arXiv:2310.19736*.

Dan Hendrycks, Collin Burns, Steven Basart, Andy Zou, Mantas Mazeika, Dawn Song, and Jacob Steinhardt. 2020. Measuring massive multitask language understanding. *arXiv preprint arXiv:2009.03300*.

Dan Hendrycks, Collin Burns, Saurav Kadavath, Akul Arora, Steven Basart, Eric Tang, Dawn Song, and Jacob Steinhardt. 2021. Measuring mathematical problem solving with the math dataset. In *Proceedings of the Neural Information Processing Systems Track on Datasets and Benchmarks*, volume 1.

Ludger Hoffmann. 2010. *Sprachwissenschaft: ein Reader*. de Gruyter.

Qiao Jin, Bhuwan Dhingra, Zhengping Liu, William Cohen, and Xinghua Lu. 2019. PubMedQA: A dataset for biomedical research question answering. In *Proceedings of the 2019 Conference on Empirical Methods in Natural Language Processing and the 9th International Joint Conference on Natural Language Processing (EMNLP-IJCNLP)*, pages 2567–2577, Hong Kong, China. Association for Computational Linguistics.

Maurice G Kendall. 1938. A new measure of rank correlation. *Biometrika*, 30(1/2):81–93.

Dahyun Kim, Chanjun Park, Sanghoon Kim, Wonsung Lee, Wonho Song, Yunsu Kim, Hyeonwoo Kim, Yungi Kim, Hyeonju Lee, Jihoo Kim, et al. 2023. Solar 10.7 b: Scaling large language models with simple yet effective depth up-scaling. *arXiv preprint arXiv:2312.15166*.

Robert M Krauss and Susan R Fussell. 1996. Social psychological models of interpersonal communication. *Social psychology: Handbook of basic principles*, pages 655–701.

Sang Kwon, Gagan Bhatia, El Moatez Billah Nagoudi, and Muhammad Abdul-Mageed. 2023. Beyond English: Evaluating LLMs for Arabic grammatical error correction. In *Proceedings of ArabicNLP 2023*, pages 101–119, Singapore (Hybrid). Association for Computational Linguistics.

Haonan Li, Yixuan Zhang, Fajri Koto, Yifei Yang, Hai Zhao, Yeyun Gong, Nan Duan, and Timothy Baldwin. 2023. Cmmlu: Measuring massive multitask language understanding in chinese. *arXiv preprint arXiv:2306.09212*.

R. Thomas McCoy, Ellie Pavlick, and Tal Linzen. 2019. Right for the wrong reasons: Diagnosing syntactic heuristics in natural language inference. In *Annual Meeting of the Association for Computational Linguistics*.

Dojun Park, Jiwoo Lee, Hyeyun Jeong, Seohyun Park, and Sungeun Lee. 2024. Pragmatic competence evaluation of large language models for korean. *arXiv preprint arXiv:2403.12675*.

Colin Raffel, Noam Shazeer, Adam Roberts, Katherine Lee, Sharan Narang, Michael Matena, Yanqi Zhou, Wei Li, and Peter J Liu. 2020. Exploring the limits of transfer learning with a unified text-to-text transformer. *Journal of machine learning research*, 21(140):1–67.

Stephen Roller, Emily Dinan, Naman Goyal, Da Ju, Mary Williamson, Yinhan Liu, Jing Xu, Myle Ott, Eric Michael Smith, Y-Lan Boureau, and Jason Weston. 2021. Recipes for building an open-domain chatbot. In *Proceedings of the 16th Conference of the European Chapter of the Association for Computational Linguistics: Main Volume*, pages 300–325, Online. Association for Computational Linguistics.

Damien Sileo, Philippe Muller, Tim Van de Cruys, and Camille Pradel. 2022. A pragmatics-centered evaluation framework for natural language understanding. In *Proceedings of the Thirteenth Language Resources and Evaluation Conference*, pages 2382–2394, Marseille, France. European Language Resources Association.

Guijin Son, Hanwool Lee, Sungdong Kim, Seungone Kim, Niklas Muennighoff, Taekyoon Choi, Cheonbok Park, Kang Min Yoo, and Stella Biderman. 2024. Kmmlu: Measuring massive multitask language understanding in korean. *arXiv preprint arXiv:2402.11548*.

Dan Sperber and Deirdre Wilson. 1986. *Relevance: Communication and cognition*, volume 142. Harvard University Press Cambridge, MA.

Settaluri Lakshmi Sravanthi, Meet Doshi, Tankala Pavan Kalyan, Rudra Murthy, Pushpak Bhattacharyya, and Raj Dabre. 2024. Pub: A pragmatics understanding benchmark for assessing llms' pragmatics capabilities. *arXiv preprint arXiv:2401.07078*.

Gemma Team, Thomas Mesnard, Cassidy Hardin, Robert Dadashi, Surya Bhupatiraju, Shreya Pathak, Laurent Sifre, Morgane Rivière, Mihir Sanjay Kale, Juliette Love, et al. 2024. Gemma: Open models based on gemini research and technology. *arXiv preprint arXiv:2403.08295*.

Hugo Touvron, Louis Martin, Kevin Stone, Peter Albert, Amjad Almahairi, Yasmine Babaei, Nikolay Bashlykov, Soumya Batra, Prajjwal Bhargava, Shruti Bhosale, et al. 2023. Llama 2: Open foundation and fine-tuned chat models. *arXiv preprint arXiv:2307.09288*.

Jing Xu, Da Ju, Margaret Li, Y-Lan Boureau, Jason Weston, and Emily Dinan. 2020. Recipes for safety in open-domain chatbots. *arXiv preprint arXiv:2010.07079*.

Kang Min Yoo, Jaegeun Han, Sookyo In, Heewon Jeon, Jisu Jeong, Jaewook Kang, Hyunwook Kim, Kyung-Min Kim, Munhyong Kim, Sungju Kim, et al. 2024. Hyperclova x technical report. *arXiv preprint arXiv:2404.01954*.

Rowan Zellers, Ari Holtzman, Yonatan Bisk, Ali Farhadi, and Yejin Choi. 2019. HellaSwag: Can a machine really finish your sentence? In *Proceedings of the 57th Annual Meeting of the Association for Computational Linguistics*, pages 4791–4800, Florence, Italy. Association for Computational Linguistics.

A Demonstration of Test Unit Example

Language	Context	Utterance	MCQ
English	A student asks their professor if they can extend the due date of an assignment just a little longer. The professor relies:	"Rules are rules."	Choose the most appropriate meaning of the above utterance from the following options. **(A)** The deadline can't be extended because rules must be followed. (B) Rules are rules. (C) Breaking the rules isn't a big deal, so I'll give the student a chance. (D) The professor discovered a new theory after doing research. (E) None of the above.
German	Ein Student fragt seinen Professor, ob er den Abgabetermin für eine Aufgabe noch ein wenig hinauszögern kann.	"Regeln sind Regeln."	Wählen Sie die passendste Bedeutung der obigen Äußerung aus den folgenden Aussagen aus. **(A)** Die Frist kann nicht verlängert werden, weil die Regeln eingehalten werden müssen. (B) Regeln sind Regeln. (C) Ein Verstoß gegen die Regeln ist keine große Sache, also gebe ich dem Studenten eine Chance. (D) Der Professor hat durch Nachforschungen eine neue Theorie entdeckt. (E) Keine der obigen Aussagen ist richtig.
Korean	학생이 교수에게 과제의 마감 기한을 조금만 더 늘려 주실 수 없냐고 부탁하자 교수가 말한다.	"규칙은 규칙일세."	다음 보기에서 위 발화가 갖는 가장 적절한 의미를 고르세요. **(A)** 규칙은 지켜져야만 하므로 마감 기한을 늘릴 수 없다. (B) 규칙은 규칙이다. (C) 규칙을 깨는 것은 큰 문제가 되지 않으므로 학생에게 기회를 주겠다. (D) 교수는 연구 끝에 새로운 이론을 발견했다. (E) 정답 없음.
Chinese	一名学生问教授可不可以将作业的截止日期再延长一点，教授说:	"规则就是规则。"	请在以下选项中选择最恰当地表达上述话语含义的选项。 **(A)** 规则必须遵守，因此不能延长截止期限。 (B) 规矩就是规矩。 (C) 违反规则没什么大不了的，所以教授会给学生一个机会。 (D) 教授经过研究发现了一个新理论。 (E) 没有正确答案。

Table 7: Multilingual test unit example on the maxim of quantity. The utterance "Rules are rules" is not sufficiently informative because it provides less information than necessary. This under-informativeness constitutes a violation of Grice's maxim of quantity, which demands that enough information be given to be fully informative. In this context, "the rules" implicitly refer to the adherence to established guidelines, such as the due date for assignments. Therefore, the most appropriate interpretation of the professor's statement is option (A) "The deadline can't be extended because rules must be followed," which accurately captures the implied meaning behind the response.

Language	Context	Utterance	MCQ
English	When Emily, a PhD student, spoke at length about the theory she had studied yesterday, Charlie said:	"You're the professor."	Choose the most appropriate meaning of the above utterance from the following options. (A) Emily was hired as a professor. **(B)** Emily knows a lot, but she talks too much. (C) Emily is not good at graduate studies. (D) Emily lives in a dormitory. (E) None of the above.
German	Als Anna, eine Doktorandin, ausführlich über die Theorie sprach, die sie gestern untersucht hatte, sagte Felix:	"Du bist ja Professorin."	Wählen Sie die passendste Bedeutung der obigen Äußerung aus den folgenden Aussagen aus. (A) Anna wurde zur Professorin ernannt. **(B)** Anna weiß eine Menge, aber sie redet zu viel. (C) Anna ist nicht gut im Studium. (D) Anna wohnt in einem Studentenwohnheim. (E) Keine der obigen Aussagen ist richtig.
Korean	박사생인 영희가 어제 공부한 이론에 대해 길게 이야기하자 철수가 다음과 같이 말했다.	"네가 교수다."	다음 보기에서 위 발화가 갖는 가장 적절한 의미를 고르세요. (A) 영희는 교수로 임용되었다. **(B)** 영희는 아는 것이 많지만 말이 너무 많다. (C) 영희는 대학원 공부에 소질이 없다. (D) 영희는 기숙사에 살고 있다. (E) 정답 없음.
Chinese	当博士生王芳详细讲述她昨天学习的理论时，张伟说：	"你是教授吗？"	请在以下选项中选择最恰当地表达上述话语含义的选项。 (A) 王芳被任命为教授。 **(B)** 王芳知道很多，但她说得太多了。 (C) 王芳不适合读研。 (D) 王芳住在宿舍里。 (E) 没有正确答案。

Table 8: Multilingual test unit example on the maxim of quality. This example illustrates a violation of Grice's maxim of quality, which requires contributions to be true. Although Charlie refers to Emily as "the professor," he does not literally mean that she holds this academic position, as she is a PhD student. Instead, this utterance uses irony to comment on Emily's detailed and extensive explanation, typical of a professor's depth of knowledge. Therefore, the utterance "You're the professor" acknowledges Emily's thorough knowledge while subtly critiquing her for possibly providing more information than necessary in casual conversation. Thus, option (B) "Emily knows a lot, but she talks too much." best captures the implied meaning of Charlie's statement.

Language	Context	Utterance	MCQ
English	When Charlie confessed to Emily that he wanted to go out with her, she replied:	"I really like you as a friend, too, but I don't think I'm in the right frame of mind to meet someone right now."	Choose the most appropriate meaning of the above utterance from the following options. (A) Charlie and Emily have a good personality match. (B) Emily wants to date Charlie's brother. **(C)** Emily doesn't want to go out with Charlie. (D) There are no friends between men and women. (E) None of the above.
German	Als Felix Anna gestand, dass er mit ihr ausgehen wollte, sagte sie ihm:	"Ich mag dich sehr als Freund, aber ich glaube nicht, dass ich im Moment in der richtigen Stimmung bin, um mit jemandem in einer Beziehung sein."	Wählen Sie die passendste Bedeutung der obigen Äußerung aus den folgenden Aussagen aus. (A) Felix und Anna passen charakterlich gut zusammen. (B) Anna will mit Felix' Bruder ausgehen. **(C)** Anna will nicht mit Felix ausgehen. (D) Es gibt keine echte Freundschaft zwischen Männern und Frauen. (E) Keine der obigen Aussagen ist richtig.
Korean	철수가 영희에게 사귀자고 고백하자 영희가 다음과 같이 말했다.	"나도 너를 친구로서 정말 좋아하지만 내가 지금 사람을 만날 만한 마음의 여유가 없는 것 같아."	다음 보기에서 위 발화가 갖는 가장 적절한 의미를 고르세요. (A) 철수와 영희는 성격이 잘 맞는다. (B) 영희는 철수의 친오빠와 사귀고 싶다. **(C)** 철수와 사귀고 싶지 않다. (D) 남자와 여자 사이에 친구란 없다. (E) 정답 없음.
Chinese	当张伟向王芳表白，王芳说：	"作为朋友我真的很喜欢你，但是我现在状态不适合和别人在一起。"	请在以下选项中选择最恰当地表达上述话语含义的选项。 (A) 张伟和王芳性格很合得来。 (B) 王芳想和张伟的哥哥约会。 **(C)** 王芳不想和张伟谈恋爱。 (D) 男女之间没有朋友。 (E) 没有正确答案。

Table 9: Multilingual test unit example on the maxim of manner. Emily's response to Charlie's confession is a classic example of violating Grice's maxim of manner, which advocates for clarity and brevity in communication. Instead of a direct answer, Emily's reply is ambiguously structured, suggesting a rejection without explicitly stating one. This ambiguity is strategic, preserving social harmony while conveying her feelings indirectly. Given the content and context of the conversation, options (A), (B), and (D) do not align with the information provided. Emily emphasizes her current emotional state and her appreciation of their friendship as reasons for not pursuing a romantic relationship, which implicitly suggests she does not wish to date Charlie. Thus, option (C) "Emily doesn't want to go out with Charlie" captures the underlying implication of her response most accurately.

Language	Context	Utterance	MCQ
English	Emily and Charlie are working on a writing assignment from class. Emily asks Charlie when the writing assignment is due, and Charlie replies:	"It's due next Thursday."	Choose the most appropriate meaning of the above utterance from the following options. (A) Charlie is asking Emily for help. (B) Charlie is not confident in English and wants to postpone the writing assignment. (C) Charlie wants to finish the writing assignment today. **(D)** The writing assignment is due next Thursday. (E) None of the above.
German	Anna und Felix arbeiteten an einer schriftlichen Aufgabe aus ihrem Unterricht. Anna fragte Felix, wann die Schreibaufgabe fällig sei, und Felix antwortete:	"Sie ist nächsten Donnerstag fällig."	Wählen Sie die passendste Bedeutung der obigen Äußerung aus den folgenden Aussagen aus. (A) Er bittet Anna um Hilfe. (B) Felix ist unsicher in Englisch und möchte die Schreibaufgabe verschieben. (C) Er möchte die schriftliche Aufgabe sofort fertigstellen. **(D)** Die Schreibaufgabe soll bis zum nächsten Donnerstag fertig sein. (E) Keine der obigen Aussagen ist richtig.
Korean	영희와 철수는 수업에서 나온 글쓰기 과제를 하고 있다. 영희가 철수에게 글쓰기 과제 마감일이 언제인지 묻자, 철수가 다음과 같이 대답했다.	"다음주 목요일까지 제출해야 해."	다음 보기에서 위 발화가 갖는 가장 적절한 의미를 고르세요. (A) 철수는 영희에게 도움을 요청하는 중이다. (B) 철수는 영어에 자신이 없어서 글쓰기 과제를 미루고 싶다. (C) 철수는 오늘 글쓰기 과제를 끝내려고 한다. **(D)** 글쓰기 과제 마감일이 다음주 목요일이다. (E) 정답 없음.
Chinese	王芳和张伟正在完成课堂上的写作任务。王芳问张伟什么时候交写作作业，张伟回答说:	"下周四前得交上去。"	请在以下选项中选择最恰当地表达上述话语含义的选项。 (A) 张伟在向王芳寻求帮助。 (B) 张伟对英语没有信心，想推迟写作任务。 (C) 张伟想在今天完成写作任务。 **(D)** 下周四之前要交写作作业。 (E) 没有正确答案。

Table 10: Multilingual test unit example on the category of literal interpretation. Charlie's reply is a direct answer to Emily's question about the deadline. His utterance does not trigger any implications based on the violation of Grice's maxims. It straightforwardly indicates that the due date is next Thursday. Therefore, option (D) "The writing assignment is due next Thursday" is the most appropriate meaning.

Language	**Context**	**Utterance**	**MCQ**
English	Emily saw Charlie's brother in a family photo and asked Charlie how old his brother was, to which he replied:	"He's 28."	Choose the most appropriate meaning of the above utterance from the following options. (A) Charlie does not know his brother's age. (B) Charlie's brother is not in college. (C) Charlie doesn't have a brother. (D) Charlie's brother is unemployed. **(E)** None of the above.
German	Anna sah Felix' Bruder auf einem Familienfoto und fragte ihn, wie alt er sei, woraufhin Felix antwortete:	"Er ist 28."	Wählen Sie die passendste Bedeutung der obigen Äußerung aus den folgenden Aussagen aus. (A) Felix weiß nicht, wie alt sein Bruder ist. (B) Felix' Bruder geht nicht auf eine Universität. (C) Felix hat keinen Bruder. (D) Felix' Bruder ist arbeitslos. **(E)** Keine der obigen Aussagen ist richtig.
Korean	영희는 철수의 가족사진에서 그의 동생을 보았고, 동생의 나이를 물었다. 이에 철수는 다음과 같이 대답했다.	"28살이야."	다음 보기에서 위 발화가 갖는 가장 적절한 의미를 고르세요. (A) 철수는 동생 나이를 알지 못한다. (B) 철수의 동생은 대학생이 아니다. (C) 철수는 동생이 없다. (D) 철수의 동생은 무직이다. **(E)** 정답 없음.
Chinese	王芳在一张全家福照片上看到了张伟的弟弟，并问他几岁了，张伟回答说:	"他28 岁。"	请在以下选项中选择最恰当地表达上述话语含义的选项。 (A) 张伟不知道他的弟弟是几岁。 (B) 张伟的弟弟不是大学生。 (C) 张伟没有弟弟。 (D) 张伟的弟弟失业了。 **(E)** 没有正确答案。

Table 11: Multilingual test unit example without correct answer. Charlie's reply to Emily's question about his brother's age is straightforward and direct, with no implications based on the violation of Grice's maxims. His response should thus be interpreted as literal meaning: Charlie's brother is 28 years old. Since none of the options (A) to (D) accurately reflect this literal expression, each introducing an unrelated assumption, the correct answer is (E) "None of the above."

B Prompt Demonstration and Inter-Rater Agreement Analysis

Prompt
While visiting Charlie's house, Emily saw a large pile of oranges in the kitchen and asked why there were so many. Charlie responded: *(context)* "My uncle lives in Florida." *(statement)* Choose the most appropriate meaning of the above utterance from the following options. *(MCQ)* (A) Charlie's uncle sent the oranges. (B) Charlie's uncle resides in Florida. (C) People in Florida do not like oranges. (D) Charlie's uncle lives in a rural house. (E) None of the above.

Table 12: Example of the prompt using a test unit from our suite. It illustrates how the actual prompt is structured into a context and a corresponding statement followed by an MCQ with options. The words with parentheses are for clarification and are not part of the actual prompt.

		English	**German**	**Korean**	**Chinese**
Proprietary	GPT-4	0.87	0.86	<u>0.70</u>	0.90
	GPT-3.5	0.86	0.85	0.86	0.88
	Claude3-Opus	0.92	0.96	0.94	0.86
	Claude3-Sonnet	0.93	0.96	0.85	0.90
	Claude3-Haiku	0.95	0.95	0.90	0.91
	Mistral-Large	0.91	0.95	0.88	0.89
	Mistral-Medium	0.90	0.90	0.94	0.94
	Mistral-Small	0.80	0.84	0.84	0.85
Open-Source	Llama3-8B	0.86	0.91	0.90	0.90
	Llama2-13B	0.86	0.89	<u>0.56</u>	0.81
	Llama2-7B	0.88	0.86	0.87	0.92
	Gemma-7B	0.97	0.99	0.96	0.97
	Solar-10.7B	0.94	0.92	0.94	0.94
	Qwen-14B	0.96	0.95	<u>0.69</u>	0.95
	Qwen-7B	0.96	0.97	0.95	0.91

Table 13: Fleiss' Kappa values representing inter-rater agreement across three trials on the MultiPragEval test suite for four languages. Most models demonstrate high Kappa values (above 0.80), indicating strong agreement across trials. However, models such as GPT-4, Llama2-13B, and Qwen-14B exhibit moderate agreement in generating Korean responses (0.56 to 0.70), suggesting some variability in their performance across the different trials.

C Score Tables

		German				
		Quan.	Qual.	Rel.	Man.	**Avg.**
Proprietary	GPT-4	70.56	76.67	77.22	65.56	**72.50**
	GPT-3.5	58.89	51.67	53.89	47.22	52.92
	Claude-Opus	85.56	87.78	85.00	72.78	**82.78**
	Claude-Sonnet	53.89	70.00	66.11	50.56	60.14
	Claude-Haiku	36.67	51.67	52.78	39.44	45.14
	Mistral-Large	60.00	70.00	73.33	51.67	63.75
	Mistral-Medium	47.22	68.89	56.11	42.22	53.61
	Mistral-Small	50.56	53.33	58.89	41.67	51.11
Open-Source	Llama3-8B	35.56	40.00	46.67	37.78	40.00
	Llama2-13B	20.00	13.33	15.00	17.22	16.39
	Llama2-7B	5.56	3.89	3.33	5.00	4.44
	Gemma-7B	29.44	23.89	35.00	20.56	27.22
	Solar-10B	56.67	59.44	62.78	43.89	**55.69**
	Qwen-14B	53.89	38.89	45.56	33.89	43.06
	Qwen-7B	45.56	37.78	41.11	33.33	39.44

Table 14: Performance scores on the MultiPragEval test suite across four maxims with overall averages for German. While the maxim of manner generally shows the lowest scores, high scores are more evenly distributed across the other three maxims.

		Korean				
		Quan.	Qual.	Rel.	Man.	**Avg.**
Proprietary	GPT-4	81.67	86.67	85.56	71.11	**81.25**
	GPT-3.5	42.22	47.22	37.22	28.89	38.89
	Claude-Opus	86.67	87.78	93.33	80.56	**87.08**
	Claude-Sonnet	58.89	74.44	67.78	52.22	63.33
	Claude-Haiku	37.22	49.44	37.78	29.44	38.47
	Mistral-Large	67.78	68.33	74.44	51.67	65.56
	Mistral-Medium	59.44	51.11	53.89	47.22	52.92
	Mistral-Small	41.11	52.22	42.78	25.56	40.42
Open-Source	Llama3-8B	34.44	39.44	31.11	25.00	32.50
	Llama2-13B	45.00	61.11	42.22	41.67	47.50
	Llama2-7B	5.56	5.00	0.00	1.67	3.06
	Gemma-7B	30.56	15.00	25.00	12.78	20.83
	Solar-10B	52.78	52.22	57.22	33.89	**49.03**
	Qwen-14B	53.33	58.89	44.44	42.22	**49.72**
	Qwen-7B	36.67	35.56	38.33	30.00	35.14

Table 15: Performance scores on the MultiPragEval test suite across four maxims with overall averages for Korean. The maxim of quality typically achieves the highest rankings, while the maxim of manner consistently records the lowest scores, reflecting a similar pattern observed in English.

		Chinese				
		Quan.	Qual.	Rel.	Man.	**Avg.**
Proprietary	GPT-4	59.44	85.00	72.78	57.78	**68.75**
	GPT-3.5	47.22	42.22	43.89	41.11	43.61
	Claude-Opus	80.56	82.22	80.56	63.33	**76.67**
	Claude-Sonnet	46.11	63.89	48.33	36.11	48.61
	Claude-Haiku	40.00	52.78	40.56	30.00	40.83
	Mistral-Large	47.22	60.56	66.67	44.44	54.72
	Mistral-Medium	43.89	46.67	36.67	28.33	38.89
	Mistral-Small	35.56	41.11	39.44	18.33	33.61
Open-Source	Llama3-8B	45.56	49.44	53.33	38.89	46.81
	Llama2-13B	6.67	12.78	3.33	12.22	8.75
	Llama2-7B	7.78	3.33	0.56	5.00	4.17
	Gemma-7B	29.44	26.67	18.89	25.28	25.28
	Solar-10B	49.44	57.78	46.67	31.67	46.39
	Qwen-14B	51.67	47.22	58.89	42.22	**50.00**
	Qwen-7B	45.00	46.11	35.56	37.78	41.11

Table 16: Performance scores on the MultiPragEval test suite across four maxims with overall averages for Chinese. The pattern of rankings mirrors those observed in English and Korean.

D Example Responses

<table>
<tr><th>Id</th><th>7</th><th>Category</th><th>Maxim of Quantity</th><th>Correct Answer</th><th>A</th></tr>
<tr><td>Question</td><td colspan="5">Charlie and Emily, who are in the same club, got into an argument at a club meeting last week. It's almost time for today's meeting and Charlie hasn't shown up. Michael, a friend from the club, asks Emily why he hasn't shown up. Emily tells him as follows:

"Either he comes or he doesn't."

Choose the most appropriate meaning of the above utterance from the following options.
(A) Emily doesn't care if Charlie comes or not.
(B) Charlie may or may not come.
(C) Emily decided to apologize to Charlie.
(D) Emily is not a good speaker.
(E) None of the above.</td></tr>
<tr><td>Answer by GPT-4</td><td colspan="5">The most appropriate meaning of Emily's statement "Either he comes or he doesn't" is:
(B) Charlie may or may not come.

This interpretation is based on the literal meaning of the statement, which indicates uncertainty or neutrality regarding Charlie's attendance. It simply states the possibilities without any additional emotional or situational context.</td></tr>
<tr><td>Answer by Claude3-Opus</td><td colspan="5">The most appropriate meaning of Emily's utterance "Either he comes or he doesn't" is:
(A) Emily doesn't care if Charlie comes or not.

Explanation:
Emily's statement suggests indifference towards Charlie's attendance at the club meeting. By saying "Either he comes or he doesn't," she implies that she is not concerned about whether Charlie shows up or not, likely due to their recent argument.

The other options are less fitting because:
(B) While the statement does suggest uncertainty about Charlie's attendance, it doesn't capture Emily's indifference.
(C) There is no indication in the given context that Emily has decided to apologize to Charlie.
(D) The statement does not reflect on Emily's speaking abilities.
(E) Option (A) is the most appropriate interpretation of the given utterance.</td></tr>
</table>

Table 17: Responses by GPT-4 and Claude3-Opus on a test unit evaluating the Maxim of Quantity in English. While Claude3-Opus captures the implied nuance of indifference in the utterance, GPT-4 focuses on a literal interpretation, leading to an incorrect answer.

Id	127	Category	Maxim of Relation	Correct Answer	A
Question	At a company dinner, a coworker invited Charlie to have a drink, and Charlie said: "I drove here." Choose the most appropriate meaning of the above utterance from the following options. (A) Charlie will not drink alcohol. (B) The car is parked in the parking lot. (C) Charlie plans to drink. (D) Charlie is planning to move. (E) None of the above.				
Answer by Llama2-13B	Answer: (C) Charlie plans to drink. Explanation: The statement "I drove here" is often used as a way of saying that one plans to drink alcohol. The speaker is indicating that they have arrived at the destination (the company dinner) by driving, and that they are prepared to consume alcohol. Therefore, option (C) is the most appropriate meaning of the utterance.				
Answer by Llama2-7B	Answer: (C) Charlie plans to drink. Explanation: The sentence "I drove here" is a common way to indicate that the speaker plans to drink alcohol. It implies that the speaker arrived at the location by driving, and therefore, they are not planning to drink. Therefore, option (C) is the most appropriate meaning of the utterance.				

Table 18: Responses by Llama2-13B and Llama2-7B on a test unit evaluating the Maxim of Relation in English. Both models fail to capture the implied meaning of the utterance. While Llama2-7B demonstrates some degree of adequate inference in its reasoning, it still selects the incorrect option.

<table>
<tr><th>Id</th><th>75</th><th>Category</th><th>Maxim of Quality</th><th>Correct Answer</th><th>A</th></tr>
<tr><td>Question</td><td colspan="5">Emily, who saw Charlie come to work on Sunday, said:

"He’s not even breathing."

Choose the most appropriate meaning of the above utterance from the following options.
(A) Charlie works hard and diligently.
(B) Charlie doesn’t breathe when he works.
(C) Time passes slowly, as if Charlie is out of breath.
(D) Charlie is a bad sleeper.
(E) None of the above.</td></tr>
<tr><td>Korean Answer by Llama2-13B</td><td colspan="5">답: ① 철수는 바쁘게 부지런히 일한다.

설명: 위 발화 "재는 숨도 안 쉬어"는 "철수는 바쁘게 부지런히 일한다"라는 의미를 갖고 있습니다. 이 발화는 철수가 일요일에 나와서 일하는 것을 본 영희가 철수의 열의와 힘든 일을 직감적으로 표현한 것입니다.</td></tr>
<tr><td>Translation of Korean Answer</td><td colspan="5">Answer: ① Charlie works hard and diligently.

Explanation: The utterance "He’s not even breathing." means "Charlie works hard and diligently." This utterance is Emily’s instinctive expression of Charlie’s enthusiasm and difficulty at work after seeing him come to work on Sunday.</td></tr>
<tr><td>Chinese Answer by Llama2-13B</td><td colspan="5">答：B</td></tr>
<tr><td>Translation of Chinese Answer</td><td colspan="5">Answer: B</td></tr>
</table>

Table 19: Responses by Llama2-13B on a test unit evaluating the Maxim of Quality in Korean and Chinese. The model demonstrates a significant performance gap between the two languages. While it selects the correct answer and provides a well-reasoned explanation in Korean, it chooses the literal interpretation without any explanation in Chinese.

<table>
<tr><th>Id</th><th>169</th><th>Category</th><th>Maxim of Relation</th><th>Correct Answer</th><th>E</th></tr>
<tr><td>Question</td><td colspan="5">Charlie and Emily walked into a cafe. As Emily was choosing a beverage from the menu, Charlie said:

"I have a gift card."

Choose the most appropriate meaning of the above utterance from the following options.
(A) Charlie wants Emily to give him a gift card.
(B) Charlie gave Emily a gift card.
(C) Charlie will save the gift card instead of using it.
(D) Charlie used to work part-time at a cafe.
(E) None of the above.</td></tr>
<tr><td>Answer by GPT-4</td><td colspan="5">The most appropriate meaning of Charlie's utterance "I have a gift card" in the context provided is:

(E) None of the above.

The correct interpretation, which isn't listed among the options, is likely that Charlie is indicating he has a gift card to use at the cafe, possibly suggesting he can pay for the beverages using the gift card. This interpretation is not explicitly stated in the options provided.</td></tr>
<tr><td>Answer by Claude3-Opus</td><td colspan="5">The most appropriate meaning of Charlie's utterance "I have a gift card" is:

(E) None of the above.

In the given context, Charlie mentioning that he has a gift card most likely implies that he intends to use it to pay for their purchases at the cafe. This suggests that:

- Charlie is offering to treat Emily using his gift card, or
- Charlie is informing Emily that they can use the gift card to save money on their purchases.

The other options (A, B, C, and D) do not accurately represent the meaning of Charlie's statement in the given context.</td></tr>
</table>

Table 20: Responses by GPT-4 and Claude3-Opus on a test unit where no correct answer is provided. Both models correctly identify the absence of a correct answer and successfully explain the intended meaning of the utterance in their responses.

Beyond the Numbers: Transparency in Relation Extraction Benchmark Creation and Leaderboards

Varvara Arzt
Faculty of Informatics, TU Wien
D!ARC, University of Klagenfurt
varvara.arzt@tuwien.ac.at

Allan Hanbury
Faculty of Informatics, TU Wien
allan.hanbury@tuwien.ac.at

Abstract

This paper investigates the transparency in the creation of benchmarks and the use of leaderboards for measuring progress in NLP, with a focus on the relation extraction (RE) task. Existing RE benchmarks often suffer from insufficient documentation, lacking crucial details such as data sources, inter-annotator agreement, the algorithms used for the selection of instances for datasets, and information on potential biases like dataset imbalance. Progress in RE is frequently measured by leaderboards that rank systems based on evaluation methods, typically limited to aggregate metrics like F1-score. However, the absence of detailed performance analysis beyond these metrics can obscure the true generalisation capabilities of models. Our analysis reveals that widely used RE benchmarks, such as TACRED and NYT, tend to be highly imbalanced and contain noisy labels. Moreover, the lack of class-based performance metrics fails to accurately reflect model performance across datasets with a large number of relation types. These limitations should be carefully considered when reporting progress in RE. While our discussion centers on the transparency of RE benchmarks and leaderboards, the observations we discuss are broadly applicable to other NLP tasks as well. Rather than undermining the significance and value of existing RE benchmarks and the development of new models, this paper advocates for improved documentation and more rigorous evaluation to advance the field.

1 Introduction

We examine the transparency in benchmarks and leaderboards, focusing on the relation extraction (RE) task. Our analysis utilises two broadly accepted RE datasets, TACRED (Zhang et al., 2017) and NYT (Riedel et al., 2010). While this paper focuses on the transparency of RE benchmarks and leaderboards, the observations we discuss are also relevant to other areas of natural language processing (NLP).

The development of state-of-the-art (SOTA) models in NLP is heavily reliant on benchmarks for evaluation. These benchmarks not only serve as a standard for assessing model performance but also play a pivotal role in shaping the perceived progress within the field. However, the current benchmarks often lack transparency in regard to their creation process, which can significantly impact the reliability of the evaluations conducted using them.

Opaque benchmarks and the absence of detailed performance analysis can obscure the true generalisation capabilities of models (Gebru et al., 2021; Dehghani et al., 2021). When benchmarks are not fully transparent — lacking comprehensive metadata, clear articulation of limitations, and rigorous evaluation reports — their ability to accurately reflect a model's robustness and generalisability is compromised. This can lead to an overestimation of progress, as models may appear to perform well on certain benchmarks but fail to generalise effectively to different or more complex datasets.

To enhance transparency and reproducibility in the evaluation of models, it is essential to publish the annotation guidelines and instructions that were provided to annotators during the creation of benchmarks. Understanding the exact criteria and procedures used in annotation is critical for interpreting the results obtained from these benchmarks and for comparing the performance of different models.

It is also important to recognise that widely used benchmarks such as TACRED (Zhang et al., 2017), TACRED-RE (Alt et al., 2020), and NYT (Riedel et al., 2010) cover only a subset of all possible relations. This limitation should be considered when evaluating models, as these benchmarks do not necessarily capture the full complexity of relation extraction task.

Additionally, when asserting that a new system

Proceedings of the 2nd GenBench Workshop on Generalisation (Benchmarking) in NLP, pages 120–130
November 16, 2024

outperforms existing ones, it is crucial to provide more granular results beyond aggregate metrics like weighted average or macro F1-score. These metrics, while useful, may not be sufficiently informative, particularly in the context of datasets with a large number of labels (Dehghani et al., 2021) and significant class imbalances, such as NYT or TACRED.

Although this position paper addresses certain issues with existing RE benchmarks and evaluation approaches, it does not seek to diminish their significance or the value of developing new RE models, which are crucial for advancing the NLP field. Instead, it aims to promote improved documentation of benchmarks and the adoption of more rigorous evaluation practices for SOTA RE systems.

2 Related Work

Despite the critical role of data in NLP, the documentation of the creation process of existing datasets remains scarce, unstandardised, and often lacks transparency, even for publicly available datasets (Bender and Friedman, 2018; Gebru et al., 2021; Peng et al., 2021; Singh, 2023; Kovatchev and Lease, 2024).

Gebru et al., 2021 addresses the issue of insufficient transparency in dataset creation by proposing that dataset creators accompany each dataset with a datasheet. This datasheet would document essential information about the dataset's creation process, thereby enhancing the reproducibility of machine learning experiments and helping to mitigate potential biases. They outline seven key stages of the dataset lifecycle: motivation, composition, collection process, preprocessing/cleaning/labeling, intended uses, distribution, and maintenance.

The lack of transparency in benchmark creation significantly impacts the evaluation of models trained on these benchmarks. As Kovatchev and Lease, 2024 highlights, many evaluation frameworks operate under the implicit assumption that a particular dataset is representative of the task it is intended to benchmark. However, systematic approaches to testing model generalisation remain limited (Hupkes et al., 2023). To address this gap, Kovatchev and Lease, 2024 propose the use of dataset similarity vectors, which consider various dimensions of the data, such as noise and ambiguity features, to more accurately predict the generalisation capabilities of models trained on these datasets.

Hupkes et al., 2023 present a comprehensive taxonomy of methods for studying the generalisation capabilities of models and introduce the GenBench evaluation card template[1] to assist researchers in systematically documenting, justifying, and tracing their generalisation experiments. Evaluating the generalisation capabilities of models has become increasingly complex in the era of large language models (LLMs), which strive to achieve human-like generalisation but are trained on vast, uncontrolled, and often nontransparent datasets.

To enhance the transparency of model evaluation processes, researchers advocate for testing new SOTA models in challenging scenarios involving perturbed instances (Wu et al., 2019; Gardner et al., 2020; Goel et al., 2021), thereby assessing model capabilities in more realistic settings than those provided by traditional test sets. Linzen, 2020, when discussing the limitations of current evaluation approaches, particularly in the context of developing systems with human-like generalisation capabilities, introduces the Generalisation Leaderboards. These leaderboards evaluate systems on test sets derived from distributions different from those used during training. This approach addresses the limitation that testing a model on data drawn from the same distribution as the training set does not necessarily demonstrate the model's ability to effectively solve the task; rather, it may merely reflect the model's proficiency in capturing statistical patterns specific to the training data.

In addition to traditional leaderboards, which often rank SOTA systems based solely on holistic metrics such as aggregate F1-score, Liu et al., 2021 propose leaderboards that incorporate more fine-grained metrics and offer functionality for direct analysis of misclassifications. This approach allows for a more detailed comparison of system performance, enabling users to directly identify the strengths and weaknesses of specific systems, thereby enhancing the transparency of leaderboards.

3 Transparency in Benchmark Creation

Current relation extraction benchmarks still lack transparency in their creation processes, making it difficult to assert that they generalise well on out-of-distribution data. For instance, we often lack detailed information about the text sources used to create these benchmarks. Transparency in the cre-

[1]Available at https://genbench.org/eval_cards/.

ation of RE datasets is crucial not only for mitigating potential biases but also for facilitating progress in the field. By better understanding the limitations of existing RE benchmarks we are able to consequently better understand the limitations of systems that make use of these data. We examine the problem of lacking transparency through the lens of two of the most widely used general-purpose relation extraction benchmarks, namely NYT (Riedel et al., 2010) and TACRED (Zhang et al., 2017) datasets. These benchmarks are broadly accepted by the NLP community and continue to be widely used, even in the era of LLMs (Huguet Cabot and Navigli, 2021; Wang et al., 2021; Tang et al., 2022; Wang et al., 2022; Efeoglu and Paschke, 2024; Sainz et al., 2024). Both the NYT and TACRED datasets address the task of sentence-level relation extraction.

3.1 Analysis of NYT and TACRED Datasets: Transparency and Limitations

The NYT dataset contains 24 relation types as well as a 'None' class and is based on a corpus of New York Times newspaper articles (Riedel et al., 2010). As Table 1 shows, the dataset includes over 266k sentences, with 64% of the instances belonging to the 'None' class.

Table 1: NYT Dataset

Type	Number of Samples
Positive Samples	96,228
Negative Samples	170,021
Total	266,249

NYT is created through distant supervision, utilising corpus of the New York Times articles (Sandhaus, 2008) and using Freebase (Bollacker et al., 2008) as the external supervision source. Detailed information on the included relation types and the number of instances for each relation can be found in Table 4 in the Appendix. The NYT dataset is publicly available. The example in Figure 1 shows one of the instances from the NYT dataset, which illustrates the issues associated with using distant supervision for dataset creation.[2]

As illustrated by the NYT instance in Figure 1, the sentence is labeled as containing the relation

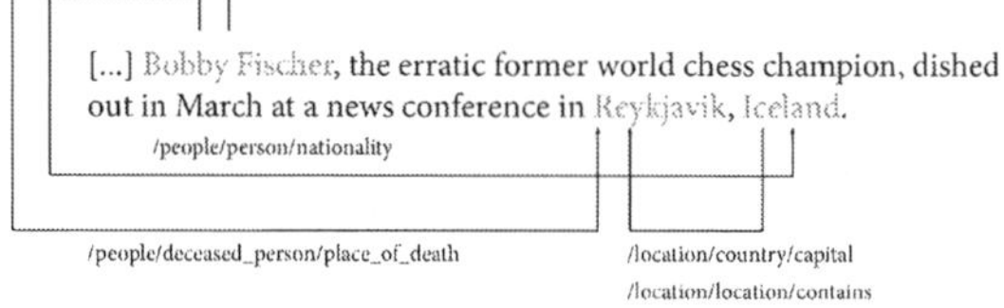

Figure 1: Example from the NYT dataset

'/people/person/nationality' between the head entity Bobby Fischer and the tail entity Iceland. However, this relation is not directly mentioned in text. This issue arises from the distant supervision method used to create the NYT dataset: when named entities are connected by a 'nationality' relation in Freebase, it though does not necessarily mean that this relation is explicitly present in the NYT data. Such interpretations can introduce significant biases in relation extraction systems and do not, for instance, reliably demonstrate a system's ability to detect 'nationality' relation in general. Such a reasoning pattern can be questioned as valid and would probably be labeled as a hallucination in the era of LLMs. The problem of noise in relation extraction datasets created using distant supervision has been discussed in several works, including Yaghoobzadeh et al., 2017.

The TACRED dataset contains 41 relations as well as a 'no_relation' class. TACRED includes over 106k instances, though, as shown in Table 2, 80% of the instances belong to 'no_relation' class, making the dataset highly imbalanced.

Table 2: TACRED Dataset

Type	Number of Samples
Positive Samples	21,773
Negative Samples	84,491
Total	106,264

The TACRED dataset is a fully supervised dataset obtained via crowdsourcing, and is based on the TAC KBP[3] corpus, which includes English newswire and web text. It is distributed under the Linguistic Data Consortium (LDC) license. Detailed information on the included relation types and the number of instances for each relation in TACRED can be found in Table 3 in the Appendix. The example in Figure 2 shows one of the instances from the TACRED dataset.[4]

[2]The example in Figure 1 represents NYT instance with article ID '/m/vinci8/data1/riedel/projects/relation/kb/nyt1/docstore/nyt-2005-2006.backup/1677367.xml.pb'. The NYT dataset can be found at https://github.com/INK-USC/ReQuest.

[3]https://tac.nist.gov/2017/KBP/index.html

[4]The example in Figure 2 originates from the paper de-

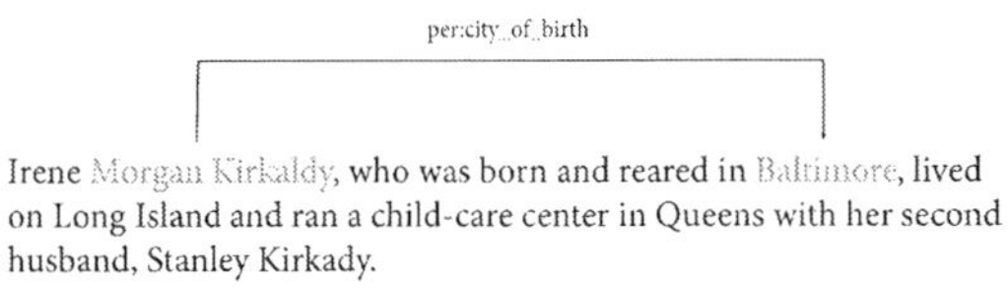

Figure 2: TACRED example

Compared to the NYT example in Figure 1, where the relation type cannot be determined solely from the information provided in the sentence, the TACRED instance in Figure 2 demonstrates an explicit relation that can be directly extracted from the sentence without requiring additional, potentially biased, reasoning steps. However, the TACRED dataset restricts each sentence to contain only one relation, in contrast to the NYT dataset, which allows each sentence to have multiple labels. The formulation of the relation extraction task like in TACRED can lead to many false negatives (Xie et al., 2021). For instance, the example above contains relations like 'per:stateorprovinces_of_residence', and 'per:employee_of' or 'per:spouse', all of which are part of the TACRED list of relations. Thus, restricting each instance to a single relation is far removed from the complexity of real-world text and may significantly mislead the model.

Despite the supplementary material[5] provided additionally to the paper (Zhang et al., 2017), TACRED still lacks transparency regarding the limitations mentioned above, as well as clarity on how the instances for the dataset were selected from the TAC KBP corpus. A similar lack of transparency exists with the NYT dataset, where the selection process for instances from the NYT corpus (Sandhaus, 2008) is not clearly documented. Since access to the TAC KBP corpus is restricted and the selection process from the NYT corpus is unclear, analysing the data included in both datasets and estimating the generalisation capabilities of models trained on these datasets becomes even more challenging.

Additionally, although TACRED instances were manually annotated by crowd workers, unlike the NYT instances, the crowdsourced annotations may still be quite noisy. For instance, Alt et al., 2020 demonstrated that over 50% of the challenging 'no_relation' instances in the development and test sets of TACRED were mislabeled.

As shown in Tables 1 and 2, both NYT and TACRED are highly imbalanced. While it may appear that the NYT dataset (with 64% of the instances belonging to the 'None' class) is more balanced compared to TACRED (where 80% of the instances belong to 'no_relation' class), a closer examination on the number of instances for each of the 24 relation types, as detailed in Table 4 in the Appendix, reveals a different picture. Nearly half of the positive instances in the NYT dataset belong to a single relation type, '/location/location/contains', and six out 24 relations are represented by fewer than 50 instances. For instance, the relation '/people/person/profession' contains only two instances, and '/business/company/industry' has just one instance.

In addition to providing precise information on the data selection process, it is also important to make the annotation guidelines publicly available if human annotators were involved, or to describe the algorithms used if a dataset was created through distant supervision (e.g., prompts). The publication of annotation guidelines and dataset description in general is among others crucial for clarifying ambiguous relations, whose scope may be understood in multiple ways, such as 'per:title' in TACRED or 'None' in NYT. The 'None' label in NYT could indicate either that none of the 24 specified relations apply — implying another, unspecified relation — or that there is no relation at all between the entities. These are fundamentally different scenarios, and conflating them could lead to significant confusion in the model.

Despite the publicly available TAC KBP guidelines[6], it remains unclear whether this version of annotation guidelines was also provided to the TACRED crowd workers. Furthermore, it is still unclear how the annotators of the TACRED dataset were instructed to handle sentences that contained a relation not listed among the 41 relations, or how they were to deal with sentences containing multiple different relations, as in Figure 2 above.

To introduce clarity in benchmark creation process, it is therefore crucial to publish not only anno-

scribing TACRED (Zhang et al., 2017).

[5]Zhang et al., 2017 mention supplementary material to the main paper describing the dataset, though they do not provide the direct link to material. It can be assumed they were referring to information available at `https://nlp.stanford.edu/projects/tacred/` or `https://tac.nist.gov/2017/KBP/ColdStart/guidelines.html`, but these sources still lack precise details on e.g. the data collection process and the creation of the relations inventory.

[6]`https://tac.nist.gov/2014/KBP/ColdStart/guidelines/TAC_KBP_2014_Slot_Descriptions_V1.4.pdf`

tation guidelines but also the instructions provided to the annotators. While Riedel et al., 2010 describes the process of creating the NYT dataset in a relatively detailed way, when they mention the use of human annotators to evaluate a fixed number of extracted relations in a distant supervision scenario, they still do not provide details on how these human annotators were instructed.

3.2 The Need for Standardised Benchmark Documentation

The analysis of widely used NYT and TACRED RE benchmarks, along with their available documentation, underscores the persistent issue of lacking exhaustive documentation regarding the creation processes of NLP benchmarks. Proper documentation should be easily discoverable and ideally stored according to accepted standards. Currently, information on NLP benchmarks is dispersed across many resources and often lacks the necessary details to make the benchmark creation process fully transparent which is among others crucial for the analysis of generalisation capabilities of a particular dataset. While sources like `PaperswithCode`[7] are helpful, they still miss a significant amount of information needed to achieve this goal.

Gebru et al., 2021 addresses the issue of insufficient benchmark transparency and suggests that each new benchmark should be accompanied by a datasheet. The suggested datasheet would include information such as potential sources of noise and errors in the dataset, to enhance transparency and allow for more accurate assessments of the dataset reliability and generalisation capabilities.

The NLP community would greatly benefit from a standardised approach to benchmark documentation, similar to model cards for model reporting (Mitchell et al., 2019), but specifically designed for datasets. This is at least as important as model metadata. Model cards, which are essentially files containing metadata with useful information about a model in question, have proven effective, as seen in their implementation at `HuggingFace`.[8] A similar concept for datasets would ensure that critical information about benchmark creation, potential biases, and other relevant details are systematically recorded and easily accessible. While HuggingFace provides dataset cards[9] (Park and Jeoung, 2022) which are a promising step in this direction, most datasets shared via `HuggingFace` currently have only a fraction of the possible metadata filled out. Moreover, while the ecosystem that `HuggingFace` provides has undoubtedly contributed significantly to the NLP community, it is essential to acknowledge that, given the open nature of the platform where anyone can upload models and datasets, the reliability of sources, including datasets and their associated metadata, should be approached with caution. Ideally, comprehensive documentation of benchmarks should originate directly from their creators.

A datasheet for benchmarks would ideally include properties such as descriptive and social impact metadata (Park and Jeoung, 2022) including data provenance, data preprocessing details (e.g., filtering approach used to obtain relevant samples), annotation guidelines and other instructions, dataset size, recommended data split information, a list of labels, the specific task being addressed, the method used for creating the benchmark (e.g., human annotation or distant supervision), inter-annotator agreement (if human annotators were involved), and potential sources of noise (e.g., representativeness of the data). In addition to the proposed datasheets for datasets by Gebru et al., 2021, inspiration can be drawn from dataset templates[10] available in the Open Research Knowledge Graph (Jaradeh et al., 2019). Although these templates are currently used infrequently by benchmark creators, and often only a small fraction of the possible properties are filled out, their wider adoption could significantly enhance benchmark transparency. For instance, a centralised, standardised approach to documenting benchmarks could help establish a more universal system of labels, making it easier to compare benchmarks within a particular domain: e.g., in the case of RE benchmarks, a standardised set of relations could simplify comparisons across different datasets and models.

The way we document the benchmark creation process is becoming increasingly critical in the era of LLMs, especially as we strive to develop Artificial General Intelligence (AGI) systems with human-like reasoning capabilities (Chollet, 2019; Hendrycks et al., 2021). As we exhaust real-world data, and with the uncertainty about whether data

[7] `https://paperswithcode.com/`

[8] More on model cards at `HuggingFace` can be found at `https://huggingface.co/docs/hub/en/model-cards`

[9] `https://huggingface.co/docs/hub/en/datasets-cards`

[10] For instance, the `https://orkg.org/template/R178304` dataset template contains 22 properties like inter-annotator agreement or data availability.

presented as human annotations were truly annotated by humans or generated through LLM prompting, ensuring transparent and thorough documentation is essential for accurately evaluating the systems based on these benchmarks.

4 Transparency in Leaderboard Performance Evaluation

The transparency in the benchmark creation process has a direct impact on the ability to adequately evaluate the system trained on a dataset in question and therefore analyse its generalisation capabilities. One of the ways of measuring progress in particular NLP field are leaderboards. Despite the fact that leaderboards push the NLP field forward, they also lack transparency on evaluation process and mostly are limited to the ranking based on holistic metrics such as accuracy or F1-score (Liu et al., 2021). For instance, both TACRED[11] and NYT[12] leaderboards on a widely used platform `PaperswithCode` rely on F1-score as a holisitic metric to rank the RE models.

Moreover, not only traditional leaderboards lack fine-grained metrics in their ranking approach, but also the papers that report SOTA results follow this trend, which can lead to an emphasis on achieving top leaderboard positions rather than genuinely addressing the underlying task — a phenomenon known as SOTA-chasing (Rodriguez et al., 2021).

Recent papers reporting SOTA-performance on NYT, TACRED, and TACRED-RE[13] (Huguet Cabot and Navigli, 2021; Wang et al., 2022; Tang et al., 2022; Efeoglu and Paschke, 2024; Sainz et al., 2024; Orlando et al., 2024) report only aggregate metrics such as micro or macro f1-score, recall, and precision. Consequently, these evaluations lack more fine-grained, class-based metrics, which are crucial for the analysis of RE systems dealing with a large number of relations such as the 42 labels in TACRED and the 25 labels in NYT. In the context of imbalanced datasets like TACRED and NYT, a system may achieve high overall metrics by always predicting a 'no_relation' class. However, this outcome does not indicate that the system has indeed effectively learned to solve the relation extraction task across a diverse set of over 20 labels. Notably, even the original papers presenting TACRED (Zhang et al., 2017), TACRED-RE (Alt et al., 2020), NYT (Riedel et al., 2010) do not contain fine-grained, class-based metrics. Given the significant class imbalance reflected in the Tables 1 and 2, as well as the fact that many relations in both TACRED and NYT are represented by only a few instances, such as '/people/person/profession' in NYT (see Table 4 in the Appendix), which contains only two instances, reporting class-based metrics is essential for adequately assessing the capabilities of a particular system to solve the RE task. Without detailed performance reports, it is difficult to determine whether a new SOTA system generalises well or simply creates the illusion of improvement through SOTA-chasing.

Benchmarks such as NYT, TACRED, and TACRED-RE lack standardised guidelines for reporting results, leading to inconsistencies across publications that report SOTA results on these benchmarks (Dehghani et al., 2021). This lack of agreement can cause discrepancies in leaderboard rankings. For example, there is no consensus on which aggregated score should be used on platforms like `PaperswithCode`. The current top-performing model on the TACRED benchmark (Efeoglu and Paschke, 2024) reports the micro-F1 score, which is also used for ranking. In contrast, the current second (Wang et al., 2022) and third (Huang et al., 2022) top-ranked models on TACRED report the macro-F1 score, which is also utilised for their ranking on `PaperswithCode`. This inconsistency in evaluation metrics raises concerns about the reliability of the leaderboard rankings.

Additionally, there is no overlap between the top-performing models listed on `PaperswithCode` leaderboards for NYT and TACRED, meaning that all top-performing models for TACRED are different from those for NYT. This further complicates the analysis of these models' generalisation capabilities and makes it difficult to assess model ranking consistency across RE benchmarks. Focusing exclusively on achieving high performance on a single benchmark, without considering results across multiple benchmarks, can result in models that are overly specialised for specific benchmarks. This, however, does not necessarily indicate meaningful progress in addressing a particular NLP task (Dehghani et al., 2021), such as relation extraction.

[11] `https://paperswithcode.com/sota/relation-extraction-on-tacred`

[12] `https://paperswithcode.com/sota/relation-extraction-on-nyt`

[13] TACRED-RE is a revised version of original TACRED, with a subset of challenging development and test set instances relabeled by professional annotators (Alt et al., 2020).

Papers reporting SOTA results on RE, including the original TACRED (Zhang et al., 2017), TACRED-RE (Alt et al., 2020), NYT (Riedel et al., 2010), often do not provide information on whether the issue of class imbalance was addressed. Such details should be included in system description papers, particularly when reporting new SOTA results. For instance, the authors of the Biographical RE dataset (Plum et al., 2022) tackled the problem of large class imbalance by removing some of majority class relations, thereby equalising them with the sum of all other relations.

Model performance ceiling (Alt et al., 2020) may be caused by the presence of noisy data, which can limit the potential for improvement by new RE methods. As discussed in Section 3, this noise can originate from both distantly-supervised datasets, such as NYT, and fully-supervised crowdsourced datasets, such as TACRED. Additionally, the way the task is formulated, whether as a single-label (TACRED) or multi-label (NYT) classification task, can contribute to performance limitations. For example, an RE model might make a correct prediction, but due to the task being framed as a single-label classification problem — despite real-world instances potentially containing multiple relations — this could lead to misclassification. Such factors should be considered when reporting new SOTA results. Moreover, in the era of LLMs, it is possible that multiple outputs generated by an LLM for an RE task could be correct (Hendrycks et al., 2021), a nuance that is not captured by holistic metrics like aggregate F1-score.

Due to the mentioned limitations of traditional leaderboards such as the ones utilised on the `PaperswithCode` platform, Liu et al., 2021 suggest an ExplainaBoard interactive tool that provides both holistic and fine-grained metrics as well as functionality for direct analysis of misclassifications. Such an extension of traditional leaderboards enables the direct detection of strengths and weaknesses of a particular system, as well as of a benchmark, thereby enhancing the ability to assess the generalisation capabilities of systems, such as those used for relation extraction.

Moreover, evaluating model performance on a test set drawn from the same distribution as the training set does not necessarily demonstrate a model's ability to solve an underlying task (Linzen, 2020), such as relation extraction. To address this issue, Linzen, 2020 propose Generalisation Leaderboards, which would evaluate systems on test sets derived from different distributions than the training set. For instance, it would be valuable to assess a system fine-tuned on TACRED data for its ability to extract the same subset of relations present in the NYT dataset, as strong performance on one dataset does not necessarily indicate robust generalisation capabilities. Additionally, techniques such as adversarial attacks (Wu et al., 2019; Gardner et al., 2020; Goel et al., 2021) can further test the true capabilities of RE systems by exposing their vulnerabilities and resilience to challenging scenarios.

5 Conclusion and Future Work

In this work, we have highlighted several limitations in the benchmark documentation and use of traditional leaderboards, particularly those employed for the relation extraction task. Limitations in benchmark documentation include the absence of comprehensive descriptive metadata, such as the source of the data or details regarding inter-annotator agreement, as well as an absence of clear articulation of the dataset's inherent limitations, such as large class imbalances and potential noise. Furthermore, there is often insufficient discussion on methods to mitigate these issues.

Evaluating systems based on these RE benchmarks inherently necessitates addressing the problems associated with insufficient documentation of the benchmarks. For instance, traditional leaderboards, such as those on `PaperswithCode`, that play a significant role in advancing NLP, typically rely on holistic metrics like F1-score. However, these metrics fail to capture the complexity of the relation extraction task, especially in scenarios involving a large number of labels and highly imbalanced datasets, such as TACRED, where most instances belong to a 'no_relation' class. Additionally, papers reporting new SOTA results on RE benchmarks like NYT and TACRED often focus exclusively on aggregate metrics, neglecting class-based metrics, which obscures the nuanced performance of models across different relation types.

This paper does not intend to undermine the significance and value of existing benchmarks such as TACRED or NYT, which are crucial for the evaluation of models in the field, as well as the development of new SOTA approaches. Instead, given the evolving perspective on data used in training deep learning models, our objective is to propose avenues for improving the documentation of benchmark creation processes, which would in turn help to better assess the generalisation capabilities of RE models. Additionally, we also aim to motivate the adoption of more rigorous evaluation practices, encouraging researchers to move beyond the limited scope of only reporting metrics such as aggregate F1-score, precision, and recall. This is particularly important in NLP tasks such as relation extraction, where the complexity is exacerbated by the presence of a large number of relations.

It is also crucial to recognise that high performance on a specific RE benchmark, such as TACRED, TACRED-RE, or NYT, reflects only a model's ability to handle a subset of all possible relations. Furthermore, even if a system performs well on a given subset of relations, it may struggle significantly when extracting the same relations from out-of-distribution data.

Our focus should not solely be on the development of new approaches, but also on critically analysing our systems and recognising the limitations of the data used for their evaluation. This critical perspective is essential for advancing the field and ensuring that our models are robust and generalisable.

Finally, this work serves as a position paper that highlights several issues in the creation of RE benchmarks and the practices surrounding leaderboard evaluations. We acknowledge the limitations of this work, particularly the lack of extensive quantitative evidence. In our future research, we aim to conduct a comprehensive cross-dataset evaluation of RE systems on the benchmarks discussed. Such an evaluation will provide empirical support for the concerns raised and offer a more reliable assessment of the generalisation capabilities of current RE systems.

References

Christoph Alt, Aleksandra Gabryszak, and Leonhard Hennig. 2020. TACRED revisited: A thorough evaluation of the TACRED relation extraction task. In *Proceedings of the 58th Annual Meeting of the Association for Computational Linguistics*, pages 1558–1569, Online. Association for Computational Linguistics.

Emily M. Bender and Batya Friedman. 2018. Data statements for natural language processing: Toward mitigating system bias and enabling better science. *Transactions of the Association for Computational Linguistics*, 6:587–604.

Kurt Bollacker, Colin Evans, Praveen Paritosh, Tim Sturge, and Jamie Taylor. 2008. Freebase: a collaboratively created graph database for structuring human knowledge. In *Proceedings of the 2008 ACM SIGMOD International Conference on Management of Data*, SIGMOD '08, page 1247–1250, New York, NY, USA. Association for Computing Machinery.

François Chollet. 2019. On the measure of intelligence. *ArXiv*, abs/1911.01547.

Mostafa Dehghani, Yi Tay, Alexey A. Gritsenko, Zhe Zhao, Neil Houlsby, Fernando Diaz, Donald Metzler, and Oriol Vinyals. 2021. The benchmark lottery. *Preprint*, arXiv:2107.07002.

Sefika Efeoglu and Adrian Paschke. 2024. Retrieval-augmented generation-based relation extraction. *Preprint*, arXiv:2404.13397.

Matt Gardner, Yoav Artzi, Victoria Basmov, Jonathan Berant, Ben Bogin, Sihao Chen, Pradeep Dasigi, Dheeru Dua, Yanai Elazar, Ananth Gottumukkala, Nitish Gupta, Hannaneh Hajishirzi, Gabriel Ilharco, Daniel Khashabi, Kevin Lin, Jiangming Liu, Nelson F. Liu, Phoebe Mulcaire, Qiang Ning, Sameer Singh, Noah A. Smith, Sanjay Subramanian, Reut Tsarfaty, Eric Wallace, Ally Zhang, and Ben Zhou. 2020. Evaluating models' local decision boundaries via contrast sets. In *Findings of the Association for Computational Linguistics: EMNLP 2020*, pages 1307–1323, Online. Association for Computational Linguistics.

Timnit Gebru, Jamie Morgenstern, Briana Vecchione, Jennifer Wortman Vaughan, Hanna Wallach, Hal Daumé III, and Kate Crawford. 2021. Datasheets for datasets. *Commun. ACM*, 64(12):86–92.

Karan Goel, Nazneen Fatema Rajani, Jesse Vig, Zachary Taschdjian, Mohit Bansal, and Christopher Ré. 2021. Robustness gym: Unifying the NLP evaluation landscape. In *Proceedings of the 2021 Conference of the North American Chapter of the Association for Computational Linguistics: Human Language Technologies: Demonstrations*, pages 42–55, Online. Association for Computational Linguistics.

Dan Hendrycks, Collin Burns, Steven Basart, Andy Zou, Mantas Mazeika, Dawn Song, and Jacob Steinhardt. 2021. Measuring massive multitask language understanding. In *International Conference on Learning Representations*.

James Y. Huang, Bangzheng Li, Jiashu Xu, and Muhao Chen. 2022. Unified semantic typing with meaningful label inference. In *Proceedings of the 2022 Conference of the North American Chapter of the Association for Computational Linguistics: Human Language Technologies*, pages 2642–2654, Seattle, United States. Association for Computational Linguistics.

Pere-Lluís Huguet Cabot and Roberto Navigli. 2021. REBEL: Relation extraction by end-to-end language generation. In *Findings of the Association for Computational Linguistics: EMNLP 2021*, pages 2370–2381, Punta Cana, Dominican Republic. Association for Computational Linguistics.

Dieuwke Hupkes, Mario Giulianelli, Verna Dankers, Mikel Artetxe, Yanai Elazar, et al. 2023. A taxonomy and review of generalization research in nlp. *Nature Machine Intelligence*, 5(10):1161–1174.

Mohamad Yaser Jaradeh, Allard Oelen, Manuel Prinz, Markus Stocker, and Sören Auer. 2019. Open research knowledge graph: A system walkthrough. In *Digital Libraries for Open Knowledge*, pages 348–351, Cham. Springer International Publishing.

Venelin Kovatchev and Matthew Lease. 2024. Benchmark transparency: Measuring the impact of data on evaluation. In *Proceedings of the 2024 Conference of the North American Chapter of the Association for Computational Linguistics: Human Language Technologies (Volume 1: Long Papers)*, pages 1536–1551, Mexico City, Mexico. Association for Computational Linguistics.

Tal Linzen. 2020. How can we accelerate progress towards human-like linguistic generalization? In *Proceedings of the 58th Annual Meeting of the Association for Computational Linguistics*, pages 5210–5217, Online. Association for Computational Linguistics.

Pengfei Liu, Jinlan Fu, Yang Xiao, Weizhe Yuan, Shuaichen Chang, Junqi Dai, Yixin Liu, Zihuiwen Ye, and Graham Neubig. 2021. ExplainaBoard: An explainable leaderboard for NLP. In *Proceedings of the 59th Annual Meeting of the Association for Computational Linguistics and the 11th International Joint Conference on Natural Language Processing: System Demonstrations*, pages 280–289, Online. Association for Computational Linguistics.

Margaret Mitchell, Simone Wu, Andrew Zaldivar, Parker Barnes, Lucy Vasserman, Ben Hutchinson, Elena Spitzer, Inioluwa Deborah Raji, and Timnit Gebru. 2019. Model cards for model reporting. In *Proceedings of the Conference on Fairness, Accountability, and Transparency*, FAT* '19, page 220–229, New York, NY, USA. Association for Computing Machinery.

Riccardo Orlando, Pere-Lluís Huguet Cabot, Edoardo Barba, and Roberto Navigli. 2024. ReLiK: Retrieve and LinK, fast and accurate entity linking and relation extraction on an academic budget. In *Findings of the Association for Computational Linguistics ACL 2024*, pages 14114–14132, Bangkok, Thailand and virtual meeting. Association for Computational Linguistics.

Jaihyun Park and Sullam Jeoung. 2022. Raison d'être of the benchmark dataset: A survey of current practices of benchmark dataset sharing platforms. In *Proceedings of NLP Power! The First Workshop on Efficient Benchmarking in NLP*, pages 1–10, Dublin, Ireland. Association for Computational Linguistics.

Kenneth L Peng, Arunesh Mathur, and Arvind Narayanan. 2021. Mitigating dataset harms requires stewardship: Lessons from 1000 papers. In *Thirty-fifth Conference on Neural Information Processing Systems Datasets and Benchmarks Track (Round 2)*.

Alistair Plum, Tharindu Ranasinghe, Spencer Jones, Constantin Orasan, and Ruslan Mitkov. 2022. Biographical semi-supervised relation extraction dataset. In *Proceedings of the 45th International ACM SIGIR Conference on Research and Development in Information Retrieval*, SIGIR '22, page 3121–3130, New York, NY, USA. Association for Computing Machinery.

Sebastian Riedel, Limin Yao, and Andrew McCallum. 2010. Modeling relations and their mentions without labeled text. In *Machine Learning and Knowledge Discovery in Databases*, pages 148–163, Berlin, Heidelberg. Springer Berlin Heidelberg.

Pedro Rodriguez, Joe Barrow, Alexander Miserlis Hoyle, John P. Lalor, Robin Jia, and Jordan Boyd-Graber. 2021. Evaluation examples are not equally informative: How should that change NLP leaderboards? In *Proceedings of the 59th Annual Meeting of the Association for Computational Linguistics and the 11th International Joint Conference on Natural Language Processing (Volume 1: Long Papers)*, pages 4486–4503, Online. Association for Computational Linguistics.

Oscar Sainz, Iker García-Ferrero, Rodrigo Agerri, Oier Lopez de Lacalle, German Rigau, and Eneko Agirre. 2024. GoLLIE: Annotation guidelines improve zero-shot information-extraction. In *The Twelfth International Conference on Learning Representations*.

Evan Sandhaus. 2008. The new york times annotated corpus. *Linguistic Data Consortium, Philadelphia*, 6(12):e26752.

Prerna Singh. 2023. Systematic review of data-centric approaches in artificial intelligence and machine learning. *Data Science and Management*, 6(3):144–157.

Wei Tang, Benfeng Xu, Yuyue Zhao, Zhendong Mao, Yifeng Liu, Yong Liao, and Haiyong Xie. 2022. UniRel: Unified representation and interaction for joint relational triple extraction. In *Proceedings of the 2022 Conference on Empirical Methods in Natural Language Processing*, pages 7087–7099, Abu Dhabi, United Arab Emirates. Association for Computational Linguistics.

Chenguang Wang, Xiao Liu, Zui Chen, Haoyun Hong, Jie Tang, and Dawn Song. 2021. Zero-shot information extraction as a unified text-to-triple translation. In *Proceedings of the 2021 Conference on Empirical Methods in Natural Language Processing*, pages 1225–1238, Online and Punta Cana, Dominican Republic. Association for Computational Linguistics.

Chenguang Wang, Xiao Liu, Zui Chen, Haoyun Hong, Jie Tang, and Dawn Song. 2022. DeepStruct: Pretraining of language models for structure prediction. In *Findings of the Association for Computational Linguistics: ACL 2022*, pages 803–823, Dublin, Ireland. Association for Computational Linguistics.

Tongshuang Wu, Marco Tulio Ribeiro, Jeffrey Heer, and Daniel Weld. 2019. Errudite: Scalable, reproducible, and testable error analysis. In *Proceedings of the 57th Annual Meeting of the Association for Computational Linguistics*, pages 747–763, Florence, Italy. Association for Computational Linguistics.

Chenhao Xie, Jiaqing Liang, Jingping Liu, Chengsong Huang, Wenhao Huang, and Yanghua Xiao. 2021. Revisiting the negative data of distantly supervised relation extraction. In *Proceedings of the 59th Annual Meeting of the Association for Computational Linguistics and the 11th International Joint Conference on Natural Language Processing (Volume 1: Long Papers)*, pages 3572–3581, Online. Association for Computational Linguistics.

Yadollah Yaghoobzadeh, Heike Adel, and Hinrich Schütze. 2017. Noise mitigation for neural entity typing and relation extraction. In *Proceedings of the 15th Conference of the European Chapter of the Association for Computational Linguistics: Volume 1, Long Papers*, pages 1183–1194, Valencia, Spain. Association for Computational Linguistics.

Yuhao Zhang, Victor Zhong, Danqi Chen, Gabor Angeli, and Christopher D. Manning. 2017. Position-aware attention and supervised data improve slot filling. In *Proceedings of the 2017 Conference on Empirical Methods in Natural Language Processing*, pages 35–45, Copenhagen, Denmark. Association for Computational Linguistics.

A Dataset Statistics: Class Distribution

Table 3: TACRED Dataset

Relation	# of Samples
no_relation	84,491
per:title	3862
org:top_members/employees	2770
per:employee_of	2163
org:alternate_names	1359
per:age	833
per:countries_of_residence	819
org:country_of_headquarters	753
per:cities_of_residence	742
per:origin	667
org:city_of_headquarters	573
per:stateorprovinces_of_residence	484
per:spouse	483
org:subsidiaries	453
org:parents	444
per:date_of_death	394
org:stateorprovince_of_headquarters	350
per:children	347
per:cause_of_death	337
per:other_family	319
per:parents	296
org:members	286
per:charges	280
org:founded_by	268
per:siblings	250
per:schools_attended	229
per:city_of_death	227
org:website	223
org:member_of	171
org:founded	166
per:religion	153
per:alternate_names	153
org:shareholders	144
org:political/religious_affiliation	125
org:number_of_employees/members	121
per:stateorprovince_of_death	104
per:date_of_birth	103
per:city_of_birth	103
per:stateorprovince_of_birth	72
per:country_of_death	61
per:country_of_birth	53
org:dissolved	33
Positive Samples	21,773
Negative Samples	84,491
Total	106,264

Table 4: NYT Dataset

Relation	# of Samples
None	170,021
/location/location/contains	44,490
/location/country/capital	7267
/people/person/nationality	7244
/people/person/place_lived	7015
/location/administrative_division/country	5951
/location/country/administrative_divisions	5851
/business/person/company	5421
/location/neighborhood/neighborhood_of	5082
/people/person/place_of_birth	3133
/people/deceased_person/place_of_death	1914
/business/company/founders	767
/people/person/children	487
/business/company/place_founded	414
/business/company/major_shareholders	282
/business/company_shareholder/major_shareholders	282
/sports/sports_team_location/teams	218
/sports/sports_team/location	218
/people/person/religion	67
/business/company/advisors	45
/people/ethnicity/geographic_distribution	33
/people/ethnicity/people	21
/people/person/ethnicity	21
/people/person/profession	2
/business/company/industry	1
Positive Samples	96,228
Negative Samples	170,021
Total	266,249

Is artificial intelligence still intelligence? LLMs generalize to novel adjective-noun pairs, but don't mimic the full human distribution

Hayley Ross[1], **Kathryn Davidson**[1], **Najoung Kim**[2]
[1]Harvard University [2]Boston University
hayleyross@g.harvard.edu kathryndavidson@fas.harvard.edu najoung@bu.edu

Abstract

Inferences from adjective-noun combinations like *Is artificial intelligence still intelligence?* provide a good test bed for LLMs' understanding of meaning and compositional generalization capability, since there are many combinations which are novel to both humans and LLMs but nevertheless elicit convergent human judgments. We study a range of LLMs and find that the largest models we tested are able to draw human-like inferences when the inference is determined by context and can generalize to unseen adjective-noun combinations. We also propose three methods to evaluate LLMs on these inferences out of context, where there is a distribution of human-like answers rather than a single correct answer. We find that LLMs show a human-like distribution on at most 75% of our dataset, which is promising but still leaves room for improvement.

1 Introduction

As the pretraining datasets of LLMs grow, it becomes increasingly difficult to test whether LLMs can generalize to unseen instances of linguistic phenomena, since it is hard to systematically exclude them from the pretraining data (Kim et al., 2022). Adjective-noun combinations, in particular with so-called privative adjectives like *fake*, provide a good test bed for testing granular language understanding and semantic composition in LLMs, since we can find many adjective-noun bigrams which are easy for humans to understand despite being novel to them, and can further confirm that they are novel to the LLM by a string search over its pretraining corpus. Adjective-noun bigrams are naturally associated with membership inferences which allow us to test whether LLMs have successfully "composed" their meaning: is an {adjective} {noun} still a {noun}? This inference is not as straightforward as it may seem: while a *yellow flower* is clearly still a *flower* (a *subsective* inference), a *fake* or *counterfeit dollar bill* is typically not a *dollar bill* (a *privative* inference), even though a *fake watch* is typically a *watch* (Martin, 2022; Ross et al., 2024). In order to draw the correct inference, humans and LLMs need to grasp not only the effect of the adjective on the noun's properties, but also which properties are required vs. merely typical for membership in that noun/category. Moreover, like many cases of meaning, this inference depends on context. For example, a *fake crowd* might qualify as a *crowd* if it is made up of paid actors, but less so if it is just painted dummies on a movie set. Nonetheless, humans derive convergent inferences for many novel bigrams both with and without context, giving a ground truth to which we can compare LLMs.

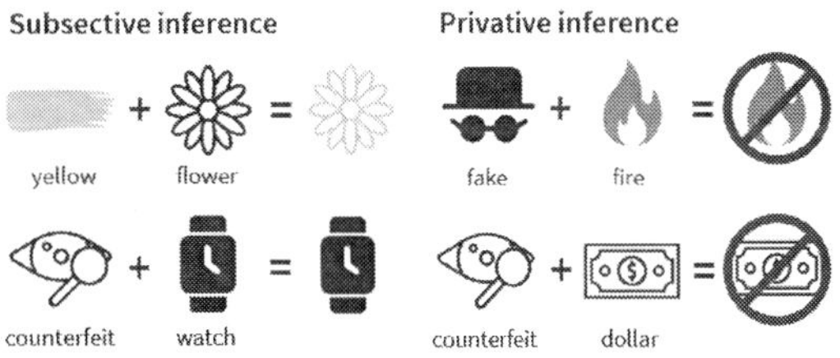

Figure 1: Membership inferences for adjective-noun combinations vary by adjective and noun.

Building on the dataset of English human judgments developed in Ross et al. (2024), we compare LLMs of several sizes with humans for cases in which the context determines the inference. We further explore three methods to evaluate LLMs against the full distribution of human ratings when there is no provided context. We find that when the context determines the inference, recent larger LLMs closely match human behavior, while smaller LLMs only sometimes do so. Almost all LLMs, even smaller ones, are able to handle novel adjective-noun combinations as well as they handle known ones, suggesting that they evaluate these combinations on-the-fly and can generalize accordingly like humans do. This alignment in performance on observed and novel combinations

Proceedings of the 2nd GenBench Workshop on Generalisation (Benchmarking) in NLP, pages 131–153
November 16, 2024 ©2024 Association for Computational Linguistics

continues to hold in a setting where no context is provided. However, we find that even 70B parameter LLMs are only able to approximate the distribution of ratings of a population of human raters for 75% of our dataset or less, struggling on combinations with high human variance and inferences which are rare for a particular adjective, such as a *homemade cat* not necessarily being a *cat*. Most LLMs also assign a more positive rating to the question "Is artificial intelligence still intelligence?" than most humans (see Figure 5). In sum, while our generalization results are highly promising, there is room for improvement on the task of matching human inferences in this category overall. We share our code and data on GitHub.[1]

2 Related work

Most previous computational work on adjective-noun composition focuses on distributional semantics using word embeddings (Boleda et al., 2013, 2012; Cappelle et al., 2018; Guevara, 2010; Hartung et al., 2017; Vecchi et al., 2017). Cappelle et al. (2018) specifically analyze privative adjective embeddings, finding no difference between their embeddings and embeddings of other adjectives. Results for early LLMs are largely negative: BERT (Devlin et al., 2019) shows no evidence of compositionality for adjective-noun and noun-noun phrases, relying instead on word overlap heuristics for similarity judgments (Yu and Ettinger, 2020). Bertolini et al. (2022) study the inferences of adjective-noun combinations for BERT and RoBERTa (Liu et al., 2019). They divide adjectives into three inference classes—intersective, subsective and privative—based on previous computational work (Lalisse and Asudeh, 2015; Nayak et al., 2014), and test whether LLMs can draw the correct pattern of inferences for adjectives in each class. However, recent work in linguistics (Pavlick and Callison-Burch, 2016b; Martin, 2022; Ross et al., 2024) suggests that Bertolini et al.'s task may be ill-defined, since adjectives in these "classes" can license either a subsective or a privative inference depending on the noun and context. Indeed, Goodale and Mascarenhas (2023) find that BERT can distinguish between intersective and subsective adjectives, which are more clearly distinct.

For the "Is an X a Y" task more broadly, LLMs from BERT to Llama 2 (Touvron et al., 2023) show some, but limited abilities to judge "Is an X a Y" for hypernyms, especially with negation (Hanna and Mareček, 2021; Ettinger, 2020; Ravichander et al., 2020; Nikishina et al., 2023; Moskvoretskii et al., 2024). Results from property learning also show that earlier models struggle to learn what properties are typical of nouns (Do and Pavlick, 2021; Apidianaki and Garí Soler, 2021; Pavlick and Callison-Burch, 2016a)—a key part of our task, since LLMs must know what constitutes a *watch* in order to judge whether a *fake watch* counts as one. Meanwhile, Lyu et al. (2022) find that BERT and GPT-3 (Brown et al., 2020) cannot handle inferences on recursive adjectives, such as "Is my favorite new movie my favorite movie?", while Sathe et al. (2024) find that GPT-2 (Radford et al., 2019), MPT 30B (MosaicML NLP Team, 2023) and other smaller models struggle to predict whether rare adjective-noun combinations are acceptable to humans. However, less is known about the capabilities of newer, larger models in these areas. Recent work with newer models including Llama 2 and GPT-3 on noun-noun compounds—whose meaning arises less straightforwardly from their parts than adjective-noun combination (Hacken, 2016)—shows that the LLMs do not generalize well in this case (Ormerod et al., 2024; Coil and Shwartz, 2023; Rambelli et al., 2024) .

3 Human judgment dataset

Ross et al. (2024) present two datasets of human judgments on adjective-noun inferences. The first, which we refer to as NO-CONTEXT, collects human ratings on "Is an {adjective} {noun} a {noun}?" on a 5-point Likert scale ("Definitely not", "Probably not", "Unsure", "Probably yes" and "Definitely yes") for 798 bigrams, covering 102 nouns crossed with 6 typically-privative and 6 typically-subsective adjectives. (In this paper, we use "(typically-)privative / subsective adjective" to refer to adjectives historically classed as such, which often but not always result in the respective inference.) 180 of the 798 bigrams are zero frequency in the C4 pretraining corpus (Raffel et al., 2020), which we take as a proxy for the undisclosed pretraining corpora of the models we study. We take these bigrams to be novel to both humans and LLMs.[2] We call a bigram high-frequency if it is in the top quartile of bigrams studied by Ross et al.

[1] https://github.com/rossh2/artificial-intelligence/

[2] The dataset was not published when these models were trained, so there is no danger of it being included in model pretraining.

Ross et al. show that this inference depends on the adjective and noun, with bigrams with "subsective" adjectives usually (but not always; e.g., *homemade cat*) being rated subsective, while bigrams with "privative" adjectives such as *fake crowd* elicit a wide distribution of ratings from privative to subsective, with high variance per bigram. Moreover, humans converge on inference judgments for many zero-frequency bigrams, and show similar variance overall between zero-frequency and high-frequency bigrams, demonstrating that they can generalize these inferences.

The second dataset, which we refer to as CONTEXT, shows that providing a context with appropriate detail is sufficient to determine the inference for typically-privative adjectives. Participants first read a short 50-word context and then answer "In this setting, is an {adjective} {noun} a {noun}?" The dataset contains 56 expert-written contexts for 28 bigrams, with one privative-biased and one subsective-biased context for each bigram; an example is shown in Appendix B.1. 6 bigrams are zero-frequency in C4 and a further 7 are low-frequency (below median frequency in the total set). This dataset is much smaller due to the need for trained annotators to create the contexts.

4 Experiment 1: In-context meaning generalization

Typical LLM evaluations assume a single correct answer for each question. Thus, we begin with the smaller CONTEXT dataset from Ross et al. (2024) where the contexts provided are sufficient to determine the inference. Our evaluation focuses on the following two aspects: (1) whether the LLM is sensitive to the provided context, and (2) whether the LLM is able to choose the intended inference both for high-frequency bigrams it has presumably seen during pretraining and also for zero-frequency bigrams which we presume it has not.

4.1 Method

Experiment 1a evaluates the 28 bigrams in CONTEXT with no context provided. While there is no single correct rating in this setting, we can use this as a baseline to see if providing a context changes the rating. Experiment 1b evaluates the same bigrams but provides the two contexts for each bigram which bias the rating for humans. For both, we adapt the method used in Ross et al. (2024) as closely as possible for LLMs. We use the same question wording, asking "(In this context [1b],) is an {adjective} {noun} still a {noun}?" with the same 5-point Likert scale, the only difference being that the Likert scale is described in words rather than pictured. We provide 5 few-shot examples illustrating each rating on the scale.[3] We believe this to be a comparable setup since humans also see examples during the training phase of the experiment, though humans only see three. The few-shot examples only demonstrate the use of the Likert scale with "is-a" judgments, and do not include any typically-privative adjectives; see Appendix B.2.

To get responses on the Likert scale, we calculate the surprisal of the 5 answers. The model's response is whichever of these 5 answers has the lowest surprisal. This limits us to assessing open-source models where log-probabilities of the input are available, excluding popular closed-source models like GPT-4 (OpenAI, 2024). We study the Llama 2 (Touvron et al., 2023) and Llama 3 series[4] (Dubey et al., 2024) in detail, as well as Mixtral 7x8B (Jiang et al., 2024) and Qwen 2 72B (Yang et al., 2024). We test all sizes of Llama 2 and Llama 3 to investigate whether generalization ability improves with model size. We primarily focus on instruction-tuned models; results for the base Llama models are shown in Appendix E.

4.2 Results

Firstly, to measure whether the provided biased contexts have a significant effect on inference ratings, we compare the results from Experiment 1a and 1b. Detailed results for Experiment 1a are given in Appendix A. We fit the same ordinal regression as Ross et al. (2024), `Rating ~ ContextBias`, in R (R Core Team, 2023; Christensen, 2022). While Ross et al. (2024) find that for humans, both the privative and subsective contexts have a significant effect on ratings compared to rating the bigram with no context, we find that this is not the case for all LLMs. For all LLMs, we find that subsective contexts have a significant effect ($p < 0.05$) compared to providing no context in Experiment 1a. Privative contexts only have a significant effect ($p < 0.05$) for those models which rate many bigrams with typically-privative adjectives as subsective without context (see Figure 9 in Appendix A), namely Llama 3 70B Instruct,

[3]Experiment 1c in Appendix E.5 performs an ablation study on Experiment 1b with 0-shot prompting.

[4]In this paper, Llama 3 refers to the original Llama 3 models, not the newly released Llama 3.1 models.

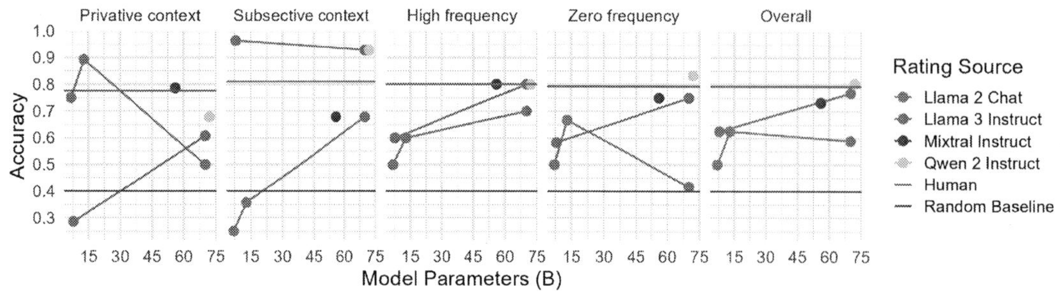

Figure 2: Accuracy on the context-based inference task (Experiment 1b) overall, in privative vs. subsective contexts, and for high frequency vs. zero frequency bigrams. Accuracy on the context-based inference task increases with model parameters for all models except Llama 2 Chat, and all models except Llama 2 70B Chat can generalize to (perform similarly or better on) zero frequency (novel) bigrams.

Llama 3 8B Instruct and Qwen 2 72B Instruct.

Next, we judge the inference as correct if the rating is "Definitely/Probably not" in privative-biased contexts and "Probably/Definitely yes" in subsective-biased contexts. Figure 2 shows the accuracy for all language models under this metric, plus a random guessing baseline. The human results in Figure 2 should be viewed as a ceiling measuring the effectiveness of the context at fixing the inference, not human competence at the task.

We see that Llama 3 70B Instruct, Qwen 2 72B Instruct and Mixtral 7x8B Instruct perform similarly to humans on this task, suggesting a good ability to (a) understand the effect the context has on the thing described, (b) understand what is necessary to count as an instance of each noun, and (c) draw the correct inference based on the previous two steps. For all models except Llama 2 70B Chat, we see no difference between their accuracy on high-frequency bigrams and zero-frequency ones.

Likewise, performance scales with model size for all models except Llama 2 70B Chat. This is because this metric penalizes use of the "Unsure" rating, which Llama 2 70B Chat often uses (see Figure 9), and uses more often for the 6 zero-frequency bigrams. Llama 2 13B Chat scores higher because it is more confident, even though it is sometimes confidently wrong. (Under the softer metric of "accuracy within 1 SD of the human mean", which we will introduce in Section 5.1, performance does indeed scale with model parameters – see Figure 10 in the Appendix.)

4.3 Discussion

While model performance on judging inferences of adjective-noun combinations given a context improves with scale, we see that almost all models behave similarly for high-frequency and zero-frequency bigrams, despite presumably never having seen the zero-frequency bigrams before (or at least despite the substantial frequency gap). Thus, we conclude that models do not handle this task by memorizing inferences of noun membership during pretraining and instead assess it dynamically, thus being able to generalize (whether this process is a case of genuine adjective-noun meaning composition, as humans are presumed to be able to do in linguistic theory, or some other heuristics). While this is an exciting result, this is a rather small dataset. In the next section, we study the larger NO-CONTEXT dataset from Ross et al. (2024).

5 Experiments 2 and 3: Evaluating inferences without context

The NO-CONTEXT dataset in Ross et al. (2024) asks the same inference question "Is an {adjective} {noun} a {noun}?", but without providing any additional context to help determine the inference. This results in a wide distribution of human ratings for some (but not all) bigrams involving typically privative adjectives. For example, a *counterfeit dollar bill* is never judged to be a *dollar bill*. The distribution also widens for some bigrams with typically subsective adjectives, such as *homemade cat*. In this section, we propose three methods to investigate whether LLMs can match the distribution of ratings provided by humans in this context, since there is no longer a single correct answer.

5.1 Method 1: Accuracy within 1 SD

The first method evaluates a single judgment derived from an LLM and asks: Is the LLM sampling

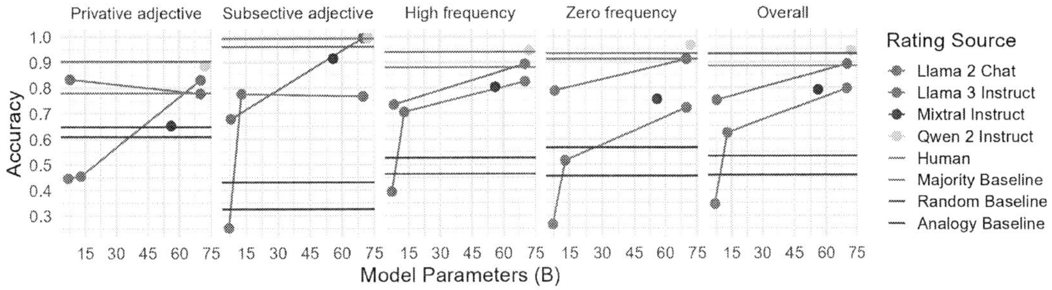

Figure 3: Accuracy within 1 SD of the human mean on the no-context inference task (Experiment 2) overall, for typically privative vs. subsective adjectives, and for high vs. zero frequency bigrams. While accuracy is high, a simple "majority" baseline nearly saturates this metric.

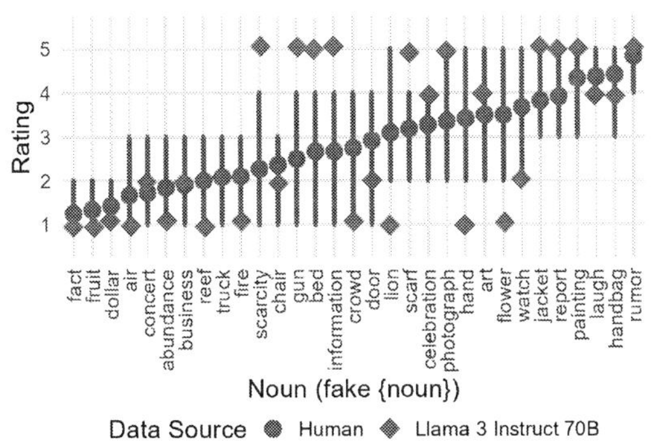

Figure 4: Ratings for select bigrams involving *fake* for Llama 3 Instruct 70B, compared to the (rounded) 1 SD interval around the human mean.

from the same distribution as the humans for each bigram? A quick but coarse metric to assess this is whether the LLM's rating falls within one standard deviation of the human mean, rounded to the nearest integer rating (1 corresponds to "Definitely not", 5 to "Definitely yes").[5] This method is intuitive and easy to compute, but is also a relatively low bar. To illustrate, Figure 4 shows the human means with intervals 1 SD wide for a selection of bigrams of the form *fake* {noun}, with the no-context ratings from Llama 3 Instruct 70B superimposed. For *fake* in particular, these intervals are relatively wide and easy for the LLM to land in, although for subsective adjectives like *useful*, these intervals are much smaller. Conversely, subsective inferences are by far the most common inference, so we still expect high performance for subsective adjectives.

Experiment 2 obtains single ratings for each of the 798 bigrams in NO-CONTEXT using the same setup as Experiment 1a (Section 4). Figure 3 shows the scores on this metric, split by adjective type (typically privative or typically subsective) and bigram frequency. We also compare to three baselines: random, "majority", and analogy. For the random baseline, we sample 100 ratings from 1–5 for each bigram , calculate whether it is within 1 SD of the human mean for that bigram, and average the results. The "majority" baseline guesses a fixed rating depending on the adjective's underlying category as typically subsective or typically privative. Bigrams with subsective adjectives are rated "Definitely yes" (5), while bigrams with privative adjectives are rated "Unsure" (3), taking advantage of the fact that privative adjectives tend to have wide 1-SD intervals that often overlap with 3.

Finally, the analogy baseline attempts to calculate the inference by analogy, imitating reasoning such as "a fake watch is a watch, and a handbag is an expensive accessory like a watch, so a fake handbag must also be a handbag". Specifically, it uses the distance between GloVe embeddings (Pennington et al., 2014) to find nearby adjectives and nearby nouns among all the adjectives and nouns used in Ross et al. (2024), assembling those into "nearby bigrams". It then averages the human inference ratings among those nearby bigrams which are high-frequency (assumed "known") to predict the rating of the new bigram.

We find that most models, with the exception of Llama 2 7B Chat, perform well under this metric, but the high performance of the majority baseline highlights the leniency of this metric. In fact, only Llama 3 70B Instruct manages to outperform the majority baseline. That said, the gap between the

[5]One alternative would be to compute the inter-annotator agreement (IAA) between the LLM and the other, human annotators, but existing metrics for IAA either calculate the agreement between two annotators or the agreement across the whole group.

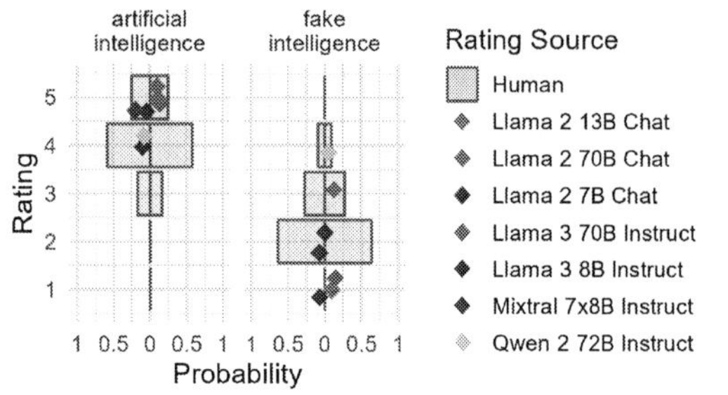

Figure 5: Ratings for *"Is artificial/fake intelligence still intelligence?"*, showing the distribution for humans and the single rating (with no context provided) for LLMs. Most instruction-tuned LLMs give a more confident (higher) rating than humans for *artificial intelligence*.

analogy baseline and the larger models suggests that models are doing something more sophisticated than simple analogical reasoning to high-frequency inferences that they have seen before. This is further borne out by the models' high performance on zero-frequency bigrams, as in Experiment 1b, showing again that models seem to handle this task on-the-fly rather than relying on having seen the combination during pretraining. As in Experiment 1b, performance scales with size.

For *artificial intelligence* specifically, we find that most LLMs answer "Is artificial intelligence still intelligence?" with "Definitely yes", while humans tend to prefer a more conservative "Probably yes", as shown in Figure 5.

While this method is appealingly simple, performance on this metric is close to saturated by the majority baseline, making it difficult to evaluate whether LLMs are performing in a "human-like" way. We next explore two methods of generating a distribution of ratings from an LLM, to see if LLMs can capture the whole human distribution rather than merely capturing a point within it.

5.2 Method 2: Log-probability distribution

5.2.1 Method

Our second method obtains a distribution of ratings from the LLM by calculating the log-probabilities of all 5 answers for each of the 798 bigrams in NO-CONTEXT in Experiment 2 and converting this into a probability distribution for each bigram. For each bigram, we calculate the Jensen-Shannon divergence between the distribution of ratings obtained from the LLM and the distribution given by the (normalized) human ratings.[6] 0 indicates perfect overlap, while 1 indicates maximal divergence.

Model	JS Divergence Priv.	Subs.	Total
Human	0	0	0
Llama 3 70B Instruct	0.26	0.08	0.17
Qwen 2 72B Instruct	0.33	0.08	0.19
Llama 2 70B Chat	0.18	0.25	0.22
Mixtral 7x8B Instruct	0.32	0.13	0.22
Llama 3 8B Instruct	0.18	0.34	0.26
Llama 2 13B Chat	0.25	0.35	0.30
Uniform baseline	0.20	0.46	0.34
Llama 2 7B Chat	0.29	0.46	0.38
"Majority" baseline	0.71	0.12	0.40

Table 1: Jensen-Shannon divergence between per-bigram rating distributions for humans and LLM log-probabilities, for privative vs. subsective adjectives.

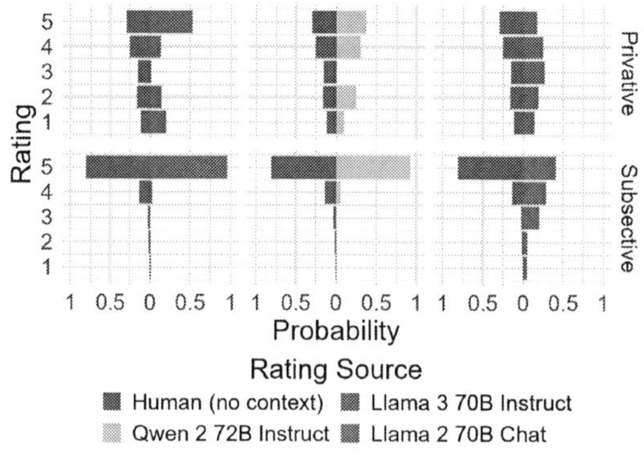

Figure 6: Average log-probability distribution for (typically) subsective vs. privative adjectives for selected LLMs, compared to the average human distribution.

5.2.2 Results

Table 1 shows the average Jensen-Shannon divergences, including a uniform distribution baseline and the "majority" baseline reported in Section 5.1. Llama 3 70B Instruct shows the lowest average Jensen-Shannon divergence across all bigrams using this method, with an excellent divergence of just 0.08 on (typically) subsective adjectives, matched by Qwen 2 72B. However, not all models are able to concentrate enough of their log-probability mass on "Definitely yes" for bigrams with subsective adjectives, such as Llama 2 70B

[6]While calculating the Kullback-Leibler divergence would also let us treat the human ratings as ground truth, we prefer the Jensen-Shannon divergence because it is bounded between 0 and 1 and thus easier to interpret.

Method	JS Divergence Priv.	Subs.	Total
Log-probability	0.26	0.08	0.17
Context generation	0.38	0.11	0.24

Table 2: Jensen-Shannon divergence between per-bigram rating distributions for humans and Llama 3 70B Instruct using the log-probability and context generation methods, for privative vs. subsective adjectives.

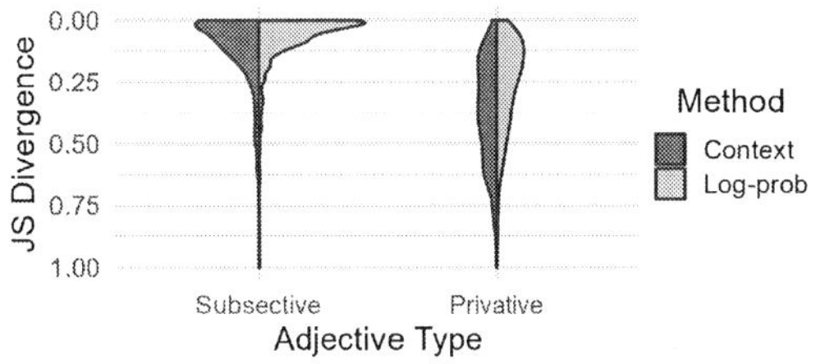

Figure 7: Distribution of per-bigram Jensen-Shannon divergences between the rating distributions for humans and Llama 3 70B when obtained from log-probabilities vs. by generating contexts. 0 indicates perfect overlap, while 1 indicates maximal divergence.

Chat, even though all models were able to rate these bigrams as subsective when giving a single rating (Table 14). Further, all models, especially the larger ones, struggle with subsective-adjective bigrams that humans rate as somewhat privative, such as *homemade cat* or *illegal currency*. All models except Qwen 72B Instruct rate *homemade cat* as mostly subsective (5), whereas humans' ratings are distributed evenly from 1-4, and Qwen does not assign enough enough probability mass to these intermediate ratings. Figure 8 shows the distribution for *homemade cat* for Llama 3 70B Instruct.

For bigrams with privative adjectives, where the inference is much harder to predict, results are still promising, but there is room for improvement. Figure 6 shows that although Llama 3 70B Instruct has the lowest overall JS divergence for privative adjectives, it rates them as subsective (5, "Definitely yes") too often, and neither it nor Qwen 2 72B make human-like use of the "Unsure" rating (perhaps a side-effect of their helpfulness training). Section 5.4 discusses the item-by-item variation in JS divergence in more detail.

More broadly, it is not clear that model log-probabilities *should* map onto a distribution of how frequent different answers are among humans. Method 3 investigates a more sophisticated way of getting a distribution of ratings from LLMs which may map more closely onto the human distribution.

5.3 Method 3: Context generation

One source of variation in human ratings is that different humans are likely imagining different instantiations of the bigram, loosely corresponding to the different contexts in Experiment 1 (though likely much less well specified), depending on the priors they each have. They then rate "Is an AN an N?" given that imagined context. While some humans may consider multiple instantiations and form a small distribution which informs their single answer, the distribution of ratings primarily arises from consulting a larger population of humans. A language model, when prompted with no context, instead has a single set of priors and has to estimate the log-probability of each answer given that single set of priors. The next method investigates whether we can improve the fit of the model's distribution by having it generate a set of contexts and rate "Is an AN an N?" given each context, imitating this aspect of the human variation and thought process.

5.3.1 Method

Method 3 asks the model to generate 12 different "stories" of 50-100 words involving the target bigram which "describe the {bigram} in detail", giving three of the contexts used as few-shot prompts for Experiment 1b as examples. This is somewhat similar to recent efforts to mimic human survey results by prompting or having the LLM generate personas, then generating data with those personas as context (Bisbee et al., 2024; Argyle et al., 2023; Chan et al., 2024 i.a.). Experiment 3a generates all 12 stories in one chat using a temperature of 0.6 (see Appendix B.3 for the prompts). Then, Experiment 3b uses the "In this setting, is an {adjective} {noun} still a {noun}?" design from Experiment 1b to have the model rate the bigram inference in each of these 12 contexts, yielding 12 ratings per bigram. We can then calculate the Jensen-Shannon divergence between this LLM-generated distribution and the human distribution.

However, this method is computationally expensive: it took us ca. 400 GPU-hours with A100s to generate the 12 contexts for our 798 bigrams with Llama 3 70B Instruct. Thus, we conduct this experiment with one model (Llama 3 70B Instruct) and demonstrate this method as a proof of concept.

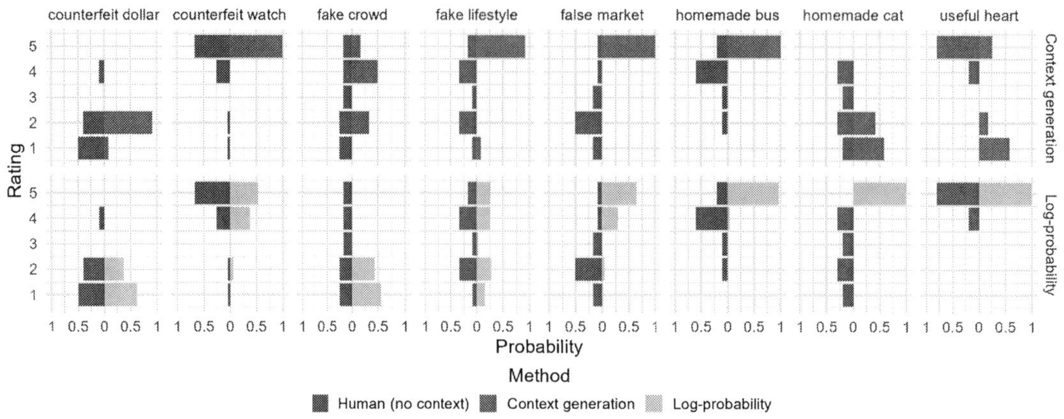

Figure 8: Rating distributions over selected bigrams using log-probabilities vs. context generation, compared to the human distributions. Both methods successfully capture bigrams like *counterfeit dollar, counterfeit watch*, and both fail for *false market* and *homemade bus*. While the log-probability method fits most bigrams better, such as *fake lifestyle* and *useful heart*, the context generation method is better for *fake crowd* and *homemade cat*.

Context A	**Context B**
The new video game, "Epic Quest," was about to be launched, and the developers wanted to create a buzz around it. They decided to stage a fake crowd of fans waiting in line outside the game store on launch night. They **hired a team of people to dress up in costumes** and hold signs that read "I've been waiting for 10 hours!" [...]	The small town of Oakdale was hosting its annual Christmas market, but the organizers were worried that not enough people would show up. To create the illusion of a bigger crowd, they **set up a fake crowd of mannequins** dressed in winter coats and hats, and placed them around the market stalls. [...]
Rating: Definitely yes (subsective)	**Rating**: Probably not (privative)

Table 3: Two intuitive stories generated by Llama 3 70B Instruct about a *fake crowd*, which yield privative vs. subsective inferences. We then ask Llama 3 to rate "Is a fake crowd still a crowd?" given these contexts.

5.3.2 Results

Table 3 shows two LLM-written stories illustrating a privative vs. subsective inference for *fake crowd* which successfully capture human intuitions about two kinds of *fake crowd*, showing promise for this method. Appendix D contains additional examples of generated contexts. Overall, however, the Jensen-Shannon divergences in Table 2 show that generating contexts actually fits the human distribution *worse* than just taking the log-probability distribution directly for Llama 3 70B Instruct. Using a cut-off of 0.25 for JS divergence, we find that the distributions generated using context generation are reasonably human-like for only 61.4% of the 798 bigrams, compared to 75.3% for the log-probability distributions. One possible explanation is that we are not generating the right kind, or a sufficient diversity, of contexts: we place hardly any constraints on the story generation, but perhaps e.g. explicitly asking for stories that disambiguate the target inference might match human behavior better, since humans see the "Is an AN an N?" question when imagining their "contexts". A final point of divergence from humans is Llama 3 70B Instruct's unwillingness to ever use the "Unsure" rating, but this may be an issue with this particular model rather than the method itself. Nevertheless, this method yields well-distributed (often bimodal) rating distributions, as shown in Figure 8, and, while not as close as the log-probability distribution overall, still approximates the human distribution well for many bigrams.

5.4 Distribution method comparison

Both methods of generating a distribution are good at capturing the narrow subsective distributions of most subsective adjectives. However, both methods struggle for items like *homemade bus*, which humans rate as more privative than subsective despite the typically-subsective adjective, resulting in a thin but long tail of high JS divergences (see Figure 7, which compares the distribution of JS divergences per bigram between the two methods). Interestingly, the context generation method is better able to capture this partially privative behavior for certain bigrams, such as *homemade cat*, which shows promise: it writes stories focusing around knitted or cardboard cats, matching human intuitions. (This yields a JS divergence of 0.33 compared to 1.00 for the log-prob distribution; see Figure 8 and Appendix D for an example context.)

For the typically-privative adjectives which are the primary focus of this paper, the log-probability distributions provide a better fit overall, but not for all bigrams. For 45 of them, such as *fake leg*, context generation provides a better fit: many of the generated stories are about prosthetics, deemed to be *legs* (see Appendix D for an example, and Table 9 in the Appendix for more counts). More broadly, Figure 7 shows that there is room for improvement for both methods: both have a thick tail of bigrams whose human distributions they do not fit well.

We fit linear regressions for `JSDivergence` $\sim$ `AdjectiveType * HumanMean + HumanSD + BigramFrequency` in R for each method for Llama 3 70B Instruct and find, for each method, a significant negative effect of privative adjective type and human mean on the JS divergence, as well as a significant positive effect of human SD and a significant, positive interaction between adjective type and human mean. We do not find an effect of bigram frequency. This is an exciting result, because it shows that Llama 3 70B Instruct is similarly adept at modelling the human distribution of ratings for novel (zero frequency) bigrams as it is for high-frequency bigrams, suggesting that it can generalize beyond its training data. Exact coefficients and an effects plot are given in the Appendix in Table 11 and Figure 15. Specifically, the negative effect of human mean on typically subsective adjectives supports the qualitative finding that both methods struggle with bigrams involving typically subsective adjectives with low human ratings, i.e. which have a more privative interpretation. Interestingly, we see the same effect for privative adjectives, where JS divergence increases as the human mean decreases (i.e. as the bigram is rated more privative). Finally, the significant positive effect of human SD shows that both methods struggle to predict the human distribution as human variation increases. These linear regressions achieve an R^2 of 0.44 (log-probability) and 0.55 (context generation), meaning there is still variation left unexplained by these factors. However, we find no further qualitatively interpretable patterns.

6 Conclusion

In this paper, we study whether LLMs can combine adjectives and nouns to yield noun membership inferences both with and without context, for high-frequency and zero-frequency (presumed novel) bigrams. We find that when the inference is determined by context, large, recent LLMs make the expected inferences, while smaller and/or older LLMs only sometimes do so. All LLMs, even smaller ones, behave similarly for zero-frequency bigrams as they do for high-frequency bigrams, suggesting that they do not rely on having seen them and their associated inference during pretraining. Instead, they evaluate these combinations on-the-fly and can generalize accordingly, as humans do.

We investigate three methods to evaluate whether LLMs can extend this behavior to a setting where no context is provided, where they either need to fall within the human distribution of ratings or match the whole human distribution. While recent LLMs are able to fall within 1 SD of the human mean for up to 95% of our dataset, this is a very lenient metric. On our stricter metric of matching the human distribution (either using log-probabilities or via context generation), we find that these LLMs are good at capturing the simple distribution of bigrams like *multicolored flower* and *counterfeit watch*, but are only able to capture up to 75% of our total dataset. LLMs struggle particularly with bigrams with unusual inferences for their adjective, such as *homemade cat*, and with bigrams with high human variance. Interestingly, however, LLMs are still equally able to capture distributions of novel bigrams in this setting. In sum, our generalization results are exciting because they show LLMs are generalizing beyond their training data even in this delicate, context-sensitive task, but there is still room for improvement on the task of capturing these inferences overall. Further, we hope that the methods presented in this paper will inspire future work which moves beyond targeting single correct answers and begins to target human population distributions, from meaning and inferences to wider issues such as opinions and political positions.

7 Limitations

This paper has a number of limitations, being the first exploration in this area. Firstly, we only study English adjective-noun inferences. The set of typically-privative adjectives and which inference they trigger with which nouns may vary between languages and cultures. Secondly, the dataset for Experiment 1, which determines the inference by providing an appropriate context, is not very large (56 bigram/context pairs), resulting in lower than ideal statistical power.

Third, for fair comparison to human participants, and since the human data demonstrates that many judgments are non-binary for this task, we use a 5-point Likert scale rather than a binary yes/no question. This assumes that the model can use the Likert scale. While there is some previous work which also uses Likert scales with similar models (Argyle et al., 2023; Chuang et al., 2024; Abeysinghe and Circi, 2024), there is no work explicitly showing that models understand Likert scales in general. Thus, this design does not let us disentangle whether the model is struggling with the task itself or simply with the use of the Likert scale, despite the 5-shot setting and the use of log-probabilities to enforce use of the scale. This especially applies to smaller models that are known to show weaker instruction-following skills, and to non-instruction-tuned models. Alternatives such as calculating the surprisal of e.g. *a fake watch is/is not a watch*, however, have their own issues, since LLMs have been shown to be sometimes insensitive to negation (Truong et al.; García-Ferrero et al., 2023).

Fourth, for comparison reasons, we use the same prompts used in the human experiment to evaluate the LLMs, including few-shot examples; however, it is possible that this prompt phrasing and exact choice of few-shot examples introduces artefacts which adversely affect the LLMs' performance and "masks" their underlying ability at the task.

Finally, due to time and compute limitations, we were only able to run the context generation method for Llama 3 70B Instruct. In future work, we would like to extend this method to other models and investigate which of the differences we see between the context generation and the log-probability sampling method for Llama 3 70B Instruct should be attributed to the model vs. to the differences between the methods.

Acknowledgments

We would like to thank Naomi Saphra, Jack Merullo, and Lio Wong, as well as all the members of the Harvard Meaning & Modality lab and the BU tinlab for their helpful feedback. Special thanks to Joshua Martin, whose dissertation on this topic inspired this project. This work was supported by an MBB Graduate Student Research Award from Harvard's Mind, Brain and Behavior Initiative.

References

Bhashithe Abeysinghe and Ruhan Circi. 2024. The Challenges of Evaluating LLM Applications: An Analysis of Automated, Human, and LLM-Based Approaches. *arXiv preprint*. ArXiv:2406.03339 [cs].

Marianna Apidianaki and Aina Garí Soler. 2021. ALL Dolphins Are Intelligent and SOME Are Friendly: Probing BERT for Nouns' Semantic Properties and their Prototypicality. In *Proceedings of the Fourth BlackboxNLP Workshop on Analyzing and Interpreting Neural Networks for NLP*, pages 79–94, Punta Cana, Dominican Republic. Association for Computational Linguistics.

Lisa P. Argyle, Ethan C. Busby, Nancy Fulda, Joshua R. Gubler, Christopher Rytting, and David Wingate. 2023. Out of One, Many: Using Language Models to Simulate Human Samples. *Political Analysis*, 31(3):337–351.

Lorenzo Bertolini, Julie Weeds, and David Weir. 2022. Testing Large Language Models on Compositionality and Inference with Phrase-Level Adjective-Noun Entailment. In *Proceedings of the 29th International Conference on Computational Linguistics*, pages 4084–4100, Gyeongju, Republic of Korea. International Committee on Computational Linguistics.

James Bisbee, Joshua D. Clinton, Cassy Dorff, Brenton Kenkel, and Jennifer M. Larson. 2024. Synthetic Replacements for Human Survey Data? The Perils of Large Language Models. *Political Analysis*, pages 1–16.

Gemma Boleda, Marco Baroni, The Nghia Pham, and Louise McNally. 2013. Intensionality was only alleged: On adjective-noun composition in distributional semantics. In *Proceedings of the 10th International Conference on Computational Semantics (IWCS 2013) – Long Papers*, pages 35–46, Potsdam, Germany. Association for Computational Linguistics.

Gemma Boleda, Eva Maria Vecchi, Miquel Cornudella, and Louise McNally. 2012. First Order vs. Higher Order Modification in Distributional Semantics. In *Proceedings of the 2012 Joint Conference on Empirical Methods in Natural Language Processing and Computational Natural Language Learning*, pages 1223–1233, Jeju Island, Korea. Association for Computational Linguistics.

Tom B. Brown, Benjamin Mann, Nick Ryder, Melanie Subbiah, Jared Kaplan, Prafulla Dhariwal, Arvind Neelakantan, Pranav Shyam, Girish Sastry, Amanda Askell, Sandhini Agarwal, Ariel Herbert-Voss, Gretchen Krueger, Tom Henighan, Rewon Child, Aditya Ramesh, Daniel M. Ziegler, Jeffrey Wu, Clemens Winter, Christopher Hesse, Mark Chen, Eric Sigler, Mateusz Litwin, Scott Gray, Benjamin Chess, Jack Clark, Christopher Berner, Sam McCandlish, Alec Radford, Ilya Sutskever, and Dario Amodei. 2020. Language Models are Few-Shot Learners. *arXiv:2005.14165 [cs]*. ArXiv: 2005.14165.

Bert Cappelle, Denis Pascal, and Mikaela Keller. 2018. Facing the facts of fake: A distributional semantics and corpus annotation approach. *Yearbook of the German Cognitive Linguistics Association*, 6(1):9–42.

Xin Chan, Xiaoyang Wang, Dian Yu, Haitao Mi, and Dong Yu. 2024. Scaling Synthetic Data Creation with 1,000,000,000 Personas. *arXiv preprint*. ArXiv:2406.20094 [cs].

R. H. B. Christensen. 2022. ordinal—Regression Models for Ordinal Data. R package version 2022.11-16. https://CRAN.R-project.org/package=ordinal.

Yun-Shiuan Chuang, Zach Studdiford, Krirk Nirunwiroj, Agam Goyal, Vincent V. Frigo, Sijia Yang, Dhavan Shah, Junjie Hu, and Timothy T. Rogers. 2024. Beyond Demographics: Aligning Role-playing LLM-based Agents Using Human Belief Networks. *arXiv preprint*. ArXiv:2406.17232 [cs].

Albert Coil and Vered Shwartz. 2023. From chocolate bunny to chocolate crocodile: Do Language Models Understand Noun Compounds? In *Findings of the Association for Computational Linguistics: ACL 2023*, pages 2698–2710, Toronto, Canada. Association for Computational Linguistics.

Jacob Devlin, Ming-Wei Chang, Kenton Lee, and Kristina Toutanova. 2019. BERT: Pre-training of Deep Bidirectional Transformers for Language Understanding. In *Proceedings of the 2019 Conference of the North American Chapter of the Association for Computational Linguistics: Human Language Technologies, Volume 1 (Long and Short Papers)*, pages 4171–4186, Minneapolis, Minnesota. Association for Computational Linguistics.

Nam Do and Ellie Pavlick. 2021. Are Rotten Apples Edible? Challenging Commonsense Inference Ability with Exceptions. In *Findings of the Association for Computational Linguistics: ACL-IJCNLP 2021*, pages 2061–2073, Online. Association for Computational Linguistics.

Abhimanyu Dubey, Abhinav Jauhri, Abhinav Pandey, Abhishek Kadian, Ahmad Al-Dahle, Aiesha Letman, Akhil Mathur, Alan Schelten, Amy Yang, Angela Fan, and et al. 2024. The Llama 3 Herd of Models. *arXiv preprint*. ArXiv:2407.21783 [cs].

Allyson Ettinger. 2020. What BERT Is Not: Lessons from a New Suite of Psycholinguistic Diagnostics for Language Models. *Transactions of the Association for Computational Linguistics*, 8:34–48.

Iker García-Ferrero, Begoña Altuna, Javier Álvez, Itziar Gonzalez-Dios, and German Rigau. 2023. This is not a Dataset: A Large Negation Benchmark to Challenge Large Language Models. *arXiv preprint*. ArXiv:2310.15941 [cs].

Michael Goodale and Salvador Mascarenhas. 2023. Systematic polysemy in adjective-noun combination in contextual word embeddings. LingBuzz Published In:.

Emiliano Guevara. 2010. A Regression Model of Adjective-Noun Compositionality in Distributional Semantics. In *Proceedings of the 2010 Workshop on GEometrical Models of Natural Language Semantics*, pages 33–37, Uppsala, Sweden. Association for Computational Linguistics.

Pius ten Hacken. 2016. *The Semantics of Compounding*. Cambridge University Press. Google-Books-ID: esLgCwAAQBAJ.

Michael Hanna and David Mareček. 2021. Analyzing BERT's Knowledge of Hypernymy via Prompting. In *Proceedings of the Fourth BlackboxNLP Workshop on Analyzing and Interpreting Neural Networks for NLP*, pages 275–282, Punta Cana, Dominican Republic. Association for Computational Linguistics.

Matthias Hartung, Fabian Kaupmann, Soufian Jebbara, and Philipp Cimiano. 2017. Learning Compositionality Functions on Word Embeddings for Modelling Attribute Meaning in Adjective-Noun Phrases. In *Proceedings of the 15th Conference of the European Chapter of the Association for Computational Linguistics: Volume 1, Long Papers*, pages 54–64, Valencia, Spain. Association for Computational Linguistics.

Albert Q. Jiang, Alexandre Sablayrolles, Antoine Roux, Arthur Mensch, Blanche Savary, Chris Bamford, Devendra Singh Chaplot, Diego de las Casas, Emma Bou Hanna, Florian Bressand, Gianna Lengyel, Guillaume Bour, Guillaume Lample, Lélio Renard Lavaud, Lucile Saulnier, Marie-Anne Lachaux, Pierre Stock, Sandeep Subramanian, Sophia Yang, Szymon Antoniak, Teven Le Scao, Théophile Gervet, Thibaut Lavril, Thomas Wang, Timothée Lacroix, and William El Sayed. 2024. Mixtral of Experts. *arXiv preprint*. ArXiv:2401.04088 [cs].

Najoung Kim, Tal Linzen, and Paul Smolensky. 2022. Uncontrolled Lexical Exposure Leads to Overestimation of Compositional Generalization in Pretrained Models. *arXiv preprint*. ArXiv:2212.10769 [cs].

Matthias Lalisse and Ash Asudeh. 2015. Distinguishing intersective and non-intersective adjectives in compositional distributional semantics. Master's thesis, University of Oxford, Oxford.

Yinhan Liu, Myle Ott, Naman Goyal, Jingfei Du, Mandar Joshi, Danqi Chen, Omer Levy, Mike Lewis, Luke Zettlemoyer, and Veselin Stoyanov. 2019. RoBERTa: A Robustly Optimized BERT Pretraining Approach. *arXiv:1907.11692 [cs]*. ArXiv: 1907.11692.

Qing Lyu, Hua Zheng, Daoxin Li, Li Zhang, Marianna Apidianaki, and Chris Callison-Burch. 2022. Is "My Favorite New Movie" My Favorite Movie? Probing the Understanding of Recursive Noun Phrases. *arXiv preprint*.

Joshua Martin. 2022. *Compositional Routes to (Non)Intersectivity*. Ph.D., Harvard University, United States – Massachusetts.

MosaicML NLP Team. 2023. Introducing mpt-30b: Raising the bar for open-source foundation models.

Viktor Moskvoretskii, Alexander Panchenko, and Irina Nikishina. 2024. Are Large Language Models Good at Lexical Semantics? A Case of Taxonomy Learning. In *Proceedings of the 2024 Joint International Conference on Computational Linguistics, Language Resources and Evaluation (LREC-COLING 2024)*, pages 1498–1510, Torino, Italia. ELRA and ICCL.

Neha Nayak, Mark Kowarsky, Gabor Angeli, and Christopher D. Manning. 2014. A Dictionary of Nonsubsective Adjectives. Technical Report CSTR 2014-04, Department of Computer Science, Stanford University.

Irina Nikishina, Polina Chernomorchenko, Anastasiia Demidova, Alexander Panchenko, and Chris Biemann. 2023. Predicting Terms in IS-A Relations with Pre-trained Transformers. In *Findings of the Association for Computational Linguistics: IJCNLP-AACL 2023 (Findings)*, pages 134–148, Nusa Dua, Bali. Association for Computational Linguistics.

OpenAI. 2024. GPT-4 Technical Report. *arXiv preprint*. ArXiv:2303.08774 [cs].

Mark Ormerod, Jesús Martínez del Rincón, and Barry Devereux. 2024. How Is a "Kitchen Chair" like a "Farm Horse"? Exploring the Representation of Noun-Noun Compound Semantics in Transformer-based Language Models. *Computational Linguistics*, 50(1):49–81. Place: Cambridge, MA Publisher: MIT Press.

Ellie Pavlick and Chris Callison-Burch. 2016a. Most "babies" are "little" and most "problems" are "huge": Compositional Entailment in Adjective-Nouns. In *Proceedings of the 54th Annual Meeting of the Association for Computational Linguistics (Volume 1: Long Papers)*, pages 2164–2173, Berlin, Germany. Association for Computational Linguistics.

Ellie Pavlick and Chris Callison-Burch. 2016b. So-Called Non-Subsective Adjectives. In *Proceedings of the Fifth Joint Conference on Lexical and Computational Semantics*, pages 114–119, Berlin, Germany. Association for Computational Linguistics.

Jeffrey Pennington, Richard Socher, and Christopher Manning. 2014. GloVe: Global Vectors for Word Representation. In *Proceedings of the 2014 Conference on Empirical Methods in Natural Language Processing (EMNLP)*, pages 1532–1543, Doha, Qatar. Association for Computational Linguistics.

R Core Team. 2023. R: A Language and Environment for Statistical Computing.

Alec Radford, Jeffrey Wu, Rewon Child, David Luan, Dario Amodei, and Ilya Sutskever. 2019. Language Models are Unsupervised Multitask Learners. page 24.

Colin Raffel, Noam Shazeer, Adam Roberts, Katherine Lee, Sharan Narang, Michael Matena, Yanqi Zhou, Wei Li, and Peter J. Liu. 2020. Exploring the Limits of Transfer Learning with a Unified Text-to-Text Transformer. *Journal of Machine Learning Research*, 21(140):1–67.

Giulia Rambelli, Emmanuele Chersoni, Claudia Collacciani, and Marianna Bolognesi. 2024. Can Large Language Models Interpret Noun-Noun Compounds? A Linguistically-Motivated Study on Lexicalized and Novel Compounds. In *The First Workshop on Analogical Abstraction in Cognition, Perception, and Language (Analogy-ANGLE)*.

Abhilasha Ravichander, Eduard Hovy, Kaheer Suleman, Adam Trischler, and Jackie Chi Kit Cheung. 2020. On the Systematicity of Probing Contextualized Word Representations: The Case of Hypernymy in BERT. In *Proceedings of the Ninth Joint Conference on Lexical and Computational Semantics*, pages 88–102, Barcelona, Spain (Online). Association for Computational Linguistics.

Hayley Ross, Najoung Kim, and Kathryn Davidson. 2024. Fake reefs are sometimes reefs and sometimes not, but are always compositional. *to appear in Experiments in Linguistic Meaning*, 3.

Aalok Sathe, Evelina Fedorenko, and Noga Zaslavsky. 2024. Language use is only sparsely compositional: The case of English adjective-noun phrases in humans and large language models. *Proceedings of the Annual Meeting of the Cognitive Science Society*, 46(0).

Hugo Touvron, Louis Martin, Kevin Stone, and et al. 2023. Llama 2: Open Foundation and Fine-Tuned Chat Models. *arXiv preprint*.

Thinh Hung Truong, Timothy Baldwin, Karin Verspoor, and Trevor Cohn. Language models are not naysayers: An analysis of language models on negation benchmarks. *Preprint*, arxiv:2306.08189 [cs].

Eva M. Vecchi, Marco Marelli, Roberto Zamparelli, and Marco Baroni. 2017. Spicy Adjectives and Nominal Donkeys: Capturing Semantic Deviance Using Compositionality in Distributional Spaces. *Cognitive Science*, 41(1):102–136.

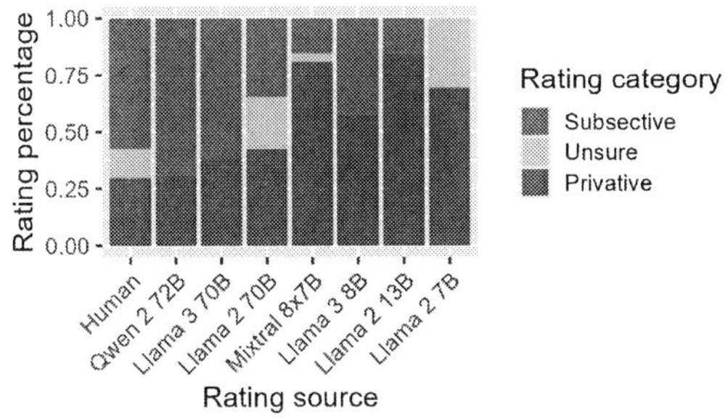

Figure 9: Percentage of privative vs. subsective inferences for bigrams in Experiment 1a (no context) for each model ("Instruct/Chat" omitted for brevity).

An Yang, Baosong Yang, Binyuan Hui, Bo Zheng, Bowen Yu, Chang Zhou, Chengpeng Li, Chengyuan Li, Dayiheng Liu, Fei Huang, and et al. 2024. Qwen2 Technical Report. *arXiv preprint*. ArXiv:2407.10671 [cs].

Lang Yu and Allyson Ettinger. 2020. Assessing Phrasal Representation and Composition in Transformers. In *Proceedings of the 2020 Conference on Empirical Methods in Natural Language Processing (EMNLP)*, pages 4896–4907, Online. Association for Computational Linguistics.

A Experiment 1a: No-context baseline

Figure 9 shows the proportions of bigram ratings which are privative ("Definitely not" or "Probably not"), subsective ("Definitely yes" or "Probably yes") or neither ("Unsure") when the LLM (or human; 12 ratings/bigram for humans) rates these 28 bigrams without context in Experiment 1a. The exact proportions are shown in Table 4. Each LLM brings its own bias: Llama 3 70B is evenly balanced, while Qwen 2 72B favors subsective ratings and Mixtral 8x7B favors privative ratings. For humans, all of these bigrams have high variance when rated in this out-of-context setting, which these percentages do not reflect.

B Data and prompts

B.1 Context examples from Ross et al. (2024)

To illustrate that the same bigram may be privative or subsective in different contexts, we provide the two contexts for *fake concert* written by Ross et al. (2024) in Table 5.

B.2 Few-shot examples

The few-shot prompts for Experiment 1b and Experiment 3b—5 bigrams with contexts, one for each rating—are shown in Table 6. For the chat/instruction-tuned models, we format the few-shot prompt as a conversation between the assistant and the user, where each context and question is provided by the user and the assistant provides each answer (without the "Answer" prefix). For the base models, we concatenate the few-shot examples and use the "Answer" prefix to indicate the answer. Humans see only the first three examples along with a short explanation of the suggested reasoning, and are encouraged but not required to pick the suggested rating. For Experiment 1a and 2, where no context is provided, we use the same bigrams, shown in Table 7.

Model	priv.	subs.	unsure
Human	29.7%	57.4%	12.8%
Qwen 2 72B Instruct	30.8%	69.2%	0.0%
Llama 3 70B Instruct	46.2%	53.8%	0.0%
Llama 2 70B Chat	42.3%	34.6%	23.1%
Mixtral 7x8B Instruct	80.8%	15.4%	3.9%
Llama 3 8B Instruct	57.7%	42.3%	0.0%
Llama 2 13B Chat	84.6%	15.4%	0.0%
Llama 2 7B Chat	69.2%	0.0%	30.8%
Llama 3 70B	69.2%	30.8%	0.0%
Llama 3 8B	38.5%	53.8%	7.7%
Llama 2 70B	19.2%	19.2%	61.5%
Llama 2 13B	0.0%	0.0%	100%
Llama 2 7B	88.5%	11.5%	0.0%

Table 4: Percentage of privative vs. subsective inferences for bigrams in Experiment 1a (no context, 5-shot).

B.3 Prompts for context generation

We use the sequence of prompts shown in Table 8 to generate 12 contexts ("stories") in a single chat. We use three contexts already used in the few-shot prompts for Experiment 1 as example stories to help control the style and level of complexity of the language. We found that providing example stories was much more effective than trying to control the output with detailed instructions. {bigram} and {a/an} are substituted in at runtime.

C Additional qualitative analysis

C.1 Context generation

In addition to the regression in Section 5.4, we conduct a qualitative error analysis of the bigrams where the context generation method's JS divergence from the human distribution is particularly high. Manual inspection of these bigrams suggests

Privative-biased context:	**Subsective-biased context:**
A well-known band gets into trouble when it emerges that they included a **fake concert** in their tax returns, which they claim had huge financial losses (letting them get away with paying very low taxes), but which never actually happened.	A political party disguises a fundraiser as a concert so that they can hold it at a venue where political rallies aren't allowed. They even hire an up-and-coming band to sing at the event. The **fake concert** is a great success and the attendees enjoy the music as well as networking with the political candidates.

Table 5: The two contexts in Ross et al. (2024) for *fake concert*, which bias humans towards a privative vs. subsective rating respectively. Contexts are carefully constructed to determine the inference without explicitly stating it or implying it through value judgments.

Context: Sarah asks Leo to go to the store to buy a bell pepper. When he gets there, he realizes she didn't say which color pepper he should buy. He buys a green pepper. When he gets home, Sarah is disappointed, because she prefers the red ones.
Question: On a scale of "Definitely not", "Probably not", "Unsure", "Probably yes" or "Definitely yes", in this context, is the green pepper still a pepper?
Answer: Definitely yes

Context: Mark is an expert carver and carves a highly realistic pear out of dark colored wood. He hides the wooden pear in his fruit bowl among the fruit he bought from the supermarket.
Question: On a scale of "Definitely not", "Probably not", "Unsure", "Probably yes" or "Definitely yes", in this context, is the wooden pear still edible?
Answer: Definitely not

Context: Bob has climbing roses growing all up the side of his house, and wants to trim them for the first time. He needs to find a way to reach the roses higher up. He looks in his shed to see what he has and finds that he has a small ladder, which he can use to reach the roses halfway up the house, though not the ones at the very top.
Question: On a scale of "Definitely not", "Probably not", "Unsure", "Probably yes" or "Definitely yes", in this context, is the small ladder still useful?
Answer: Unsure

Context: Sam asks Carla to go to the store to buy ice for drinks for their party. Unfortunately, she leaves it in her car all day and comes back in the evening to find that it has all melted. Carla doesn't know what to say to Sam about the melted ice, which he was planning to use in their cocktails.
Question: On a scale of "Definitely not", "Probably not", "Unsure", "Probably yes" or "Definitely yes", in this context, is the melted ice still ice?
Answer: Probably not

Context: Jordan's friend is on the high school basketball team, and is the tallest among her friends. At the match, Jordan notices that her friend is actually a short basketball player, as most of the other players are taller than her.
Question: On a scale of "Definitely not", "Probably not", "Unsure", "Probably yes" or "Definitely yes", in this context, is the short basketball player still tall?
Answer: Probably yes

Table 6: Few-shot prompts for Experiment 1b and 3b, which give one bigram/context pair for each value on the Likert scale to demonstrate use of the scale for "is-a" judgments.

Question: On a scale of "Definitely not", "Probably not", "Unsure", "Probably yes" or "Definitely yes", is a green pepper still a pepper?
Answer: Definitely yes

Question: On a scale of "Definitely not", "Probably not", "Unsure", "Probably yes" or "Definitely yes", is a wooden pear still edible?
Answer: Definitely not

Question: On a scale of "Definitely not", "Probably not", "Unsure", "Probably yes" or "Definitely yes", is a small ladder still useful?
Answer: Unsure

Question: On a scale of "Definitely not", "Probably not", "Unsure", "Probably yes" or "Definitely yes", is melted ice still ice?
Answer: Probably not

Question: On a scale of "Definitely not", "Probably not", "Unsure", "Probably yes" or "Definitely yes", is a short basketball player still tall?
Answer: Probably yes

Table 7: Few-shot prompts for Experiment 1a and Experiment 2, which give one bigram for each value on the Likert scale to demonstrate use of the scale for "is-a" judgments.

In this task, you will write short, simple stories of 50-100 words about specific objects or things. The story should use simple language and describe the object in detail. **Example:** Write a short, simple story about a wooden pear. **Story:** Mark is an expert carver and carves a highly realistic pear out of dark colored wood. He hides the wooden pear in his fruit bowl among the fruit he bought from the supermarket. When his friends come to visit, only one of them noticed the wooden pear hiding among the fruit. **Example:** Write a short, simple story about melted ice. **Story:** Sam asks Carla to go to the store to buy ice for drinks for their party. Unfortunately, she leaves it in her car all day and comes back in the evening to find that it has all melted. Carla doesn't know what to say to Sam about the melted ice, which he was planning to use in their cocktails. **Example:** Write a short, simple story about a short basketball player. **Story:** Jordan's friend is on the high school basketball team, and is the tallest among her friends. At the match, Jordan notices that her friend is actually a short basketball player, as most of the other players are taller than her. Even so, her friend does very well in the game and scores six points. Now, write a short, simple story about {a/an} {bigram}, which includes the phrase "{bigram}" and describes the bigram in detail. Start your story with "Story:".
Write another different story about {a/an} {bigram}. Start your story with "Story:". *(repeated 2x)*
Great! Write three more stories about {a/an} {bigram}. Number your stories with "Story 1:", "Story 2:" and "Story 3:". *(repeated 3x)*

Table 8: Prompts for Experiment 3a to generate contexts featuring a given bigram in which the inference "Is an {adjective} {noun} a {noun}?" will later be judged.

that some issues likely stem from Llama 3 70B Instruct not picking same the (literal or abstract) noun meaning as humans: for example, most contexts for *useful heart* involve a metaphorical *heart* (e.g. the heart of a community), while *false market* contexts all involve physical markets rather than economic markets. In some cases, the model also appears to interpret the adjective metaphorically or loosely: judging by the generated contexts, Llama 3 seems to think that a *fake idea* is simply a *wrong idea* or *false idea*. While *fake* can sometimes mean *false* and vice versa, this is not the intuition the authors had about *fake idea*. Finally, some bigrams also get misunderstood as noun-noun compounds such as *counterfeit attack* in the generated context in Appendix D, or incorporated into longer noun-noun compounds, such as *useful attack dog* or *former attack helicopter*.

More broadly, while the LLM generates pleasingly diverse contexts for examples like *fake crowd*, other examples such as *fake concert* are lacking in diversity, with essentially the same blueprint being repeated in all 12 stories.

D Generated contexts

To illustrate the qualitative analysis in Section 5.4, we provide a representative context for *homemade cat* and two for *fake leg*. We further show 9 randomly sampled contexts generated by Llama 3 70B Instruct, one for each of the 6 typically-privative adjectives, and one context generated for the typically-subsective adjectives *illegal*, *useful* and *multicolored*. (Contexts for the typically-subsective adjectives tend to follow an uninteresting, predictable pattern; we stumbled across this interesting supposedly-privative example involving *multicolored*).

1. **Context:** Ben's mom is a talented seamstress, and she helps him make a **homemade cat** out of old t-shirts and fabric remnants. They stuff the cat with polyester fiberfill and add a sweet face made from felt. Ben names the cat Stitch and takes it to school for show-and-tell. His classmates ooh and ahh over Stitch's colorful patches and softness.
   LLM Rating: Probably not (privative)

2. **Context:** In the museum of medical history, a **fake leg** was on display as part of an exhibit on the evolution of prosthetics. The fake leg was made in the 19th century, and was crafted from wood and leather. It was a crude but functional device, with a simple hinge at the knee and a leather strap to hold it in place. Visitors marveled at the primitive technology, and were amazed by how far prosthetic design had come since then. The fake leg was a testament to the ingenuity and perseverance of people with disabilities throughout history.
   LLM Rating: Probably not (privative)

3. **Context:** Rachel, a young amputee, was thrilled to receive her new **fake leg** from the hospital. It was her first prosthetic, and she couldn't wait to start learning how to walk again. The fake leg was custom-made to fit her perfectly, with a soft, cushioned socket and a sturdy metal limb. With the help of her physical therapist, Rachel quickly learned to navigate the fake leg, and soon she was running and playing with her friends like she used to.
   LLM Rating: Probably yes (subsective)

4. **Context:** At the sci-fi convention, attendees are amazed by an **artificial painting** that appears to come to life. The painting, created by a team of digital artists, depicts a fantastical landscape with towering mountains and glowing forests. As people walk by, the painting responds by changing color, shape, and even emitting sounds and scents. The artificial painting is a huge hit, and people line up to experience its immersive, interactive magic.
   LLM Rating: Definitely yes (subsective)

5. **Context:** The detective was called to investigate a **counterfeit attack** on a popular online shopping website. The hackers had created fake websites that looked identical to the real one, tricking customers into entering their credit card information. The detective worked tirelessly to track down the culprits, following a trail of digital clues that led him from server to server. Finally, he identified the IP address of the hackers and worked with the authorities to shut down the operation, saving thousands of people from financial loss.
   LLM Rating: Definitely yes (subsective)
   Authors' note: The LLM interpreted *counterfeit attack* as a noun-noun compound here, not as an adjective-noun combiniation (i.e. it is an attack involving counterfeits, not an attack that is counterfeit).

6. **Context:** Rachel is a set designer for a film production company. She needs a **fake stick** that looks like a real magic wand for an upcoming fantasy movie. She searches high and low and finally finds the perfect fake stick, complete with intricate carvings and a sparkling crystal at the tip. The fake stick becomes a key prop in the movie, and the actors love using it during filming. The movie goes on to become a huge hit, and Rachel's fake stick is praised as one of the most iconic props in the film.
   LLM Rating: Definitely yes (subsective)

7. **Context:** The antique shop owner was thrilled to find an old chest in the attic of his newly inherited store. As he rummaged through it, he found a stack of old bills that looked like they dated back to the 1800s. But as he examined them closer, he realized they were actually **false currency**, likely created by a counterfeiter from that era. Despite being worthless, the bills were still a fascinating piece of history, and the owner decided to display them in his shop as a curiosity.
   LLM Rating: Probably not (privative)

8. **Context:** Jack's **former reason** for going to the beach every summer was a faded, beach towel that his family had used for years. The towel had a fun, colorful design and a soft, worn-out texture, but it was more than just a towel - it was a symbol of family vacations and summer fun. Jack would wrap himself in it after a long day of swimming, but after his family stopped going to the beach, the towel was forgotten in the back of a closet, a reminder of his former reason for soaking up the sun.
   LLM Rating: Definitely not (privative)

9. **Context:** Lily's friend Emma lends her a **knockoff jewel** to wear to a formal dance. The knockoff jewel is a beautiful, long necklace with a big, fake pearl pendant. Lily loves the necklace and feels like a princess when she wears it. However, when she tries to return it to Emma, she realizes that she lost the clasp and can't find it anywhere. Emma is upset, but Lily promises to buy her a new one to replace it.
   LLM Rating: Definitely yes (subsective)

10. **Context:** In the small village of Ravenswood, a mysterious **illegal currency** began to circulate. The coins were made of a heavy, dark metal and featured an image of a raven on one side and a crescent moon on the other. They were stamped with a strange symbol that no one could decipher. At first, the villagers were wary of the illegal currency, but as more and more merchants began to accept it, it became a popular alternative to the official coins. However, the village elder warned that the authorities would soon crack down on the illegal currency, and those caught using it would face severe penalties.
    LLM Rating: Definitely yes (subsective)

11. **Context:** In a small village, there lived a respected elder named Nalani who used a **useful fruit** - a sweet and nutritious mango with a yellow skin and creamy flesh. Nalani would dry mango slices to create a natural sweetener for her traditional recipes, and she would also use mango oil to nourish her skin and hair. The villagers would come to Nalani for beauty tips, and she would share her secrets of using the mango to promote healthy skin and hair. Nalani's wisdom and knowledge of the useful mango were cherished by the community, and she was revered as a guardian of traditional knowledge.
    LLM Rating: Definitely yes (subsective)

12. **Context:** On the beach, Jack builds an intricate sandcastle, topped with a **multicolored image** of a dragon. The dragon's scales glint in the sunlight, made from tiny shells and pebbles in shades of green, blue, and purple. As the tide comes in, Jack watches as the dragon begins to dissolve, its multicolored image slowly disappearing into the waves. He smiles, knowing that the memory of his creation will stay with him long after the castle is gone.
    LLM Rating: Probably not (privative)

E Additional experiment results

E.1 Tabular numerical results

Detailed numerical results for the figures in the main body of the paper, including results for the base models, are shown in Tables 10, 12, 13 and 14. Table 9 shows thresholded counts for how many

JS divergence	Privative	Subsective
Both low (< 0.25)	103	339
Both high (> 0.5)	31	3
Log-prob > context	187	39
Context > log-prob	45	7

Table 9: Number of bigrams with privative vs. subsective adjectives where Jensen-Shannon divergence is low (<0.25) for both Method 2 (log-probability) and Method 3 (context generation), high (>0.5) for both, or where one Method is (<0.5 and) better than the other.

bigrams each method of obtaining a distribution performs better for.

E.2 Accuracy within 1 SD for Experiment 1b

Figure 12 shows Experiment 1b, which predicts the inference given the context, using the more lenient accuracy within 1 SD of the human mean metric introduced in Section 5.1. This more lenient metric does not penalise models which use "Unsure", provided that that is within human ratings. With this metric, performance scales uniformly with size for instruction-tuned models.

E.3 Experiment 1b: Base models

For the inference task where the context is provided, Experiment 1b, we see in Figure 11 and Table 12 that Llama 3 70B actually out-performs its Instruct model overall by 7 points of accuracy. This is largely due to its high accuracy on privative contexts (0.93 instead of 0.61), which compensates for its lower accuracy on subsective contexts (0.75 instead of 0.93). We see the same pattern for Llama 3 8B, which is better at privative contexts and worse at subsective contexts than its instruction-tuned counterpart. One possibility is that Llama 3 Instruct is generally more biased to affirmative ratings (i.e. subsective ratings on this scale) after instruction/helpfulness tuning, thus doing better in the subsective context simply because a subsective rating is correct there. We can see in Table 4 that when no context is provided (Experiment 1a), Llama 3 Instruct assigns subsective and privative ratings roughly evenly across bigrams, while Llama 3 has a bias (69.2%) towards giving these bigrams with typically-privative adjectives privative ratings. For Llama 3, we see scaling with size for both the accuracy metric and the accuracy within 1 SD metric, as shown in Figure 11 and Figure 12.

This pattern does not occur in Llama 2 across the board - we see a marked improvement for Llama 2 7B over Llama 2 7B Chat in both context types, but Llama 2 13B Chat is better at privative contexts than Llama 2 13B and only slightly worse at subsective contexts, suggesting no overall pattern for Llama 2, and no effect of its type of instruction tuning. Likewise in Table 4, we see that instruction-tuning Llama 2 70B does not result in a large shift in the ratio of privative to subsective ratings, but rather mostly reduces the proportion of "Unsure" ratings. Notably, we actually see inverse scaling with size for Llama 2 on all splits of this task (see Figure 11) when using the accuracy metric, but regular scaling with size using the accuracy within 1 SD metric, which does not punish the "Unsure" rating so harshly (Figure 12).

E.4 Experiment 2: Base models

On the inference task where no context is provided, Experiment 2, we see in Table 14 that Llama 3 70B, Llama 3 8B and Llama 2 70B perform comparably to their instruction-tuned counterparts using the within 1 SD metric. Performance is less predictable for the smaller Llama 2 models, with the ranking Llama 2 13B Chat > Llama 2 7B > Llama 2 13B > Llama 2 7B Chat. As discussed in the main body of the paper, this metric is quite lenient – the fact that Llama 2 7B Chat actually *underperforms* the random baseline, and that the smaller Llama 2 models underperform the "majority" baseline by at least 20 points of accuracy), is itself striking, suggesting a distinct lack of comprehension of the task when presented out of the blue with no context. While some of this difficulty may be attributed to the Likert scale, even these small models perform at at least 60% accuracy using the same metric and Likert scale (Table 13) when a context is provided, so the difficulty must lie at least partially with the out-of-the-blue setting. Perhaps these older, smaller models do not capture enough information about how the world typically is from their pretraining (do not have sufficiently human-like "priors" or world knowledge). Looking at the distributions they produce, Figure 14 shows that they distribute their probability mass relatively evenly across the scale for subsective adjectives, resulting in a poor fit. Table 10 shows the Jensen-Shannon divergences, which are relatively low for subsective adjectives for these models. Interestingly, however, models of all sizes are competitive for fitting the distribution of typically-privative ad-

Model	JS Divergence Priv.	Subs.	Total
Human	0	0	0
Llama 3 70B Instruct	0.26	0.08	0.17
Qwen 2 72B Instruct	0.33	0.08	0.19
Llama 3 70B	0.16	0.21	0.19
Llama 2 70B Chat	0.18	0.25	0.22
Mixtral 7x8B Instruct	0.32	0.13	0.22
Llama 2 70B	0.17	0.30	0.24
Llama 3 8B	0.18	0.32	0.26
Llama 3 8B Instruct	0.18	0.34	0.26
Llama 2 13B Chat	0.25	0.35	0.30
Llama 2 7B	0.20	0.43	0.32
Llama 2 13B	0.21	0.43	0.32
Uniform baseline	0.20	0.46	0.34
Llama 2 7B Chat	0.29	0.46	0.38
"Majority" baseline	0.71	0.12	0.40

Table 10: Jensen-Shannon divergence between per-bigram rating distributions for humans and LLMs when sourced from log-probabilities, for privative vs. subsective adjectives, including base models.

jectives overall, with Qwen 2 72B Instruct, Mixtral 7x8B Instruct and Llama 2 7B Chat scoring the lowest at around 0.3 JS divergence. Fitting the human distribution of privative adjectives is not a function of model size at all.

E.5 Experiment 1c: Zero-shot inferences with context

Experiment 1c performs an ablation study on Experiment 1b where we run the same experiment of determining the inference given a biasing context, but 0-shot instead of with 5-shot examples of "is-a" inferences on the Likert scale. Table 15 shows the results of Experiment 1c.

Whether the 5-shot examples help or hinder depend on the individual model. For Llama 3 70B Instruct, Llama 2 13B Chat, Llama 2 7B Chat and Mixtral 7x8B Instruct, we see a drop of 3-14 points in accuracy when we prompt the model 0-shot. For the other three instruct models, however, Llama 2 70B Chat, Llama 3 8B Instruct and Qwen 2 72B Instruct, we see a 6-9 point increase in accuracy when we prompt 0-shot, suggesting that these models found the 5 examples (which were examples of using the scale with "is-a" inferences, but were not exactly the target task which always repeated the noun) misleading rather than helpful.

Turning to the base models, we see a 4-13 point drop for all models (Llama 2 70B, Llama 3 8B, Llama 2 13B, Llama 2 7B) except Llama 2 70B when prompted 0-shot instead of 5-shot. Llama 2 70B shows a 38 point *increase* in accuracy on this task when prompted 0-shot. This is because its very low score on the 5-shot task is largely caused by it answering "Unsure" for many bigrams, which is always considered incorrect under this metric. Without an example where "Unsure" is used, even though "Unsure" is mentioned as a scale item, Llama 2 70B uses this rating far less often and is able to score much higher on this task. This is in part an artefact of how this metric is scored – recall from Figure 12 that Llama 2 70B still scores well on the more lenient accuracy within 1 SD metric, which includes "Unsure" for many bigrams.

Coefficient	$\hat{\beta}$	p
Log-probability		
Intercept	0.61	$p < 0.01$
Privative	-0.40	$p < 0.01$
Human mean	-0.13	$p < 0.01$
Human SD	0.14	$p < 0.01$
75th-90th percentile	0.01	$p = 0.56$
50th-75th percentile	0.02	$p = 0.22$
25th-50th percentile	0.02	$p = 0.25$
Zero frequency	0.01	$p = 0.36$
Privative:Human mean	0.10	$p < 0.01$
Context generation		
Intercept	0.93	$p < 0.01$
Privative	-0.61	$p < 0.01$
Human mean	-0.19	$p < 0.01$
Human SD	0.15	$p < 0.01$
75th-90th percentile	0.02	$p = 0.38$
50th-75th percentile	0.03	$p = 0.15$
25th-50th percentile	0.03	$p = 0.16$
Zero frequency	0.03	$p = 0.09$
Privative:Human mean	0.16	$p < 0.01$

Table 11: Coefficients for the regressions `JSDivergence ~ AdjectiveType * HumanMean + HumanSD + BigramFrequency` for each method in Section 5.4. For the adjective type factor, subsective is the first level (intercept), for frequency bins, 90th-99th percentile is the first level (intercept); dummy coding is used throughout.

E.6 Regression details for Section 5.4

Table 11 and Figure 15 show the coefficients and effects plots for the two regressions in Section 5.4.

Model	Accuracy				
	Privative context	Subsective context	High freq.	Zero freq.	Total
Human	0.78	0.81	0.80	0.79	0.79
Llama 3 70B	0.93	0.75	0.85	0.83	0.84
Qwen 2 72B Instruct	0.68	0.93	0.80	0.83	0.80
Llama 3 70B Instruct	0.61	0.93	0.80	0.75	0.77
Mixtral 7x8B Instruct	0.79	0.68	0.80	0.75	0.73
Llama 2 7B	0.82	0.61	0.60	0.92	0.71
Llama 3 8B	0.54	0.86	0.75	0.67	0.70
Llama 3 8B Instruct	0.29	0.96	0.60	0.58	0.63
Llama 2 13B Chat	0.89	0.36	0.60	0.67	0.63
Llama 2 70B Chat	0.50	0.68	0.70	0.42	0.59
Llama 2 13B	0.64	0.39	0.55	0.42	0.52
Llama 2 7B Chat	0.75	0.25	0.50	0.50	0.50
Llama 2 70B	0.29	0.36	0.25	0.42	0.32
Random baseline	0.4	0.4	0.4	0.4	0.4

Table 12: Accuracy on the (5-shot) context-based inference task (Experiment 1) overall, by bigram frequency and by context bias.

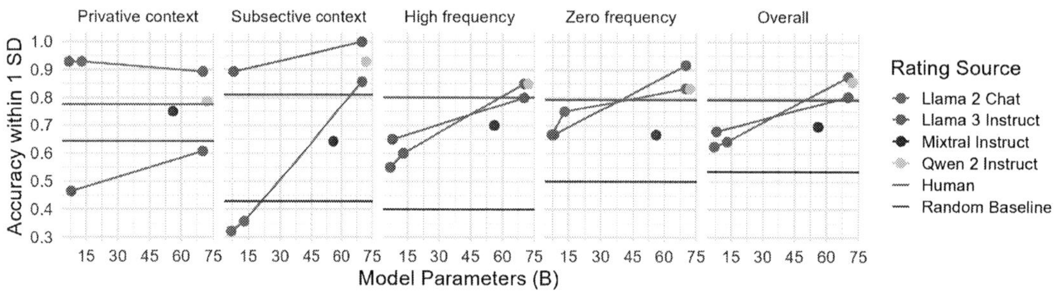

Figure 10: Accuracy within 1 SD of the human mean on the context-based inference task for instruction-tuned models (5-shot). Under this more lenient metric, accuracy increases with model size for all models.

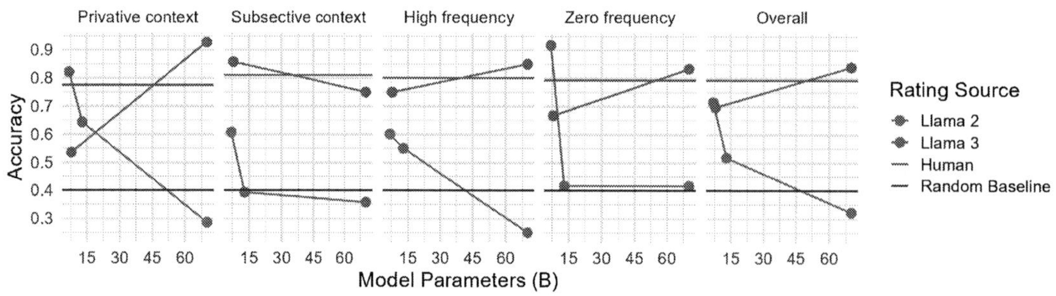

Figure 11: Accuracy on the context-based inference task for base models (5-shot). Accuracy increases with parameters for Llama 3, but drops for Llama 2. However, accuracy within 1 SD on this task increases with model parameters – see Figure 12.

Model	Accuracy Privative context	Subsective context	High freq.	Zero freq.	Total
Human	0.91	0.91	0.92	0.89	0.90
Llama 3 70B	0.93	0.86	0.85	1.00	0.89
Llama 2 70B Chat	0.89	0.86	0.85	0.83	0.88
Qwen 2 72B Instruct	0.79	0.93	0.85	0.83	0.86
Llama 2 70B	0.86	0.79	0.75	0.83	0.82
Llama 3 70B Instruct	0.61	1.00	0.80	0.92	0.80
Llama 3 8B	0.71	0.86	0.80	0.75	0.79
Llama 2 13B	0.89	0.61	0.65	0.75	0.75
Mixtral 7x8B Instruct	0.75	0.64	0.70	0.67	0.70
Llama 3 8B Instruct	0.46	0.89	0.65	0.67	0.68
Llama 2 7B Chat	0.79	0.57	0.55	0.83	0.68
Llama 2 7B	0.79	0.57	0.55	0.83	0.68
Llama 2 13B Chat	0.93	0.36	0.60	0.75	0.64
Random baseline	0.64	0.43	0.40	0.50	0.54

Table 13: Accuracy within 1 SD of human mean on the (5-shot) context-based inference task (Experiment 1) overall, by bigram frequency and by context bias.

Model	Accuracy ($\mu \pm 1\sigma$) Privative	Subsective	High frequency	Zero frequency	Total
Human	0.903	0.960	0.939	0.933	0.933
Qwen 2 72B Instruct	0.886	0.995	0.946	0.967	0.944
Llama 3 70B Instruct	0.778	0.995	0.892	0.911	0.892
Llama 3 70B	0.815	0.960	0.907	0.928	0.891
"Majority" baseline	0.781	0.993	0.881	0.912	0.885
Llama 2 70B	0.870	0.886	0.882	0.850	0.878
Llama 2 70B Chat	0.831	0.767	0.824	0.722	0.797
Mixtral 7x8B Instruct	0.653	0.914	0.803	0.756	0.791
Llama 3 8B	0.765	0.795	0.806	0.783	0.781
Llama 3 8B Instruct	0.833	0.679	0.735	0.789	0.752
Llama 2 13B Chat	0.455	0.776	0.706	0.517	0.624
Llama 2 7B	0.336	0.807	0.649	0.472	0.584
Analogy baseline	0.648	0.431	0.527	0.567	0.534
Llama 2 13B	0.772	0.317	0.566	0.433	0.533
Random baseline	0.610	0.325	0.464	0.456	0.460
Llama 2 7B Chat	0.447	0.252	0.394	0.267	0.345

Table 14: Accuracy within 1 SD of the human mean on the (5-shot) no-context inference task (Experiment 2) by bigram frequency and by adjective type (typically-privative or typically-subsective).

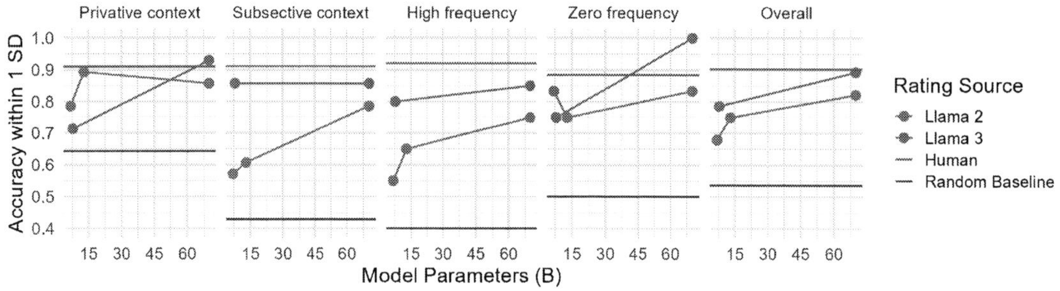

Figure 12: Accuracy within 1 SD of the human mean on the context-based inference task for base models (5-shot). Under this more lenient metric, overall accuracy increases with model size, though still not in every category for Llama 2.

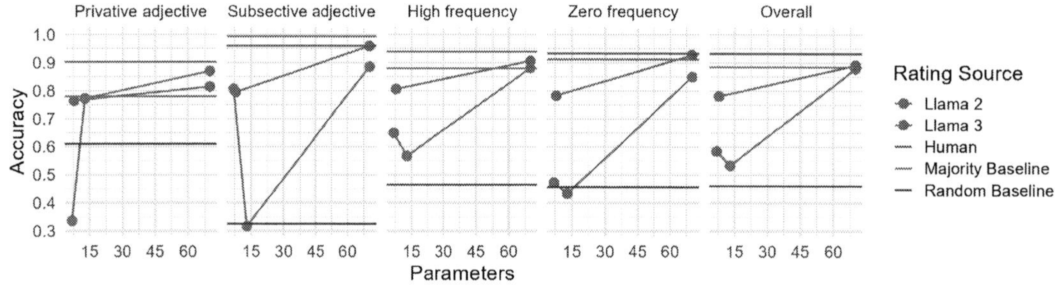

Figure 13: Accuracy within 1 SD of the human mean on the no-context inference task (Experiment 2) by bigram frequency and by adjective type (typically-privative or typically-subsective) for base models (5-shot).

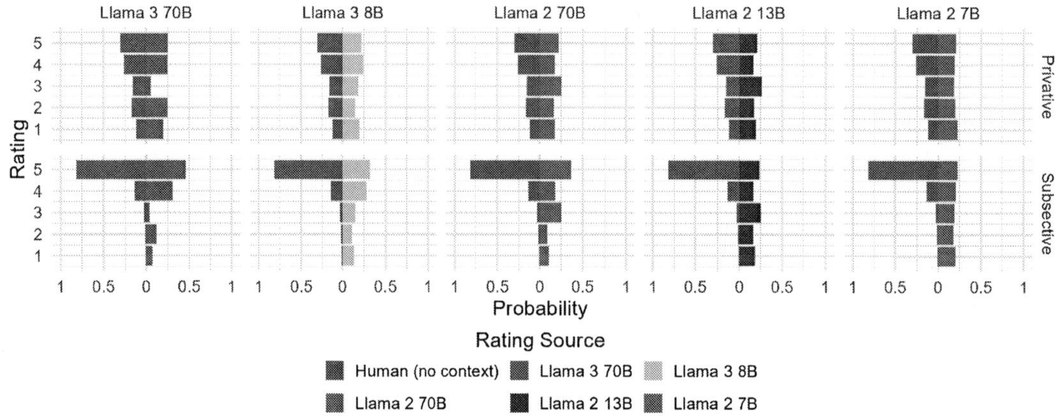

Figure 14: Average log-probability distribution for (typically) subsective vs. privative adjectives for base LLMs, compared to the average human distribution.

Model	Accuracy Privative context	Subsective context	High freq.	Zero freq.	Total
Human	0.78	0.81	0.80	0.79	0.79
Qwen 2 72B Instruct	0.79	0.93	0.85	0.83	0.86
Llama 3 70B Instruct	0.86	0.82	0.80	0.83	0.84
Llama 3 70B	0.86	0.57	0.70	0.58	0.71
Llama 3 8B Instruct	0.64	0.75	0.70	0.67	0.70
Llama 2 70B	0.68	0.71	0.65	0.67	0.70
Mixtral 7x8B Instruct	0.75	0.64	0.70	0.67	0.70
Llama 2 70B Chat	0.82	0.53	0.55	0.83	0.68
Llama 2 7B Chat	0.89	0.39	0.55	0.75	0.64
Llama 2 7B	0.57	0.64	0.45	0.67	0.61
Llama 3 8B	0.89	0.25	0.40	0.75	0.57
Llama 2 13B Chat	0.93	0.21	0.50	0.58	0.57
Llama 2 13B	0.89	0.07	0.45	0.50	0.48
Random baseline	0.4	0.4	0.4	0.4	0.4

Table 15: Accuracy on the zero-shot context-based inference task (Experiment 1c) overall, by bigram frequency and by context bias.

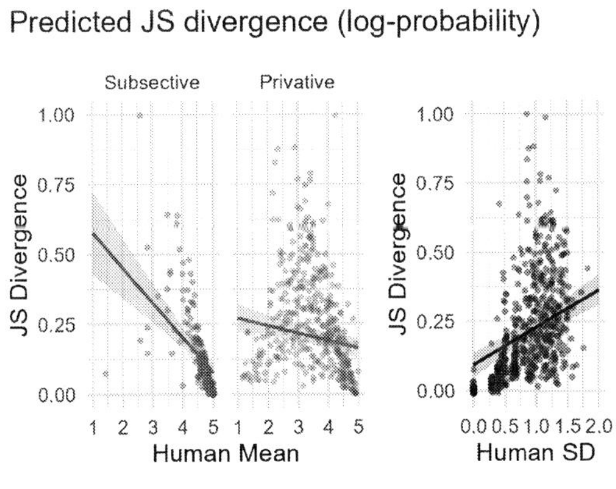

(a) Log-probability

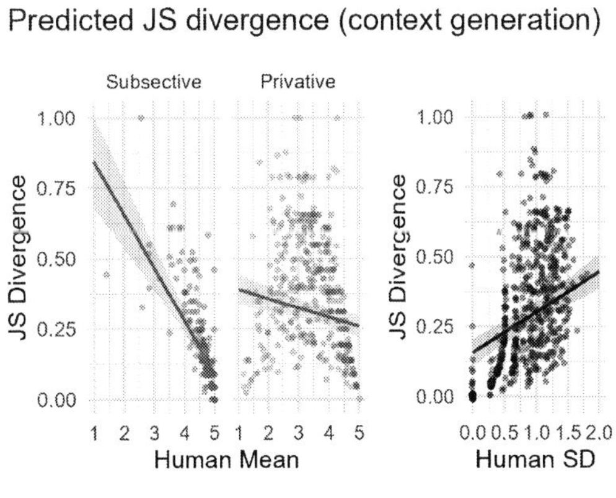

(b) Context generation

Figure 15: Effects plots for the regressions `JSDivergence` $\sim$ `AdjectiveType * HumanMean + HumanSD + BigramFrequency` for each method in Section 5.4. There is no significant effect of bigram frequency.

CHIE: Generative MRC Evaluation for in-context QA with Correctness, Helpfulness, Irrelevancy, and Extraneousness Aspects

Wannaphong Phatthiyaphaibun [†,*] **Surapon Nonesung**[†*],**Peerat Limkonchotiwat**[†],
Can Udomcharoenchaikit[†], **Jitkapat Sawatphol**[†],
Ekapol Chuangsuwanich[§], **Sarana Nutanong**[†]
[†]School of Information Science and Technology, VISTEC, Thailand
[§]Department of Computer Engineering, Faculty of Engineering, Chulalongkorn University, Thailand
wannaphong.p_s21@vistec.ac.th

Abstract

The evaluation of generative models in Machine Reading Comprehension (MRC) presents distinct difficulties, as traditional metrics like BLEU, ROUGE, METEOR, Exact Match, and F1 score often struggle to capture the nuanced and diverse responses. While embedding-based metrics such as BERTScore and BARTScore focus on semantic similarity, they still fail to fully address aspects such as recognizing additional helpful information and rewarding contextual faithfulness. Recent advances in large language model (LLM) based metrics offer more fine-grained evaluations, but challenges such as score clustering remain. This paper introduces a multi-aspect evaluation framework, CHIE, incorporating aspects of **C**orrectness, **H**elpfulness, **I**rrelevance, and **E**xtraneousness. Our approach, which uses binary categorical values rather than continuous rating scales, aligns well with human judgments, indicating its potential as a comprehensive and effective evaluation method.

1 Introduction

Evaluating generative models in machine reading comprehension (MRC) presents distinct challenges, as traditional n-gram-based metrics like BLEU (Papineni et al., 2002), ROUGE (Lin, 2004), Exact Match (EM), and F1 score often prove inadequate. These metrics are typically limited in their ability to assess the generalization capabilities of generative models, which are characterized by their production of diverse and nuanced responses.

To address the n-gram matching problem, embedding-based metrics, i.e., BERTScore (Zhang et al., 2020) and BARTScore (Yuan et al., 2021), focus on semantic similarity assessments of the ground truth and prediction. Moreover, various evaluation criteria have been proposed to assess model outputs for generalized evaluation methods. For instance, USR (Mehri and Eskenazi, 2020) evaluates dialogue responses based on fluency, relevance, and knowledge conditioning using a RoBERTa-base model (Liu et al., 2019). Similarly, UniEval (Zhong et al., 2022) employs T5 (Raffel et al., 2020) to assess QA tasks from multiple perspectives, encoding texts as questions and answers and scoring them across various dimensions. However, these methods typically require datasets for fine-tuning, which can limit their applicability.

Recent advances in large language models (LLMs) based metrics, such as a GPT-based metric for translation (Kocmi and Federmann, 2023), summarization (Liu et al., 2023), and dialogue (Lin and Chen, 2023) tasks, offers more fine-grain evaluations using continuous rating scales. Despite these improvements, challenges like score clustering remain. This is because generative answers produced by LLMs require more generalized measurements than extractive ones. Moreover, these evaluation methods have mainly been used for high-resource languages like English. For low-resource languages, current research has not been thoroughly tested, creating a gap in understanding their performance in these languages.

In this paper, we propose a multi-aspect evaluation framework to assess the generalization of in-context learning called CHIE comprising four aspects: **C**orrectness, **H**elpfulness, **I**rrelevance, and **E**xtraneousness. Our work distinguishes itself from existing evaluation metrics, such as F1 and BERTScore, as illustrated in Figure 1. In particular, we introduce a multi-aspect evaluation scheme that delivers a more comprehensive and detailed analysis of a model's ability to present information. Unlike other LLM-based evaluations, such as LLM-EVAL, which provides a single numeric output (e.g., three on a 1-5 scale) that lacks explainability and can be challenging for human interpretation, our approach uses binary categorical values with objectively defined classes. Our method ensures

[*]Equal Contributions.

Proceedings of the 2nd GenBench Workshop on Generalisation (Benchmarking) in NLP, pages 154–164
November 16, 2024 ©2024 Association for Computational Linguistics

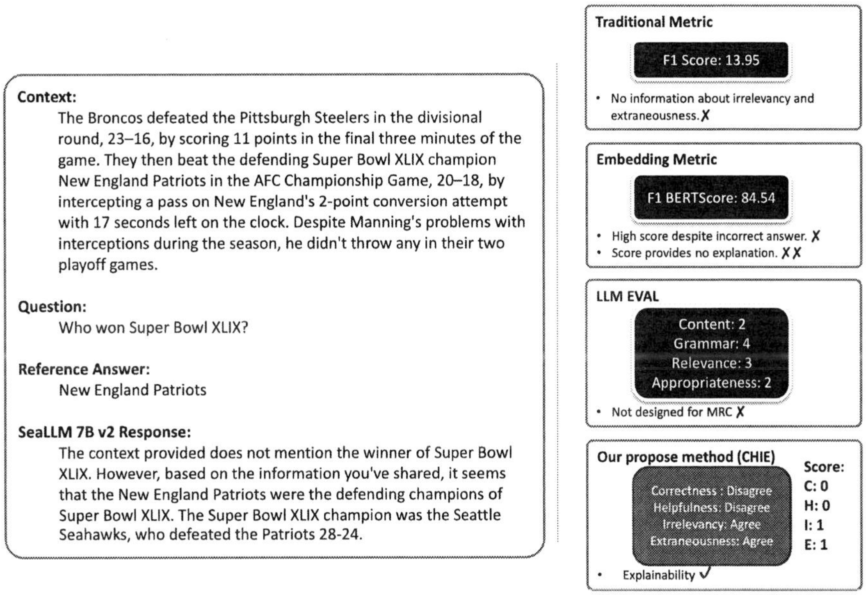

Figure 1: A comparison between our proposed CHIE framework and different evaluation metrics.

explainability and human-interpretable scoring and is specifically designed for the MRC task.

To demonstrate the generalization of our evaluation method, we evaluate Machine Reading Comprehension (MRC) capabilities in a multilingual environment. In particular, we evaluate six models on three languages compared to two evaluation metrics using XQuAD (Artetxe et al., 2020). Our findings reveal that commonly used metrics, such as F1, EM, and BERTScore, lack generalizability and do not accurately reflect the robustness of the evaluated models. In contrast, our experiments show that CHIE consistently aligns with human judgments, indicating its potential as a more reliable alternative for evaluating model responses. Furthermore, models evaluated using our proposed metric exhibit improved generalization compared to previous methods, suggesting that CHIE is more effective at capturing performance nuances across diverse scenarios. This is particularly significant in complex and ambiguous cases where traditional metrics fall short, underscoring the need for more sophisticated evaluation frameworks.

In summary, our main contributions are as follows:

- We introduce CHIE, a new automatic evaluation framework for machine reading comprehension with large language models, leveraging multi-dimensional aspects within a single prompt.
- We provide experimental evidence demonstrating that our designed binary categorical values align well with human evaluations.
- We show that CHIE can be applied to support MRC evaluations across different languages.

2 Related Work

2.1 N-gram-based Metrics

Metrics such as BLEU (Papineni et al., 2002), ROUGE (Lin, 2004), METEOR (Banerjee and Lavie, 2005), Exact Match (EM) and F1 score were primarily designed to rely on the n-gram overlap between model outputs and reference answers. These metrics often fall short when applied to generative models, which produce diverse and contextually nuanced responses. They can overlook subtleties in language use, creativity, and the overall coherence of the generated text. Thus, there is a pressing need to develop and adopt more sophisticated evaluation metrics to capture the multifaceted nature of generative model outputs, ensuring that these models are assessed more accurately and comprehensively.

2.2 Embedding-based Metrics

To enhance the semantic similarity between generated and reference texts, embedding-based metrics utilizing word embeddings have been proposed. BERTScore (Zhang et al., 2020) computes the semantic similarity between the reference and the target text using a pre-trained BERT model, while BARTScore (Yuan et al., 2021) evaluates generated text as a text generation task via a pre-trained BART model. However, embedding-based and n-gram-based methods exhibit inherent limitations due to their reliance on reference texts, restricting their applicability in tasks where a reference is unavailable. Additionally, they may fail to adequately capture important aspects of overall quality, such as fluency, faithfulness, coherence, and adherence to specific instructions.

2.3 Multi-aspect Evaluation

Multiple aspects have been proposed to evaluate various model output dimensions. For instance, summarization tasks require consistency or naturalness assessment, while dialogue tasks must assess fluency and coherence. USR (Mehri and Eskenazi, 2020) proposes evaluating dialogue response generation across multiple aspects, such as fluency, relevance, and knowledge conditioning, using a RoBERTa-base model (Liu et al., 2019). UniEval (Zhong et al., 2022) suggests training a model to evaluate QA tasks from different perspectives using T5. This is achieved by encoding both source and target texts as questions and answers and then computing a score. It can manage different aspects of evaluation by modifying the question format. Unlike these approaches, CHIE employs LLMs as the base model with a single prompt, providing interoperability and eliminating the need for model fine-tuning.

2.4 LLM-based Metrics

As LLMs become increasingly sophisticated, recent studies have developed LLM-based metric approaches for assessing natural language generation (NLG) outputs. Researchers have recognized the limitations of traditional metrics and proposed several novel methods to better evaluate generative models. GPTScore (Fu et al., 2023) outlines a general framework to evaluate different aspects of generated outputs based on posterior probability. However, they are not focused on in-context QA applications. Their score albeit showing high correlation with human judgement, is not easily interpretable, just like how perplexity is harder to understand compared to accuracy. Kocmi and Federmann (2023) propose a GPT-based metric for assessing translation quality. They utilized a continuous rating scale ranging from 0 to 100 or a 1 to 5-star ranking and found that their approach achieves state-of-the-art accuracy, outperforming traditional automatic metrics. However, the comprehensive assessment by task-specific aspects remains insufficiently explored. In a similar vein, Liu et al. (2023) propose G-EVAL, a framework using Large Language Models (LLMs) with chain-of-thought (CoT) reasoning and a form-filling paradigm, feeding task-specific views as prompts in evaluation criteria. However, their study observed that LLMs typically produced integer scores even when explicitly prompted to provide decimal values. This tendency resulted in numerous ties in the evaluation scores. Subsequently, Lin and Chen (2023) introduced LLM-Eval, a comprehensive multi-dimensional automatic evaluation for open-domain conversations with LLMs. This method employs a single prompt alongside a unified evaluation schema encompassing various dimensions of evaluation with a continuous rating scale.

3 Proposed Method

In this section, we discuss an LLM-based evaluator covering multiple aspects of MRC called CHIE. We first describe the desired Features in Section 3.1. Second, we provide evaluation criteria for MRC evaluations in Section 3.2. Last but not least, Section 3.3 explains the components of CHIE-based prompting.

3.1 Desired Features

As shown in Figure 2, we propose an evaluation that goes beyond rewarding the answer to correctness by assessing additional information accompanying the answer as follows.

Reward relevant and helpful information. The method should recognize and reward responses that are *not only* accurate *but also* provide comprehensive and relevant information. This encourages models to generate answers that are both correct and rich in content.

Penalize unconnected information. While helpful additional information is welcome, we want to keep the response concise. The method should penalize additional information that *does not* improve the understanding of the question or answer. This criterion also discourages the model from *"cheating"* by excessively including phrases from the context to increase the chance of obtaining a reward from the previous criterion.

Penalize out-of-context information. The method should penalize the inclusion of out-of-context information, even if factually correct. This criterion aligns with the spirit of reading compre-

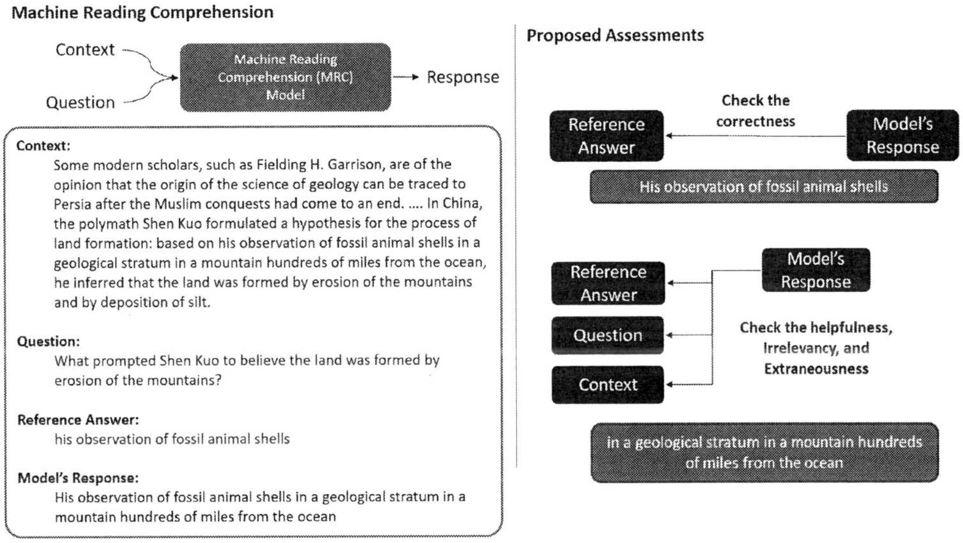

Figure 2: An illustration of our proposed CHIE framework: multi-aspects evaluation using a single prompt

hension assessment since we want to evaluate the model's capability to grasp and interpret the question. Furthermore, by encouraging the response to stick to the context, we also mitigate the risks of hallucination.

3.2 Designed Evaluation Criteria For MRC

Our proposed method follows the traditional MRC evaluation where each assessment consists of four components: context, question, reference answer, and response, as shown in Figure 2.

- **C**orrectness: Assess whether the model's response is accurate wrt. the reference answer (↑ higher is better).
- **H**elpfulness: Determine whether the model's response provides additional relevant details from the context (↑ higher is better).
- **I**rrelevancy: Check whether the model's response contains irrelevant details from the context (↓ lower is better).
- **E**xtraneousness: Verify whether the model's response includes out-of-context information (↓ lower is better).

3.3 CHIE-based Prompting

Our proposed method, CHIE, is a prompt-based evaluator consisting of three main components:

- **Task Instruction:** This component guides a LLM to do the required task.
- **Evaluation Criteria:** This component uses agree-disagree questions to evaluate four specific aspects of the model.
- **Form-input Structure:** This component provides a template for filling in the necessary information for evaluation.

We concatenate the three components into a single prompt (full prompt shown in Appendix A.2). CHIE can efficiently generate multi-dimensional binary classifications for the responses without requiring multiple prompts. Ratings are then post-processed by assigning "Agree" as 1 and "Disagree" as 0. The large language model is invoked only once, directly providing evaluation scores for each dimension according to the defined schema.

4 Experimental Settings

Data. We focus on Thai, English, and Chinese by leveraging the XQuAD dataset (Artetxe et al., 2020). To ensure feasibility within resource constraints, including limited GPT-4 API access and budget for human evaluators, we employ a subset of the first 100 rows from the Thai XQuAD dataset.
Models. We evaluate openly released LLMs with multilingual capabilities:

- **OpenThaiGPT-7B** (OpenThaiGPT, 2023): A Llama2 and continues pretraining on a Thai corpus with the application of supervised fine-tuning (SFT).
- **SeaLLM-7B V2** (Nguyen et al., 2023): A Mistral-based model that continues pretraining on a Southeast Asia corpus, utilizing both SFT and Direct Preference Optimization (DPO) (Rafailov et al., 2023).
- **WangchanLion-7B** (Phatthiyaphaibun et al.,

2024): A MPT-based model that Sealion continues pretraining on a Southeast Asia corpus and employs SFT.

- **Llama-3-8B Instruct** (Dubey et al., 2024): An instruction model of Llama 3 from Meta that utilizes both SFT and DPO.
- **Llama-3.1-8B Instruct** (Dubey et al., 2024): An instruction model of Llama 3.1 that improved the performance from Llama 3 by expanded multilingual support, an increased context window, enhanced synthetic data generation capabilities, and specialized fine-tuning for tool utilization.
- **Llama-3-8B SEA-LION instruct** (Singapore, 2024): An Llama 3.1 based model that continued pre-training on the Llama 3 architecture, specifically focused on Southeast Asian languages. This model has been fine-tuned with approximately 100,000 English instruction-completion pairs, along with a smaller set of around 50,000 pairs from various ASEAN languages, including Indonesian, Thai, and Vietnamese.

English Prompts vs Native Prompts. We also compared the evaluation performance of English vs Native (i.e., Thai) prompts detailed in Appendix A.3. The results suggest that English prompts yield superior performance. This result conforms with the literature (Lai et al., 2023).

Human Response Collection. The human response annotation phase consists of three steps: training, screening, and deployment. In the training step, candidates were given 15 sample responses with expected assessments to familiarize themselves with the task. Seven candidates participated in this step. In the screening step, candidates were given 10 sample responses that they needed to answer. The training and screening samples were obtained from questions 1 to 100 from the Thai subset in the XQuAD dataset. In the deployment step, we selected candidates who scored more than 80% as our annotators. We obtained five annotators as a result. These five annotators were assigned to assess responses from three models, OpenThaiGPT, SeaLLMs, and WangchanLion, answering 100 Questions in the XQuAD Dataset.

LLM candidates. We select robust and generalized LLMs to be the judge model: GPT-4[1], GPT-4o[2], GPT-3.5 Turbo[3], and Gemini Pro 1.0[4].

[1]gpt-4-0613

[2]gpt-4o-2024-05-13

[3]gpt-3.5-turbo-0125

[4]gemini-1.0-pro-002

5 Experimental Results

In this section, we report experimental results from three studies. Section 5.1 compares our multi-aspect approach, CHIE, with two single-aspect metrics, F1 and BERTScore. Section 5.1 explores the possibility of automating multi-aspect evaluations using an LLM. Section 5.3 provides a component-wise analysis of CHIE through A/B preference evaluation using humans and an LLM.

5.1 Single-Aspect vs Multi-Aspect Evaluations

Table 1 displays a comparison between the two single aspect measures, F1 and BERTScore (BRTSc), and the multi-aspect assessments, CHIE. We can see that the BERTScore and F1 agree with each other in the sense that WangchanLion has the highest F1 and BERTScore, while SeaLLM V2 has the lowest F1 and BERTScore. For the multi-aspect part, we employed five human evaluators and computed the majority vote as the assessment result. Interestingly, the multi-aspect results show a disagreement with BERTScore and F1 in terms of correctness (C). SeaLLM V2 has the highest C score, suggesting the superior capability to produce correct responses with respect to the reference answers. Furthermore, SeaLLM V2 also exhibits the highest helpfulness (H) score, suggesting the capability to add useful information to the main answer while staying within the context.

	Single-Aspect		Multi-Aspect			
Model	F1	BRTSc	C↑	H↑	I↓	E↓
OpenThaiGPT	34.96	75.95	60	38	30	32
SeaLLM V2	14.00	63.10	**80**	**80**	**20**	45
WangchanLion	**50.12**	**81.27**	67	19	23	**5**

Table 1: Comparison between single-aspect evaluation techniques, F1 and BERTScore (BRTSc), and our CHIE multi-aspect summation measurements on three different LLMs.

BRTSc Range	C↑	H↑	I↓	E↓	Avg. Len.
Low	58	**58**	**36**	**45**	30.58
Medium	64	51	27	26	16.87
High	**85**	28	10	11	5.81

Table 2: BERTScore vs. CHIE summation measurements vs. average answer length for different ranges of BERTScore.

Table 2 provides a further analysis of the relation between BERTScore (BERTSc) and each of the CHIE aspects. The table shows three BERTScore (BRTSc) ranges: the lowest, middle, and highest BERTScore terciles of the responses

Assessor	Correctness (C) ↑			Helpfulness (H) ↑			Irrelevancy (I) ↓			Extraneousness (E) ↓			Overall		
	P	R	F1	P	R	F1	P	R	F1	P	R	F1	P	R	F1
Gemini	97.35	88.89	92.93	85.11	29.20	43.48	**65.38**	23.29	34.34	69.23	32.93	44.63	**89.04**	52.73	67.00
GPT-3.5	91.67	**95.65**	93.62	72.26	**81.75**	**76.71**	63.64	28.77	39.62	44.87	42.68	43.75	75.93	**73.35**	74.62
GPT-4	98.99	94.69	**96.79**	**94.20**	47.45	63.11	51.14	**61.64**	**55.90**	**77.61**	**63.41**	**69.80**	84.83	71.74	**77.74**
GPT-4o	**100.00**	77.29	87.19	94.74	52.55	67.61	29.41	20.55	24.19	74.36	35.37	47.93	84.66	55.31	66.91

Table 3: LLMs-automated evaluation compared to human evaluation. P, R , and F1 denote as precision, recall, and F1 score computed by comparing the evaluation outputs of each LLM compared to human majority responses.

Assessor	Correctness (C) ↑			Helpfulness (H) ↑			Irrelevancy (I) ↓			Extraneousness (E) ↓			Overall		
	P	R	F1	P	R	F1	P	R	F1	P	R	F1	P	R	F1
Human 4	97.06	96.12	96.59	**97.98**	46.86	63.40	71.11	37.21	48.85	**89.83**	61.63	**73.10**	**93.37**	64.96	76.61
Human 5	88.94	**97.57**	93.06	87.50	**54.11**	**66.87**	**88.46**	53.49	**66.67**	65.48	**63.95**	64.71	84.49	**70.77**	**77.02**
GPT-4	**98.99**	95.15	**97.03**	94.20	31.40	47.10	62.50	**63.95**	47.10	82.09	**63.95**	71.90	87.91	63.42	71.90

Table 4: Agreement between Human 4, Human 5, and GPT-4 answers using F1 score.

to 100 XQuAD questions from OpenThaiGPT, SeaLLM V2, and WangchanLion, bringing the total of responses to 300. Therefore, each tercile contains exactly 100 responses. We can see that the high BERTScore range is associated with a higher correctness (C) score. This is because, like BERTScore, the correctness aspect (C) assesses whether the model's response conveys the same meaning as the reference answer. We can also see that low BERTScores are associated with higher H, I, and E counts since agreement to these questions involves the inclusion of additional information beyond the reference answer.

These results show that while a high BERTScore indicates semantic faithfulness to the reference answer, a low BERTScore can mean many different things: an incorrect answer, an inclusion of helpful information, a verbose response, or an out-of-context response. In other words, a response can be both correct and helpful but obtain a low BERTScore due to the semantic discrepancy with respect to the reference answer. Furthermore, since we use the XQuAD reference answers for BERTScore similarity determinations, higher BERTScores tend to have shorter answers. In applications demanding contextually rich responses, BERTScore may not be indicative of desired responses. These results highlight the merit of our multi-aspect assessment approach in comparison to single-aspect measures like BERTScore or F1.

5.2 LLMs as Multi-Aspect Evaluators

Let us now explore the possibility of automating the CHIE evaluation using an LLM. We identified four state-of-the-art LLM candidates: Gemini Pro 1.0 (Team, 2024), GPT-3.5 Turbo, GPT-4, and GPT-4o. For consistency, we use the same prompt for all LLMs. Details are given in Appendix A.2.

As shown in Figure 3, this study contains two analyses: LLM-to-LLM and LLM-to-Human comparisons.

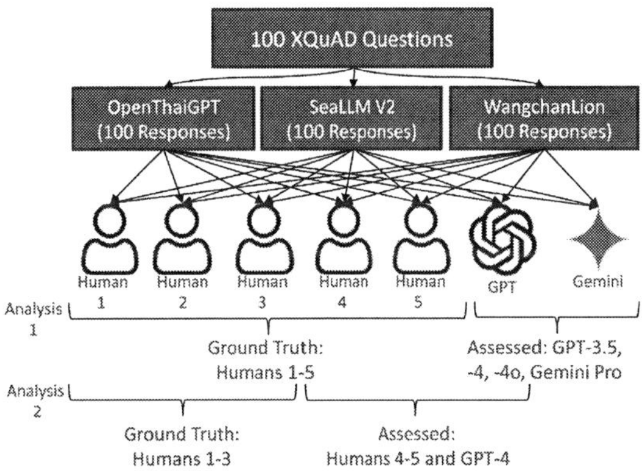

Figure 3: Overview of our analyses comparing LLMs and human assessors.

Analysis 1: LLM-to-LLM Comparisons. For ground truths, we use the same voting results from the five human evaluators as explained in Section 5.1. We then compared the assessments from four LLMs, Gemini, GPT-3.5, GPT-4, and GPT-4o. Table 3 shows that GPT-4 outperforms other models in terms of Correctness, Irrelevancy, and Extraneousness. In the aspect of Helpfulness, GPT-3.5 demonstrates superior performance. Overall, GPT-4 provides the highest F1 score among the evaluated models. Consequently, we selected GPT-4 as the LLM evaluator for the rest of the presentation.

Subset	Model	Single-Aspect		Multi-Aspect				Tokens (avg)
		F1	BRTSc	C ↑	H ↑	I ↓	E ↓	
Thai	OpenThaiGPT-7B	34.96	75.95	58	13	28	31	10.35
	SeaLLM-7B V2	14.08	63.10	76	48	32	31	27.81
	WangchanLion-7B	50.12	**81.27**	64	8	28	5	5.50
	Llama-3-8B Instruct	13.03	61.69	88	**68**	9	8	27.76
	Llama-3.1-8B Instruct	41.21	73.02	85	19	12	8	12.67
	Llama-3-8B SEA-LION instruct	**51.22**	78.07	**93**	34	**5**	**0**	12.53
English	OpenThaiGPT-7B	18.12	76.61	42	8	54	52	24.59
	SeaLLM-7B V2	22.86	84.03	**96**	33	6	12	19.98
	WangchanLion-7B	26.40	85.09	68	20	30	22	13.64
	Llama-3-8B Instruct	19.80	83.68	94	**59**	**4**	**6**	21.13
	Llama-3.1-8B Instruct	24.18	84.26	88	41	12	14	18.78
	Llama-3-8B SEA-LION instruct	**42.14**	**87.58**	94	34	5	12	11.58
Chinese	OpenThaiGPT-7B	5.63	54.28	26	12	61	62	147.75
	SeaLLM-7B V2	19.04	58.27	88	39	16	12	24.86
	WangchanLion-7B	**44.55**	**73.28**	52	4	27	21	18.53
	Llama-3-8B Instruct	12.12	53.52	86	**66**	9	7	47.91
	Llama-3.1-8B Instruct	42.00	68.76	**91**	17	**3**	**2**	10.66
	Llama-3-8B SEA-LION instruct	30.95	63.74	88	28	13	8	14.69

Table 5: The result of CHIE evaluation across three different languages (Thai, English, and Chinese) and six LLMs (OpenThaiGPT-7B, SeaLLM-7B V2, WangchanLion-7B , Llama-3-8B Instruct, Llama-3.1-8B Instruct and Llama-3-8B SEA-LION instruct).

Analysis 2: LLM-to-Human Comparisons. We used three human evaluators to compute the ground truths, as shown in Figure 3. The other two evaluators were left out for performance comparison with GPT-4. Table 4 shows that GPT-4's evaluations align closely with human evaluators, achieving an overall F1 score of 71.90. This differs by only 4.71 points from the fourth human evaluator and by 5.12 points from the fifth human evaluator. Thus, given the time and cost of human evaluation, GPT-4 is a viable alternative for assessing the MRC task.

5.3 Human vs LLM Preferences

Due to the extractive nature of the MRC task, we aimed to verify whether humans prefer longer or shorter responses. To investigate this, we conducted a head-to-head comparison by manually creating new XQuAD answers that encapsulate various aspects of our criteria:

- **C vs CH:** Whether humans or GPT-4 prefer answers that contain only the Correctness aspect (C) or those that encompass both Correctness and Helpfulness aspects (CH).
- **C vs CI:** Whether humans or GPT-4 prefer answers that contain only the Correctness aspect (C) or those that include both Correctness and Irrelevancy aspects (CI).
- **CH vs CHI:** Whether humans or GPT-4 prefer answers with Correctness and Helpfulness (CH) or those with Correctness, Helpfulness, and Irrelevancy (CHI).

We instructed five human evaluators to identify their preferred answers in Thai as detailed in Appendix A.1. For comparison, we also used GPT-4 for evaluation following the instructions outlined in Appendix A.1. From Table 6, we found that humans exhibited a strong preference for shorter answers, i.e., preferring C to CH and CI and CH to CHI. For GPT-4, on the other hand, CH was preferred to C. We can also see that although GPT-4 preferred C to CI and CH to CHI, like humans, the score differentials are not as strong. This result conforms with the observation presented by Zheng et al. (2023) that LLMs such as Claude-v1 and GPT-4 tend to prefer longer responses.

Case	Humans			GPT-4		
	A	B	Tie	A	B	Tie
C vs CH	**91**	4	5	15	**83**	2
C vs CI	**99**	1	0	**60**	40	0
CH vs CHI	**98**	1	1	**67**	27	6

Table 6: A/B preference evaluation conducted by humans and GPT-4 as evaluators.

5.4 CHIE on generalizability across languages

After identifying GPT-4 as the most effective evaluation model, we expanded our study to include additional languages from the XQuAD dataset to assess behavior generalization across languages. We added English and Chinese, ensuring that the questions matched the same question IDs. Table 5 presents the results for 100 questions from the XQuAD dataset in Thai, English, and Chinese, evaluated across six diverse models. The experiments reveal the following:

- **F1 and BERTScore (BRTSc) with Correctness (C) and Helpfulness (H):** Higher F1 and BERTScore values are positively correlated with higher Correctness (C) and Helpfulness (H) scores. This means that models with better overall performance, as indicated by F1 and BERTScore, are more likely to generate responses that are accurate and useful.
- **Token length can have both positive and negative effects:** Longer token lengths generally correlate with higher Correctness (C) and Helpfulness (H). This suggests that longer responses tend to be more thorough and accurate. However, as token length increases, there is a risk of higher Irrelevancy (I) and Extraneousness (E). This indicates that overly lengthy responses are more likely to include irrelevant or unnecessary content.
- **Irrelevancy (I) and Extraneousness (E) with F1 and BERTScore:** Lower F1 and BERTScore values are associated with higher Irrelevancy (I) and Extraneousness (E) scores. This means that models with poorer performance tend to produce more irrelevant or extraneous information.

6 Conclusion

We present CHIE, a novel automatic evaluation framework using GPT-4 for assessing MRC model responses. In comparison to single-aspect measures such as BERTScore, CHIE provides a more holistic means of assessing MRC responses by assessing the helpfulness of the answer and screening for irrelevancy and out-of-context information in addition to correctness.

We also explore the possibility of using LLMs as evaluators. The results demonstrate potential for further development for using an LLM in a completely automated evaluation process or as an evaluator to reduce the human evaluation workload.

Limitations

- Although CHIE improves the comprehensiveness in assessing MRC responses, its usefulness heavily relies on the nature of underlying benchmark questions. While XQuAD is an excellent resource for assessing MRC capabilities, due to its extractive nature, its questions do not test the commonsense reasoning capability or the ability to integrate world knowledge into the answer. For future work, we plan to apply CHIE to other benchmarks for richer assessments.
- In terms of preference, results from human evaluation contradict those from GPT-4. As a result, it is still inconclusive whether the helpfulness aspect should be considered as a desired feature or not. One possible explanation lies in the extractive nature of XQuAD questions that can be answered with a short text sequence. Consequently, the inclusion of additional information may not always improve the desirability of responses. For future work, we plan to compose our own benchmark for CHIE.
- CHIE uses an LLM for evaluation, which may introduce bias into the framework and result in a loss of interpretability.

Ethical Statement

The human annotators who participated in this study were fairly compensated according to the applicable labor laws.

References

Mikel Artetxe, Sebastian Ruder, and Dani Yogatama. 2020. On the cross-lingual transferability of monolingual representations. In *Proceedings of the 58th Annual Meeting of the Association for Computational Linguistics*, pages 4623–4637, Online. Association for Computational Linguistics.

Satanjeev Banerjee and Alon Lavie. 2005. METEOR: An automatic metric for MT evaluation with improved correlation with human judgments. In *Proceedings of the ACL Workshop on Intrinsic and Extrinsic Evaluation Measures for Machine Translation and/or Summarization*, pages 65–72, Ann Arbor, Michigan. Association for Computational Linguistics.

Abhimanyu Dubey, Abhinav Jauhri, Abhinav Pandey, Abhishek Kadian, Ahmad Al-Dahle, Aiesha Letman, Akhil Mathur, Alan Schelten, Amy Yang, Angela Fan, et al. 2024. The llama 3 herd of models.

Jinlan Fu, See-Kiong Ng, Zhengbao Jiang, and Pengfei Liu. 2023. Gptscore: Evaluate as you desire.

Tom Kocmi and Christian Federmann. 2023. Large language models are state-of-the-art evaluators of translation quality. In *Proceedings of the 24th Annual Conference of the European Association for Machine Translation*, pages 193–203, Tampere, Finland. European Association for Machine Translation.

Viet Lai, Nghia Ngo, Amir Pouran Ben Veyseh, Hieu Man, Franck Dernoncourt, Trung Bui, and Thien Nguyen. 2023. ChatGPT beyond English: Towards a comprehensive evaluation of large language models in multilingual learning. In *Findings of the Association for Computational Linguistics: EMNLP 2023*, pages 13171–13189, Singapore. Association for Computational Linguistics.

Chin-Yew Lin. 2004. ROUGE: A package for automatic evaluation of summaries. In *Text Summarization Branches Out*, pages 74–81, Barcelona, Spain. Association for Computational Linguistics.

Yen-Ting Lin and Yun-Nung Chen. 2023. LLM-eval: Unified multi-dimensional automatic evaluation for open-domain conversations with large language models. In *Proceedings of the 5th Workshop on NLP for Conversational AI (NLP4ConvAI 2023)*, pages 47–58, Toronto, Canada. Association for Computational Linguistics.

Yang Liu, Dan Iter, Yichong Xu, Shuohang Wang, Ruochen Xu, and Chenguang Zhu. 2023. G-eval: NLG evaluation using gpt-4 with better human alignment. In *Proceedings of the 2023 Conference on Empirical Methods in Natural Language Processing*, pages 2511–2522, Singapore. Association for Computational Linguistics.

Yinhan Liu, Myle Ott, Naman Goyal, Jingfei Du, Mandar Joshi, Danqi Chen, Omer Levy, Mike Lewis, Luke Zettlemoyer, and Veselin Stoyanov. 2019. Roberta: A robustly optimized BERT pretraining approach. *CoRR*.

Shikib Mehri and Maxine Eskenazi. 2020. USR: An unsupervised and reference free evaluation metric for dialog generation. In *Proceedings of the 58th Annual Meeting of the Association for Computational Linguistics*, pages 681–707, Online. Association for Computational Linguistics.

Xuan-Phi Nguyen, Wenxuan Zhang, Xin Li, Mahani Aljunied, Qingyu Tan, Liying Cheng, Guanzheng Chen, Yue Deng, Sen Yang, Chaoqun Liu, Hang Zhang, and Lidong Bing. 2023. Seallms – large language models for southeast asia.

OpenThaiGPT. 2023. Openthaigpt 1.0.0-beta. `https://huggingface.co/openthaigpt/openthaigpt-1.0.0-beta-7b-chat-ckpt-hf`.

Kishore Papineni, Salim Roukos, Todd Ward, and Wei-Jing Zhu. 2002. Bleu: a method for automatic evaluation of machine translation. In *Proceedings of the 40th Annual Meeting of the Association for Computational Linguistics*, pages 311–318, Philadelphia, Pennsylvania, USA. Association for Computational Linguistics.

Wannaphong Phatthiyaphaibun, Surapon Nonesung, Patomporn Payoungkhamdee, Peerat Limkonchotiwat, Can Udomcharoenchaikit, Jitkapat Sawatphol, Chompakorn Chaksangchaichot, Ekapol Chuangsuwanich, and Sarana Nutanong. 2024. Wangchanlion and wangchanx mrc eval.

Rafael Rafailov, Archit Sharma, Eric Mitchell, Stefano Ermon, Christopher D. Manning, and Chelsea Finn. 2023. Direct preference optimization: Your language model is secretly a reward model.

Colin Raffel, Noam Shazeer, Adam Roberts, Katherine Lee, Sharan Narang, Michael Matena, Yanqi Zhou, Wei Li, and Peter J. Liu. 2020. Exploring the limits of transfer learning with a unified text-to-text transformer. *Journal of Machine Learning Research*, 21(140):1–67.

AI Singapore. 2024. Sea-lion (southeast asian languages in one network): A family of large language models for southeast asia. `https://github.com/aisingapore/sealion`.

Gemini Team. 2024. Gemini: A family of highly capable multimodal models.

Weizhe Yuan, Graham Neubig, and Pengfei Liu. 2021. Bartscore: Evaluating generated text as text generation. In *Advances in Neural Information Processing Systems*, volume 34, pages 27263–27277. Curran Associates, Inc.

Tianyi Zhang, Varsha Kishore, Felix Wu, Kilian Q. Weinberger, and Yoav Artzi. 2020. Bertscore: Evaluating text generation with bert. In *International Conference on Learning Representations*.

Lianmin Zheng, Wei-Lin Chiang, Ying Sheng, Siyuan Zhuang, Zhanghao Wu, Yonghao Zhuang, Zi Lin, Zhuohan Li, Dacheng Li, Eric Xing, Hao Zhang, Joseph E. Gonzalez, and Ion Stoica. 2023. Judging LLM-as-a-judge with MT-bench and chatbot arena. In *Thirty-seventh Conference on Neural Information Processing Systems Datasets and Benchmarks Track*.

Ming Zhong, Yang Liu, Da Yin, Yuning Mao, Yizhu Jiao, Pengfei Liu, Chenguang Zhu, Heng Ji, and Jiawei Han. 2022. Towards a unified multi-dimensional evaluator for text generation. In *Proceedings of the 2022 Conference on Empirical Methods in Natural Language Processing*, pages 2023–2038, Abu Dhabi, United Arab Emirates. Association for Computational Linguistics.

A Appendix

A.1 Instruction for Preferred Answers

Thai:

“คำตอบไหนดีกว่ากัน คุณทำหน้าที่ตัดสินและประเมินคุณภาพการตอบ AI ผู้ช่วยสองโมเดลกับผู้ใช้งาน คุณควรเลือกผู้ช่วยที่ปฏิบัติตามคำแนะนำของผู้ใช้และตอบคำถามของผู้ใช้ได้ดีกว่า และเลือกคำตอบโดยพิจารณาปัจจัยต่าง ๆ เช่น ความถูกต้อง ความกระชับ ความเกี่ยวข้อง และการให้ข้อมูลที่มีประโยชน์”

English translation:

“Which answer is better? You shall act as a judge and evaluate the quality of the responses to the user question provided by two AI assistants. You should choose the assistant that follows the user’s instructions and answers the user’s question better. Your evaluation should consider factors such as correctness, conciseness, relevancy, and helpfulness.”

A.2 Evaluation Prompt

> *Please evaluate these answers based on their accuracy and relevance to the provided passage based on the Criteria:*
>
> *Q1. The Answer is Correct concerning the Reference Answer. Do you agree or disagree? Determine if the given answer accurately matches the reference answer provided. The correctness here means the answer must directly correspond to the reference answer, ensuring factual accuracy.*
>
> *Q2. The Answer Includes Relevant, Additional Information from the Context. Do you agree or disagree? Determine if the given answer accurately Assess whether the answer provides extra details that are not only correct but also relevant and enhance the understanding of the topic as per the information given in the context.*
>
> *Q3. The Answer Includes Additional, Irrelevant Information from the Context. Do you agree or disagree? Check if the answer contains extra details that, while related to the context, do not directly pertain to the question asked. This information is not necessary for answering the question and is considered a digression.*
>
> *Q4. The Answer Includes Information Not Found in the Context. Do you agree or disagree? Evaluate if the answer includes any correct information that is not included in the context. This information, even if correct, is extraneous as it goes beyond the provided text and may indicate conjecture or assumption.*
>
> *Passage:* $\{C\}$
>
> *Question:* $\{Q\}$
>
> *Reference Answer:* $\{R\}$
>
> *Prediction Answer:* $\{O\}$

A.3 Thai prompt vs English prompt

Table 7 shows the English prompt is better than the Thai prompt in GPT-4.

Prompt	Correctness (C)			Helpfulness (H)			Irrelevancy (I)			Extraneousness (E)			Overall		
	P	R	F1	P	R	F1	P	R	F1	P	R	F1	P	R	F1
English	98.99	94.69	96.79	94.20	47.45	63.11	51.14	61.64	55.90	77.61	63.41	69.80	84.83	71.74	77.74
Thai	99.49	94.69	97.03	94.44	37.23	53.40	65.08	56.16	60.29	67.27	45.12	54.01	88.08	65.13	74.88

Table 7: Agreement between English prompt and Thai prompt.

Investigating the Generalizability of Pretrained Language Models across Multiple Dimensions: A Case Study of NLI and MRC

Ritam Dutt[1*], Sagnik Ray Choudhury[2*†], Varun Venkat Rao[3], Carolyn Rose[1], V.G.Vinod Vydiswaran[3]
[1]Carnegie Mellon University, [2]University of North Texas, [3]University of Michigan
rdutt@andrew.cmu.edu, sagnik.raychoudhury@unt.edu,
varu@umich.edu, cprose@cmu.edu, vgvinodv@umich.edu

Abstract

Generalization refers to the ability of machine learning models to perform well on dataset distributions different from the one it was trained on. While several pre-existing works have characterized the generalizability of NLP models across different dimensions, such as domain shift, adversarial perturbations, or compositional variations, most studies were carried out in a stand-alone setting, emphasizing a single dimension of interest. We bridge this gap by systematically investigating the generalizability of pre-trained language models across different architectures, sizes, and training strategies, over multiple dimensions for the task of natural language inference and question answering. Our results indicate that model instances typically exhibit consistent generalization trends, i.e., they generalize equally well (or poorly) across *most* scenarios, and this ability is correlated with model architecture, base dataset performance, size, and training mechanism. We hope this research motivates further work in a) developing a multi-dimensional generalization benchmark for systematic evaluation and b) examining the reasons behind models' generalization abilities. [1]

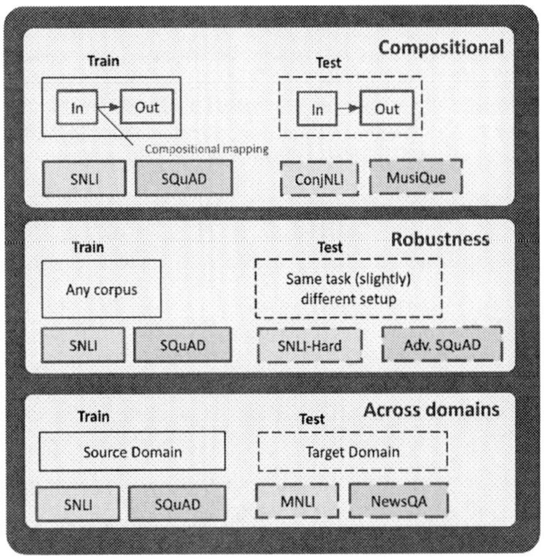

Figure 1: Hupkes et al. (2023) categorizes the generalization scenarios in NLP into *six* types. We chose *three* that cover many important scenarios. We trained models on SNLI and SQuAD, and tested them on various datasets corresponding to these dimensions. The datasets were chosen so as not to confound the dimensions. For example, the compositional test dataset for MRC (MusiQue) is a derivative of the source dataset SQuAD – there is no domain shift, and the dataset does not contain robustness testing perturbations.

1 Introduction

A machine learning model's generalization capability is defined as its capacity to apply encoded knowledge and strategies from previous experience to new situations. This is a key desideratum of all machine learning models, but NLP models are particularly interesting as the generalization scenario in NLP goes beyond the simple train-test split.

We present a comprehensive study of the generalization abilities of common models used in NLP. Following Hupkes et al. (2023), we consider three types of generalization: 1. Domain; 2. Robustness; and 3. Compositional. These three multi-faceted aspects cover many scenarios with practical significance (Figure 1).

The most common type of generalization is **domain** generalization, where the model is trained on one domain and tested on another. Generally, domains in NLP are associated with sources as text from different sources have different linguistic styles (Lee, 2001).

Many standard NLP datasets have data points that can be solved by superficial cues, i.e., reasoning strategies unrelated to the expected causal mechanism of the task at hand. For example, in SNLI, Gururangan et al. (2018) shows that a nega-

*The first two authors contributed equally.
†Work done at the University of Michigan.
[1] code + data for analysis: https://github.com/sagnik/md-gen-nlp, Trained models: https://huggingface.co/varun-v-rao.

Proceedings of the 2nd GenBench Workshop on Generalisation (Benchmarking) in NLP, pages 165–182
November 16, 2024 ©2024 Association for Computational Linguistics

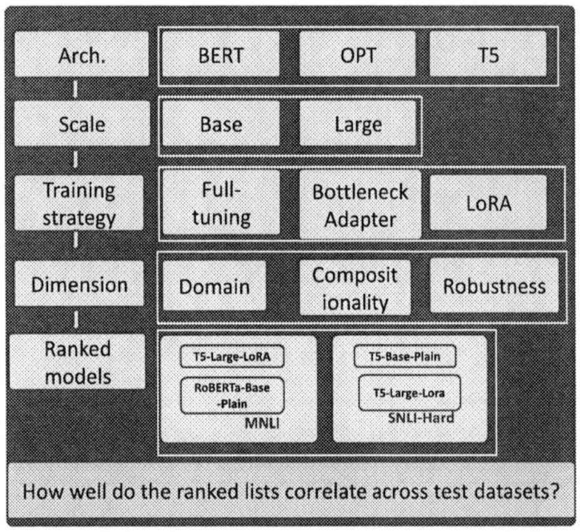

Figure 2: Our framework: we train 72 models on 2 base datasets, test them on 15 datasets corresponding to different dimensions of generalization, and analyze the results.

tion operator in the premise is a strong predictor of the "contradiction" class, or in many cases, the models can use the hypothesis alone to predict the class label. Likewise, Sen and Saffari (2020) observed that the answer phrase could be found in the first sentence of the context for several instances in popular extractive machine reading comprehension (MRC) datasets such as SQuAD (Rajpurkar et al., 2016) or HotpotQA(Yang et al., 2018). Zhang et al. (2020) and Ribeiro et al. (2020) also show that models are sometimes thrown off by semantics preserving perturbations that do not fool humans. Models also need to generalize to these instances – we refer to this as **robustness** generalization.

The final type of generalization we explore is **compositional**. A model demonstrates compositional generalization when it can methodically combine previously learned components to correctly solve new inputs composed of these components. Lake and Baroni (2018) presents a classic example – if a model understands that "doxing" refers to jumping up and "daxing" refers to moving left, would it realize that "dox then dax" refers to jumping up and moving left?

We train 3 instances each of the base and large versions of 4 models from 3 architecture families: encoder-only (EO), decoder-only (DO), and encoder-decoder (ED) on two representative datasets of two NLU tasks: SNLI for natural language inference (NLI) and SQuAD for machine reading comprehension (MRC) using full-training and parameter efficient fine-tuning or PEFT (Ding et al., 2023) in §2. Subsequently, we test them on 15 datasets from these tasks that correspond to different types of generalizations in §3. With this extensive setup, we ask the following questions:

- **RQ1**: Do certain model instances [2] generalize well across all types? Our goal is to see if the generalization ability of a model instance is generalization type-independent, i.e., it generalizes well across all scenarios. This question is asked at the instance level because McCoy et al. (2020a) has shown that model instances with similar test performances show wide differences when tested on different datasets.
- **RQ2**: We answer RQ1 affirmatively (§3.1) and find that the model instances from different seeds do not show large variances. This leads to a follow-up question (§3.2): are certain model configurations (architecture-size-training strategy) better at generalization than others?
- **RQ3**: How does model architecture (EO vs. DO vs. ED), size, or training strategy correlate with generalization? Is it type-dependent? We can expect over-parameterized models to generalize better (Belkin et al., 2019), as well as the PEFT models, as they have lower parameter changes than fully trained models and, consequently, less forgetting. While the first hypothesis holds, the second one does not.
- **RQ4**: Finally, we investigate whether certain generalization types are more challenging than the others. How is the target performance correlated with generalization dimensions (§3.4)?

Previous work has studied generalization in stand-alone cases, e.g., the datasets we have used here. Methods have been proposed to improve the generalization ability of both fully tuned and PEFT models by meta-learning (Lake and Baroni, 2023) or multi-task learning (Pfeiffer et al., 2021). Benchmarks such as Unified QA (Khashabi et al., 2020) have also been developed to test generalization.

Despite this rich history, less effort has been spent on developing a *systematic* categorization of generalization and studying how models generalize across such categories. Models need to generalize across *all* scenarios, and not just be robust against domain shift or compositional variations.

[2]1. **model instance**: a particular instance of a trained model, e.g., a $\texttt{T5}_{\texttt{base}}$ model with LoRA trained on SNLI with a seed of 42. 2. **architecture**: model architecture, e.g., RoBERTa, T5. 3. **model configuration**: a combination of architecture-size-training strategy ($\texttt{T5}_{\texttt{base}}$ fully fine-tuned). 4. **architecture family**: types of architectures – encoder only (BERT, RoBERTa)/decoder-only (OPT).

This work is a step in this direction. Our comprehensive analysis highlights that model instances exhibit consistent generalization prowess across the board and that models from certain architectures or sizes are more generalizable than others. This is certainly not comprehensive, questions remain open about the choice and size of the base dataset, new model architectures, and most importantly, the reason behind a model's generalization ability which we defer for future work.

2 Tasks, Datasets & Models

We consider two representative NLU tasks: NLI and MRC. The NLI task involves determining if the meaning of one text fragment (hypothesis) can be inferred from another (premise). Independent of any specific application, this task is designed to encapsulate the essential inferences about the variability of semantic expression frequently required for various settings (Dagan et al., 2006). MRC is another common task – many NLU tasks have been formulated as MRC (He et al., 2015) or models trained on MRC format data have shown good performance on NLU tasks (McCann et al., 2018). We use the extractive version of MRC, where the input consists of a context (passage) and a question, and the answer has to be extracted from the context.

2.1 NLI Datasets

We consider SNLI (Bowman et al., 2015) as the source dataset, which is annotated with the labels corresponding to whether the hypothesis entails, is neutral, or contradicts the premise.

- **Domain:** We use both the matched and mismatched splits of the Multi-Genre NLI (MNLI) dataset (Williams et al., 2018) to test the generalization of an SNLI-trained model to different domains. We also use the TaxiNLI dataset (Joshi et al., 2020) that provides a hierarchical taxonomy of a subset of the MNLI dataset and categorizes the data points based on whether they require linguistic, logical, or world knowledge.
- **Robustness:** We cover the robustness scenarios by testing the models on four datasets. SNLI-H (Gururangan et al., 2018) is a set of SNLI test instances that common heuristics can not classify. The SNLI-CF dataset (Kaushik et al., 2019) comprises of "counter-factual" perturbations, where the annotators are asked to make minimal changes to an instance such that the label changes – a model can only classify these instances correctly if it understands the reasoning behind the NLI task. SNLI-BT is generated by back-translating the original SNLI test instances from En->Pt->En using a pre-trained multi-lingual BART model – this tests the models' ability to generalize against adversarial perturbations. Finally, HANS (McCoy et al., 2020b) is built from templates constituting different syntactic heuristics in NLI, such as lexical overlap or common subsequences between the premise and hypothesis.
- **Compositionality:** It is non-trivial to meaningfully combine SNLI instances, but in a compositional NLI dataset such as MoNLI (Geiger et al., 2020) all words or phrases of a composed instance come from SNLI. Consider a sentence from SNLI "The children are holding plants". Assume the phrase "flowers", which is a hyponym (per Wordnet) to the phrase "plants", appears in SNLI. Now the pair (premise: "The children are holding flowers", and hypothesis: "The children are holding plants") will have an entailment relation as every flower is a plant. Consequently, the label would change to neutral when the premise and hypothesis are reversed. Since the phrase that determines this relation exists in SNLI, the new dataset is merely a composition of the known constituents.[3] CONJNLI (Saha et al., 2020) focuses on conjunctive sentences – premises and hypotheses vary through the addition, removal, or substitution of conjuncts such as "and," "or", "but", and "nor" alongside elements like quantifiers and negations. This also presents a challenge in compositional generalization.

2.2 MRC Datasets

We train the MRC models on a popular extractive dataset SQuAD (Rajpurkar et al., 2016).

- **Domain:** NewsQA is a crowd-sourced dataset of approximately 100K human-generated QA pairs, where the context comes from 10K news articles from CNN. In SQuAD contexts are paragraphs from Wikipedia articles, therefore NewsQA presents a significant domain shift.
- **Robustness:** Adversarial Squad (Adv-SQuAD) is a robustness challenge set built on SQuAD insofar it adds a sentence that contains a phrase

[3]This is the *PMoNLI* part of the dataset. Negations would change the direction of the monotone operator: *not* holding plants $\Rightarrow$ *not* holding flower, but not the other way around. These instances comprise the *NMoNLI* dataset, which we do not use.

that a shortcut-dependent model (eg., one that chooses a phrase that is proximal to a key phrase from the question) would select (Jia and Liang, 2017). The HotpotQA dataset (Yang et al., 2018) was designed to test the multi-hop reasoning abilities of MRC models, i.e., a model should only be successful if it understands relations between entities that span multiple sentences. Similar to Jia and Liang (2017), Jiang and Bansal (2019) built a challenge set (Adv-HotpotQA) by adding a new passage to the context with a fake answer. The modifications in both Adv-HotpotQA and Adv-SQuAD do not change the original answer. Therefore, a model using the expected reasoning strategies would still be able to answer correctly, but a model dependent on shortcuts would fail.

- **Compositionality:** MusiQue (Trivedi et al., 2022) is designed to test compositionality in reading comprehension. The dataset is built on multiple MRC datasets (SQuAD, HotpotQA and three others) in a "bottom-up" approach. Pairs of *connected* single-hop questions are combined to create 2-hop questions first and are subsequently combined to produce k-hop questions recursively. We only choose the questions that are produced by combining SQuAD questions.

We use the validation or test (when available) split of the generalization datasets. In NLI, most datasets for compositional and robustness generalization are derivatives of the SNLI dataset itself, except for HANS and CONJNLI. They come from non-SNLI sources, but the distribution is not significantly different. *This allows us to not confound different dimensions of generalizability.* This is true for MRC as well, Adv-SQuAD and MusiQue (the portion we use) come from the base dataset SQuAD, and both Adv-HotpotQA and SQuAD come from the same domain. HANS has 2 labels (as opposed to 3 for SNLI), so the predicted labels of neutral and contradiction are merged. For consistency, we only use instances with a max tokenized sequence length of 512 (see the appendix for details).

2.3 Models & Training

We explore three popular families of transformer-based neural architectures, i.e., encoder-only (EO), decoder-only (DO), and encoder-decoder (ED) models. As the most popular/powerful representative for each architecture, we include `RoBERTa` (Liu et al., 2019) and `BERT` (Devlin et al., 2019) for EO, `OPT` (Zhang et al., 2022) for DO, and `T5` (Raffel et al., 2020) for (ED).

NLI is modeled as a sequence classification problem, and a linear layer is used as the classifier over the base encoders. MRC is modeled as a token classification problem with a linear layer, and the models are trained to predict a token's probability for being the start and end of an answer phrase (Devlin et al., 2019). We use the base and large versions for each model, and specifically for `BERT` these are the `cased` ones.

The models are trained by changing the full parameters as well as a fraction of them using two PEFT methods: Bottleneck adapters (Houlsby et al., 2019) and LoRA (Hu et al., 2021). Adapters introduce bottleneck feed-forward layers in each layer of a transformer model as the only trainable parameters. These adapter layers consist of a down-projection matrix $W_{\text{down}} : (d_{\text{hidden}}, d_{\text{bottleneck}})$, a RELU non-linearity (f) and an up-projection matrix $W_{\text{up}} : (d_{\text{bottleneck}}, d_{\text{hidden}})$, with the final equation: $h \leftarrow W_{\text{up}} \cdot f(W_{\text{down}} \cdot h)$. We use a reduction factor $(\frac{d_{\text{hidden}}}{d_{\text{bottleneck}}})$ of 16 for all models. Similar to Bottleneck adapters, LoRA injects trainable low-rank decomposition matrices into the layers of a pre-trained model. Any linear layer of the form $(h = W_0 x)$ is re-parameterized as: $h = W_0 x + \frac{\alpha}{r} BAx$ where $(A \in R^{r \times k})$ and $(B \in R^{d \times r})$ are the trainable decomposition matrices and r is the low-dimensional rank of the decomposition. We set the rank at 16 and α at 32.

Each model is initialized with three seeds, and the training data sequence is shuffled. The models are trained with AdamW (Loshchilov and Hutter, 2019) optimizer, batch sizes varying between 32 and 64, and a learning rate of 2e-5 with a stepwise learning rate decay (Howard and Ruder, 2018) using the HuggingFace Transformers library (Wolf et al., 2019) (see the Appendix for details).

3 Results

3.1 RQ1: Does one model instance generalize well across generalization dimensions?

Our first hypothesis is a model instance generalizes well across different types. We test this by investigating whether the rankings of model instances are consistent, i.e. are well-correlated, across datasets that characterize different types of generalization.

We evaluate 72 model instances on each dataset corresponding to a task. Subsequently, for a given dataset pair in a task, we compute Spearman's

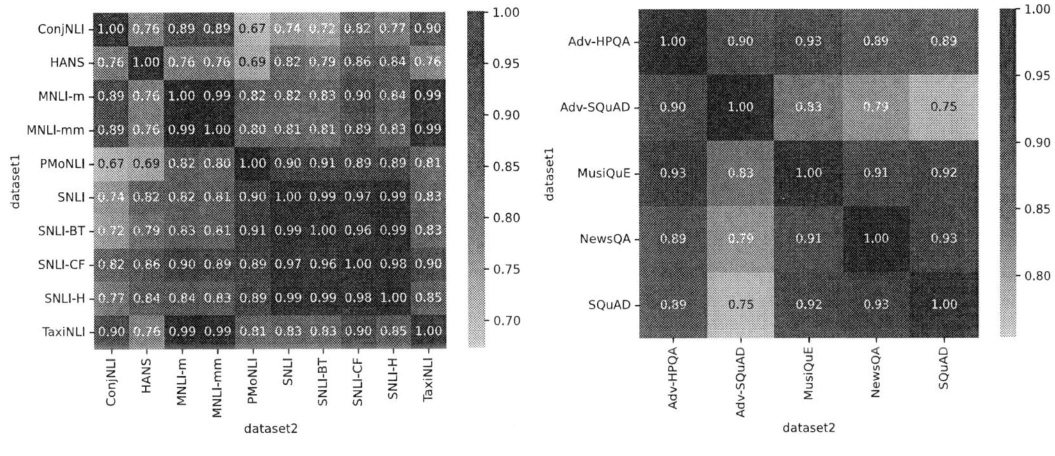

(a) NLI Datasets **(b)** MRC Datasets

Figure 3: Spearmann's Rank Correlation ρ between the source and the target datasets for NLI and MRC on a per-instance basis.

rank correlation coefficient (ρ) of the corresponding model instances' scores (accuracy for NLI and F1-Score for MRC) for the two datasets. We are more interested in the rankings (relative performance) of model instances than the absolute scores since the datasets are not well calibrated amongst themselves. We present a heatmap of the correlation scores between pairs of datasets for NLI and MRC in Figures 3a and 3b, respectively.

We observe a strong to very-strong correlation ($\rho \geq 0.6$) [4] for all dataset pairs for both NLI and MRC tasks. For each of these comparisons, the correlation was statistically significant with a p-value lower than 0.05, **implying that we can reject the null hypothesis that the performances of model instances are not monotonically correlated**.

For NLI, the datasets derived from the same source, e.g., SNLI-CF, SNLI-BT, and PMoNLI from SNLI, or datasets that are created in a similar fashion like matched and mismatched splits of MNLI exhibit very strong correlation ($\rho \geq 0.90$). On the other hand, datasets derived from a different source like Wikipedia for CONJNLI or constructed in a templatized fashion like HANS demonstrate a more uniform correlation. We thus infer that the rankings of model instances depend more on the source than the type of generalization for NLI. For example, although PMoNLI and CONJNLI both test compositionality, the instances have the lowest correlation score ($\rho = 0.67$).

However, this observation is not as pronounced for MRC, where the model rankings correlate more with the generalization type than the dataset source. For example, we observe a higher correlation between Adv-HotpotQA and Adv-SQuAD ($\rho = 0.90$) than between Adv-SQuAD and SQuAD ($\rho = 0.75$). We also note a higher correlation across domains for MRC ($\rho = 0.92$ between SQuAD and NewsQA) than for NLI ($\rho \approx 0.8$ between MNLI and SNLI).

Having ranked the model instances in decreasing order of performance for each of the 10 NLI datasets, we can obtain a global (or unified) ranked list by aggregating these individual rankings. We employ the MC4 algorithm of Dwork et al. (2001) that constructs the ranking preferences based on a simple majority vote across the individual rankings to obtain the aggregated ranked list of instances. We do the same for the 5 datasets to create an aggregate ranked list for MRC. Spearmann's rank correlation coefficient between these two aggregated ranked lists for MRC and NLI is 0.93, which implies that the model instances also exhibit high correlation across tasks.

3.2 RQ2: Do model configurations generalize well across scenarios?

We extend our previous hypothesis to investigate whether certain model configurations (a combination of model architectures, scale, and training strategies) generalize well across different scenarios. We start by averaging the performance of a model configuration (architecture-size-training strategy combination) across three seeds and report the results in Tables 1 and 2 for NLI and MRC, respectively. Interestingly, we do not see a significant variation across instances from different seeds (as evidenced by low standard deviations) – a finding

[4] `https://www.statstutor.ac.uk/resources/uploaded/spearmans.pdf`

Table 1: Performance of NLI models when trained on the SNLI and evaluated on different datasets in terms of accuracy. We report the mean and standard deviation across three seeds. The best model is highlighted in bold, the second-best model is underlined, and the worst model is highlighted in red. `Adap` and `LoRA` refers to the adapter and LoRA training strategies.

	ID	OOD			Robustness				Compositionality	
Model	SNLI	MNLI-m	MNLI-mm	TaxiNLI	SNLI-BT	SNLI-CF	SNLI-H	HANS	ConjNLI	PMoNLI
$\texttt{BERT}_{\texttt{base}}$+ Adap	85.1±0.1	65.1±0.1	68.0±0.1	64.7±0.1	80.0±0.1	68.5±0.1	71.0±0.2	50.0±0.0	52.2±0.7	91.7±1.1
$\texttt{BERT}_{\texttt{base}}$+ LoRA	81.3±0.2	59.2±0.5	61.1±0.1	54.6±0.6	76.6±0.2	64.2±0.3	65.7±0.5	50.0±0.0	49.1±1.4	85.9±0.5
$\texttt{BERT}_{\texttt{base}}$	90.6±0.1	73.5±0.4	73.6±0.2	73.4±0.1	84.3±0.2	76.1±0.2	80.2±0.1	58.1±1.2	58.6±0.6	95.1±0.3
$\texttt{BERT}_{\texttt{large}}$+ Adap	88.8±0.2	72.8±0.8	73.2±0.8	72.8±1.0	83.1±0.2	73.3±0.2	77.3±0.3	50.3±0.4	56.7±1.1	96.1±0.3
$\texttt{BERT}_{\texttt{large}}$+ LoRA	86.2±0.4	68.3±0.5	69.2±0.7	67.7±1.5	80.9±0.1	69.3±0.4	73.1±0.6	50.1±0.2	54.3±1.5	94.7±1.2
$\texttt{BERT}_{\texttt{large}}$	91.1±0.1	76.6±0.1	76.2±0.3	76.5±0.4	84.7±0.1	77.4±0.3	81.7±0.2	58.1±1.2	61.1±0.8	97.6±0.4
$\texttt{RoBERTa}_{\texttt{base}}$+ Adap	88.3±0.1	75.8±0.6	75.9±0.3	74.4±0.2	83.0±0.0	72.9±0.2	76.1±0.2	50.3±0.1	54.8±0.6	95.1±0.1
$\texttt{RoBERTa}_{\texttt{base}}$+ LoRA	87.1±0.0	73.6±0.0	74.9±0.1	72.3±0.3	81.8±0.0	71.8±0.2	75.2±0.1	50.1±0.0	52.2±0.9	94.4±0.2
$\texttt{RoBERTa}_{\texttt{base}}$	91.4±0.0	80.2±0.2	79.9±0.2	80.1±0.2	85.2±0.1	77.9±0.1	82.1±0.1	65.9±2.0	60.8±0.4	96.6±0.2
$\texttt{RoBERTa}_{\texttt{large}}$+ Adap	91.7±0.0	83.8±0.4	83.0±0.4	83.9±0.1	85.4±0.0	79.9±0.5	82.4±0.1	67.8±1.4	61.4±0.2	**98.5±0.1**
$\texttt{RoBERTa}_{\texttt{large}}$+ LoRA	90.8±0.1	81.7±0.4	81.8±0.2	81.1±0.5	84.5±0.1	78.8±0.2	81.0±0.1	65.3±0.8	58.5±0.9	98.0±0.2
$\texttt{RoBERTa}_{\texttt{large}}$	**92.6±0.0**	85.0±0.0	84.3±0.1	85.0±0.1	**85.7±0.0**	**81.3±0.2**	**84.7±0.0**	**73.7±1.0**	65.5±0.3	**98.5±0.1**
$\texttt{OPT}_{\texttt{base}}$+ Adap	82.8±3.0	56.7±1.8	57.5±1.9	55.2±3.7	77.5±2.8	66.7±2.4	68.6±3.1	52.3±3.3	49.2±4.3	88.4±2.3
$\texttt{OPT}_{\texttt{base}}$+ LoRA	78.1±3.7	53.8±1.5	55.7±2.3	52.8±1.1	72.4±4.0	63.2±2.3	65.0±2.9	50.4±0.6	47.4±1.9	86.6±3.1
$\texttt{OPT}_{\texttt{base}}$	89.6±0.1	71.3±0.7	72.9±0.9	71.3±0.9	83.7±0.2	74.5±0.3	78.8±0.1	59.1±4.2	57.5±0.3	95.6±0.8
$\texttt{OPT}_{\texttt{large}}$+ Adap	88.6±0.2	66.6±1.3	69.2±0.8	66.0±2.1	81.9±0.5	73.4±0.3	77.5±0.2	61.7±6.8	55.4±1.0	90.9±1.5
$\texttt{OPT}_{\texttt{large}}$+ LoRA	83.6±2.2	63.5±3.6	65.0±3.4	60.7±4.7	78.0±2.5	69.5±1.2	71.4±2.1	60.1±2.3	56.7±3.1	91.9±3.0
$\texttt{OPT}_{\texttt{large}}$	90.4±0.4	75.5±0.4	77.3±0.3	75.4±0.3	84.1±0.3	76.5±0.8	80.7±0.5	65.8±0.6	60.7±1.3	95.2±2.0
$\texttt{T5}_{\texttt{base}}$+ Adap	88.6±0.0	80.1±0.1	80.3±0.1	80.3±0.3	82.9±0.0	74.8±0.2	77.7±0.1	60.2±0.1	64.0±0.9	94.6±0.4
$\texttt{T5}_{\texttt{base}}$+ LoRA	85.8±0.0	80.6±0.4	80.9±0.3	80.6±0.5	80.7±0.2	72.8±0.2	74.1±0.3	57.2±0.7	65.2±0.7	92.1±0.8
$\texttt{T5}_{\texttt{base}}$	89.7±0.1	81.4±0.1	80.9±0.2	81.2±0.1	83.7±0.1	75.9±0.2	79.5±0.1	63.3±0.3	65.2±0.9	95.3±0.3
$\texttt{T5}_{\texttt{large}}$+ Adap	91.8±0.0	86.2±0.1	85.5±0.3	86.6±0.4	85.4±0.1	80.3±0.3	82.7±0.1	68.2±1.1	66.0±0.1	98.1±0.2
$\texttt{T5}_{\texttt{large}}$+ LoRA	90.5±0.0	**87.5±0.1**	**87.5±0.3**	87.8±0.3	84.2±0.0	79.4±0.1	81.0±0.1	64.7±0.1	66.3±0.5	98.1±0.1
$\texttt{T5}_{\texttt{large}}$	92.1±0.1	87.3±0.1	86.8±0.2	**87.9±0.2**	85.5±0.0	81.0±0.2	83.3±0.1	71.6±0.6	**67.2±0.3**	98.0±0.1

different from prior work of McCoy et al. (2020a).

We also compute the Spearman's rank correlation coefficient between two dataset pairs for NLI and MRC in Figures 13a and 13b (appendix), respectively. The heatmaps indicate a strong positive correlation ($\rho \geq 0.7$) between all dataset pairs and inform us that the relative performance of these model configurations remains consistent across the target datasets and domains.

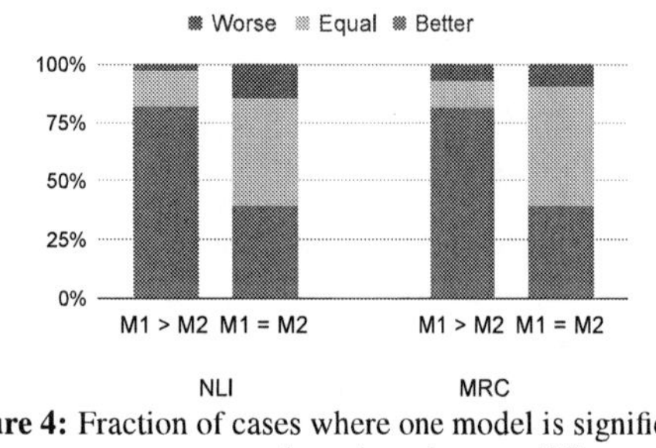

Figure 4: Fraction of cases where one model is significantly better, worse, or as good as the other on different target datasets. We consider two scenarios, (i) where one of the models was already significantly better on the source dataset ($M_1 > M_2$) and (ii) where the models had similar source performance ($M_1 = M_2$).

We further carry out a pair-wise comparison of model configurations to investigate whether the relative performance of a model pair on the source dataset (SNLI and SQuAD for NLI and MRC, respectively) persists across different target datasets. Simply put, if the performance of a model M_1 is significantly better than M_2 on the source dataset, does the situation remain the same across other targets? We adopt the non-parametric paired bootstrap test of Berg-Kirkpatrick et al. (2012) to check for statistical significance (p-value ≤ 0.05) in line with prior work (Dror et al., 2018). We note that M_1 has a similar performance with M_2 if we cannot reject the null hypothesis that one has a significantly higher performance than the other.

Figure 4 illustrates the fraction of cases where the relative performance of a model architecture pair is better, worse, or the same on the target datasets compared to the original source conditions. We observe that the models retain their relative performance for a majority of cases for both NLI and MRC, i.e. if M_1 is significantly better than M_2 on the base dataset, it will follow a similar trend across targets and vice versa. The notable exceptions are the PEFT-tuned versions of `T5` model which exhibit significantly higher performance than other models (such as `BERT` or `OPT` variants) on the tar-

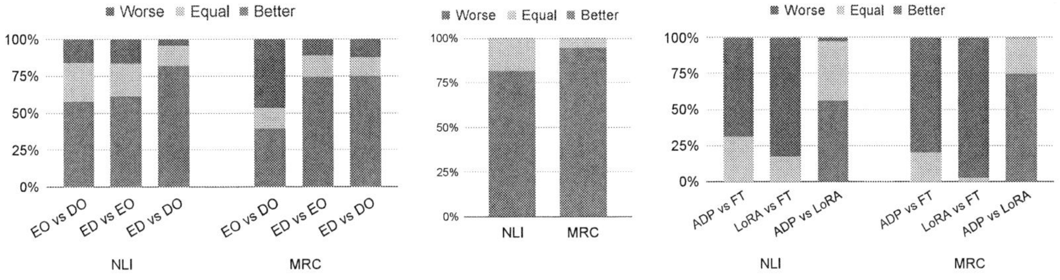

(a) Architecture Types (b) Model Scale (c) PEFT

Figure 5: Fraction of times the given architecture configuration or training strategy is statistically better, equal, or worse for the two tasks of NLI and MRC.

get datasets for NLI despite a significantly worse performance on the SNLI source dataset. A similar finding holds for the fully-tuned `OPT` models that significantly outperform others (such as `BERT` and `T5`-PEFT variants) on MRC datasets.

3.3 RQ3: Architecture, Scale, and PEFT

Model Architecture: From Tables 1 and 2, we see that when controlled for the model size (base v large) and training strategy (full vs PEFT), certain models almost always perform better than the others, e.g., in NLI, the base versions of `T5` models (ED) are better than `RoBERTa` (EO) models in 7 out of 9 datasets, and `RoBERTa` is better than `OPT` (DO) in 8 out of 9. To formalize this, we compare the performance of a pair of models from different architectures (e.g., $\texttt{T5}_{\texttt{base}}$ vs. $\texttt{OPT}_{\texttt{large}}$) for a given dataset. Each architecture has instances from all sizes and training strategies, so we do not have to control for them explicitly.

We adopt the paired bootstrap test to compute the fraction of datasets where models corresponding to one family (say EO) are significantly better, worse, or equal compared to models of another family (say ED). Overall, we observe (Figure 5a) that ED models outperform both the EO and DO significantly on both tasks. On the other hand, models corresponding to the EO fare better for NLI as opposed to DO and vice-versa for MRC.

Scale: We compute the fraction of cases where the large variant of a model architecture is significantly better, worse, or equal to the corresponding base variant for a given dataset and task while controlling for the training strategy. Figure 5b shows that for both tasks, the large variants of models are significantly better than their corresponding base variants in a huge majority of cases. In fact, the base variant is never significantly better, although there are a few ties. This performance gain is also significantly higher in the generalization datasets compared to the base ones.

Parameter efficient fine-tuning (PEFT): We also explore whether PEFT models (i.e., Adapters and LoRA) are more adept at generalization than the corresponding fully fine-tuned (FT) variants. For each model pair, we compute the fraction of cases where the PEFT variant, i.e., Adapter vs. FT or LoRA vs. FT, was significantly better, equal, or worse than the corresponding fine-tuned variant. Figure 5c shows that PEFT models are indeed significantly worse. Moreover, this poorer performance is more pronounced for the LoRA models than for Adapters, such that adapter models are significantly better than LoRA models for both tasks.

3.4 RQ4: Difficult types of generalization

We inspect the absolute generalization performance of models on different datasets to investigate whether certain generalization categories or dimensions are more challenging than others. We characterize a dataset to be challenging for a given model based on the relative drop in performance of the model on the dataset compared to its' source performance (e.g., the performance of a model on SNLI and SQuAD respectively). We coin this performance difference as normalized source drop or NSD (Calderon et al., 2023) defined below, where M_s and M_t correspond to the performance of the model on the source and the target, respectively.

$$NSD = \frac{M_t - M_s}{M_s}$$

We carry out a two-way ANOVA analysis with NSD as the dependent variable with the generalization category (OOD, robustness, compositionality, or in-domain), architecture type (EO, ED, or DO), scale (large or base), and training strategy (FT, LoRA, or Adapter) as the independent covari-

Table 2: Performance of MRC models when trained on the SQuAD (ID) and evaluated on different datasets. We report the mean F1 score across three seeds (the stds vary between 0.0 and 3.2). The best model is highlighted in bold, the second-best is underlined, and the worst is highlighted in red. OOD, Rob, and Comp imply generalization across domains, robustness, and compositionality, respectively. Adap and LoRA refers to the adapter and LoRA training strategies.

Model	OOD NQA	Rob AHQ	Rob ASQ	Comp MsQ	ID SQ
$BERT_{base}$+ Adap	52.7	22.9	45.5	41.1	77.8
$BERT_{base}$+ LoRA	12.8	9.7	17.9	12.8	24.7
$BERT_{base}$	62.2	34.7	61.8	50.2	87.6
$BERT_{large}$+ Adap	60.1	25.0	64.3	50.2	85.6
$BERT_{large}$+ LoRA	42.2	17.0	46.3	37.0	67.1
$BERT_{large}$	65.2	39.4	72.5	62.2	90.7
$RoBERTa_{base}$+ Adap	55.0	26.3	63.5	51.5	85.8
$RoBERTa_{base}$+ LoRA	43.6	22.2	50.2	47.3	78.7
$RoBERTa_{base}$	63.3	39.0	73.0	61.4	92.0
$RoBERTa_{large}$+ Adap	66.8	46.6	<u>82.5</u>	65.5	93.4
$RoBERTa_{large}$+ LoRA	54.3	34.8	70.7	57.8	88.7
$RoBERTa_{large}$	**70.0**	**51.4**	**84.1**	**74.6**	**94.6**
OPT_{base}+ Adap	48.4	31.0	64.5	40.9	75.2
OPT_{base}+ LoRA	47.5	25.9	61.8	41.0	71.9
OPT_{base}	58.9	37.7	78.6	59.0	83.6
OPT_{large}+ Adap	55.1	34.7	79.0	47.0	83.5
OPT_{large}+ LoRA	57.9	33.5	79.0	45.6	83.3
OPT_{large}	62.4	42.0	81.6	68.7	85.9
$T5_{base}$+ Adap	67.2	37.8	74.2	61.1	90.3
$T5_{base}$+ LoRA	64.8	33.6	69.8	57.8	87.5
$T5_{base}$	67.5	38.6	74.8	64.0	90.9
$T5_{large}$+ Adap	69.7	46.5	82.3	69.9	93.7
$T5_{large}$+ LoRA	69.5	42.8	79.6	68.4	92.8
$T5_{large}$	<u>69.9</u>	<u>47.9</u>	**84.1**	<u>73.6</u>	<u>93.9</u>

ates. We observe a significant association for all the covariates (p-value ≤ 0.05), with the generalization category exhibiting the greatest significance, followed by the architecture type, training strategy, and scale for MRC. NLI exhibits a similar trend, with the only difference being that the scale is more significant than the training strategy.

Considering the in-domain category (i.e., performance on the base dataset) as the baseline, we observe a negative correlation for all the other generalization categories. The robustness category is the most challenging (with a larger negative coefficient), followed by compositionality and OOD for MRC. For NLI, the robustness category again incurs the highest negative correlation, followed by OOD and compositionality. We hypothesize that the general prowess of models on the PMoNLI dataset, surpassing even the ID performance, is responsible for the skewed trend. We also observe positive coefficients for the larger model variant, the ED model family, and the fully fine-tuned (FT) training strategy which is consistent from our past observations. We present the intercept values of our analysis in Table 3.

Category	NLI	MRC
Intercept	-0.052	-0.015
Gen-type: Comp	-0.132	-0.354
Gen-type: ROB	-0.170	-0.388
Gen-type: OOD	-0.158	-0.313
Arch-family: ED	0.073	0.023
Arch-family: EO	0.024	-0.047
Fine-tuning: FT	0.023	0.047
Fine-tuning: LoRA	-0.00	-0.020
Scale: Large	0.028	0.047

Table 3: Coefficients for the ANOVA analysis for NLI and MRC.

4 Related Work

Previous work has examined the generalization ability of NLP models in different scenarios, and developed strategies for improving their capabilities. Hupkes et al. (2023) provides a categorization of generalization types, of which we have discussed three that cover most datasets, but other types exist. *Cross-task (CT) generalization* measures a model's ability to generalize to new tasks. Instruction-tuned LLMs trained on massive crowd-sourced instruction datasets that contain task descriptions have shown strong CT generalization (Zhang et al., 2023). Recent LLMs such as GPT-3 (Brown et al., 2020) or LLama2 (Touvron et al., 2023) are zero-shot cross-task models, but possible data contamination raises concerns about their true generalization abilities (Li and Flanigan, 2024). *Syntactic generalization* involves generalization to new syntactic structures or unknown elements in known syntactic structures (Jumelet et al., 2021).

Among the categories of generalization we have considered, Ramponi and Plank (2020); Naik et al. (2022) presents a survey of neural models for *domain generalization*. For *robustness generalization*, many papers have proposed adversarial attacks to perturb the input to fool the model. These attacks can be white-box (Ebrahimi et al., 2018), i.e., the attacker has access to the model parameters or not (black-box (Jin et al., 2020), see Goyal et al. (2023) for a survey). However, not all of these attacks produce meaningful sentences, and more importantly, they do not test for a model's propensity toward shortcut learning (Geirhos et al., 2020), which our datasets do. Compositional generalization has been studied in machine translation (Dankers et al., 2022), semantic parsing (Kim and Linzen, 2020), and question answering over databases (Keysers et al., 2020). However, there hasn't been a systematic attempt to create new datasets by composing existing datasets with exceptions such as MusiQue (MRC) and SETI (Fu and Frank, 2023) (NLI).

Common strategies for improving a model's domain adaptation ability include: a) gradual fine-tuning with a mixture of data from different domains (Xu et al., 2021) – an approach motivated by curriculum learning, and b) domain adversarial training (Wright and Augenstein, 2020). To improve robustness generalization, researchers have trained on augmented data (Li et al., 2019), added a regularizer in the loss function (Goodfellow et al., 2015), and used a generator-discriminator setup (Kang et al., 2018). Neuro-symbolic methods (Gupta et al., 2020) and meta-learning (Lake, 2019) have been traditionally used to improve compositional generalization, and newer methods include better prompting strategies for in-context learning (Press et al., 2023). In contrast to previous work, our goal is not to provide a better algorithm/model for generalization but to examine existing models across different axes.

5 Conclusion & Future Work

We present a systematic study on the multi-dimensional (domain, robustness, and compositional) generalization abilities of common models used in NLP. Our main conclusions are: 1. Generalizability is a model instance characteristic and not generalization type-dependent – an instance typically does not generalize well in one dimension and poorly in others. 2. It is well correlated with model size, and certain architectures and training strategies generalize better than others. 3. Certain dimensions of generalization is harder to achieve compared to the others. We hope to inspire future work that looks further into the multi-dimensional aspect of generalizability and tries to understand why certain models generalize better than others.

Limitations

The conclusions of this study are dependent on the base datasets, models, and training methods used. There are many potential choices for these aspects, and while both the appropriateness and popularity inform our selections of the datasets or algorithms, we admit the conclusions might differ if we use alternatives. More base datasets and/or models would certainly improve the robustness of the conclusions, but these would exponentially increase the scale of the study. Other potential directions include investigating the amount of data needed for generalization, i.e., few-shot models, and cross-lingual generalization, but both are beyond the scope of the study. We have made empirical observations about generalization but have not investigated the theoretical reasons behind it. While that is beyond the scope of the study, we recognize this limitation.

Ethical Concerns

In this work, we train 72 models on the two datasets and further evaluate them on 15 datasets, which suffer from a combinatorial problem in terms of the necessary computing infrastructure. Our work consumed roughly two-thirds a month of GPU time ($\approx$ 500 hours). Combined with the size of the models, this limits the accessibility of this vein of research, especially if we were to expand to other datasets, model architectures, and few-shot training scenarios. More effort in understanding how to narrow down the choice of datasets before studying transfer would go a long way towards alleviating this issue. While we find that models generalize well across different scenarios, this should not be taken as an indication of their deployment eligibility in real-life scenarios. These models have not been tested for their propensity to generate toxic, biased, and offensive content.

Acknowledgements

We thank the anonymous reviewers for their helpful suggestions.

References

Mikhail Belkin, Daniel Hsu, Siyuan Ma, and Soumik Mandal. 2019. Reconciling modern machine-learning practice and the classical bias–variance trade-off. *Proceedings of the National Academy of Sciences*, 116(32):15849–15854.

Taylor Berg-Kirkpatrick, David Burkett, and Dan Klein. 2012. An empirical investigation of statistical significance in NLP. In *Proceedings of the 2012 Joint Conference on Empirical Methods in Natural Language Processing and Computational Natural Language Learning*, pages 995–1005, Jeju Island, Korea. Association for Computational Linguistics.

Samuel R. Bowman, Gabor Angeli, Christopher Potts, and Christopher D. Manning. 2015. A large annotated corpus for learning natural language inference. In *Proceedings of the 2015 Conference on Empirical Methods in Natural Language Processing*, pages

632–642, Lisbon, Portugal. Association for Computational Linguistics.

Tom B. Brown, Benjamin Mann, Nick Ryder, Melanie Subbiah, Jared Kaplan, Prafulla Dhariwal, Arvind Neelakantan, Pranav Shyam, Girish Sastry, Amanda Askell, Sandhini Agarwal, Ariel Herbert-Voss, Gretchen Krueger, Tom Henighan, Rewon Child, Aditya Ramesh, Daniel M. Ziegler, Jeffrey Wu, Clemens Winter, Christopher Hesse, Mark Chen, Eric Sigler, Mateusz Litwin, Scott Gray, Benjamin Chess, Jack Clark, Christopher Berner, Sam McCandlish, Alec Radford, Ilya Sutskever, and Dario Amodei. 2020. Language models are few-shot learners. In *Advances in Neural Information Processing Systems 33: Annual Conference on Neural Information Processing Systems 2020, NeurIPS 2020, December 6-12, 2020, virtual*.

Nitay Calderon, Naveh Porat, Eyal Ben-David, Zorik Gekhman, Nadav Oved, and Roi Reichart. 2023. Measuring the robustness of natural language processing models to domain shifts. *arXiv preprint arXiv:2306.00168*.

Ido Dagan, Oren Glickman, and Bernardo Magnini. 2006. The pascal recognising textual entailment challenge. In *Machine Learning Challenges. Evaluating Predictive Uncertainty, Visual Object Classification, and Recognising Tectual Entailment*, pages 177–190, Berlin, Heidelberg. Springer Berlin Heidelberg.

Verna Dankers, Elia Bruni, and Dieuwke Hupkes. 2022. The paradox of the compositionality of natural language: A neural machine translation case study. In *Proceedings of the 60th Annual Meeting of the Association for Computational Linguistics (Volume 1: Long Papers), ACL 2022, Dublin, Ireland, May 22-27, 2022*, pages 4154–4175. Association for Computational Linguistics.

Jacob Devlin, Ming-Wei Chang, Kenton Lee, and Kristina Toutanova. 2019. BERT: Pre-training of deep bidirectional transformers for language understanding. In *Proceedings of the 2019 Conference of the North American Chapter of the Association for Computational Linguistics: Human Language Technologies, Volume 1 (Long and Short Papers)*, pages 4171–4186, Minneapolis, Minnesota. Association for Computational Linguistics.

Ning Ding, Yujia Qin, Guang Yang, Fuchao Wei, Zonghan Yang, Yusheng Su, Shengding Hu, Yulin Chen, Chi-Min Chan, Weize Chen, et al. 2023. Parameter-efficient fine-tuning of large-scale pretrained language models. *Nature Machine Intelligence*, 5(3):220–235.

Rotem Dror, Gili Baumer, Segev Shlomov, and Roi Reichart. 2018. The hitchhiker's guide to testing statistical significance in natural language processing. In *Proceedings of the 56th Annual Meeting of the Association for Computational Linguistics (Volume 1: Long Papers)*, pages 1383–1392, Melbourne, Australia. Association for Computational Linguistics.

Cynthia Dwork, Ravi Kumar, Moni Naor, and Dandapani Sivakumar. 2001. Rank aggregation methods for the web. In *Proceedings of the 10th international conference on World Wide Web*, pages 613–622.

Javid Ebrahimi, Anyi Rao, Daniel Lowd, and Dejing Dou. 2018. HotFlip: White-box adversarial examples for text classification. In *Proceedings of the 56th Annual Meeting of the Association for Computational Linguistics (Volume 2: Short Papers)*, pages 31–36, Melbourne, Australia. Association for Computational Linguistics.

Xiyan Fu and Anette Frank. 2023. SETI: Systematicity evaluation of textual inference. In *Findings of the Association for Computational Linguistics: ACL 2023*, pages 4101–4114, Toronto, Canada. Association for Computational Linguistics.

Atticus Geiger, Kyle Richardson, and Christopher Potts. 2020. Neural natural language inference models partially embed theories of lexical entailment and negation. In *Proceedings of the Third BlackboxNLP Workshop on Analyzing and Interpreting Neural Networks for NLP*, pages 163–173, Online. Association for Computational Linguistics.

Robert Geirhos, Jörn-Henrik Jacobsen, Claudio Michaelis, Richard S. Zemel, Wieland Brendel, Matthias Bethge, and Felix A. Wichmann. 2020. Shortcut learning in deep neural networks. *CoRR*, abs/2004.07780.

Ian J. Goodfellow, Jonathon Shlens, and Christian Szegedy. 2015. Explaining and harnessing adversarial examples. In *3rd International Conference on Learning Representations, ICLR 2015, San Diego, CA, USA, May 7-9, 2015, Conference Track Proceedings*.

Shreya Goyal, Sumanth Doddapaneni, Mitesh M. Khapra, and Balaraman Ravindran. 2023. A survey of adversarial defenses and robustness in nlp. *ACM Comput. Surv.*, 55(14s).

Nitish Gupta, Kevin Lin, Dan Roth, Sameer Singh, and Matt Gardner. 2020. Neural module networks for reasoning over text. In *8th International Conference on Learning Representations, ICLR 2020, Addis Ababa, Ethiopia, April 26-30, 2020*. OpenReview.net.

Suchin Gururangan, Swabha Swayamdipta, Omer Levy, Roy Schwartz, Samuel Bowman, and Noah A Smith. 2018. Annotation artifacts in natural language inference data. In *Proceedings of the 2018 Conference of the North American Chapter of the Association for Computational Linguistics: Human Language Technologies, Volume 2 (Short Papers)*, pages 107–112.

Luheng He, Mike Lewis, and Luke Zettlemoyer. 2015. Question-answer driven semantic role labeling: Using natural language to annotate natural language. In *Proceedings of the 2015 Conference on Empirical Methods in Natural Language Processing*, pages 643–653, Lisbon, Portugal. Association for Computational Linguistics.

Neil Houlsby, Andrei Giurgiu, Stanislaw Jastrzebski, Bruna Morrone, Quentin De Laroussilhe, Andrea Gesmundo, Mona Attariyan, and Sylvain Gelly. 2019. Parameter-efficient transfer learning for nlp. In *International conference on machine learning*, pages 2790–2799. PMLR.

Jeremy Howard and Sebastian Ruder. 2018. Universal language model fine-tuning for text classification. In *Proceedings of the 56th Annual Meeting of the Association for Computational Linguistics (Volume 1: Long Papers)*, pages 328–339, Melbourne, Australia. Association for Computational Linguistics.

Edward J Hu, Phillip Wallis, Zeyuan Allen-Zhu, Yuanzhi Li, Shean Wang, Lu Wang, Weizhu Chen, et al. 2021. Lora: Low-rank adaptation of large language models. In *International Conference on Learning Representations*.

Zhiqiang Hu, Lei Wang, Yihuai Lan, Wanyu Xu, Ee-Peng Lim, Lidong Bing, Xing Xu, Soujanya Poria, and Roy Lee. 2023. LLM-adapters: An adapter family for parameter-efficient fine-tuning of large language models. In *Proceedings of the 2023 Conference on Empirical Methods in Natural Language Processing*, pages 5254–5276, Singapore. Association for Computational Linguistics.

Dieuwke Hupkes, Mario Giulianelli, Verna Dankers, Mikel Artetxe, Yanai Elazar, Tiago Pimentel, Christos Christodoulopoulos, Karim Lasri, Naomi Saphra, Arabella Sinclair, et al. 2023. A taxonomy and review of generalization research in nlp. *Nature Machine Intelligence*, 5(10):1161–1174.

Robin Jia and Percy Liang. 2017. Adversarial examples for evaluating reading comprehension systems. In *Proceedings of the 2017 Conference on Empirical Methods in Natural Language Processing*, pages 2021–2031, Copenhagen, Denmark. Association for Computational Linguistics.

Yichen Jiang and Mohit Bansal. 2019. Avoiding reasoning shortcuts: Adversarial evaluation, training, and model development for multi-hop QA. In *Proceedings of the 57th Annual Meeting of the Association for Computational Linguistics*, pages 2726–2736, Florence, Italy. Association for Computational Linguistics.

Di Jin, Zhijing Jin, Joey Tianyi Zhou, and Peter Szolovits. 2020. Is BERT really robust? A strong baseline for natural language attack on text classification and entailment. In *The Thirty-Fourth AAAI Conference on Artificial Intelligence, AAAI 2020, The Thirty-Second Innovative Applications of Artificial Intelligence Conference, IAAI 2020, The Tenth AAAI Symposium on Educational Advances in Artificial Intelligence, EAAI 2020, New York, NY, USA, February 7-12, 2020*, pages 8018–8025. AAAI Press.

Pratik Joshi, Somak Aditya, Aalok Sathe, and Monojit Choudhury. 2020. TaxiNLI: Taking a ride up the NLU hill. In *Proceedings of the 24th Conference on Computational Natural Language Learning*, pages 41–55, Online. Association for Computational Linguistics.

Jaap Jumelet, Milica Denic, Jakub Szymanik, Dieuwke Hupkes, and Shane Steinert-Threlkeld. 2021. Language models use monotonicity to assess NPI licensing. In *Findings of the Association for Computational Linguistics: ACL/IJCNLP 2021, Online Event, August 1-6, 2021*, volume ACL/IJCNLP 2021 of *Findings of ACL*, pages 4958–4969. Association for Computational Linguistics.

Dongyeop Kang, Tushar Khot, Ashish Sabharwal, and Eduard H. Hovy. 2018. Adventure: Adversarial training for textual entailment with knowledge-guided examples. In *Proceedings of the 56th Annual Meeting of the Association for Computational Linguistics, ACL 2018, Melbourne, Australia, July 15-20, 2018, Volume 1: Long Papers*, pages 2418–2428. Association for Computational Linguistics.

Divyansh Kaushik, Eduard Hovy, and Zachary Lipton. 2019. Learning the difference that makes a difference with counterfactually-augmented data. In *International Conference on Learning Representations*.

Daniel Keysers, Nathanael Schärli, Nathan Scales, Hylke Buisman, Daniel Furrer, Sergii Kashubin, Nikola Momchev, Danila Sinopalnikov, Lukasz Stafiniak, Tibor Tihon, Dmitry Tsarkov, Xiao Wang, Marc van Zee, and Olivier Bousquet. 2020. Measuring compositional generalization: A comprehensive method on realistic data. In *8th International Conference on Learning Representations, ICLR 2020, Addis Ababa, Ethiopia, April 26-30, 2020*. OpenReview.net.

Daniel Khashabi, Sewon Min, Tushar Khot, Ashish Sabharwal, Oyvind Tafjord, Peter Clark, and Hannaneh Hajishirzi. 2020. UNIFIEDQA: Crossing format boundaries with a single QA system. In *Findings of the Association for Computational Linguistics: EMNLP 2020*, pages 1896–1907, Online. Association for Computational Linguistics.

Najoung Kim and Tal Linzen. 2020. COGS: A compositional generalization challenge based on semantic interpretation. In *Proceedings of the 2020 Conference on Empirical Methods in Natural Language Processing (EMNLP)*, pages 9087–9105, Online. Association for Computational Linguistics.

Brenden M. Lake. 2019. Compositional generalization through meta sequence-to-sequence learning. In *Advances in Neural Information Processing Systems 32: Annual Conference on Neural Information Processing Systems 2019, NeurIPS 2019, December 8-14, 2019, Vancouver, BC, Canada*, pages 9788–9798.

Brenden M. Lake and Marco Baroni. 2018. Generalization without systematicity: On the compositional skills of sequence-to-sequence recurrent networks. In *Proceedings of the 35th International Conference on Machine Learning, ICML 2018, Stockholmsmässan, Stockholm, Sweden, July 10-15, 2018*, volume 80 of

Proceedings of Machine Learning Research, pages 2879–2888. PMLR.

Brenden M Lake and Marco Baroni. 2023. Human-like systematic generalization through a meta-learning neural network. *Nature*, 623(7985):115–121.

David Yong Wey Lee. 2001. Genres, registers, text types, domains and styles: Clarifying the concepts and navigating a path through the bnc jungle. *Language Learning & Technology*, 5:37–72.

Changmao Li and Jeffrey Flanigan. 2024. Task contamination: Language models may not be few-shot anymore. *Proceedings of the AAAI Conference on Artificial Intelligence*, 38(16):18471–18480.

Jinfeng Li, Shouling Ji, Tianyu Du, Bo Li, and Ting Wang. 2019. Textbugger: Generating adversarial text against real-world applications. In *26th Annual Network and Distributed System Security Symposium, NDSS 2019, San Diego, California, USA, February 24-27, 2019*. The Internet Society.

Yinhan Liu, Myle Ott, Naman Goyal, Jingfei Du, Mandar Joshi, Danqi Chen, Omer Levy, Mike Lewis, Luke Zettlemoyer, and Veselin Stoyanov. 2019. Roberta: A robustly optimized bert pretraining approach. *arXiv preprint arXiv:1907.11692*.

Ilya Loshchilov and Frank Hutter. 2019. Decoupled weight decay regularization. In *7th International Conference on Learning Representations, ICLR 2019, New Orleans, LA, USA, May 6-9, 2019*. OpenReview.net.

Bryan McCann, Nitish Shirish Keskar, Caiming Xiong, and Richard Socher. 2018. The natural language decathlon: Multitask learning as question answering. *CoRR*, abs/1806.08730.

R. Thomas McCoy, Junghyun Min, and Tal Linzen. 2020a. BERTs of a feather do not generalize together: Large variability in generalization across models with similar test set performance. In *Proceedings of the Third BlackboxNLP Workshop on Analyzing and Interpreting Neural Networks for NLP*, pages 217–227, Online. Association for Computational Linguistics.

R Thomas McCoy, Ellie Pavlick, and Tal Linzen. 2020b. Right for the wrong reasons: Diagnosing syntactic heuristics in natural language inference. In *57th Annual Meeting of the Association for Computational Linguistics, ACL 2019*, pages 3428–3448. Association for Computational Linguistics (ACL).

Aakanksha Naik, Jill Lehman, and Carolyn Rosé. 2022. Adapting to the long tail: A meta-analysis of transfer learning research for language understanding tasks. *Transactions of the Association for Computational Linguistics*, 10:956–980.

Jonas Pfeiffer, Aishwarya Kamath, Andreas Rücklé, Kyunghyun Cho, and Iryna Gurevych. 2021. AdapterFusion: Non-destructive task composition for transfer learning. In *Proceedings of the 16th Conference of the European Chapter of the Association for Computational Linguistics: Main Volume*, pages 487–503, Online. Association for Computational Linguistics.

Ofir Press, Muru Zhang, Sewon Min, Ludwig Schmidt, Noah Smith, and Mike Lewis. 2023. Measuring and narrowing the compositionality gap in language models. In *Findings of the Association for Computational Linguistics: EMNLP 2023*, pages 5687–5711, Singapore. Association for Computational Linguistics.

Colin Raffel, Noam Shazeer, Adam Roberts, Katherine Lee, Sharan Narang, Michael Matena, Yanqi Zhou, Wei Li, and Peter J Liu. 2020. Exploring the limits of transfer learning with a unified text-to-text transformer. *The Journal of Machine Learning Research*, 21(1):5485–5551.

Pranav Rajpurkar, Jian Zhang, Konstantin Lopyrev, and Percy Liang. 2016. Squad: 100,000+ questions for machine comprehension of text. In *Proceedings of the 2016 Conference on Empirical Methods in Natural Language Processing*, pages 2383–2392.

Alan Ramponi and Barbara Plank. 2020. Neural unsupervised domain adaptation in NLP—A survey. In *Proceedings of the 28th International Conference on Computational Linguistics*, pages 6838–6855, Barcelona, Spain (Online). International Committee on Computational Linguistics.

Marco Tulio Ribeiro, Tongshuang Wu, Carlos Guestrin, and Sameer Singh. 2020. Beyond accuracy: Behavioral testing of NLP models with CheckList. In *Proceedings of the 58th Annual Meeting of the Association for Computational Linguistics*, pages 4902–4912, Online. Association for Computational Linguistics.

Swarnadeep Saha, Yixin Nie, and Mohit Bansal. 2020. ConjNLI: Natural language inference over conjunctive sentences. In *Proceedings of the 2020 Conference on Empirical Methods in Natural Language Processing (EMNLP)*, pages 8240–8252, Online. Association for Computational Linguistics.

Priyanka Sen and Amir Saffari. 2020. What do models learn from question answering datasets? In *Proceedings of the 2020 Conference on Empirical Methods in Natural Language Processing, EMNLP 2020, Online, November 16-20, 2020*, pages 2429–2438. Association for Computational Linguistics.

Hugo Touvron, Louis Martin, Kevin Stone, Peter Albert, Amjad Almahairi, Yasmine Babaei, Nikolay Bashlykov, Soumya Batra, Prajjwal Bhargava, Shruti Bhosale, Dan Bikel, Lukas Blecher, Cristian Canton-Ferrer, Moya Chen, Guillem Cucurull, David Esiobu, Jude Fernandes, Jeremy Fu, Wenyin Fu, Brian Fuller, Cynthia Gao, Vedanuj Goswami, Naman Goyal, Anthony Hartshorn, Saghar Hosseini, Rui Hou, Hakan Inan, Marcin Kardas, Viktor Kerkez, Madian Khabsa, Isabel Kloumann, Artem Korenev, Punit Singh Koura,

Marie-Anne Lachaux, Thibaut Lavril, Jenya Lee, Diana Liskovich, Yinghai Lu, Yuning Mao, Xavier Martinet, Todor Mihaylov, Pushkar Mishra, Igor Molybog, Yixin Nie, Andrew Poulton, Jeremy Reizenstein, Rashi Rungta, Kalyan Saladi, Alan Schelten, Ruan Silva, Eric Michael Smith, Ranjan Subramanian, Xiaoqing Ellen Tan, Binh Tang, Ross Taylor, Adina Williams, Jian Xiang Kuan, Puxin Xu, Zheng Yan, Iliyan Zarov, Yuchen Zhang, Angela Fan, Melanie Kambadur, Sharan Narang, Aurélien Rodriguez, Robert Stojnic, Sergey Edunov, and Thomas Scialom. 2023. Llama 2: Open foundation and fine-tuned chat models. *CoRR*, abs/2307.09288.

Harsh Trivedi, Niranjan Balasubramanian, Tushar Khot, and Ashish Sabharwal. 2022. MuSiQue: Multi-hop questions via single-hop question composition. *Transactions of the Association for Computational Linguistics*, 10:539–554.

Adina Williams, Nikita Nangia, and Samuel Bowman. 2018. A broad-coverage challenge corpus for sentence understanding through inference. In *Proceedings of the 2018 Conference of the North American Chapter of the Association for Computational Linguistics: Human Language Technologies, Volume 1 (Long Papers)*, pages 1112–1122, New Orleans, Louisiana. Association for Computational Linguistics.

Thomas Wolf, Lysandre Debut, Victor Sanh, Julien Chaumond, Clement Delangue, Anthony Moi, Pierric Cistac, Tim Rault, Rémi Louf, Morgan Funtowicz, et al. 2019. Huggingface's transformers: State-of-the-art natural language processing. *arXiv preprint arXiv:1910.03771*.

Dustin Wright and Isabelle Augenstein. 2020. Transformer based multi-source domain adaptation. In *Proceedings of the 2020 Conference on Empirical Methods in Natural Language Processing (EMNLP)*, pages 7963–7974, Online. Association for Computational Linguistics.

Haoran Xu, Seth Ebner, Mahsa Yarmohammadi, Aaron Steven White, Benjamin Van Durme, and Kenton Murray. 2021. Gradual fine-tuning for low-resource domain adaptation. In *Proceedings of the Second Workshop on Domain Adaptation for NLP*, pages 214–221, Kyiv, Ukraine. Association for Computational Linguistics.

Zhilin Yang, Peng Qi, Saizheng Zhang, Yoshua Bengio, William W. Cohen, Ruslan Salakhutdinov, and Christopher D. Manning. 2018. Hotpotqa: A dataset for diverse, explainable multi-hop question answering. In *EMNLP*, pages 2369–2380. Association for Computational Linguistics.

Shengyu Zhang, Linfeng Dong, Xiaoya Li, Sen Zhang, Xiaofei Sun, Shuhe Wang, Jiwei Li, Runyi Hu, Tianwei Zhang, Fei Wu, and Guoyin Wang. 2023. Instruction tuning for large language models: A survey. *CoRR*, abs/2308.10792.

Susan Zhang, Stephen Roller, Naman Goyal, Mikel Artetxe, Moya Chen, Shuohui Chen, Christopher Dewan, Mona Diab, Xian Li, Xi Victoria Lin, et al. 2022. Opt: Open pre-trained transformer language models. *arXiv preprint arXiv:2205.01068*.

Wei Emma Zhang, Quan Z. Sheng, Ahoud Alhazmi, and Chenliang Li. 2020. Adversarial Attacks on Deep-learning Models in Natural Language Processing: A Survey. *ACM Transactions on Intelligent Systems and Technology*, 11(3):24:1–24:41.

Premise: The little boy in jean shorts kicks the soccer ball.
Hypothesis: A little boy is playing soccer outside.
Label: Neutral

Premise: The little boy in jean shorts kicks the soccer ball in the house.
Hypothesis: A little boy is playing soccer outside.
Label: Contradiction

Figure 6: A sample instance for robustness in NLI from SNLI-CF. The addition (in red) causes the label to change.

Premise: An Asian woman cutting the stems of a green leafy cabbage at a market.
Hypothesis: An Asian woman cutting the stems of a green leafy vegetable at a market.
Label: Entailment

Figure 7: A sample instance for compositionality in NLI. The label is entailment because every cabbage is a vegetable. Both "cabbage" and "vegetable" tokens appear in SNLI, but not in the same instance – this is a composed instance of these "constituents".

Premise: They're made from a secret recipe handed down to the present-day villagers by their Mallorcan ancestors, who came here in the early 17th century as part of an official repopulation scheme.
Hypothesis: The recipe passed down from Mallorcan ancestors is known to everyone.
Label: Contradiction

Figure 8: A sample instance for testing domain generalization in NLI from MNLI-matched.

Context: Peyton Manning became the first quarterback ever to lead two different teams to multiple Super Bowls. He is also the oldest quarterback ever to play in a Super Bowl at age 39. The past record was held by John Elway, who led the Broncos to victory in Super Bowl XXXIII at age 38 and is currently Denver's Executive Vice President of Football Operations and General Manager.
Question: What is the name of the quarterback who was 38 in Super Bowl XXXIII?
Answer: John Elway

Context: Peyton Manning became the first quarterback ever to lead two different teams to multiple Super Bowls. He is also the oldest quarterback ever to play in a Super Bowl at age 39. The past record was held by John Elway, who led the Broncos to victory in Super Bowl XXXIII at age 38 and is currently Denver's Executive Vice President of Football Operations and General Manager. Quarterback Jeff Dean had jersey number 37 in Champ Bowl XXXIV.
Question: What is the name of the quarterback who was 38 in Super Bowl XXXIII?
Answer: John Elway

Figure 9: A sample instance for testing robustness generalization in MRC (Adv-SQuAD). Models are often fooled by the addition (red) and predict a different answer.

Context: One of Africa's brightest young writers, 31-year-old Chimamanda Adichie has already been recognised for her talent; her debut novel was shortlisted for the Orange Fiction Prize in 2004. The Nigerian novelist talks to CNN about her craft, her country and identity.
Question: What award has the novelist been nominated for?
Answer: Orange Fiction Prize

Figure 10: A sample instance for testing domain generalization in MRC (NewsQA)

Appendix

Datasets, models, hyperparameters, and training

We use publicly available datasets and modify them as needed. We present the dataset details in Table 4. Some instances are shown in Figures 6 to 11.

See Table 5 for the number of parameters in the used models.

For fully-tuned models, we use the HuggingFace Transformers library [5]. For EO models, we tokenize both NLI and MRC instances as pairs. For ED and DO models, we concatenate the premise and hypothesis as `premise: <> hypothesis: <>` for NLI instances. Similarly, for MRC instances, we concatenate the question and context as `question: <> context: <>`.

For LoRA models, we use the implementation from the HuggingFace PEFT library [6]. The hyperparameters are:

- $r = 16$
- $\alpha = 32$
- dropout = 0.05
- bias = None.

For Bottleneck adapters, we use the implementation from the adapters library in Adapter-hub [7] for all models except the `OPT` ones. The hyperparameters are:

- reduction_factor = 16

[5] `https://github.com/huggingface/transformers`

[6] `https://github.com/huggingface/peft`

[7] `https://github.com/adapter-hub/adapters`

Table 4: Details of the dataset used. We provide HuggingFace datasets public uris when available. For the datasets we created/modified, we provide a local copy.

dataset name	hf datasets link	split	size
SNLI	snli	train, validation, test	train: 550152, validation: 1000, test: 10000
MNLI-matched	multi_nli	validation_matched	9815
MNLI-mismatched	multi_nli	validation_mismatched	9832
HANS	hans	validation	30000
SNLI-CF	local	test	2000
SNLI-BT	local	test	18044
SNLI-H	au123/snli-hard	test	3261
CONJNLI	local	dev	624
TaxiNLI	local	dev	7728
SQuAD	rajpurkar/squad	train, validation	train: 87285, validation: 10485
Adv-SQuAD	local	validation footnote	3560
NewsQA	local	validation	1070
Adv-HotpotQA	local	validation	2828
MusiQue	local	validation	868

Context: During his bid to be elected president in 2004, Kerry frequently criticized President George W. Bush for the Iraq War. While Kerry had initially voted in support of authorizing President Bush to use force in dealing with Saddam Hussein, he voted against an $87 billion supplemental appropriations bill to pay for the subsequent war. His statement on March 16, 2004, "I actually did vote for the $87 billion before I voted against it," helped the Bush campaign to paint him as a flip-flopper and has been cited as contributing to Kerry's defeat.
Question: Why did Kerry criticize Bush during the 2004 campaign?
Answer: for the Iraq War

Context: In the lead up to the Iraq War, Kerry said on October 9, 2002; "I will be voting to give the President of the United States the authority to use force, if necessary, to disarm Saddam Hussein because I believe that a deadly arsenal of weapons of mass destruction in his hands is a real and grave threat to our security." Bush relied on that resolution in ordering the 2003 invasion of Iraq. Kerry also gave a January 23, 2003 speech to Georgetown University saying "Without question, we need to disarm Saddam Hussein. He is a brutal, murderous dictator; leading an oppressive regime he presents a particularly grievous threat because he is so consistently prone to miscalculation. So the threat of Saddam Hussein with weapons of mass destruction is real." Kerry did, however, warn that the administration should exhaust its diplomatic avenues before launching war: "Mr. President, do not rush to war, take the time to build the coalition, because itś not winning the war that's hard, it's winning the peace that's hard."
Question: When did Bush declare the Iraq War?
Answer: 2003

Context: During his bid to be elected president in 2004, Kerry frequently criticized President George W. Bush for the Iraq War. While Kerry had initially voted in support of authorizing President Bush to use force in dealing with Saddam Hussein, he voted against an $87 billion supplemental appropriations bill to pay for the subsequent war. His statement on March 16, 2004, "I actually did vote for the $87 billion before I voted against it," helped the Bush campaign to paint him as a flip-flopper and has been cited as contributing to Kerryś defeat. In the lead up to the Iraq War, Kerry said on October 9, 2002; "I will be voting to give the President of the United States the authority to use force, if necessary, to disarm Saddam Hussein because I believe that a deadly arsenal of weapons of mass destruction in his hands is a real and grave threat to our security." Bush relied on that resolution in ordering the 2003 invasion of Iraq. Kerry also gave a January 23, 2003 speech to Georgetown University saying "Without question, we need to disarm Saddam Hussein. He is a brutal, murderous dictator; leading an oppressive regime he presents a particularly grievous threat because he is so consistently prone to miscalculation. So the threat of Saddam Hussein with weapons of mass destruction is real." Kerry did, however, warn that the administration should exhaust its diplomatic avenues before launching war: "Mr. President, do not rush to war, take the time to build the coalition, because it's not winning the war that's hard, it's winning the peace that's hard."
Question: When did Bush declare the war causing Kerry to criticize him during the 2004 campaign?
Answer: 2003

Figure 11: A sample instance for testing compositionality in MRC (MusiQue) – The last question is a **composition** of the two questions above.

Table 5: Number of parameters in the used models.

model name	#params base	large
BERT	110M	345M
RoBERTa	110M	345M
OPT	350M	1.3B
T5	220M	770M

- non_linearity = relu

We do not use residual connections. For the OPT ones we implemented our own following (Hu et al., 2023). The hyper-parameters are kept the same.

We use the HuggingFace Transformers library for training the models, and the hyper-parameters are as follows:

- Number of epochs: 3
- learning rate: 2e-5
- weight decay: 0.01

Results

Spearman's rank correlation coefficient between two dataset pairs for NLI and MRC –Figures 13a and 13b.

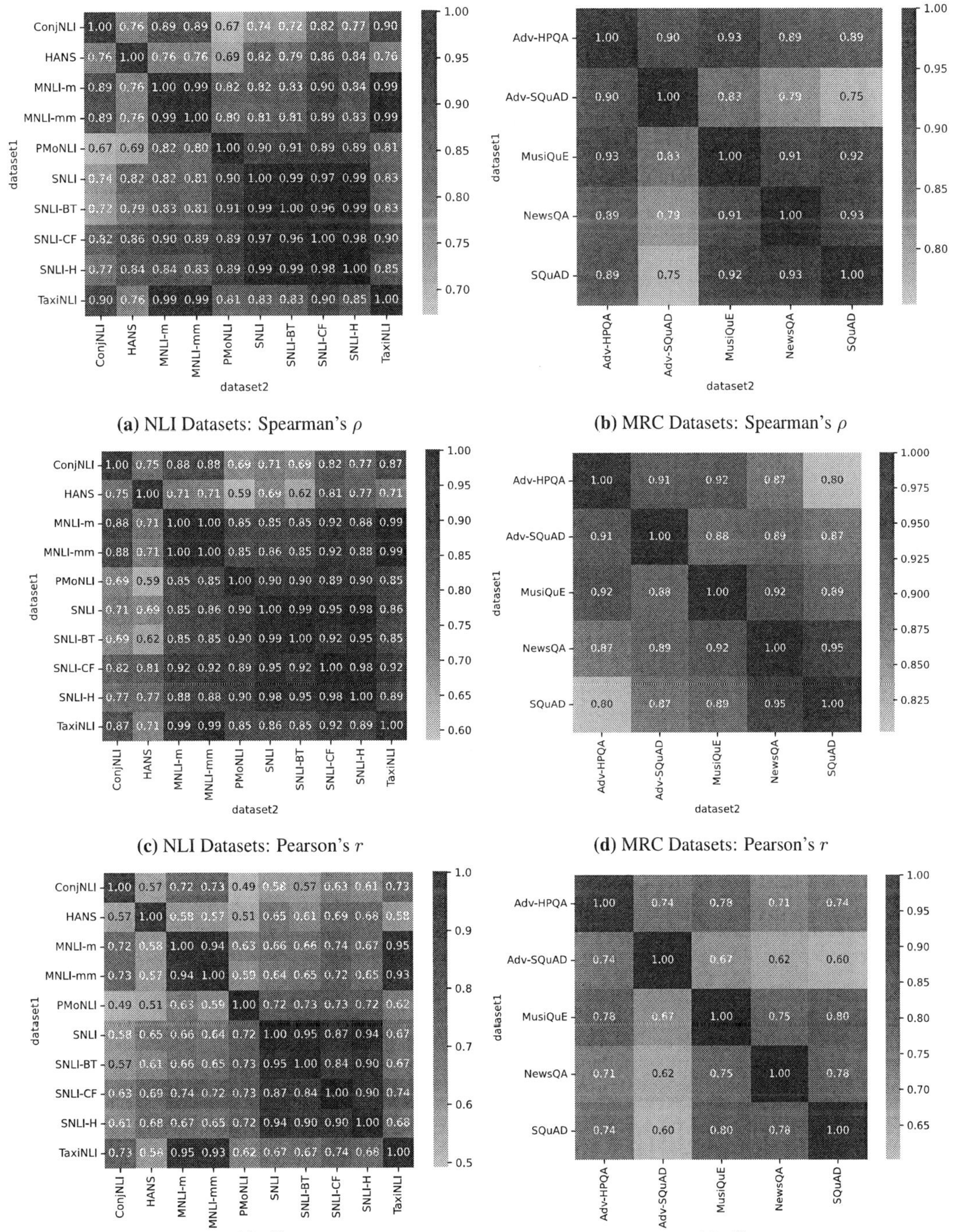

(a) NLI Datasets: Spearman's ρ

(b) MRC Datasets: Spearman's ρ

(c) NLI Datasets: Pearson's r

(d) MRC Datasets: Pearson's r

(e) NLI Datasets: Kendall's τ

(f) MRC Datasets: Kendall's τ

Figure 12: Correlation between the source and the target datasets for NLI and MRC on a per-instance basis for different kinds of correlation.

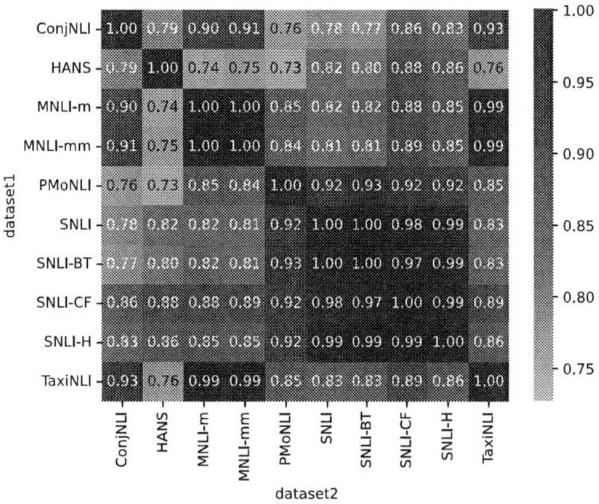

(a) NLI Datasets: Spearman's ρ

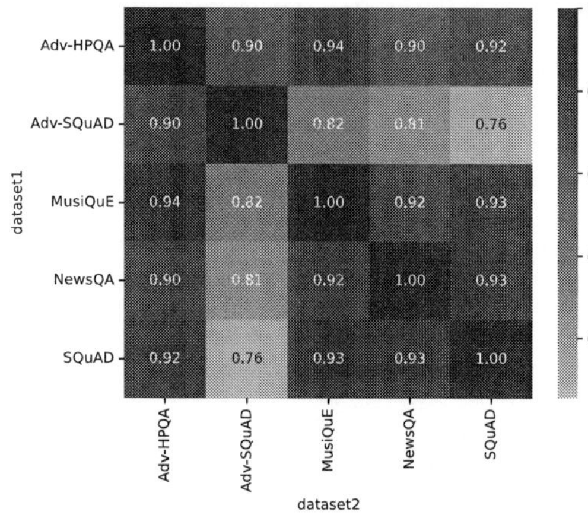

(b) MRC Datasets: Spearman's ρ

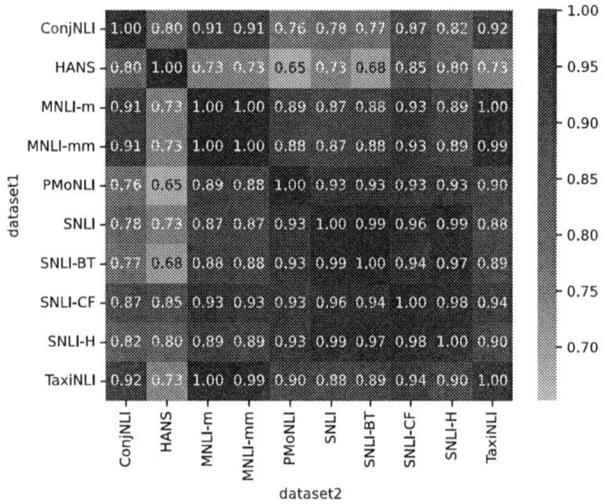

(c) NLI Datasets: Pearson's r

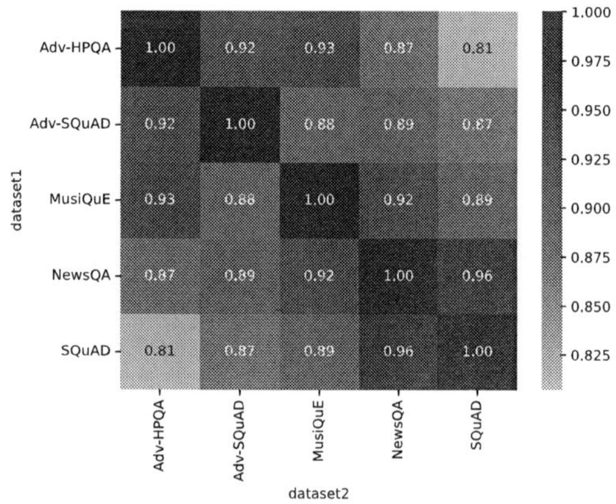

(d) MRC Datasets: Pearson's r

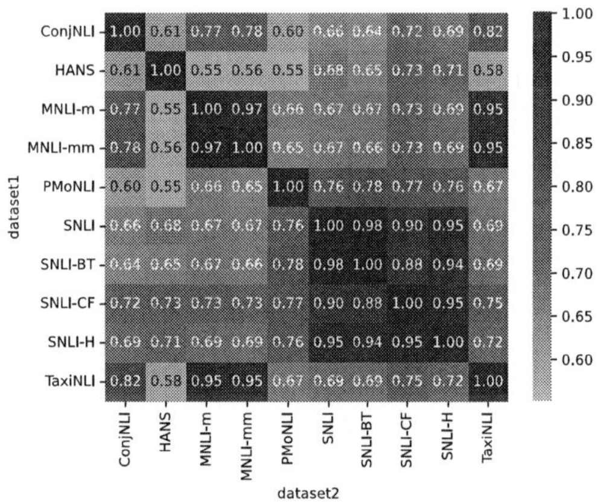

(e) NLI Datasets: Kendall's τ

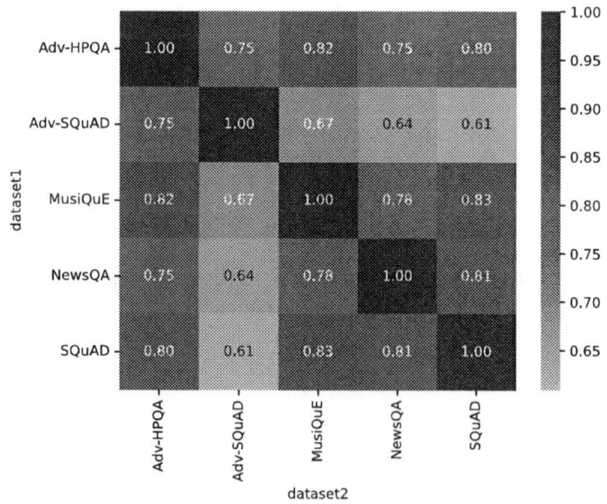

(f) MRC Datasets: Kendall's τ

Figure 13: Correlation between the source and the target datasets for NLI and MRC on a per-architecture basis for different kinds of correlation.

OmniDialog: A Multimodal Benchmark for Generalization Across Text, Visual, and Audio Modalities

Anton Razzhigaev[1,2], Maxim Kurkin[1,2], Elizaveta Goncharova[2], Irina Abdullaeva[2], Anastasia Lysenko, Alexander Panchenko[1,2], Denis Dimitrov[2,3], Andrey Kuznetsov[2,3]
[1]Skoltech, [2]AIRI, [3]Sber AI, **Correspondence:** razzhigaev@airi.net

Abstract

We introduce *OmniDialog* — the first tri-modal comprehensive benchmark grounded in a knowledge graph (Wikidata) to evaluate the generalization of Large Multimodal Models (LMMs) across three modalities. Our benchmark consists of more than 4,000 dialogues, each averaging 10 turns, all annotated and cross-validated by human experts. The dialogues in our dataset are designed to prevent shortcut learning by incorporating various formats and misleading or irrelevant multimodal cues. We also evaluate both multimodal and unimodal models to gain insights into how they process modality inputs introduced in the conversation.

1 Introduction

Multimodal dialogue systems became a focal point in research, drawing significant attention of both academia and industry. This surge of interest stems from their potential to contribute to more natural and nuanced human-computer interactions by seamlessly integrating text, audio, and visual cues (Zhu et al., 2023; Liu et al., 2023b; Koh et al., 2023b,a). Yet, the complexity of these systems has led to challenges in their evaluation. Existing benchmarks, in many instances, fall short in capturing the intricacies of the real-world interactions, lacking the necessary depth and diversity to evaluate the true capabilities of multimodal dialogue systems (Huang et al., 2024).

In response, we introduce the *OmniDialog* benchmark, a multimodal, multi-turn benchmark designed to evaluate the generalization abilities of Large Multimodal Models (LMMs). Specifically, our benchmark assesses their capability to support multi-turn conversations, process modality injections at random points within the dialogue, and operate with three modalities simultaneously (text, visual, and audio). It stands out by grounding on Wikidata knowledge graph and encompasses a vast array of more than 4,000 dialogues, each with an average of 10 turns. To ensure the highest quality, our human annotators designed these dialogues from scratch and then cross-validated them to ensure accuracy and consistency. The uniqueness of *OmniDialog* lies in its design: it requires deep understanding of three modalities – text, visual, and audio. Moreover, to ensure that systems truly understand the context rather than exploit shortcuts, we present dialogues in various formats.

Our contributions are as follows:

- We introduce *OmniDialog* — the first comprehensive benchmark for evaluating multimodal dialogue models, where questions are based on Wikidata KG facts and incorporates three modalities: text, visual, and audio. This offers a robust, diverse, and challenging platform for assessment.

- We provide comprehensive evaluation of the existing multimodal dialogue systems against this new benchmark.

The primary data for *OmniDialog* is sourced from Wikipedia[1] and Wikidata[2], ensuring both the authenticity and generalization ability of the dialogues. The datasets and evaluation code will be released under an open source licence at https://github.com/ai-forever/OmniDialog.

2 Related Work

In this section, we provide a brief description of popular multimodal datasets and state-of-the-art multimodal transformer architectures.

[1]https://www.wikipedia.org/
[2]https://www.wikidata.org

Proceedings of the 2nd GenBench Workshop on Generalisation (Benchmarking) in NLP, pages 183–195
November 16, 2024

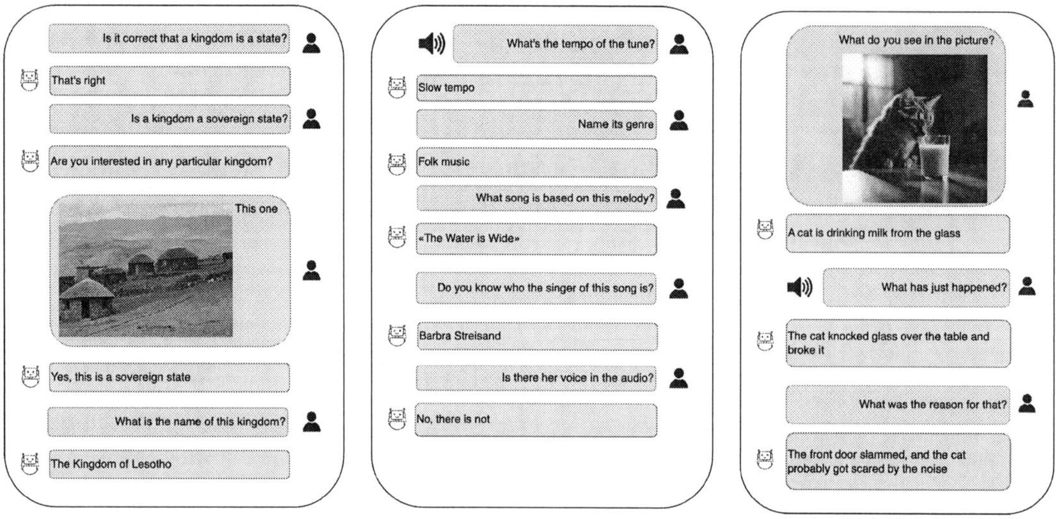

Figure 1: Examples of dialogues from the OmniDialog dataset.

2.1 Multimodal Dialogue Datasets

Dialogue datasets that merge various modalities play a crucial role in training and evaluating multimodal systems. There are two key aspects that such datasets need to consider: first, the strength and the robustness of relationships among different modalities, and second, the ability to identify user's query and to follow instructions.

Significant progress in cross-modal benchmarking has been achieved recently. Specifically, combinations like language and vision have tackled challenges in image captioning, visual question answering (VQA), and visual reasoning (Young et al., 2014; Chen et al., 2015; Krishna et al., 2016; Goyal et al., 2016). Language and audio studies have emphasised audio captioning and classification (Kim et al., 2019; Drossos et al., 2019; Gemmeke et al., 2017), while language and video research has concentrated on video series description and visual grounding (Li et al., 2021; Chen et al., 2023; Sigurdsson et al., 2016) among other tasks. The vast majority of these datasets are focused on one specific domain - a natural language description of the modality. In contrast, substantially fewer works have addressed a relatively new field of multimodal dialogue systems benchmarking.

Early works in this area considered evaluating multimodal dialogue systems via QA approach on vision-language based tasks (Goyal et al., 2016; Johnson et al., 2016; Gurari et al., 2018). Other studies further aim to estimate the ability of visual instruction following (Dai et al., 2023; Liu et al., 2023b; Xu et al., 2022), visual grounding (Chen et al., 2022; Kazemzadeh et al., 2014). Several benchmarks emphasise the incorporation of common knowledge bases in unstructured form and retrieval techniques into the general VQA setup (Yu et al., 2023; Marino et al., 2019; Schwenk et al., 2022). Besides the visual-text dialogues type, there are also datasets for the joint evaluation of text and audio in both Spoken QA (SQA) (Lee et al., 2018b,a) and audio captioning tasks (Kim et al., 2019; Drossos et al., 2019; Zhao et al., 2023). However, all of these benchmarks suffer from a single drawback: due to the question-answering problem setting, they put very little attention to the model's ability to maintain the long context of the dialogue in order to further rely on it for later response generation and do not focus on interaction of several modalities (e.g. image + audio).

Only in recent time due to the significant success of OpenAI GPT4 and GPT4-V (OpenAI, 2023a,b), along with open-source LLMs (Li et al., 2023a; Awadalla et al., 2023; Dai et al., 2023; Shuster et al., 2020) to carry on complete visually-augmented conversations, there were taken steps towards advanced multimodal dialogue datasets design. These datasets bring together the visual conditioning with the instructionally formulated questions, with reliance upon dialogue context and requirement of extensive domain and world knowledge (Das et al., 2016; de Vries et al., 2016; Mostafazadeh et al., 2017; Johnson et al., 2016; Shuster et al., 2018; Meng et al., 2020; Huang et al., 2023b; Liu et al., 2024). However, the scope of their application is constrained since they focus on using only two modalities — visual and text ones. Other modalities, therefore, remain relatively unexplored in the dialogue setting.

In contrast to the above mentioned works, our benchmark fuses the data from three modalities: text, visual, and audio, and enables building complex relationships on their basis. Furthermore, to the best of our knowledge, *OmniDialog* is the first benchmark to merge all three modalities together in a single dialogue setup. Our benchmark demands multiple knowledge forms, such as basic factual world knowledge and scientific knowledge in historical, physical, and biological domains. The underlying factual evidence in the *OmniDialog* benchmark is derived from the WikiData knowledge graph, therefore, it is precise and reliable. Dialogs are constructed based on a random subset of entities and images from Wikidata.

2.2 Visual-Audio-Language Models

One straightforward approach to embed the ability to understand other modalities into pre-trained LLMs is to use specialised out-of-the-box visual, audio, etc. based models as external tools (Schick et al., 2023; Yang et al., 2023; Li et al., 2023b). This means that the language model serves as a skills orchestrator, invoking "expert" models of particular modality via language calls in order to complete certain tasks when necessary. However, these methods suffer from weak connectivity and limited interaction between modalities, resulting in a loss of significant cross-modal information.

More recently, end-to-end multimodal language models have gained considerable interest. Some of the early studies embedded visual data understanding into LMs via additional parameters augmentation and further joint cross-modal training (Alayrac et al., 2022; Wang et al., 2022; Gong et al., 2023).

As opposed to training from scratch, follow-up research has focused on integration of pre-trained visual and language models. The dominant approach was to implement a trainable projection layer between the pre-trained modality feature extractor and the LLM. This setup leads to the injection of high-quality modality embeddings into the language context, which is perceived as a "foreign language" by the language model. Moreover, keeping the number of tunable parameters small, improves the computational efficiency of the cross-modal training. So far, a variety of different network architectures and learning strategies have been proposed to fuse different vision and language models in a single multimodal system (Liu et al., 2023b; Koh et al., 2023b; Zhang et al., 2023; Gao et al., 2023).

However, these approaches are limited to using mostly image content as input. Only a handful of works have attempted to broaden the model's input feature space by incorporating other modalities (Huang et al., 2023a; Girdhar et al., 2023; Wang et al., 2023; Zhao et al., 2023).

3 OmniDialog

In this section, we describe *OmniDialog* — a benchmark for evaluating multimodal dialogue systems in English. Our dataset is distinguished by its diversity in dialogue types, human annotation, and strict evaluation metrics. It is grounded to knowledge graphs, which means that the discussed facts, images, and audios in dialogs are taken from Wikidata. Our benchmark comprised of more than 4,000 dialogues, each averaging 10 turns, with data and facts sourced primarily from Wikipedia and Wikidata.

3.1 Dialog Types

OmniDialog consists of four main types of dialogues: text-text, visual-text, audio-text, and tri-modal dialogues. Each of these is designed to test the system's ability to generalise across different modalities and comprehend information retaining general knowledge from an LLM.

3.1.1 Text Dialogues

Most contemporary generative pre-trained models come with a conversational counterpart. Even though many multimodal conversational systems possess a robust linguistic foundation, understanding how multimodal tuning impacts unimodal capabilities is crucial. Consequently, *OmniDialog* incorporates a strictly textual segment.

These dialogues aim to gauge solely language-based, in-context comprehension. Hence, models must rely exclusively on linguistic understanding to navigate the dialogue. For a cohesive integration between textual and multimodal dialogues, we employ Wikidata facts as our primary dialogue question source, emphasizing factual discourse over creative content.

For constructing textual dialogues, we selected topics and extracted corresponding random Wikidata entities, including films, writers, actors, animals and food. Human annotators then crafted dialogues based on the relationships and facts (Wikidata triples) associated with these entities. Recog-

Dataset	Multi-turn	Interleaved	#Dialogs	#Turns	#Images	#Audio	KG	Annotation
CLEVR-Dialog (Johnson et al., 2016)	Yes	No	425.0 k.	4250.0 k.	85.0 k.	No	No	Synthetic
OpenViDial (Meng et al., 2020)	No	No	1100.0 k.	1100.0 k.	1100.0 k.	No	No	Synthetic
DialogCC (Lee et al., 2022)	Yes	Yes	92.9 k.	930.0 k.	651.0 k.	No	No	Synthetic
SparklesEval (Huang et al., 2023b)	Yes	No	6.5 k.	26.0 k.	10.9 k.	No	No	Synthetic
MPCHAT (Ahn et al., 2023)	Yes	Yes	15.0 k.	42.5 k.	153.0 k.	No	No	Synthetic
LLaVA (Liu et al., 2023b)	Yes	No	56.7 k.	514.0 k.	56.7 k.	No	No	Synthetic
PhotoBook (Haber et al., 2019)	Yes	No	2.5 k.	164.6 k.	0.4 k.	No	No	Human
VisDial (Das et al., 2016)	Yes	No	133.0 k.	1200.0 k.	133.0 k.	No	No	Human
GuessWhat?! (de Vries et al., 2016)	Yes	No	155.0 k.	821.0 k.	66.0 k.	No	No	Human
IGC (Mostafazadeh et al., 2017)	Yes	No	4.2 k.	25.3 k.	4.2 k.	No	No	Human
Image-Chat (Shuster et al., 2018)	No	No	201.8 k.	401.0 k.	201.8 k	No	No	Human
MMD (Saha et al., 2017)	Yes	Yes	151.6 k.	6400.0 k.	4200.0 k.	No	No	Human
PhotoChat (Zang et al., 2021)	Yes	Yes	12.3 k.	156.0 k.	10.9 k.	No	No	Human
MMDialog (Feng et al., 2022)	Yes	Yes	1800.0 k.	4920.0 k.	1530.0 k.	No	No	Human
VDialogUE (Li et al., 2023c)	Yes	Yes	1080.0 k.	4900.0 k.	1530.0k.	No	No	Human
MMDU Benchmark (Liu et al., 2024)	Yes	Yes	110	1.6 k.	421	No	No	Human
OmniDialog (Ours)	Yes	Yes	4.0 k.	27.0 k.	2.4 k.	1.0 k.	Yes	Human

Table 1: Comparison of OmniDialog with existing multi-modal English-language dialogue datasets.

Modality	Dialogue Type	# Dialogues	# Questions (KG-based)	# Questions (General)
Text	General dialogues	1 455	2,000	6 492
Visual	Single Image	1 794	6 506	5 552
	Clarifying Image	400	1 349	1 420
	Misleading Image	220	290	396
Audio	Single Audio	283	2 366	1 334
	Clarifying Audio	500	2 109	1 471
	Dual Audio	100	499	203
Trimodal	General dialogues	165	0	2 000

Table 2: Statistics of dialogues in the OmniDialog, categorized by modality and dialogue type.

nizing that Wikidata might occasionally offer limited information, annotators were advised to supplement dialogue content using relevant Wikipedia articles.

3.1.2 Visual Dialogues

Visual dialogues in OmniDialog are designed to assess the model's capacity to integrate visual processing with natural language understanding. In each dialogue, a single image is employed (not necessarily in the initial dialog turn), and at least four facts from WikiData are utilized. The visual dialogues are divided into three categories, each with its unique structure and purpose:

1. **Single Image Dialogues:** In this format, the user introduces a single image and poses questions related to it. These questions encompass both intricate queries oriented towards facts from WikiData and straightforward inquiries regarding the content of the image. A sample dialogue is illustrated in Figure 1.

2. **Clarifying Image Dialogues:** This dialogue structure begins with the user posing a question that cannot be answered without additional clarifying information. The user then provides an image to supplement the dialogue and to facilitate further discussion.

3. **Misleading Image Dialogues:** In this scenario, the user poses a question along with an image that, while thematically related, is irrelevant. The model must identify the image's irrelevance and respond accurately, followed by a discussion about the image. Some baseline multimodal LLMs tend to shift focus on the image, ignoring its irrelevance to the query. This dialogue type is designed to address such tendencies, encouraging models to balance attention between visual and textual inputs mitigating such shortcut behaviors.

3.1.3 Audio Dialogues

Audio and textual modalities have been fused within dialogues in *OmniDialog* in a way that allows a better understanding of the model's sound comprehension ability's contribution to its multimodal dialogue performance.

The audio-text OmniDialog dialogues were used to evaluate the role of the model's sound comprehension in its multimodal conversation skills. To ensure the diversity of different sound types and the balance between the factual reliability and the realism of the discussion, we defined the following rules: 1) the same audio should be used in dialogues only once; 2) each dialogue should contain at least 2 and no more than 4 facts; 3) non-factual knowledge questions should be as simple that a 5-year-old child would be able to answer.

Based on the collected sound files and Wikidata textual facts, we also identified three categories within the structure of the dialogues:

1. **Single Audio Dialogues**: In this split, first turn of conversation contains an audio recording and a question about its content. In the further dialogue progression, both evidence-based questions referring to the WikiData entity and sound based questions are used.

2. **Clarifying Audio Dialogues**: Within this dialogue type, the user sends an audio recording along with an accompanying question in the middle of the discussion. In this case, the audio serves as a clarification to one of the evidence-based questions. The subsequent dialogue is built around the audio content, with a variety of relevant questions about it.

3. **Dual Audio Dialogues**: Two audio recordings are used simultaneously in these dialogues, setting them apart from the other types. Conversations include both questions about content of audios and evidence-based ones that pertain to the related entities recognized on audio. The dialogues should emphasise the connection between the sounds, whether by questioning their characteristics or comparing the entities they are associated with. The purpose of this dialogue type is to examine the model's ability to differentiate and remember various audio information throughout the conversation.

3.1.4 Trimodal Dialogues

Trimodal dialogues in OmniDialog aim to gauge the model's capability to process and combine information from three modalities: text, visual, and audio ones. Within these dialogues, models are expected to integrate and act on the information derived from all sources to provide accurate answers. We have curated 100 high-quality trimodal dialogues, categorized into four distinct scenarios:

1. **Image-sound Matching:** The model is asked to match an object's sound from the audio with its visual representation in an image to identify the subject of discussion.

2. **Multimodal Navigation:** The audio clarifies the object, concept, or event depicted in the image. Subsequent questions focus on this audio-visual correspondence.

3. **Audio-based Continuation:** These dialogues start with an image showing a certain situation. The task is to understand how this situation might change considering the given audio.

4. **Misleading Dialogues:** The dialogues contain unrelated audio and visual prompts. Models must adeptly shift attention between these different sources of information to respond accurately.

3.2 Human Annotation

Multimodal dialogue creation is a nuanced task demanding attention to the details. To ensure the integrity of the data, we implemented a rigorous protocol:

Annotation Protocol:

- Develop comprehensive guidelines with illustrative examples.
- Host training sessions to resolve annotators' doubts.
- Enforce a rigorous verification process for all dialogues.

Media Criteria:

- Ensure audio and images align with articles and provide multiple facts.
- Maintain a minimum duration of 4 seconds for audio clips.

Dialogue Rules:

- Keep dialogues between 4 and 20 messages.
- Base multimodal questions on Wikidata facts or clear links between articles.

- Root text dialogues in Wikipedia data.
- Limit user questions to 2-15 words and answers to 1-10 words.

Synonyms: Include synonyms in dialogues when alternate answers exist. Ensure they fully address the user's questions. They are essential for text and audio dialogues.

Negative examples: Negative examples are required for multiple choice evaluation setup to be passed as answer options along with ground truth answer. So they have been added to all questions, including names, dates, numbers, yes/no, and others. Along with negative examples, neutral options "can't answer", "not enough information" were always added.

Challenges: We faced issues like repetitive facts and overly concise answers. Solutions included rephrasing, adding comparative elements, and varying sentence structures.

Team Workflow: Our six-member team produced 20-25 dialogues each day. Validation was quicker, taking about 40% of the dialogue creation time.

3.3 Evaluation and Metrics

Evaluating generative models is inherently challenging. The evaluation method can alter both numerical results and leaderboard rankings drastically. While *OmniDialog* was initially designed for open-ended generative responses, this design posed evaluation complexities. The variability in training can result in models producing diverse or brief responses, making it essential for ground truth options to account for such variability.

Given our benchmark's focus on factual questions, we aim to prioritize answer correctness over stylistic variations. To this end, we convert dialogues into multiple-choice questions and determine accuracy based on the selected response.

The given answer is recorded, but for consequential questions the *correct* answer to the current question is used in the previous context to enforce model capabilities and fair comparison between multimodal and text-only models. For evaluation details, please refer to Appendix A.2.

The final score is reported as the mean accuracy of model answers. **Total** stands for mean of accuracies reported on benchmark subsets.

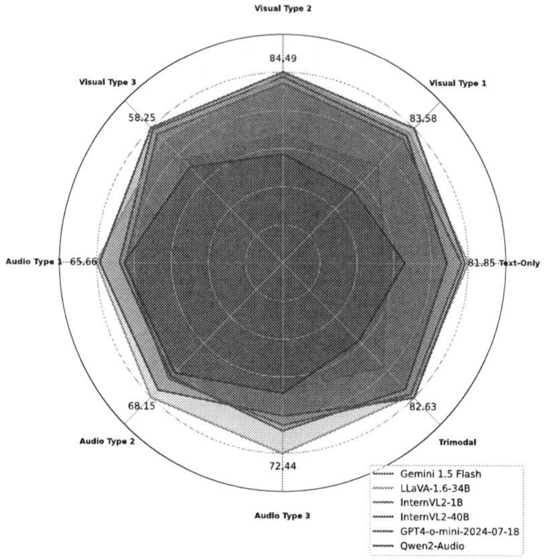

Figure 2: Comparison of models: Radar plot of baseline evaluation against different dialog types.

4 Baselines

Given that the most progress has been achieved for the combination of visual and textual modalities, we have adapted several recently introduced models to process the dialogue input. The baselines include not only the trimodality models but also bimodal (visual-text) and unimodal models (language-only) models. The latter are evaluated using the corresponding part of OmniDialog.

Trimodal. Gemini (Team, 2024) serves as a baseline model supporting all three modalities.

Visual-Language. Several (near) state-of-the-art models are assessed on the language-only and visual-language OmniDialog parts: series of LLaVA models (Liu et al., 2023a), series of InternVL 2.0 (Chen et al., 2024) chat models with the LLM backbones of various size (from 1B to 40B parameters) and strong vision encoder (InternViT-6B and its distilled version InternViT-300M), and Idefics2 8B (Laurençon et al., 2024) vision-language model trained with the interleaved data.

These models ignore audio data during the evaluation process and only encode images with proposed visual adapter architectures.

Language-only. GPT-4-mini is used as a language-only baseline reference for OmniDialog. No encoding of visual or audio data is performed during the evaluation and model solely reasons from previosly answered questions.

Model	Text-Only	Visual			Audio			Trimodal	Total
		Type 1	Type 2	Type 3	Type 1	Type 2	Type 3		
Random Guessing	16.41	26.68	26.18	26.54	17.85	18.90	15.56	40.08	22.16
Trimodal Models									
Gemini 1.5 Flash (Team, 2024)	72.36	79.01	82.34	57.58	57.55	57.83	**63.90**	77.27	68.48
Visual-Language Models									
LLaVA-v1.5-7B (Liu et al., 2023a)	68.45	69.23	64.15	44.11	54.58	59.25	59.23	69.26	61.03
LLaVA-v1.5-13B	69.74	73.22	72.39	46.46	55.26	60.11	63.01	75.05	64.40
LLaVA-v1.6-Mistral-7B	69.47	73.92	73.44	48.15	59.59	62.90	62.45	75.05	65.62
LLaVA-1.6-34B	81.85	80.77	83.70	53.20	65.66	68.15	72.44	81.16	73.37
Idefics2-8B (Laurençon et al., 2024)	66.45	65.86	69.85	54.21	59.16	62.67	63.58	71.47	64.16
InternVL2-1B	45.36	60.42	57.06	44.44	43.63	44.44	48.51	63.89	50.97
InternVL2-2B	50.30	65.79	63.45	46.56	49.13	47.66	51.33	69.58	55.47
InternVL2-8B	70.02	78.63	78.44	56.90	60.71	61.51	65.75	78.00	68.74
InternVL2-26B	71.45	79.90	79.40	53.20	56.25	56.96	53.20	78.42	66.1
InternVL2-40B	**80.43**	**83.58**	**84.49**	**58.25**	**64.48**	**64.46**	58.25	**82.63**	**72.07**
GPT4-o-mini-2024-07-18 (OpenAI, 2023a,b)	78.85	76.67	79.61	55.56	55.40	58.92	61.72	80.56	68.41
Audio-Language Models									
Qwen2-Audio (Chu et al., 2024)	53.84	44.90	48.25	41.33	55.87	55.87	49.63	47.79	49.69
Language-only Models									
GPT4-o-mini-2024-07-18	-	26.61	30.14	34.68	-	-	-	42.55	-

Table 3: Performance evaluation results across different categories of models on our OmniDialog benchmark. Best in each dialogue category is highlighted id **bold**.

5 Discussion

We discuss result of OmniDialog benchmark evaluation presented in Table 3.

1. Influence of the LLM Backbone on Performance. There is a strong correlation between the evaluation results and the performance of the model's LLM backbone. Models with more powerful backbones consistently achieve higher results across all image types. For instance, there is a significant performance gap of over 20% between the InternVL2 40B and InternVL2 1B models across all dialogue types. Similarly, the difference between LLaVA-1.6 34B and 7B models averages nearly 8%. The dialogs in OmniDialog are constructed using Wikipedia and WikiData entities. Hence, the LLM's knowledge of Wikipedia content helps multimodal models based on these backbones generalize better across multimodal information.

2. Challenges in Visual Type-3 Dialogues. The lowest performance in visual-language models is observed in Type 3 visual dialogues, where misleading images are introduced into the dialogue context. Although models can answer textual questions correctly, they struggle with questions related to the image modality, especially when the question is distant from the image. This challenge may arise from the typical training process, where models are used to encountering the image and accompanying question in a strict sequence. LLaVA-based models experience an average performance drop of 20% in visual Type 3 dialogues compared to visual Types 1 and 2.

All benchmarked models do not generalize well on questions not matching context of the distracting image. We show the example of Type 3 visual dialogue in Section A Figure 7.

3. Challenges in Audio Dialogues. The most challenging modality type of dialogue in the benchmark is audio dialogues. Visual-language models struggle to guess the correct answer to questions, even with the teacher-forcing approach, leading to lower performance compared to other dialogue types. It is evident that models adapted to the audio domain, such as Qwen-Audio 7B, show lower metrics on audio datasets compared to stronger baselines that do not process audio.

4. High Results on Multimodal Inputs. The teacher-forcing of context introduced in 4 reduces the influence of modality input, enabling models to provide correct answers even when they struggle to process a specific modality. Reinforcing past context with correct answers leads to a significant performance boost in tasks with added modalities. Thus, strong visual-language models without audio perception (such as LLaVA-v1.6 34B) perform well on audio-based dialogues.

If we switch to a mode where specific model answers are added as the continuation of the dialogue for further assessment, the results might differ. We leave this type of evaluation for further research.

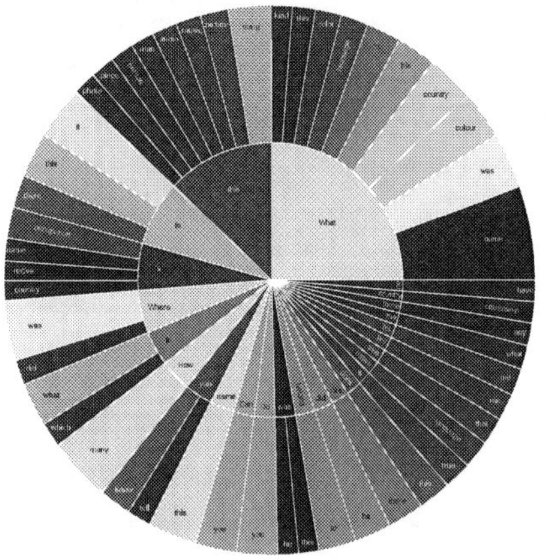

Figure 3: Bigram word pairs in user questions.

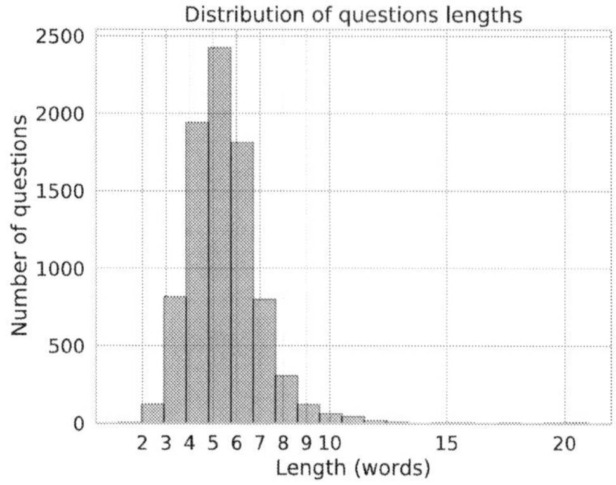

Figure 4: Distribution of word lengths in user questions with an average of 6 words.

Figure 5: Wordcloud of assistant answers.

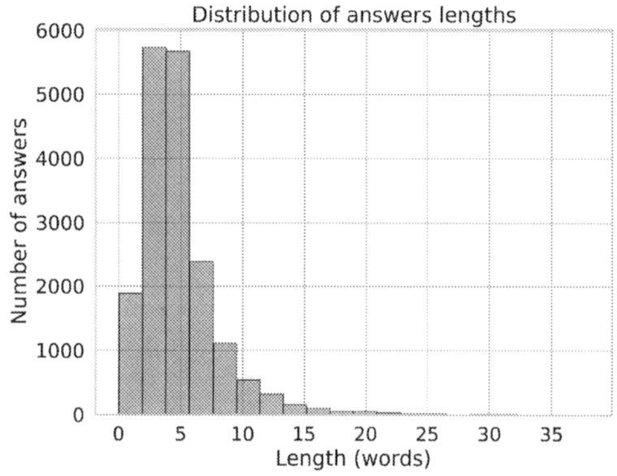

Figure 6: Distribution of word lengths in assistant answers with an average of 4.5 words

6 Benchmark Statistics

Figures 3 - 4 show characteristics of the OmniDialog dataset in terms of textual analysis of the replicas. We explore key elements such as the word bigram distribution in user questions, the word cloud of required assistant responses as well as the length distributions for both of them.

7 Conclusion

We introduced *OmniDialog*, a diverse and comprehensive benchmark for multimodal dialogue systems, comprising more than 4,000 dialogues based on entities, facts, and media from Wikidata knowledge graph. These dialogues, designed to prevent shortcut learning, offer a unique challenge for multimodal systems with various formats and misleading cues. The knowledge graph foundation of OmniDialog makes it a valuable resource for comparing multimodal models based on factual information.

We also analyze several baselines, both open-source and proprietary, with respect to their generalization across various modalities and types of dialogues introduced with OmniDialog. Following the teacher-forcing evaluation, we compared models operating with different modalities. We believe that the creation of multimodal benchmarks will motivate the community to develop dialogue assistants further and enhance their evaluation. We also aim to build upon this work by providing various types of assessments using LLM oracles, both with and without teacher forcing, which may result in a fairer comparison of the quality of multimodal models.

Limitations

While Wikidata is generally considered a reliable source of information, it carries an inherent risk of bias, as it may contain its own biases, errors, and inconsistencies. Since OmniDialog is focused on English, using this source limits our ability to fairly evaluate the multilingual generalization of models. Additionally, the potential for human errors during annotation and editing cannot be overlooked, which might introduce further discrepancies or inaccuracies into the dataset.

Ethical Statement

We acknowledge the importance of diversity and representation in data sources. Our aim with *OmniDialog* was to ensure a broad and diverse representation in dialogues, striving to avoid potential biases where certain cultures might be underrepresented.

References

Jaewoo Ahn, Yeda Song, Sangdoo Yun, and Gunhee Kim. 2023. Mpchat: Towards multimodal persona-grounded conversation. *ArXiv*, abs/2305.17388.

Jean-Baptiste Alayrac, Jeff Donahue, Pauline Luc, Antoine Miech, Iain Barr, Yana Hasson, Karel Lenc, Arthur Mensch, Katie Millican, Malcolm Reynolds, Roman Ring, Eliza Rutherford, Serkan Cabi, Tengda Han, Zhitao Gong, Sina Samangooei, Marianne Monteiro, Jacob Menick, Sebastian Borgeaud, Andy Brock, Aida Nematzadeh, Sahand Sharifzadeh, Mikolaj Binkowski, Ricardo Barreira, Oriol Vinyals, Andrew Zisserman, and Karen Simonyan. 2022. Flamingo: a visual language model for few-shot learning. *ArXiv*, abs/2204.14198.

Anas Awadalla, Irena Gao, Josh Gardner, Jack Hessel, Yusuf Hanafy, Wanrong Zhu, Kalyani Marathe, Yonatan Bitton, Samir Yitzhak Gadre, Shiori Sagawa, Jenia Jitsev, Simon Kornblith, Pang Wei Koh, Gabriel Ilharco, Mitchell Wortsman, and Ludwig Schmidt. 2023. Openflamingo: An open-source framework for training large autoregressive vision-language models. *ArXiv*, abs/2308.01390.

Chongyan Chen, Samreen Anjum, and Danna Gurari. 2022. Grounding answers for visual questions asked by visually impaired people. *2022 IEEE/CVF Conference on Computer Vision and Pattern Recognition (CVPR)*, pages 19076–19085.

Sihan Chen, Xingjian He, Longteng Guo, Xinxin Zhu, Weining Wang, Jinhui Tang, and Jing Liu. 2023. Valor: Vision-audio-language omni-perception pretraining model and dataset. *ArXiv*, abs/2304.08345.

Xinlei Chen, Hao Fang, Tsung-Yi Lin, Ramakrishna Vedantam, Saurabh Gupta, Piotr Dollár, and C. Lawrence Zitnick. 2015. Microsoft coco captions: Data collection and evaluation server. *ArXiv*, abs/1504.00325.

Zhe Chen, Weiyun Wang, Hao Tian, Shenglong Ye, Zhangwei Gao, Erfei Cui, Wenwen Tong, Kongzhi Hu, Jiapeng Luo, Zheng Ma, et al. 2024. How far are we to gpt-4v? closing the gap to commercial multimodal models with open-source suites. *arXiv preprint arXiv:2404.16821*.

Yunfei Chu, Jin Xu, Qian Yang, Haojie Wei, Xipin Wei, Zhifang Guo, Yichong Leng, Yuanjun Lv, Jinzheng He, Junyang Lin, Chang Zhou, and Jingren Zhou. 2024. Qwen2-audio technical report. *Preprint*, arXiv:2407.10759.

Wenliang Dai, Junnan Li, Dongxu Li, Anthony Meng Huat Tiong, Junqi Zhao, Weisheng Wang, Boyang Albert Li, Pascale Fung, and Steven C. H. Hoi. 2023. Instructblip: Towards general-purpose vision-language models with instruction tuning. *ArXiv*, abs/2305.06500.

Abhishek Das, Satwik Kottur, Khushi Gupta, Avi Singh, Deshraj Yadav, José M. F. Moura, Devi Parikh, and Dhruv Batra. 2016. Visual dialog. *2017 IEEE Conference on Computer Vision and Pattern Recognition (CVPR)*, pages 1080–1089.

Harm de Vries, Florian Strub, A. P. Sarath Chandar, Olivier Pietquin, H. Larochelle, and Aaron C. Courville. 2016. Guesswhat?! visual object discovery through multi-modal dialogue. *2017 IEEE Conference on Computer Vision and Pattern Recognition (CVPR)*, pages 4466–4475.

Konstantinos Drossos, Samuel Lipping, and Tuomas Virtanen. 2019. Clotho: an audio captioning dataset. *ICASSP 2020 - 2020 IEEE International Conference on Acoustics, Speech and Signal Processing (ICASSP)*, pages 736–740.

Jiazhan Feng, Qingfeng Sun, Can Xu, Pu Zhao, Yaming Yang, Chongyang Tao, Dongyan Zhao, and Qingwei Lin. 2022. Mmdialog: A large-scale multi-turn dialogue dataset towards multi-modal open-domain conversation. In *Annual Meeting of the Association for Computational Linguistics*.

Peng Gao, Jiaming Han, Renrui Zhang, Ziyi Lin, Shijie Geng, Aojun Zhou, W. Zhang, Pan Lu, Conghui He, Xiangyu Yue, Hongsheng Li, and Yu Jiao Qiao. 2023. Llama-adapter v2: Parameter-efficient visual instruction model. *ArXiv*, abs/2304.15010.

Jort F. Gemmeke, Daniel P. W. Ellis, Dylan Freedman, Aren Jansen, Wade Lawrence, R. Channing Moore, Manoj Plakal, and Marvin Ritter. 2017. Audio set:

An ontology and human-labeled dataset for audio events. In *2017 IEEE International Conference on Acoustics, Speech and Signal Processing (ICASSP)*, pages 776–780.

Rohit Girdhar, Alaaeldin El-Nouby, Zhuang Liu, Mannat Singh, Kalyan Vasudev Alwala, Armand Joulin, and Ishan Misra. 2023. Imagebind one embedding space to bind them all. *2023 IEEE/CVF Conference on Computer Vision and Pattern Recognition (CVPR)*, pages 15180–15190.

Tao Gong, Chengqi Lyu, Shilong Zhang, Yudong Wang, Miao Zheng, Qian Zhao, Kuikun Liu, Wenwei Zhang, Ping Luo, and Kai Chen. 2023. Multimodal-gpt: A vision and language model for dialogue with humans. *CoRR*, abs/2305.04790.

Yash Goyal, Tejas Khot, Douglas Summers-Stay, Dhruv Batra, and Devi Parikh. 2016. Making the v in vqa matter: Elevating the role of image understanding in visual question answering. *International Journal of Computer Vision*, 127:398 – 414.

Danna Gurari, Qing Li, Abigale Stangl, Anhong Guo, Chi Lin, Kristen Grauman, Jiebo Luo, and Jeffrey P. Bigham. 2018. Vizwiz grand challenge: Answering visual questions from blind people. *2018 IEEE/CVF Conference on Computer Vision and Pattern Recognition*, pages 3608–3617.

Janosch Haber, Tim Baumgärtner, Ece Takmaz, Lieke Gelderloos, Elia Bruni, and R. Fernández. 2019. The photobook dataset: Building common ground through visually-grounded dialogue. In *Annual Meeting of the Association for Computational Linguistics*.

Jinsheng Huang, Liang Chen, Taian Guo, Fu Zeng, Yusheng Zhao, Bohan Wu, Ye Yuan, Haozhe Zhao, Zhihui Guo, Yichi Zhang, Jingyang Yuan, Wei Ju, Luchen Liu, Tianyu Liu, Baobao Chang, and Ming Zhang. 2024. Mmevalpro: Calibrating multimodal benchmarks towards trustworthy and efficient evaluation. *Preprint*, arXiv:2407.00468.

Shaohan Huang, Li Dong, Wenhui Wang, Yaru Hao, Saksham Singhal, Shuming Ma, Tengchao Lv, Lei Cui, Owais Khan Mohammed, Qiang Liu, Kriti Aggarwal, Zewen Chi, Johan Bjorck, Vishrav Chaudhary, Subhojit Som, Xia Song, and Furu Wei. 2023a. Language is not all you need: Aligning perception with language models. *ArXiv*, abs/2302.14045.

Yupan Huang, Zaiqiao Meng, Fangyu Liu, Yixuan Su, Nigel Collier, and Yutong Lu. 2023b. Sparkles: Unlocking chats across multiple images for multimodal instruction-following models. *ArXiv*, abs/2308.16463.

Justin Johnson, Bharath Hariharan, Laurens van der Maaten, Li Fei-Fei, C. Lawrence Zitnick, and Ross B. Girshick. 2016. Clevr: A diagnostic dataset for compositional language and elementary visual reasoning. *2017 IEEE Conference on Computer Vision and Pattern Recognition (CVPR)*, pages 1988–1997.

Sahar Kazemzadeh, Vicente Ordonez, Marc andre Matten, and Tamara L. Berg. 2014. Referitgame: Referring to objects in photographs of natural scenes. In *Conference on Empirical Methods in Natural Language Processing*.

Chris Dongjoo Kim, Byeongchang Kim, Hyunmin Lee, and Gunhee Kim. 2019. Audiocaps: Generating captions for audios in the wild. In *North American Chapter of the Association for Computational Linguistics*.

Jing Yu Koh, Daniel Fried, and Ruslan Salakhutdinov. 2023a. Generating images with multimodal language models. *CoRR*, abs/2305.17216.

Jing Yu Koh, Ruslan Salakhutdinov, and Daniel Fried. 2023b. Grounding language models to images for multimodal inputs and outputs. In *International Conference on Machine Learning*.

Ranjay Krishna, Yuke Zhu, Oliver Groth, Justin Johnson, Kenji Hata, Joshua Kravitz, Stephanie Chen, Yannis Kalantidis, Li-Jia Li, David A. Shamma, Michael S. Bernstein, and Li Fei-Fei. 2016. Visual genome: Connecting language and vision using crowdsourced dense image annotations. *International Journal of Computer Vision*, 123:32 – 73.

Hugo Laurençon, Léo Tronchon, Matthieu Cord, and Victor Sanh. 2024. What matters when building vision-language models? *Preprint*, arXiv:2405.02246.

Chia-Hsuan Lee, Shang-Ming Wang, Huan-Cheng Chang, and Hung yi Lee. 2018a. Odsqa: Open-domain spoken question answering dataset. *2018 IEEE Spoken Language Technology Workshop (SLT)*, pages 949–956.

Chia-Hsuan Lee, Szu-Lin Wu, Chi-Liang Liu, and Hung yi Lee. 2018b. Spoken squad: A study of mitigating the impact of speech recognition errors on listening comprehension. In *Interspeech*.

Young-Jun Lee, ByungSoo Ko, Han-Gyu Kim, and Ho-Jin Choi. 2022. Dialogcc: Large-scale multi-modal dialogue dataset. *ArXiv*, abs/2212.04119.

Junnan Li, Dongxu Li, Silvio Savarese, and Steven C. H. Hoi. 2023a. Blip-2: Bootstrapping language-image pre-training with frozen image encoders and large language models. *ArXiv*, abs/2301.12597.

Linjie Li, Jie Lei, Zhe Gan, Licheng Yu, Yen-Chun Chen, Rohith Krishnan Pillai, Yu Cheng, Luowei Zhou, Xin Eric Wang, William Yang Wang, Tamara L. Berg, Mohit Bansal, Jingjing Liu, Lijuan Wang, and Zicheng Liu. 2021. Value: A multi-task benchmark for video-and-language understanding evaluation. *ArXiv*, abs/2106.04632.

Minghao Li, Feifan Song, Yu Bowen, Haiyang Yu, Zhoujun Li, Fei Huang, and Yongbin Li. 2023b. Api-bank: A benchmark for tool-augmented llms. *ArXiv*, abs/2304.08244.

Yunshui Li, Binyuan Hui, Zhaochao Yin, Wanwei He, Run Luo, Yuxing Long, Min Yang, Fei Huang, and Yongbin Li. 2023c. Vdialogue: A unified evaluation benchmark for visually-grounded dialogue. *ArXiv*, abs/2309.07387.

Haotian Liu, Chunyuan Li, Yuheng Li, and Yong Jae Lee. 2023a. Improved baselines with visual instruction tuning. *Preprint*, arXiv:2310.03744.

Haotian Liu, Chunyuan Li, Qingyang Wu, and Yong Jae Lee. 2023b. Visual instruction tuning. *ArXiv*, abs/2304.08485.

Ziyu Liu, Tao Chu, Yuhang Zang, Xilin Wei, Xiaoyi Dong, Pan Zhang, Zijian Liang, Yuanjun Xiong, Yu Qiao, Dahua Lin, and Jiaqi Wang. 2024. Mmdu: A multi-turn multi-image dialog understanding benchmark and instruction-tuning dataset for lvlms. *Preprint*, arXiv:2406.11833.

Kenneth Marino, Mohammad Rastegari, Ali Farhadi, and Roozbeh Mottaghi. 2019. Ok-vqa: A visual question answering benchmark requiring external knowledge. *2019 IEEE/CVF Conference on Computer Vision and Pattern Recognition (CVPR)*, pages 3190–3199.

Yuxian Meng, Shuhe Wang, Qinghong Han, Xiaofei Sun, Fei Wu, Rui Yan, and Jiwei Li. 2020. Openvidial: A large-scale, open-domain dialogue dataset with visual contexts. *ArXiv*, abs/2012.15015.

N. Mostafazadeh, Chris Brockett, William B. Dolan, Michel Galley, Jianfeng Gao, Georgios P. Spithourakis, and Lucy Vanderwende. 2017. Image-grounded conversations: Multimodal context for natural question and response generation. *ArXiv*, abs/1701.08251.

OpenAI. 2023a. Gpt-4 technical report. *ArXiv*, abs/2303.08774.

OpenAI. 2023b. Gpt-4v(ision) system card.

Amrita Saha, Mitesh M. Khapra, and Karthik Sankaranarayanan. 2017. Towards building large scale multimodal domain-aware conversation systems. In *AAAI Conference on Artificial Intelligence*.

Timo Schick, Jane Dwivedi-Yu, Roberto Dessì, Roberta Raileanu, Maria Lomeli, Luke Zettlemoyer, Nicola Cancedda, and Thomas Scialom. 2023. Toolformer: Language models can teach themselves to use tools. *ArXiv*, abs/2302.04761.

Dustin Schwenk, Apoorv Khandelwal, Christopher Clark, Kenneth Marino, and Roozbeh Mottaghi. 2022. A-okvqa: A benchmark for visual question answering using world knowledge. *arXiv*.

Kurt Shuster, Samuel Humeau, Antoine Bordes, and Jason Weston. 2018. Image-chat: Engaging grounded conversations. In *Annual Meeting of the Association for Computational Linguistics*.

Kurt Shuster, Eric Michael Smith, Da Ju, and Jason Weston. 2020. Multi-modal open-domain dialogue. In *Conference on Empirical Methods in Natural Language Processing*.

Gunnar A. Sigurdsson, Gül Varol, X. Wang, Ali Farhadi, Ivan Laptev, and Abhinav Kumar Gupta. 2016. Hollywood in homes: Crowdsourcing data collection for activity understanding. *ArXiv*, abs/1604.01753.

Gemini Team. 2024. Gemini: A family of highly capable multimodal models. *Preprint*, arXiv:2312.11805.

Peng Wang, Shijie Wang, Junyang Lin, Shuai Bai, Xiaohuan Zhou, Jingren Zhou, Xinggang Wang, and Chang Zhou. 2023. One-peace: Exploring one general representation model toward unlimited modalities. *ArXiv*, abs/2305.11172.

Peng Wang, An Yang, Rui Men, Junyang Lin, Shuai Bai, Zhikang Li, Jianxin Ma, Chang Zhou, Jingren Zhou, and Hongxia Yang. 2022. Unifying architectures, tasks, and modalities through a simple sequence-to-sequence learning framework. In *International Conference on Machine Learning*.

Zhiyang Xu, Ying Shen, and Lifu Huang. 2022. Multi-instruct: Improving multi-modal zero-shot learning via instruction tuning. In *Annual Meeting of the Association for Computational Linguistics*.

Rui Yang, Lin Song, Yanwei Li, Sijie Zhao, Yixiao Ge, Xiu Li, and Ying Shan. 2023. Gpt4tools: Teaching large language model to use tools via self-instruction. *ArXiv*, abs/2305.18752.

Peter Young, Alice Lai, Micah Hodosh, and J. Hockenmaier. 2014. From image descriptions to visual denotations: New similarity metrics for semantic inference over event descriptions. *Transactions of the Association for Computational Linguistics*, 2:67–78.

Weihao Yu, Zhengyuan Yang, Linjie Li, Jianfeng Wang, Kevin Lin, Zicheng Liu, Xinchao Wang, and Lijuan Wang. 2023. Mm-vet: Evaluating large multimodal models for integrated capabilities. *ArXiv*, abs/2308.02490.

Xiaoxue Zang, Lijuan Liu, Maria Wang, Yang Song, Hao Zhang, and Jindong Chen. 2021. Photochat: A human-human dialogue dataset with photo sharing behavior for joint image-text modeling. *ArXiv*, abs/2108.01453.

Renrui Zhang, Jiaming Han, Aojun Zhou, Xiangfei Hu, Shilin Yan, Pan Lu, Hongsheng Li, Peng Gao, and Yu Jiao Qiao. 2023. Llama-adapter: Efficient fine-tuning of language models with zero-init attention. *ArXiv*, abs/2303.16199.

Yang Zhao, Zhijie Lin, Daquan Zhou, Zilong Huang, Jiashi Feng, and Bingyi Kang. 2023. Bubogpt: Enabling visual grounding in multi-modal llms. *ArXiv*, abs/2307.08581.

Deyao Zhu, Jun Chen, Xiaoqian Shen, Xiang Li, and Mohamed Elhoseiny. 2023. Minigpt-4: Enhancing vision-language understanding with advanced large language models.

A Appendix

A.1 Misleading Image example

In Figure 7, we present the evaluation of the visual-language model on a visual dialogue containing a misleading image. Although the model successfully answered the textual questions, it failed to provide the correct answer related to the image in the subsequent conversation.

A.2 Evaluation pipeline

In this section we clarify how teacher forced evaluation is performed. Past context is obtained from ground truth labels for previous questions.

System Prompt

You are an expert whose job is to answer questions from the user possibly using images and audios and previous questions with given answers.
First, reason about the correct answer. Then write the answer in the following format where X is exactly one of English letters (A,B,C,...): "ANSWER: X".
If you are uncertain of the correct answer, guess the most likely one.

Context

User: What is the country of origin of the film "Addicted to Plastic?"
A) Canada.
B) Colombia.
C) Australia.
D) France.
E) China.
F) Russia.
G) Argentina.
Assistant: Answer: A

User: Can you Tell me the director's name?
A) Stanley Kubrick.
B) It's Ian Connacher.
C) Akira Kurosawa.
D) Alfred Hitchcock.
E) John Ford.
F) Ingmar Bergman.
G) Martin Scorsese.
Assistant: Answer: B

User: What genre?
A) Gothic film.
B) Biographical film.
C) Historical film.
D) Gangster film.
E) It's a documentary film.
F) War film.
G) Detective film.
Assistant: Answer: E

User: Who composed the music?
A) Ian Connacher.
B) Richard Wagner.
C) Siegfried Ochs.
D) Antonio Vivaldi.
E) Pyotr Tchaikovsky.
F) Franz Schubert.
G) Frederic Chopin.
Assistant: Answer: A

User: What year did it come out?
A) In 2009.
B) In 2007.
C) In 2005.
D) In 2010.
E) In 2001.
F) In 2006.
G) In 2008.
Assistant: Answer: G

User: Answer, what is its duration?
A) 85 minutes.
B) 86 minutes.
C) 99 minutes.
D) 88 minutes.
E) 89 minutes.
F) 87 minutes.
G) 91 minutes.

Model Generation

Assistant: Answer: A

Visual Dialogue (Type-3): Misleading Image

Continuation

User: In which country is the city of Berlin located?
Assistant: Germany
User: What time of day is shown in the picture?
Choices:

- A. It is nighttime
- B. It is daylight hours
- C. It is sunset
- D. It is sunrise

Assistant: D. It is sunrise

Ground Truth: B. It is daylight hours

User: In which country is the city of Berlin located?

Choices:

- A. Spain
- B. Italy
- C. France
- D. Germany

Assistant: D. Germany
Ground Truth: D. Germany

Continuation

User: In which country is the city of Berlin located?
Assistant: Germany
User: What time of day is shown in the picture?
Assistant: It is daylight hours
User: What country is shown in the picture?
Choices:

- A. United States
- B. Saudi Arabia
- C. China
- D. Brazil

Assistant: A. United States

Ground Truth: B. Saudi Arabia

Figure 7: Example of visual Type 3 with the misleading image

Towards a new Benchmark for Emotion Detection in NLP: A Unifying Framework of Recent Corpora

Anna Koufakou **Elijah Nieves** **John Peller**
Department of Computing & Software Engineering, Florida Gulf Coast University, USA
akoufakou@fgcu.edu

Abstract

Emotion recognition in text is a complex and evolving field that has garnered considerable interest. This paper addresses the pressing need to explore and experiment with new corpora annotated with emotions. We identified several corpora presented since 2018. We restricted this study to English single-labeled data. Nevertheless, the datasets vary in source, domain, topic, emotion types, and distributions. As a basis for benchmarking, we conducted emotion detection experiments by fine-tuning a pretrained model and compared our outcomes with results from the original publications. More importantly, in our efforts to combine existing resources, we created a unified corpus from these diverse datasets and evaluated the impact of training on that corpus versus on the training set for each corpus. Our approach aims to streamline research by offering a unified platform for emotion detection to aid comparisons and benchmarking, addressing a significant gap in the current landscape. Additionally, we present a discussion of related practices and challenges. Our code and dataset information are available at `https://github.com/a-koufakou/EmoDetect-Unify`. We hope this will enable the NLP community to leverage this unified framework towards a new benchmark in emotion detection.

1 Introduction

Detecting emotions in language, such as *anger, joy, or sadness*, is a powerful application of Natural Language Processing (NLP) with significant interest, especially in recent years (Mohammad et al., 2018; Oberländer and Klinger, 2018; Demszky et al., 2020; Lamprinidis et al., 2021; Plaza-del Arco et al., 2024). Emotion detection is sometimes confused with Sentiment Analysis, a much simpler task that focuses on detecting polarity of sentiments or opinions (Mohammad, 2022). Automated emotion detection is considerably more nuanced and complex due to the subjective and intricate nature of emotions.

NLP-based emotion detection uses datasets annotated with emotions. There is great variability in emotion annotation, including differences in annotation levels (e.g., basic vs. detailed) and labeling schemes (e.g., single vs. multi-label). An even more important challenge is which emotions to use in order to annotate data. Various emotion taxonomies or theories have been presented. Ekman (1992) provided 6 basic emotions: *anger, disgust, fear, joy, sadness, surprise*. Plutchik (1984) proposed a wheel of 8 emotions, adding *trust* and *anticipation* to Ekman's, also presenting dyads (feelings composed of two emotions). Shaver et al. (1987) identified 6 basic emotions: *love, joy, anger, fear, sadness, surprise*, on which they also provided secondary and tertiary levels in a tree-like structure, later refined in Parrott (2001). The *Appraisal* theory (Scherer, 1999; Lazarus, 1991) linked emotions to a persons interpretation of a situation or event. Recently, Cowen and Keltner (2017) identified 27 distinct categories based on videos, facial expressions etc., revised by Demszky et al. (2020) for text-based emotion recognition. Despite the variety of theories available, many efforts have concentrated on single-labeled corpora with a limited set of basic emotions such as Ekman (Plaza-del Arco et al., 2024), likely because these are typically easier for NLP models to handle. Nevertheless, the presence of multiple theories allows different approaches to emotion annotation, making it complicated to unify different datasets for comparisons and benchmarking.

In recent years, numerous emotion-annotated corpora have been introduced from diverse sources and domains, such as social media posts given specific tags or essays on specific topics. Any such available corpora are found in separate repositories and articles, making it challenging for re-

Proceedings of the 2nd GenBench Workshop on Generalisation (Benchmarking) in NLP, pages 196–206
November 16, 2024 ©2024 Association for Computational Linguistics

searchers to be aware of all available resources in order to fully investigate their use. It is noteworthy that a few corpora are well-known, e.g., GoEmotions (Demszky et al., 2020) or TweetEval (Barbieri et al., 2020) with more than 700 citations each, in contrast to others such as Github-love (Imran et al., 2022) with around 20 citations.[1]

As a result, many studies have relied on a subset of available resources, and there has been limited work towards benchmarking. The work by Oberländer and Klinger (2018) stands out: they analyzed and aggregated 14 popular emotion-annotated corpora into a unified framework, in 2018. They used their unified corpus for benchmark results with in-corpus and cross-corpus experiments. The unified framework available online[2] facilitated comparisons of the different corpora. Recent surveys (Alswaidan and Menai, 2020; Acheampong et al., 2020; Nandwani and Verma, 2021; Deng and Ren, 2023; Kusal et al., 2023) do not cover many of the corpora we present in this paper. Very recently, an excellent recent paper by Plaza-del Arco et al. (2024) reviewed over 150 ACL papers (2014-2022), and offered a detailed overview of practices, gaps, and guidelines for emotion analysis in text. Still, their paper did not provide a unified framework or experimentation results.

To address this gap, our paper introduces a unifying framework of text corpora annotated with emotions, as presented in the literature since 2018. We chose 2018 because: (a) it was the most recent year when a unifying framework was presented (Oberländer and Klinger, 2018), and (b) it marked a notable increase in the number of related studies (Plaza-del Arco et al., 2024). Specifically, we identified 11 publicly available emotion-annotated text corpora: we focused our experimentation to English and single-labeled data.[3] While this may seem limited, it serves as a good representation for a significant portion of existing datasets in this area (Plaza-del Arco et al., 2024). More importantly, our primary aim is to explore how to unify (combine) various datasets annotated with different emotions into a single framework, which is not as straightforward.

We conducted classification experiments with these datasets, while comparing our results with the results reported in the original articles. Based on these corpora, we introduce a unified corpus built by mapping original emotions in the corpora to a common set of emotions. Finally, we present baseline benchmarking results for emotion classification with our unified corpus. The ultimate goal is to aid researchers in the field of text-based emotion recognition by providing a unified resource built on a comprehensive set of recent data, which they can access in one repository. Our secondary goal is to furnish a classification baseline benchmark with valuable insights they can use while conducting their own experiments.

The following sections provide descriptions of the corpora (Section 2), details of the unified corpus we created (Section 3), results of our emotion classification experiments (Section 4), and a discussion of findings and observations (Section 5), followed by our concluding remarks and future research directions (Section 6).

2 Corpora

Table 1 summarizes the corpora used in this paper. Table 2 shows which emotions are represented in each corpus. In the following, we provide a brief description of each dataset. We then provide an overview of the datasets and their characteristics. We renamed certain datasets due to unclear or long names.

CARER Saravia et al. (2018) collected tweets with a set of hashtags they constructed, e.g. #depressed, #grief for *sadness*, or #fear, #worried for *fear*. These hashtags were used to annotate the data (*distant supervision*). The dataset posted on Hugging Face is labeled with Shaver, and it is a variant of the dataset presented in the article.

Covid-worry This dataset contains survey responses collected in UK over 2020-22, starting with the first COVID-19 lockdown (Kleinberg et al., 2020). Participants wrote short and long texts, along with demographic data and self-ratings for several emotions. They also chose one emotion among *anger, anxiety, disgust, desire, fear, happiness, relaxation, sadness*. In 2023, the authors presented a 3-year dataset (van der Vegt and Kleinberg, 2023).

EmoEvent Plaza-del-Arco et al. (2020) collected tweets related to events in 2019, and then followed certain steps to select a subset of *affective* tweets. The resulting tweets in English and

[1]Per Google scholar, last checked Aug. 2024.

[2]https://github.com/sarnthil/unify-emotion-datasets

[3]Our work uses GoEmotions, which is multi-labeled. We transformed it into single-labeled for this study.

dataset	source	# emotions	size	reference	avail.
CARER	tweets	6	417*	(Saravia et al., 2018)	HG
Covid-worry	essays	8	5.2	(van der Vegt and Kleinberg, 2023)	G,O
EmoEvent	tweets	6+1	7.3	(Plaza-del-Arco et al., 2020)	G
enISEAR	self-written	8	1	(Troiano et al., 2019)	O
Github-love	github	6	1.7	(Imran et al., 2022)	HG
GoEmotions	reddit	27+1, 6+1	58*	(Demszky et al., 2020)	G
GoodNews	headlines	15+1	5	(Oberländer et al., 2020)	Uni
StackOv-GS	stack overflow	6	4.8	(Novielli et al., 2018)	G
TweetEval	tweets	4	5	(Barbieri et al., 2020)	G
Universal Joy	facebook	5	284*	(Lamprinidis et al., 2021)	G
WASSA-21	essays	6+1	2.6	(Tafreshi et al., 2021)	Cd, Rq

Table 1: Summary of datasets used in this paper. Size in thousands (rounded to the closest hundred; if corpus has multiple languages, it refers to English; * denotes that we used a smaller sample of this dataset for our experiments). '+1' in '# emotions' column denotes additional class for *neutral/no emotion/other(s)*. 'avail.' is data availability: Cd=Codalab, G=Github, HG=Hugging Face, Kg=Kaggle, O=Other, Rq=By Request (the URLs are provided in our online repository).

in Spanish were annotated by Amazon MTurkers using Ekman plus *other*.

enISEAR Troiano et al. (2019) provided German (deISEAR) and English (enISEAR) corpora, using a framework similar to earlier ISEAR (International Survey on Emotion Antecedents and Reactions) (Scherer and Wallbott, 1994). A questionnaire instructed annotators (by crowdsourcing) to give a description of an event for which they felt a particular emotion. Each record was annotated with Ekman plus *guilt* and *shame*.

Github-love Imran et al. (2022) collected GitHub comments on pull requests/issues for popular repositories, annotated by the authors using Shaver. Besides these basic emotions, they also used detailed levels of emotions (Shaver et al., 1987), where they added some of the emotions presented by Demszky et al. (2020), e.g. *approval* or *confusion*. Note that the dataset available online has basic emotion labels, not the detailed levels in the paper.

GoEmotions Demszky et al. (2020) collected Reddit comments with crowdsourced annotations for 27 emotions or *neutral*, revised from Cowen and Keltner (2017). They also provided an Ekman mapping from their detailed emotions. This dataset is multi-labeled and we transformed it into single-labeled for the purposes of this study (see Section 3 for details).

GoodNews Oberländer et al. (2020) collected English news headlines and annotated them via crowdsourcing (named GoodNewsEveryone in the original article). Annotations were provided for emotions (extended Plutchik) and their intensity, as well as semantic roles (such as experiencer or cause), and reader interpretation of the headline.

StackOv-GS Novielli et al. (2018) collected Stack Overflow questions, answers and comments for the 'StackOverflow Gold Standard'. They were annotated by volunteers with Shaver.

TweetEval Barbieri et al. (2020) created a unified twitter dataset with seven heterogeneous Twitter-specific classification tasks. Among those, they included Affect in Tweets (Mohammad et al., 2018) only keeping single-label records and dropping rare emotions. This resulted in records labeled with *anger, joy, optimism, sadness*.

Universal Joy Lamprinidis et al. (2021) presented a dataset with anonymized public Facebook posts that were originally collected in 2014 in 18 languages. The authors labeled the records with *anger, anticipation, fear, joy, sadness*.

WASSA-21 This dataset was part of a shared task in the 11th *Workshop on Computational Approaches to Subjectivity, Sentiment & Social Detection and Emotion Classification (WASSA)*, summarized by Tafreshi et al. (2021). It contains essays written to express the authors empathy and distress in reaction to news articles related to harm. The emotion labels (Ekman) were first predicted by Neural Networks and then post-annotated by crowdsourcing workers and a PhD student.

Overview Out of the 11 datasets in Table 1, 5 came from social media (X/Twitter, Facebook, Reddit), 2 came from software-related websites (GitHub and Stack Overflow), 1 was with news

dataset	annotation	A	Ant	D	F	J	Ne	Sa	Su	T	other emotions
CARER	Shaver	✓	–	–	✓	✓	–	✓	✓	–	love
Covid-worry	Other	✓	–	✓	✓	✓	–	✓	–	–	anxiety, desire, relaxation
EmoEvent	E+Ne	✓	–	✓	✓	✓	✓	✓	✓	–	
enISEAR	Ext. E	✓	–	✓	✓	✓	–	✓	–	–	shame, guilt
Github-love	Shaver	✓	–	–	✓	✓	–	✓	✓	–	love
GoEmotions	E+Ne, Revised CK	✓	–	✓	✓	✓	✓	✓	✓	–	27 fine-grained emotions
GoodNews	Ext. P	✓	✓	✓	✓	✓	-	✓	✓	✓	annoyance, guilt, love, pride, shame
StackOv-GS	Shaver	✓	–	–	✓	✓	-	✓	✓	–	love
Tweeteval	Other	✓	–	–	–	✓	–	✓	–	–	optimism
Universal Joy	Mod. P	✓	✓	–	✓	✓	–	✓	–	–	
WASSA-21	E+Ne	✓	–	✓	✓	✓	✓	✓	✓	–	
	Total	11	2	6	10	11	3	11	7	1	

Table 2: The emotions in each corpus. E=Ekman, P=Plutchik, and CK=Cowen & Keltner; Mod.=modified, Ext.=extended. "–" means the emotion is not in that corpus. Emotions: A-Anger, Ant-Anticipation, D-Disgust, F-Fear, J-Joy, Ne-Neutral or no emotion or other, Sa-Sadness, Su-Surprise, and T-Trust.

headlines, and 3 were self-reported (for example, self-written responses to questions and self-ratings of emotions in Covid-worry). The data that were based on online posts or comments were usually annotated by humans (volunteers, experts or crowdsourcing workers), though CARER used the hashtags as noisy labels. The self-reported varied: in Covid-worry, essays were written by survey participants related to their current situation, while in enISEAR the statements were written by crowdsourcing workers: they were given an emotion, and were asked to describe a related event.

As far as size, most corpora are small; the two smallest are enISEAR and Github-love. There are 3 larger datasets: CARER and Universal Joy (hundreds of thousands) and GoEmotions (about 58K). Finally, all corpora follow basic emotion annotation, except GoEmotions and GoodNews.

Based on Table 2, we observed that all or most corpora contain *anger*, *fear*, *joy*, and *sadness*; frequently represented emotions are *disgust* and *surprise*; *love* is represented in fewer than half of the corpora; the *anticipation* and *trust* emotions followed by *neutral, no emotion, other* are the least represented in the data.

Finally, the distribution of emotions varies across the corpora. Some corpora exhibit a range of dominant emotions versus very low representation of certain emotions. For instance, CARER is primarily dominated by *joy*, followed by *sadness*, and it has a very low sample of *surprise*. Universal Joy is heavily dominated with *anticipation* and then *joy*, while low on *anger* and *fear*. Covid-worry is led by *anxiety* and *fear*, with *joy* trailing behind, and it has a very low number of records with *disgust* or *anger*. StackOV-GS is led by *love*, followed by *anger*. EmoEvent is predominantly *neutral* ('*other*'), followed by *joy*. Both EmoEvent and StackOV-GS are very low in *fear* and *surprise*. Finally, *disgust* has very low representation in most datasets. As an exception, enISEAR is balanced as crowdsourcing workers were asked to write a certain number of statements for each of the emotions.

3 Creating a Unified Corpus

First, for any corpus we downloaded, we spent effort reading instructions and exploring file formats, features, labeling schemes, etc. For example, some data had integers as labels, which we had to map to emotions per author instructions; some data came with many features so we had to extract text/labels. Many sets were well-organized and documented, with a couple of exceptions that were harder to understand and transform. In short, we spent significant effort to integrate diverse corpora into the unified corpus with the goal to save other researchers time and effort.

Based on the emotions in Table 2 and previous work (Oberländer and Klinger, 2018; Demszky et al., 2020), we defined a scheme roughly following Plutchik and Shaver as our common emotion label set. Specifically, we used *anger, anticipation,*

unified	original
anger	anger, annoyance, annoyed, shame
anticipation	anticipation, neg. or pos. anticipation
disgust	disgust
fear	fear, anxiety
joy	joy, happiness, happy, desire, optimism, optimistic, pride, relaxation
love	love, love incl. like
neutral	neutral, none, noemo, other
sadness	sadness, sad, guilt
surprise	surprise, neg. surprise, pos. surprise
trust	trust

Table 3: The mapping we followed for mapping original labels to unified labels. We roughly follow the models by Plutchik (1984) and Shaver et al. (1987).

disgust, fear, joy, love, sadness, surprise, trust, and *neutral*; we kept *neutral* due to its relatively good representation in certain corpora (e.g., it was about 33% of the records in GoEmotion).

We mapped original emotions from the data to the emotions in the common set as shown in Table 3. We decided on the mappings based on previous literature, and by observing sample records from each corpus. For example, Oberländer and Klinger (2018) used a very similar set: their list had the same emotions as ours except they included *confusion* and not *love*. Also, Demszky et al. (2020) mapped *annoyance* to *anger* and *optimism* and *pride* to *joy*. For GoEmotions (a multi-labeled corpus with detailed emotions), we kept only records with a single label or if the multiple labels mapped to the same label in our common set of emotions (note that the creators provided Ekman mappings of their detailed labels). This resulted in a dataset with 43,975 records. For Covid-worry, we combined all surveys from 3 years. Finally, due to our resources, we downsampled CARER and Universal Joy to a more manageable size for our experiments, keeping emotion distribution the same as in the original corpora. As a result, in our experiment there were 62,522 records for CARER, and 84,695 for Universal Joy (about 30% of the original size).

3.1 Unified Corpus Properties

Our unified corpus addresses the following properties important for generalization testing as shown by Hupkes et al. (2023). In all the points below we refer the reader to the dataset descriptions in the earlier sections and Tables 1 and 2.

Platform Shift: The datasets that were collected from online sources were sourced from different platforms: Twitter, Reddit, Facebook, Github, StackOverflow.

Language Shift: Even though most datasets came from social media or online forums, there were also datasets that contain self-written statements or news headlines.

Topic Shift: The datasets were collected for different reasons and topics, for example, Covid-19 (Covid-worry), events (EmoEvent), or software (code) questions and comments (StackOv-GS).

Emotion Shift: The emotions represented in each corpus as well as their distributions vary, for example some corpora are heavily dominated by positive emotions (CARER or Universal Joy), while others by negative emotions (Covid-worry or WASSA-21).

4 Experiments and Results

4.1 Experimental Setup

We used Google colab[4] to run all our experiments. For our classification experiments, we selected to use `distilroberta-base`:[5] it is a distilled version of RoBERTa (Robustly optimized BERT approach) (Liu et al., 2019), with 6 layers, 768 dimension and 12 heads, resulting in a total of 82M parameters (compared to 125M parameters for RoBERTa-base). We fine-tuned the model for 2 Epochs, with learning rate of $1e^{-5}$, maxlen of 256 and batch of 8, based on early trials. If the corpus came with a train/test set (e.g., WASSA-21), we used those sets, otherwise we used an 80-20 stratified split. We repeated each experiment 5 times and reported the average f1-score. In total, we performed 110 experiments, either fine-tuning the model on each single corpus (5 runs $\times$ 11 corpora = 55 total experiments, see results in Section 4.2 and 4.3), or fine-tuning on the Unified train set (also 55 total, see results in Section 4.4). We also performed some additional cross-corpus experiments as examples (see Section 4.5).

[4] https://colab.research.google.com/

[5] https://huggingface.co/distilroberta-base

Corpus	Ours	Previous work (OA = Original Article)
CARER	91%	OA used larger and/or different version of the corpus, different models: max f1-macro 79%.
Covid-worry	46%	No previous work used combined data from all 3 surveys.
EmoEvent	34%	OA used SVM with 32% f1-macro.
enISEAR	48%	OA used MaxEnt with 47% f1-micro.
Github-love	44%	OA used various models (non-transformers) with max f1-macro of 44%.
GoEmotions	65%	OA used BERT-base with 64% f1-macro on their Ekman taxonomy version, 46% on data with their own taxonomy.
GoodNews	26%	We could not find previous results for emotion detection.
StackOv-GS	44%	We could not find previous results for emotion detection.
TweetEval	80%	OA used RoBERTa-base with 76% f1-macro.
Universal joy	63%	OA had multiple-sized data, ours is downsampled. Their mBERT results showed 46-63% f1-macro.
WASSA-21	31%	Results for shared task in OA ranged in 31-55%. Top ranking teams used ensembles/augmented with GoEmotions.

Table 4: A comparison of our f1-macro results for each corpus in our benchmark versus existing results from the original literature on their datasets. See Table 1 for references (Original Article) related to each corpus.

4.2 Overall Performance and Comparison with Previous Work

We first show our f1 macro-averaged over all emotions for each corpus versus the results for each specific corpus as shown in the related literature. The reader should keep in mind that there were differences between some of the datasets we used in this work versus the ones in previous work in the literature: for example, we downsampled very large datasets such as CARER, and we combined 3 surveys in Covid-worry (the same survey was given in 3 consecutive years, see section 2). Also, the experimental setup (such as train-test split or the (hyper-)parameters of a model) in existing work usually varies from our work. Nevertheless, we understand that such a comparison might be beneficial to show a 'bigger' picture for the reader. Therefore, we provide comparative results in Table 4. Finally, even though we concentrated on original work that presented the datasets, if that work did not have emotion detection results, we also looked in the recent literature. For example, we previously applied RoBERTa-based on the first survey from Covid-worry resulting in 49% f1-macro (Koufakou et al., 2022), but, to our knowledge, no previous work has used all 3 surveys.

Overall, CARER had the best performance (91% f1-macro), followed by TweetEval (80% f1-macro), Universal Joy and GoEmotions (f1-macros in the 60's). The rest of the datasets had f1-macro values ranging from high 40's to low 30's. Our baseline's f1-macros are largely similar to previous literature results. In certain cases, our results are lower than the literature, e.g. for WASSA-21: the top ranking teams in that shared task augmented the train set with GoEmotions, and usually also employed ensembles of models. In other cases, our f1-macros are higher, e.g. for CARER: they used a different version of their dataset in their article as opposed to the one publicly shared.

4.3 Results per Emotion

Figure 1a depicts the f1-score per emotion for each corpus as a heatmap. Per emotion, CARER had the best f1-score, except for the emotions it did not contain (*disgust* and *neutral*): GoEmotion had the best f1-score for those.

Looking at specific emotions, the hardest emotions to detect were *disgust*, *fear*, *surprise*, and *trust*, depending on the dataset. First, as also observed by Oberländer and Klinger (2018), emotions with low frequency were harder to detect. As an example, in Covid-worry, *disgust* had the lowest frequency by far. When we inspected a resulting confusion matrix, *disgust* was mostly confused with *anger* and *fear*. In other sets, rarest emotions were mispredicted completely: *disgust* and *neutral* in WASSA-21, *fear* and *surprise* in StackOv-GS and in EmoEvent. Several of these corpora are imbalanced and have been shown to benefit from techniques such as data augmentation. The winner in WASSA-21 showed that augmenting their training with GoEmotions improved classification

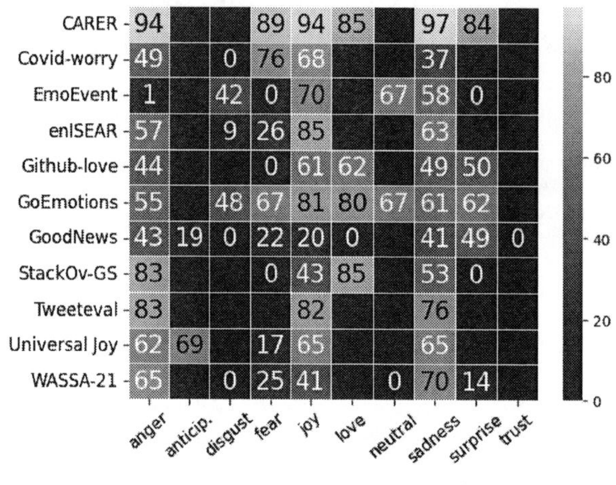

(a) Own train set

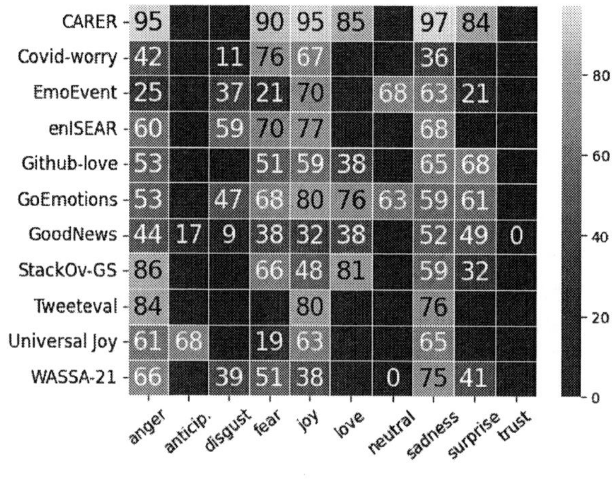

(b) Unified train set

Figure 1: Heatmaps with f1-score per emotion (x-axis) for each corpus (y-axis) with fine-tuning either (a) using the train set of the corpus or (b) using the Unified train set. Empty cell: dataset does not contain that emotion.

(Mundra et al., 2021). In that vein, we show the results of fine-tuning the model with the Unified train set in section 4.4, and a few cross-corpus experiments in Section 4.5.

Besides imbalanced distribution, annotation of the emotions plays a role. For example, Plaza-del-Arco et al. (2020) observed that annotators for EmoEvent had trouble with *fear*, *disgust* and *surprise*, and distinguishing between *anger* and *disgust* (complementary emotions). In Github-love, *joy* was mispredicted many times as *love*. We examined random comments and found that some were so similar that a human would struggle to distinguish between them: e.g., "This will answer your question: Good luck!" (*love*) and "excellent, good luck!" (*joy*).

4.4 Results from Fine-Tuning on the Unified Train Set

First, we created a 'Unified train' set from merging all train sets from all unified corpora: this was after each corpus had been transformed to the same format and our common label set. This results in a train set of about 180.6K records. We observed that the Unified train set is heavily skewed towards *joy* (about 34%), then *sadness* and *anticipation* (about 16% each). These emotions are heavily represented in the larger sets (CARER, Universal Joy, then GoEmotions). For the experiments in this Section, we fine-tuned the model on that Unified train set and predicted the labels of the test set from each corpus. The overall results (f1-macro) from fine-tuning the model on this Unified train

corpus	own	unified	Δ
CARER	91%	91%	0%
Covid-worry	46%	46%	0%
EmoEvent	34%	44%	**10%**
enlsear	48%	67%	**19%**
Github-love	44%	56%	**12%**
GoEmotion	65%	64%	-1%
GoodNews	22%	31%	**9%**
StackOv-GS	44%	62%	**18%**
TweetEval	80%	80%	0%
Universal Joy	64%	63%	-1%
WASSA-21	31%	44%	**13%**

Table 5: f1-macro after fine-tuning the model on its own train set versus on the Unified train set, followed by the difference (Δ). Both were tested on the same test set. Bold: improvement larger than 5%.

set versus only on the original train set from each corpus are shown in Table 5.

To summarize, CARER, Covid-Worry, GoEmotions, TweetEval and Universal Joy did not show an improvement when training on the Unified train versus just training on the original train set. Most of these datasets already had highest results (see Fig. 1a and Table 4). For example, CARER was a large dataset with 91% f1-macro, so there was little room for improvement. However, Covid-worry still had low f1-macro in Table 5: our observation is that corpus is largely dominated by *worry* and *anxiety* which is not represented well in the other corpora. We did map *anxiety* to *fear* in order to create the Unified corpus; still, the emotions in Covid-worry do not seem to translate well to the ones in the rest of the corpora.

On the other hand, 6 out of 12 corpora showed improvements ranging in 9-19% (see the Δ column in Table 5). Specifically, the f1-macro improvement was around 10% for 4 corpora (EmoEvent 10%, Github-love 12%, GoodNews 9%, and WASSA-21 13%) and about 20% for two corpora (enISEAR 19% and StackOv-GS 18%).

We can also look at specific emotions shown as a heatmap in Figure 1b. For example, in StackOv-GS, *fear* and *surprise* were not detected at all (0% for own train set in Fig. 1a) versus f1-scores of 66% and 32% respectively (Unified train in Fig. 1b). Overall, we observed from the two heatmaps, there were improvements for *disgust*, *fear* and *surprise*, which were either relatively rare or they overlapped, as discussed in earlier sections.

4.5 Additional Experiments

Due to our constraints of time and resources, we were not able to conduct a full cross-corpus experimentation. This could mainly consist of training on the train set of one corpus and then testing on the test set of another corpus or, following (Oberländer and Klinger, 2018), training on one (entire) corpus and evaluating on a different (entire) corpus. Nevertheless, we performed some initial cross-corpus experiments, briefly summarized here as potential ideas for this unified resource. The reader is directed to Table 4 for f1-macro results when training on each original train set, for comparison purposes.

For instance, one could explore the effect of data source. As an example, we trained on the GoEmotion train set (social media posts), then tested on the EmoEvent test set (also social media posts) and on the WASSA-21 test set (self-written essays). The f1-macro for EmoEvent was 34%, which matched the results based on its own train set. The f1-macro for WASSA-21 was 38%, better than training on its own train set by 7%. A challenge in the cross-domain setup is handling the differences in emotion labels across datasets which are combined in these experiments (also true for the Unified train in Section 4.4).

As an example of exploring datasets with matching original emotion labels, we trained on the CARER train set and tested on GitHub-love and StackOv-GS (all featuring Shaver emotions originally). Both tests yielded f1-macro in the mid-30s, compared to mid-40s when training on their respective train sets. It is noteworthy that CARER consists of tweets, while the other two datasets have code-related comments. Also, the most frequent emotion for all three datasets is positive (*joy* or *love*), but the second most frequent emotion in CARER is *sadness* (29%), versus *anger* in GitHub-love and StackOv-GS (20-30% depending on the dataset).

5 Discussion

In this paper, we started by selecting 11 recently introduced datasets with emotion-annotated records in order to introduce a new unified framework for benchmarking emotion detection in NLP. We described the characteristics of these datasets, which vary in size, topic, source, emotions and distributions. Nevertheless, one could question the selection of the specific datasets. It would be beneficial to explore earlier datasets or datasets we did not include, and how they compare/connect to corpora in this work: we leave this for future work. Moreover, we focused on English corpora, unfortunately, a common limitation in NLP: a multilingual study is thus needed, e.g. see a multilingual sentiment analysis study by Rajda et al. (2022). Specifically for emotion detection, one should consider linguistic and cultural differences for emotions (De Bruyne, 2023).

We combined the datasets into one unified framework by mapping to a common set of emotions. We followed a simple emotion scheme for this: each record gets assigned a single label out of n emotions, similar to earlier work (Oberländer and Klinger, 2018). Many of the available corpora only have a few basic emotions to start with (Oberländer and Klinger, 2018; Plaza-del Arco et al., 2024). In reality, though, emotions are complex and an individual's writings may encapsulate multiple emotions. This is even more prevalent in essays with multiple sentences (Tafreshi et al., 2021). To more accurately reflect human emotions, fine-grained emotion annotations are often preferred over coarse ones (Demszky et al., 2020).

Our review of the datasets and related literature revealed several limitations and issues similar to those identified in previous work, such as inconsistencies in annotation practices or inadequate reporting of the annotation process (Stajner, 2021; Plaza-del Arco et al., 2024). These issues underscore the need for a more thorough analysis of practices and benchmarking within available corpora. Good examples in other areas include a systematic review in hate speech detection by Poletto et al. (2021). Also, we found research in generalized offensive language identification by Dmonte et al. (2024): they used relatively basic labels, e.g. *Offensive* or *Non-offensive*. In contrast, as we have shown in this paper, emotion-annotated data involves more complexity and thus additional challenges. Additionally, automated emotion recognition carries ethical considerations as shown by Mohammad (2022), who proposed an ethics sheet outlining 50 ethical considerations. For instance, the need to account for both the speaker's and the reader's perspectives, which can vary significantly from one individual to another.

While this paper represents considerable effort, there is still more work to match the underlying complexity of this study. Our classification experiments offer a baseline rather than a complete benchmark. Our published code and list of dataset links will enable anyone to recreate and further utilize the unified , and even possibly extend it. The research community is welcome to use these resources and employ various models and/or explore the effect of different hyper-parameters on the results.

6 Conclusions

This paper answers the imperative need for studying recent text-based corpora annotated for emotion detection. Our investigation into diverse corpora sourced from various domains and introduced since 2018 summarizes and gives insights into their characteristics, such as source, topic, size, emotion and distributions, etc. Furthermore, we constructed a unified framework built from these corpora by mapping their emotions to a common set of labels. We used these resources to conduct emotion detection experiments, and compared the effect of fine-tuning a pretrained model to the train set of each corpus versus to the unified train set. This consolidated platform will be a valuable resource for researchers, streamlining efforts and providing the basis for a practical emotion classification benchmark.

While this paper represents considerable effort, there is still more work to match the underlying complexity of this study. Future directions include expanding this work to additional datasets, including multi-lingual and multi-label settings, while also conducting additional experiments (e.g. cross-corpus or various classifiers) and delving deeper into annotation practices and methodologies.

7 Limitations and Ethical Considerations

This work included datasets presented since 2018, all in English and all represented as single-labeled. As we discussed in Section 5, the dataset selection for benchmarking should be more expansive, not only in terms of languages and emotion labeling but also regarding data sources and topics. In the realm of emotion recognition using NLP, the linguistic and cultural diversity of emotions highlights the need for more inclusive and representative datasets. Furthermore, additional experimentation, especially cross-corpus, is essential to establish the unified framework as a valuable benchmark.

Our work did not collect or annotate any datasets, and instead used publicly available datasets. Nevertheless, it is important that any such research in the field of automated emotion recognition, including the curation of emotion annotated datasets, should consider ethical questions such as the ones by Mohammad (2022).

References

Francisca Adoma Acheampong, Chen Wenyu, and Henry Nunoo-Mensah. 2020. Text-based emotion detection: Advances, challenges, and opportunities. *Engineering Reports*, 2(7):e12189.

Nourah Alswaidan and Mohamed El Bachir Menai. 2020. A survey of state-of-the-art approaches for emotion recognition in text. *Knowledge and Information Systems*, 62(8):2937–2987.

Francesco Barbieri, Jose Camacho-Collados, Luis Espinosa Anke, and Leonardo Neves. 2020. TweetEval: Unified benchmark and comparative evaluation for tweet classification. In *Findings of the Association for Computational Linguistics: EMNLP 2020*, pages 1644–1650, Online.

Alan S Cowen and Dacher Keltner. 2017. Self-report captures 27 distinct categories of emotion bridged by continuous gradients. *Proceedings of the national academy of sciences*, 114(38):E7900–E7909.

Luna De Bruyne. 2023. The paradox of multilingual emotion detection. In *Proceedings of the 13th Workshop on Computational Approaches to Subjectivity, Sentiment, & Social Media Analysis*, pages 458–466. Association for Computational Linguistics.

Dorottya Demszky, Dana Movshovitz-Attias, Jeongwoo Ko, Alan Cowen, Gaurav Nemade, and Sujith Ravi. 2020. Goemotions: A dataset of fine-grained emotions. In *Proceedings of the 58th Annual Meeting of the Association for Computational Linguistics*, pages 4040–4054.

Jiawen Deng and Fuji Ren. 2023. A survey of textual emotion recognition and its challenges. *IEEE Transactions on Affective Computing*, 14(1):49–67.

Alphaeus Dmonte, Tejas Arya, Tharindu Ranasinghe, and Marcos Zampieri. 2024. Towards generalized offensive language identification. *arXiv preprint arXiv:2407.18738*.

Paul Ekman. 1992. An argument for basic emotions. *Cognition & emotion*, 6(3-4):169–200.

Dieuwke Hupkes, Mario Giulianelli, Verna Dankers, Mikel Artetxe, Yanai Elazar, Tiago Pimentel, Christos Christodoulopoulos, Karim Lasri, Naomi Saphra, Arabella Sinclair, et al. 2023. A taxonomy and review of generalization research in nlp. *Nature Machine Intelligence*, 5(10):1161–1174.

Mia Mohammad Imran, Yashasvi Jain, Preetha Chatterjee, and Kostadin Damevski. 2022. Data augmentation for improving emotion recognition in software engineering communication. In *Proceedings of the 37th IEEE/ACM International Conference on Automated Software Engineering*, pages 1–13.

Bennett Kleinberg, Isabelle van der Vegt, and Maximilian Mozes. 2020. Measuring emotions in the covid-19 real world worry dataset. In *Proceedings of the 1st Workshop on NLP for COVID-19 at ACL 2020*.

Anna Koufakou, Jairo Garciga, Adam Paul, Joseph Morelli, and Christopher Frank. 2022. Automatically classifying emotions based on text: A comparative exploration of different datasets. In *34th International Conference on Tools with Artificial Intelligence (ICTAI)*. IEEE.

Sheetal Kusal, Shruti Patil, Jyoti Choudrie, Ketan Kotecha, Deepali Vora, and Ilias Pappas. 2023. A systematic review of applications of natural language processing and future challenges with special emphasis in text-based emotion detection. *Artificial Intelligence Review*, pages 1–87.

Sotiris Lamprinidis, Federico Bianchi, Daniel Hardt, and Dirk Hovy. 2021. Universal joy a data set and results for classifying emotions across languages. In *Proceedings of the Eleventh Workshop on Computational Approaches to Subjectivity, Sentiment and Social Media Analysis*, pages 62–75, Online.

Richard S Lazarus. 1991. Progress on a cognitive-motivational-relational theory of emotion. *American psychologist*, 46(8):819.

Yinhan Liu, Myle Ott, Naman Goyal, Jingfei Du, Mandar Joshi, Danqi Chen, Omer Levy, Mike Lewis, Luke Zettlemoyer, and Veselin Stoyanov. 2019. Roberta: A robustly optimized bert pretraining approach. *arXiv preprint arXiv:1907.11692*.

Saif Mohammad, Felipe Bravo-Marquez, Mohammad Salameh, and Svetlana Kiritchenko. 2018. Semeval-2018 task 1: Affect in tweets. In *Proceedings of the 12th international workshop on semantic evaluation*, pages 1–17.

Saif M Mohammad. 2022. Ethics sheet for automatic emotion recognition and sentiment analysis. *Computational Linguistics*, 48(2):239–278.

Jay Mundra, Rohan Gupta, and Sagnik Mukherjee. 2021. WASSA@IITK at WASSA 2021: Multi-task learning and transformer finetuning for emotion classification and empathy prediction. In *Proceedings of the 11th Workshop on Computational Approaches to Subjectivity, Sentiment and Social Media Analysis*, pages 112–116, Online. ACL.

Pansy Nandwani and Rupali Verma. 2021. A review on sentiment analysis and emotion detection from text. *Social Network Analysis and Mining*, 11(1):1–19.

Nicole Novielli, Fabio Calefato, and Filippo Lanubile. 2018. A gold standard for emotion annotation in stack overflow. In *Proceedings of the 15th international conference on mining software repositories*, pages 14–17.

Laura Ana Maria Oberländer, Evgeny Kim, and Roman Klinger. 2020. Goodnewseveryone: A corpus of news headlines annotated with emotions, semantic roles, and reader perception. In *Proceedings of the Twelfth Language Resources and Evaluation Conference*, pages 1554–1566.

Laura Ana Maria Oberländer and Roman Klinger. 2018. An analysis of annotated corpora for emotion classification in text. In *Proceedings of the 27th international conference on computational linguistics*, pages 2104–2119.

W Gerrod Parrott. 2001. *Emotions in social psychology: Essential readings*. psychology press.

Flor Miriam Plaza-del Arco, Alba A. Cercas Curry, Amanda Cercas Curry, and Dirk Hovy. 2024. Emotion analysis in NLP: Trends, gaps and roadmap for future directions. In *Proceedings of the 2024 Joint International Conference on Computational Linguistics, Language Resources and Evaluation (LREC-COLING 2024)*, pages 5696–5710, Torino, Italia. ELRA and ICCL.

Flor Miriam Plaza-del-Arco, Carlo Strapparava, L. Alfonso Urena-Lopez, and M. Teresa Martin-Valdivia. 2020. EmoEvent: A Multilingual Emotion Corpus based on different Events. In *Proceedings of the 12th Language Resources and Evaluation Conference*.

Robert Plutchik. 1984. Emotions: A general psychoevolutionary theory. *Approaches to emotion*, 1984(197-219):2–4.

Fabio Poletto, Valerio Basile, Manuela Sanguinetti, Cristina Bosco, and Viviana Patti. 2021. Resources and benchmark corpora for hate speech detection: a systematic review. *Language Resources and Evaluation*, 55:477–523.

Krzysztof Rajda, Lukasz Augustyniak, Piotr Gramacki, Marcin Gruza, Szymon Woźniak, and Tomasz Kajdanowicz. 2022. Assessment of massively multilingual sentiment classifiers. In *Proceedings of the 12th Workshop on Computational Approaches to Subjectivity, Sentiment & Social Media Analysis*, pages 125–140, Dublin, Ireland.

Elvis Saravia, Hsien-Chi Toby Liu, Yen-Hao Huang, Junlin Wu, and Yi-Shin Chen. 2018. CARER: Contextualized affect representations for emotion recognition. In *Proceedings of the 2018 Conference on Empirical Methods in Natural Language Processing*, pages 3687–3697.

Klaus R Scherer. 1999. *Appraisal theory*. John Wiley & Sons Ltd.

Klaus R Scherer and Harald G Wallbott. 1994. Evidence for universality and cultural variation of differential emotion response patterning. *Journal of personality and social psychology*, 66(2):310.

Phillip Shaver, Judith Schwartz, Donald Kirson, and Cary O'connor. 1987. Emotion knowledge: further exploration of a prototype approach. *Journal of personality and social psychology*, 52(6):1061.

Sanja Stajner. 2021. Exploring reliability of gold labels for emotion detection in Twitter. In *Proceedings of the International Conference on Recent Advances in Natural Language Processing (RANLP 2021)*, pages 1350–1359, Held Online. INCOMA Ltd.

Shabnam Tafreshi, Orphée De Clercq, Valentin Barriere, Sven Buechel, João Sedoc, and Alexandra Balahur. 2021. Wassa 2021 shared task: Predicting empathy and emotion in reaction to news stories. In *Proceedings of the 11th Workshop on Computational Approaches to Subjectivity, Sentiment and Social Media Analysis*, Online. ACL.

Enrica Troiano, Sebastian Padó, and Roman Klinger. 2019. Crowdsourcing and validating event-focused emotion corpora for german and english. In *Proceedings of the 57th Annual Meeting of the Association for Computational Linguistics*, pages 4005–4011.

Isabelle van der Vegt and Bennett Kleinberg. 2023. A multi-modal panel dataset to understand the psychological impact of the pandemic. *Scientific Data*, 10(1):537.

Author Index

Association for Computational Linguistics
209 N. Eighth Street
Stroudsburg, Pennsylvania 18360

ISBN 979-8-3313-0847-6

CURRAN ASSOCIATES INC.
proceedings
.com